——THE——
KAISER'S DAWN

1

Published in 2018 by
Uniform, an imprint of Unicorn Publishing Group LLP
101 Wardour Street
London
W1F 0UG
www.unicornpublishing.org

ISBN 978-1-911604-39-6

THE
KAISER'S DAWN

JOHN HUGHES-WILSON

UNIFORM

INTRODUCTION

This is book is an historical narrative, based on one explosive and hitherto untold secret of the Great War. The basic facts are true.

After a battlefield tour to the Western Front in 2002, one of the travellers sent a CD as a souvenir to the guide. This historical treasure trove contained downloaded details of his great uncle's Royal Flying Corps log book and photographs of his service with 25 Squadron. Included among the effects of Lt A.R.Watts MC, RFC, with the breathtaking claim that he had taken part in a secret British mission to kill the Kaiser.

This extraordinary secret was confirmed by further research at the RAF museum and the RAF Historical Branch. The startling, but never before revealed, story was true. On 2nd June 1918, at the height of the final German attack of WW1, the newly formed RAF tried to assassinate the Kaiser when he was visiting the Western Front.

The facts are borne out in never-before-published notebooks, maps and pilots' flying records, kept secret for a century. Copies of these records are in the author's possession and are backed up by details tucked away in 25 Squadron's records. But the facts of this secret attack raise many new and disturbing questions.

Exactly who ordered an attack to kill the Kaiser? Was it sanctioned by Sir Douglas Haig? By the War Office? Was the King informed? Was Lloyd George, the Prime Minister asked? All very unlikely. The Official History makes no mention of any attack, and public records say nothing. Even the RAF Museum has no official record: but the attack really did take place, of that there is no doubt. 25 Squadron's documents and log books prove it. So someone did give an order to kill the Kaiser.

But who?

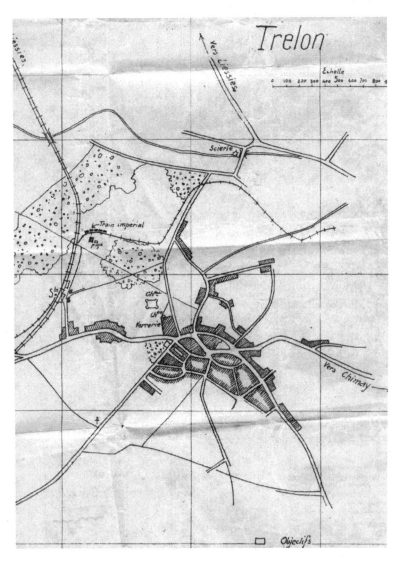

French Intelligence map showing
***Château* Trélon and the Kaiser's Train siding.**
(Author's collection)

**The Warlords: Hindenburg and Ludendorff,
Germany's real rulers, 1918.**
(Public domain)

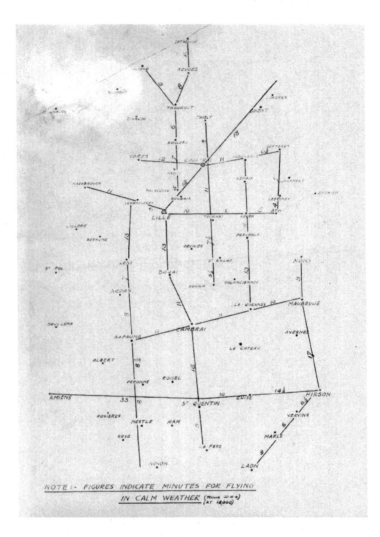

25 Squadron RAF flying times, early 1918.
(Author's collection)

25 Squadron 1918; DH4 light bomber and crew.
(Author's collection)

**Captain Archie Watts
25 Squadron, RAF 1918.**
(Author's collection)

Bomb raid on Kaiser's château at Thélon. Started at dawn 3.45 am Crossed the lines at 14,000ft and lost height over Le Cateau; came down to 500 ft and dropped bombs in turn and climbed up in formation again. Observers fired at Village and train. One machine seen to land and burnt by pilot and observer. 1 A.A gun near Chateau and AA near Cambrai very active. No huns seen

Bomb raid on Douai Visibility Very bad owing to low clouds. Machine not climbing well.

Test flight near Aerodrome. Bomb raid on Peronne. Machine very slow at climbing. 10,000ft in 24 mts. 1 Hun 2 seater shot

The 'smoking gun:' a page from a 25 Squadron pilot's log book, 2 June 1918.

(RAF Museum, Hendon)

**The Target (1):
Kaiser Wilhelm II,
Germany's Emperor.**
(Public)

The Target (2): *Château* Trélon at Hirson.
(Author's collection)

11

CONTENTS

CHAPTER 1

25 SQN

The Western Front, January 1918

Roberts had no idea that he was going to be killed quite so quickly.

Considering his youth and inexperience, it all seemed monstrously unfair. After all, it was only his third real flight in France.

Around him the world was a frozen, pale blue dome of icy January sky. Against this vivid backdrop, twenty other biplanes hung motionless, while his young brain slowly took in the sheer injustice of his imminent death.

He could even see his killer quite clearly.

It was a Pfalz, and it was very close. The distinctive 'V' struts were just like the recognition pictures on the walls of the squadron hut back at St Omer. The Pfalz was black, he noticed; the German pilot's flying helmet was black, too. He could even see the man's goggles glinting at him in the cold winter sun.

He wondered if it would hurt – being shot. Would the bullets smash like a kick in rugger or burn like a hot iron? Odd, only last season he'd been kicked in the head playing for the school first fifteen. That had hurt.

His pang of self-pity was overwhelmed by a sudden surge of guilt. In the back seat of his DH4, behind four feet of petrol tank and out of communication sat Cartwright, his observer and gunner.

If he died, then poor old Jimmy Cartwright was dead too. As a team it was universally acknowledged that two seater crews lived and died together. Poor old Jimmy! It was his own, Robert's, stupidity and slowness that was going to kill them both. Roberts' young world, suspended six thousand feet above the Flanders plain, held its breath, frozen in time and space.

The Pfalz fired.

Flickering lights danced along the engine cowling and a steady bang, bang, bang over his shoulder told him that Cartwright was firing back. By his right eye, as bright and shiny as a new copper penny, a bullet suddenly appeared as if by magic in the wing strut, half-embedded in the freshly splintered wood. He wanted to move, to do something, but seemed to be as frozen as the world around him, a metal band clamped tight round his chest. Smoking bullet trails whipped between the wings. More bullets smacked into the canvas alongside him.

Suddenly a black guillotine sliced across his vision, as a German aeroplane loomed like an oncoming cliff-face filling the windscreen. It was so close Roberts could see the soundless horror of the pilot's mouth as they stared at each other, only feet apart. Flinching with panic, Roberts pulled the trigger of the forward-firing Vickers gun, and at the same time heaved back on the stick as hard as he could. The German disappeared below as fast as he'd appeared, leaving the DH4 rearing vertically in the air like a startled horse, spraying bullets all over the sky.

It was an impossible manoeuvre. Somewhere beneath him, out of the corner of his eye the black Pfalz skidded past before the DH4 fell out of the air backwards, tail first, then kicking viciously into the dizzying chaos of an out of control nose-down spin.

By the time the world had stopped whirling round they were three thousand feet lower, alone in an empty air. Below, lay a brown jumble of anonymous fields. Above, the lacquer blue of the winter sky was devoid of any sign of the twenty odd aircraft that had been tumbling in the air only seconds before. Roberts' heart pounded under his ribs - his mouth was parched, dry. "Was that fear?" he wondered, as the aeroplane settled down.

He took a deep breath and looked around. Nothing.

The DH4 seemed all right. Behind him, Cartwright was hunched over his Lewis guns watching the sky behind. Far off in the distance he could see puffs of white smoke and the livid scar that marked the front line. He swung the DH4 gratefully westwards, and with a scared glance over his shoulder put the nose down and headed for home. At least they were still alive.

He had met his first enemy and survived.

*   *   *

Serjeant Jack Doughty was a watcher.

For nearly two years, since the spring of 1916, he had stood on various French fields, gazing at the eastern sky, hearing the canvas hangars flap behind him, trying to catch the first drone of the returning aeroplanes. He rarely heard them first. Usually the younger ground crew heard them long before him.

Doughty put this down to the fact that the wind usually blew from the West and the Royal Flying Corps' gaze was fixedly to the East, so the wind blew any sound towards Hunland. Other times he thought that the junior NCOs were younger, with sharper ears.

It never occurred to him that he was half-deaf, his hearing dulled by the shell fire and guns of nearly two years of front-line infantry soldiering. St Doughty had been out since '14 and had transferred to the Royal Flying Corps at the end of 1915.

Sometimes the others joked about this, but never to his face. 'Pop' Doughty was a regular non-commissioned officer in the Notts and Derbys, The Sherwood Foresters, with pre-war ideas of how the Army worked. He was not a man to be trifled with. So the little huddle of four ground crew shivered in the January cold and stared out to the East, their breath steam in the sharp air. To left and right similar little groups stamped their feet to keep warm, making idle conversation. All gazed fixedly at the eastern sky.

Somewhere out there were their aeroplanes.

Holmes, the airframe rigger, heard them first. A taciturn Hampshire man, brought up in the country, he always heard them early. He nodded; as he did so, others shielded their eyes until Cooper the cockney lance corporal pointed. "There they are!" Sure enough, black specks could be seen far off to the East. Sjt Doughty said nothing, waiting to count the numbers. He had seen too many not return.

Suddenly the 'planes were roaring over the boundary hedge at the far end of the aerodrome, bucking and bouncing onto the frozen turf before rocking towards their little knots of groundcrew, engines bellowing. As each aircraft nosed up to its handlers, the propeller stopped and the ground staff surrounded their charges like grooms round a Grand National winner.

Excited chatter drifted across the field. A cheerful pilot was doused in champagne, pouring off his brown leather helmet like a frothing waterfall. His observer laughed and grabbed the bottle to swig from it.

No DH4 moved up to Sjt Doughty's crew. Alone, of the twelve groups of groundcrew, they stood, forlorn, without a focus. The minutes ticked by. Aeroplanes were wheeled into hangers by chattering groundcrew and the brown-coated aircrew gathered in knots before drifting towards the grey wooden hut to report to Squadron HQ. A few glanced at Doughty's team standing alone, not talking, motionless.

As the field cleared, one of the aircrew walked across, breaking into the tight-faced séance staring east.

"I say," said the young pilot, embarrassed, returning Sjt Doughty's stony-faced salute. "Look, we saw Mr. Roberts and Mr. Cartwright going down, in a spin. Pretty bad, actually, but no one saw them crash. They may have landed somewhere else, eh? They could be all right, what?" He seemed to be about to say something else, but nodded and walked off towards the huts.

Cooper, broke the silence. "Bleedin' marvellous! We freeze our whatsits off and what for? Nuffink!" He spat disgustedly on the ground.

Doughty fixed him with a cold and slightly bloodshot eye. "Shut tha' croaking, Corporal." It was a tough, Derby voice, heavy with the authority of accustomed command. The 'corporal' hung in the air. "We'll see the officers in, rain or shine. It's wuss in't trenches, lad, a lot wuss: so shoot it."

Cooper opened his mouth and then "shut it".

He had arrived four weeks before, one of the new breed of engine mechanics, conscripted in the spring of 1917 and selected for mechanic training by the fledgling Royal Flying Corps.

At his recruiting interview, ever fly, Cooper had informed the Attesting Officer that he had worked in a garage in Bermondsey. This was a barefaced lie, designed to save a reluctant Cooper from the rigours of the Royal Fusiliers and the discomforts of the infantry in the trenches. He was banking that no-one was going to check up on him. He was right. However, by an irony of fate, in mechanic training, Albert Cooper had taken to the mysteries of the aero engine with surprising speed.

He had explained his new-found enthusiasm to Holmes, the airframe rigger, his first evening in the wet canteen over bottles of Bass.

"See, Holmsey, the way I look at it is, it stops me goin' in them bleeding trenches an' it gets me a job arter this is all over. A nice warm job in a garridge. We might as well get summink out of this war, eh?"

Now Holmes was looking stolidly ahead, staring out into the distance. The seconds turned to minutes. Suddenly he pointed: "'Ere they come," and a lone DH4 clattered low over the horizon to turn into the wind, black puffs of smoke blipping from its exhaust. "At bleedin' last," whined Cooper. "Abaht time, too."

"I'll not tell thee again, lad," Doughty said. "Shut it."

"All right, keep yer 'air on."

The Serjeant's head swivelled away from the khaki box kite bucketing across the grass towards them to eye the younger man with genuine surprise.

"Serjeant. 'All right, *Serjeant*'," Doughty said, slowly and deliberately. "You call me Serjeant. Have you got that, *Corporal* Cooper?"

Cooper, thin, pale, quick as a whippet, looked at the senior NCO's brown cracked face, ruined by tropical sun, crevassed like a seventy-year old. The heavy brown moustache fanged down, the older man's gaze unblinking.

It reminded Cooper of his father, a tough London docker, with quick hands and a quicker temper. Suddenly he was nervous, frightened. "All right then, Serjeant." The other mechanics had hinted that Pop Doughty's authority came from his fists as much as from the three stripes on his arm. For the hundredth time he eyed the faded medal ribbons on Doughty's tunic. "Bleedin' regulars", he thought. "All bull." He said nothing.

Doughty remained unmollified. "I'll have no croaking, Corporal. Now go and see to that engine." He looked at the East End boy unblinkingly, as the DH4 bumped heavily up to its waiting ground crew.

The big propeller clattered to a halt. The four men crowded round and across the field relieved faces popped out of the squadron office, noting the latecomer's arrival.

Roberts levered himself up out of the front seat and stretched. Even though his mouth was dry and his knees weak with reaction, he knew he must behave like the other pilots. It was expected of an officer. "Ah, there you are, Sarn't Doughty. One DH4 airframe, safely returned." he drawled.

"Well done, sir." Doughty's eyes took in the ragged bullet holes in the canvas. "Trouble?"

"A bit," admitted the young officer as he began to climb down, stiff and cold, from the wing. "But we saw them off, didn't we Jimmy?" He addressed the remark to the observer's cockpit, where his rear seater was still hunched over his twin Lewis guns. Cartwright grunted.

Doughty looked hard at the observer. "Making the guns safe, sir?"

Cartwright grunted again. This time the noise was more of a gurgle, like a man being sick.

Doughty swung up onto the side of the fuselage. "You all right, Mr. Cartwright?"

Again the observer gurgled, head down over his guns. Doughty noticed the guns were still armed, the observer's fingers hooked hard onto the firing levers. "Mr. Cartwright?" repeated Doughty. He touched the leather clad form.

The observer screamed, a high seagull wail that choked off in a gurgle.

The bustle of aircrew round the DH4 froze. Willing arms helped the brown clad form of Jimmy Cartwright out of the rear cockpit and laid him on the icy grass. The face was chalk white, the lips reddened with blood where he had bitten them to stop screaming in pain. The eyes were screwed tight shut.

Gently, they eased off the leather helmet. Roberts bent over his partner, rubbing Cartwright's hands and pleading with the white silent face.

Doughty addressed himself to Cope, the armourer, "Make sure those guns are made safe, lad. Then run and get the MO. Quickly, now."

"Yes, Sarn't." With a frightened glance at the recumbent form, Cope scuttled off.

"What's up, Jimmy?" pleaded Roberts, desperate and anxious. "Are you hit? What?" No reply came from the white face, although the mouth worked.

"Let's get his suit open and take a look shall we, sir?" Doughty began to pull back the brown leather flying coat. "Corporal Cooper, get that suit open. Let's have a look at the officer."

Cooper knelt by the body. The observer began to breathe noisily, panting gasps that ended in little choking noises. His eyes opened wide, then closed tight. Cooper's nose wrinkled as he pulled open the leather coat.

"'E's shit 'imself, Serjeant, that's wot. 'E stinks!"

"There's no wound," said Roberts. "Jimmy, are you hurt? I can't see a wound." Cooper rolled his eyes sardonically, then flinched from the Serjeant's hostile glare. The last flap of the fur-lined Sidcot flying suit flopped open.

As it did, Cartwright's intestines burst out, spilling shiny and purple. Blood welled out, trickling and dripping steadily onto the frozen turf. A foul stench steamed up in the frosty air.

"Oh, shit!" exclaimed Cooper, pulling back in disgust as the smell hit them.

Roberts stared uncomprehendingly at the horror.

The skin on his observer's belly was peeled back, purple loops of bowel and gut slithering slowly onto the ground. A bullet had sliced across the lower stomach, slitting it open as cleanly as any butcher's knife. Cartwright started to wail and clutched the gaping void that had been his belly. His fingers clawed into the mess and came away scarlet. He wailed again, a high-pitched keening.

Roberts reared up and staggered away from the group. He was no stranger to death, having been to the funerals of two of his friends, both killed in crashes during flying training. But this was the first time the boy had seen the butcher's-shop reality of soldiering close up. He bent over and vomited helplessly onto the frozen turf. Men running across the grass towards them skidded round the heaving shoulders of the young pilot. Doughty held the observer's bloodied hands to prevent further damage.

"Get the doctor! Get the fucking doctor! Now!" he bellowed. The parade ground voice echoed off the huts a hundred yards away. "Now!"

Suddenly all was movement. A frenzied struggle between Cartwright's bloodied hands flailing in the air, while Doughty and a chalk-faced Roberts fought desperately to stop the wounded observer doing any more damage to the ruin that had been his belly.

Corporal Cooper recoiled, eyes wide in horror. Holmes sprinted towards the huts, shouting "Stretcher bearers!" Men came running towards them, one clutching a doctor's bag.

Cartwright's shrill scream cut the air. "Mummy!" A series of wails tailed off as he started to cry. A thread of bright red blood dribbled from his mouth and he started to pant like a woman in labour.

The Squadron Medical Officer knelt by him, panting from the run. At the sight of the wound he too pulled back, nose wrinkling. Roberts looked across at the doctor, lips forming a question. Acting Captain Joshua Moon, US Army Medical Corps, one of the many US doctors seconded to British units to gain experience since America had entered the war the previous autumn, shook his head. In the two months since the young American had been with the British, this was the worst he'd seen – and still living, too. The boy was disembowelled.

He spoke to the crunched up face. "Hey, Jimmy. How're you doin'?" The Alabama voice was soft, gentle. "C'mon boy, speak to me. How're you doin'?"

Slowly, the dying observer's eyes fluttered open. First they seemed to stare at the sky, an infinity above them, then slowly focussed on the little group bending over him. He started to cry. Tears trickled down his face. "It hurts," he said, matter of factly. He recognised the doctor. "Hello, doc. Help me," he pleaded. "Please help me."

The doctor scrabbled in his bag and put two grey tablets under the bloody tongue. "They'll take the pain away, Jimmy." He plunged back into the leather bag and began to fill a glass hypodermic.

Halfway through he stopped and looked down at the crucified figure of the weeping boy, bowels spilling out onto the ground, arms held firmly by Sgt Doughty and Lt. Roberts. They looked up at his hesitation, puzzled by the delay.

The American doctor's jaw closed and he continued to draw deeper into the syringe. For a long moment, he looked down at the young man on the ground. Then he pushed the needle firmly down into the shoulder between throat and collarbone. Roberts looked across at him, questioning. Doughty held the observer's arms and stared down fixedly at the wounded man's face, avoiding the doctor's eye. He'd seen this before. The syringe came out. Doc Moon mechanically wiped away the tiny smear of blood.

For a long minute the little group looked down at the wounded man. Slowly the observer's face cleared and the eyes opened, taking in the anxious faces bent over him. He smiled weakly. "Hello, Doc. That feels better. Am I going to be all right?"

"Yes. I guess it does, Jimmy. You're gonna be fine now. No more pain. Now you rest awhile. Go to sleep. You jes' rest quiet, now". Moon's voice was tired and compassionate.

"Thanks doc…" The observer's eyes fluttered, unfocussed, one last time. Looking deep into some unfathomable space far above them he said very quietly, "I can see everything. But it's very dark." The voice was calm and slightly puzzled. "Not night. No, sleepy dark." Suddenly the eyes opened wide in astonishment as if seeing some vision. "Got to sleep; see Mama…" he breathed softly, and sighed. Then his eyes frosted blank forever.

So, Second Lieutenant James Antony Cartwright, Royal Flying Corps, just twenty years old at Christmas, died on the frozen grass of a French airfield, victim of a fatal abdominal wound and a massive overdose of morphine.

Moon and Roberts stood up. The doctor avoided eye contact as he packed his bag. Sjt Doughty pulled the leather coat over the ruined stomach and gestured to the waiting stretcher-bearers.

"Coom on, lads. Get 'im out of 'ere. Gently mind," he added.

Roberts leant against the side of the DH4. Absently his finger traced a bullet hole in the fuselage, behind the observer's cockpit. His shoulders began to heave and suddenly he was crying, shock and the awfulness of it all stripping away the 20-year-old's veneer of control. Just eighteen months before he had still been a schoolboy, only too impatient to join the heroic fliers of the RFC and get to the war.

"C'mon Robbie," said the doctor, patting his shoulder. "There's nothing anyone of us could do. C'mon, boy. Let's you and me go and have a drink. I guess you need it."

Roberts rounded on him accusingly. "You! You! You ...!" He stopped, gasping. "You did, didn't you? You...finished him?"

Moon looked at the boy and nodded. "Sure I did, Robbie. Jimmy was my friend; yours too. I did what was right. You know I did. You saw him. You wanted him to suffer? I wouldn't put my dawg through that, boy and I'm darned if I'll see a friend and a good man suffer. I'd do the same for you, you damned idiot. Now come on, let's go and have a drink. It's cold. There's nothing to do here."

Roberts looked at the group. Two bearers were loading the body onto a stretcher. The lifeless hands kept flopping sideways, despite Cope the armourer's attempts to keep them on the stretcher. Sjt Doughty was checking the observer's flight bag. Holmes was buttoning the leather coat over the white skin of the dead man's body. Cooper stood apart, mouth open, shaking his head in disgust. Roberts nodded slowly to his groundcrew and allowed himself to be led away, shoulders heaving, towards the waiting knot of pilots by the huts. All that was left of Jimmy Cartwight's Calvary was a smear of dark blood on the grass.

Suddenly, only the four ground crew were left by the aeroplane.

Cooper's London whine broke the silence. "Well, I never thought I'd see a bleedin' officer behave like that. Bein' sick like that. Crying like a fuckin' girl."

Sjt Doughty looked at the sneering face.

Officers. From somewhere deep down in the vaults of his memory, an old vision of Lieutenant Oldfield screaming in the mud of Ypres one autumn afternoon in 1914 floated into his mind.

The Notts and Derbys had been desperately trying to stem wave after wave of German attacks. A shell had blown off both Mr. Oldfield's legs. From the thighs down he had looked like raw dog meat splattered on the earth. Mr. Oldfield had looked at where his legs should have been and screamed. He had gone on screaming for over a minute until he died.

Then Doughty remembered Tommy Hallam from Chesterfield croaking in a stinking shellhole in February of 1915 near Neuve Chappelle.

Tommy Hallam had been in India with him. First Battalion men. They'd made corporal together, pulled in the winning tug of war team at the Battalion sports and got drunk together. He knew his missus. But then Tommy had been dying; half his lungs torn out by a shell splinter, shiny bright red blood and splintered white bones showing.

"For Christ's sake, Jack. Shoot me! Shoot me!" he had shrieked, bubbles of bright blood swelling and spattering from his lips. The pain-crazed eyes had shrieked from the red smeared face. Then Jack Doughty had crashed the brass bound butt of his Lee Enfield rifle down on his old chum's head to stop the screams, crunching again and again until the pleading stopped and poor Tommy Hallam was just another lifeless bundle of rags in the rain soaked mud, clawed fingers still twitching in death.

The memories stirred deep in Doughty's mind and his eyes took in Corporal Cooper, thin, whining, moaning about dying officers; disembowelled too. Nasty way to go.

What did this scrawny six-month apology for a soldier, let alone a non-commissioned officer, know of real soldiering, of the war? Whining little bastard. Knew nowt. Never heard the dull *whap*! of a bullet hitting flesh. Never seen a shell burst, never seen a friend dying in agony? Knew bugger all. Moaning little bastard. All Doughty's own fears, his frustrations and the loss of what he genuinely thought of as another of 'his officers' surged in his mind as he stared at Cooper's pale, ferrety face.

So Jack Doughty hit him.

It was a hard controlled upward blow, the experienced punch of a deputy from Chesterfield pit, not meant to leave a mark on his man but smashing into the Cockney corporal's solar plexus, driving every ounce of wind out of his lungs. Cooper collapsed, choking for air, eyes bulging with disbelief.

"I'll not tell thee again, Corporal," said Sjt Doughty calmly. "I'll have no disrespect on my crew. When tha's soldiered a bit then tha' can say summat. Till then – shoot it!" The Derbyshire accent was strong.

Cooper had fallen to his knees, mouth working soundlessly, like a landed fish on a riverbank, gasping for air.

Sjt Doughty turned to Holmes and Cope, impassive, silent observers of the drama. "C'mon then, lads. Let's put this bird away in the hangar."

As an afterthought he added, "You too, Corporal Cooper. I'll have no scrimshanking on my crew."

Slowly, the three men pushed the DH4 back into the flapping canvas hangar.

From the squadron commander's hut the Adjutant looked out and wondered why Corporal Cooper appeared to be having difficulties pushing the wing.

CHAPTER 2

During that bitter winter of 1917/18, the Western Front in France and Flanders was a mass of movement. The normally quiet period, when snow and ice made just keeping warm the most important battle of all, was that year a time of frantic activity on both sides. Either side of the 'murdered strip of nature' that was no-man's land, the fighting troops prepared for the storms to come.

Instead of huddling in their dugouts, the British, in particular, were busy digging new defensive trenches, staking out barbed wire and patrolling every night to find out exactly what the Germans were up to.

For their part, the Germans generally kept an ominous quiet. But, on cold clear nights, the British could hear them. In the South, along the old Somme battlefield, frozen sentries, cursing the cold and stamping their boots to stay warm, heard the rumble of distant gun wheels moving behind the German lines. Sometimes they heard the unmistakable clink of spade on stone as the hitherto comfortably ensconced Germans dug mysterious new earthworks just behind their front.

The man responsible for this disruption of the conventions of normal winter soldiering had taken the decision long before the turn of the year, long before the snow and ice had arrived. In a meeting, just over the Belgian border at Mons, on 11th November 1917, a group of senior German staff officers had gathered round a table.

The irony of their meeting place and its date would only become clear exactly one year later. But, that November, their leader had leaned over a map of the Western Front and determined the fate of millions of men. Bull necked, heavily moustached, and crop haired, the carmine stripes of a full general on the Great German General Staff betrayed his trade.

Germany's warlord, First QuarterMaster General Erich von Ludendorff, began to speak.

"Gentlemen, the assessment of Germany's military position is, for the first time in three years, firmly in our favour. The English and French are tired and weak. They are praying for the Americans to arrive, to arrive and save them. That will take another year. The forces in the West are therefore in balance."

The gruff low voice went on, "But in the East the war is over. Russia is finished. The Revolution of the Reds has finally brought their government down. Thanks to the Bolsheviks, the Russian Army is no longer a fighting force. I tell you, we could march on Moscow tomorrow should we wish. Between our 5th Army and Saint Petersburg, the only Russian soldiers we can see are heading east as fast as they can run, and throwing away their rifles as they go. Their government has collapsed. Trotsky and his Bolshevist scum are already begging Berlin for peace. Gentlemen, the war in the East is over. Germany has triumphed. In the East, we are victorious!"

He looked at his rapt audience.

"We therefore have an opportunity. An unbelievable chance. For the first time since 1914 we can end this struggle in Germany's favour. *Oberstleutnant* Hentsch's intelligence section estimates 60 English divisions and 105 French divisions oppose us in the West. As you know, we ourselves already have 150 divisions facing them."

"But – but - if we transfer our armies from the East, Operations assure me that by 1st of March next year, we will have at least another 40 divisions in France: maybe more. We will then outnumber the combined French and British. This, Gentlemen, gives us our historic opportunity. It also at last gives us a chance for total victory!" He smashed a clenched fist down on the map.

A rumble of approval greeted these last words.

The chief operational planners of the German Army in France and Flanders knew, or had deduced, these facts as well as their master. But they also knew that time was running out for Germany. The casualties of Verdun, the Somme and Passchendaele had bled the Army dry over the past two years. Half-trained youths and surly conscripted civilians now filled the ranks of what had once been the finest professional army in the world.

Worse, they knew that in one vital respect the war was nearly lost already. The '*materialschlacht*', the logistics war, was ripping the guts out of the army. The British blockade was strangling the Fatherland. Supplies were drying up. Food was scarce and when it arrived, of dreadful quality. There was no more rubber for tyres. Even bandages for the wounded were being made of crepe paper. Only ammunition and weaponry were in full supply, as Germany's faltering economy struggled to fight a war on two fronts with a starving civilian population and waves of strikes and food riots sweeping the big cities. Everyone knew that the social unrest at home was building into a national crisis.

Even the civilian politicians in Berlin no longer supported the war. Socialist deputies in the Reichstag openly demanded an end to the fighting. For the Imperial General Staff, and for the old Germany, time was fast running out.

Ludendorff eyed his staff. He knew what they were thinking, from the too-clever-by-half Hentsch of Intelligence, to the stolid von Tzschirner of Logistics: was there still time?

"Gentlemen," he went on, this time pounding the table gently with his palm to emphasise his words, "There is still time. But we cannot afford any delay."

He paused for effect.

"I have therefore made an historic decision. For the first time since 1914 we can outnumber our enemies in the west. We have developed new tactics. We have developed new artillery techniques and the guns and ammunition to make them work. We are assembling a new Army: an army of elite *Jäger* and Stormtroops; an army trained to infiltrate and get through the thickest defensive line."

He stared at the staff officers, now hanging onto their chief's words.

"Gentlemen, our hour has come. The enemy now is England. France cannot fight on without her strong right arm. Look at the French armies. They are sullen. Some divisions we know are in a state of near collapse. Every day we hear more evidence of their weakness. We even hear rumours of mutinies. Mutinies! I tell you, without England, France is finished."

He raised his voice.

"Our target, therefore, must be England. The Navy and the U Boats have failed to bring the British to their knees. They are hungry but stubborn. It is therefore up to us, the Army, to finish this war. So now we go on the offensive in the West! In the spring, when the weather is good, we will attack and drive the *verdammter* Tommies into the sea, where they belong! And then the war is won! We will attack with the greatest offensive the world has ever seen: then full victory shall be ours! This war will be won! *Deutschland, unser Vaterland*, will triumph!"

A low growl of approval greeted his rhetoric. Ludendorff stared at them, satisfied with the result of his little speech.

"Well, Gentlemen?" he asked. "Comments? Questions?"

The rigid conventions of the Great German General Staff now demanded that the logic and appreciation of the situation, even of the most senior officer, must be put to his staff experts for comment. And approval.

Von Zelle the HQ Coordination Colonel was the first to speak, clicking his heels. "*Jawohl, Herr General.* What of the *FeldMarschall?*"

Ludendorff nodded. A notable absentee from the gathering at Mons was Field Marshal Paul von Hindenburg, officially head of the German armies, and ostensibly Ludendorff's boss. Hentsch of Intelligence eyed von Zelle, wondering from Ludendorff's staged reaction if the question was a planted one.

"Ja, the Field Marshal," replied Ludendorff.

He dropped his chin. The jowls bulged in rolls of fat above the stand-up uniform collar. "You will be glad to know that this attack decision has the full approval of the highest military command in the land. The *FeldMarschall* is delighted that our armies are to attack at last. He is as confident of victory as I am!"

"I'll bet," thought Hentsch, the Chief of the Intelligence Bureau. It was an open secret that tensions were emerging between the Chief of Staff of the German Army and his deputy, the 'First Quartermaster General', whatever that rank was supposed to mean.

Some said that Ludendorff had even invented the title deliberately to place himself as Hindenburg's equal when the victors of the Battle of Tannenburg had been promoted eighteen months before as the team to run Germany's war effort. Rumour said that Hindenburg and Ludendorff now ran everything else in the Fatherland as well, with the Chancellor and politicians in Berlin coming begging, asking to be told what to do next, and following their bidding like obedient puppies.

Hentsch clicked his heels.

Ludendorff scowled. The head of the Intelligence Branch was not popular with the general staff, particularly Ludendorff's favoured *protégés* in Operations. Hentsch had been the bearer of much bad news in the autumn of 1917. The fact that he had been right only made it worse.

"What of the All Highest, *Herr General?*" he enquired politely.

"Ah, yes, Hentsch, the Kaiser." Ludendorff switched his gaze to the rest of the Staff. "What a good question …" He nodded for effect, pursing his lips.

"Gentlemen, you will be delighted to know that the Kaiser himself has approved our great attack in the spring. His Serene Majesty himself has welcomed the triumph of Germany's arms. You will be able to tell your children that you took part in the planning of the greatest battle the world has ever known. You will be able to say that you planned the "*Kaiserschlacht*". For the Kaiser has even suggested to me that the offensive should go forward under his own name!"

A buzz of approval swept round the table. The assembled staff nodded, exchanged looks and smiled. 'The Kaiser's Battle!' Surely this time they must be successful. Victory at last. *Gott sei Dank.*

"And now, Gentlemen," said Ludendorff, raising his voice above the noise. "To work. There is much to be done and little time. We have over 100 divisions to move and to train for battle before the spring. Railway Section?"

The head of the General Staff Railway Movement Planning Section stepped up to the map table to explain the implications of the great task ahead. For the moment, any doubts and uncertainties of the Great German General Staff would be submerged and sedated by the familiar narcotic of hard work and military planning.

CHAPTER 3

The British Expeditionary Force

GENERAL HEADQUARTERS, GENERAL STAFF
INTELLIGENCE BRANCH, FRANCE

January 1918

Second Lieutenant Roberts of the Royal Flying Corps knew nothing of Ludendorff's momentous conference at Mons.

What he did know was the impact on his own life of the German decision made two months before. It was killing his friends. Every day in that icy winter of early 1918, whenever the weather permitted, 25 Squadron's DH4s flew off to the East to see what was going on, or to try and bomb any target of value. And every day German scouts tried to stop them. The combination of German fighters and the accidents caused by the winter weather emptied seats around the St Omer mess table.

As Robbie sprawled near the mess stove, listening to the after dinner chatter of his fellow airmen he realised that he had already lost three chums in the short time he had been with the squadron. He felt a pang of self-pity, a memory of some long forgotten misery. It reminded him of his first term at boarding school. He looked around the crowded, dimly hit mess hut, and felt again the same memory of homesickness, the cold, and the fear of not doing the right thing in front of others. "Be a brave boy", his mother had said, sniffing. "You'll be all right my boy," his father had said, rather gruffly and pushed five shillings into the eight-year-old's hand. Five whole shillings! But then a successful Kent doctor could easily afford five shillings.

Now, in a wave of dejection, he realised he might just as well be back in a strange new school. Major Duffus the CO had seemed cool and remote since his interview on arrival. The other pilots all knew each other. They all seemed so confident and noisy and rowdy. He didn't know half of them. And Jimmy, his only real chum had gone west. On his, Roberts, first operational mission. He wondered if the old hands were laughing at him behind his back, secretly despising his weakness for breaking down when Jimmy died. He didn't know. He was always cold. A wave of misery swept over him.

"Do you know, I've never known a month like this," said Smith, the

Squadron Intelligence Officer.

Outside, the wind shrieked from the East and flurries of wet snow blattered against the wooden mess hut. The assembled young aircrew, huddled in sagging armchairs round the stove, looked up at him. Smithy, wheezing from terrible chest wounds sustained in Loos in 1915, and which would eventually kill him in 1920, went on, "Well, I remember last April. I mean, we lost a lot of good chaps, but then we were covering the show at Arras. You expect to lose chaps in an attack. But this ..." he gestured hopelessly with this glass at the two empty seats.

"It was an accident, Smithy," said one of the younger pilots.

"Yes, I know. But why? Why are we flying in conditions like this? It's stupid. That's two good crews gone west since Christmas. Not shot down by the Huns, mind: all silly accidents caused by bad weather flying. It ain't right."

"But it's the big push, Smithy. Everyone knows that the Jerries are going to attack. That's why we've got to fly."

Another voice chimed in, "And I hate to tell you, Smithy, but it's your bally photographs we're risking over necks to get!"

A laugh greeted this. Temporary Captain E. S. Smith drew hard on his cigarette and coughed pitifully.

The door of the hut burst open, and for a second the wind whipped round the hut. A puff of smoke belched from the stove. A cry of 'SHUT THE DOOR!' faded as thirty anxious faces turned to the newcomer. Tall, cadaverous, with a black eye patch, leaning heavily on a blackthorn stick, the Squadron Adjutant advanced into the yellow puddle of lamplight and looked down at a purple duplicated sheet of foolscap in his black-gloved hand.

"Right, gentlemen," he spoke in a dry measured tone. "The Squadron will be flying patrols at dawn tomorrow – weather permitting."

A groan greeted this announcement.

"'A' Flight: you're stood down. B Flight: Arty Observation, take off first light. Patrol towards Hazebrouck, details in the morning. C Flight: ready for take off as ordered from nine ack emma onwards."

The single beady eye swept round the room. The fire-ravaged face of Captain Peter Coachman, late the 60th Rifles, leaned heavily on his stick. In the lamplight the livid scars gleamed red and white. "Now, my advice to you chaps is to get some sleep. Duty flight commanders come with me please."

And with that 25 Squadron's Adjutant and operations officer limped off to the far end of the hut.

The warm, cosy spell was broken. The knot of aircrew that had been slumped round the stove or against the walls, rose, stretched, exchanged good nights and scattered, the hut door banging in the wind. Only the dozen or so of 'A' Flight stayed behind. Someone called for another whisky. Chairs were moved closer to the warmth of the stove. Not for 'A' Flight the sleepless night, the call in the blackness before dawn, the stewed tea, the bleary-eyed breakfast of greasy eggs and bacon eaten in a dark and silent mess hut, and then the lumbering walk in the frozen sunrise out to the waiting aeroplanes, with their chilled and anxious ground crews.

"Well, rather them than us," said Jack Armstrong, 'A' Flight's commander, a pale, dark-eyed veteran of twenty-two.

"Probably won't fly with this wind," said the whisky drinker.

"Lucky beggars."

"I wish we'd had weather like this yesterday morning."

"Why?"

"Then we'd not have had to fly yesterday – and Bunny and Slugs would still be here."

"That's rot," cut in Armstrong. He threw a cigarette savagely into the stove and replaced the metal lid with a bang. He ran a hand over his brilliantined black hair.

"It's just luck. It could happen to any of us, at any time. Anyway," he added, "We don't want anyone in this flight talking like that. Miserable stuff. Don't help anyone, what?"

'A' Flight absorbed their commander's rebuke.

"Anyway," said Armstrong, "We're off tomorrow. Have we got the envelopes?"

Tradition in 25 Squadron demanded that every newly arrived pilot or observer placed a £5 note in an envelope which was then pinned to the Officers' Mess notice board. A dozen eyes scanned the forest of labelled envelopes by the door.

"No," said the whisky drinker, "They're still there. I'll get them"

He rose and unpinned the two envelopes, bringing them to Armstrong.

"Drinks," he said sharply, and A Flight rose to their feet. Armstrong clawed open the first envelope, drawing out a crumpled and rather grubby five-pound note. With it was a note scrawled on a page ripped from an observer's notebook. Armstrong read it and smiled.

"It's Slugs. He says, 'If you miserable sinners are reading this, then I've gone west. Don't spend it all on drink…'" His voice tailed off.

"And what did Bunny say, skipper?"

Armstrong ripped open the second envelope, unfolding a brand new fiver, which gleamed white in the light as he unfolded it. With it was a blue note and another envelope. He read the note in silence then pocketed the sealed envelope.

"Well?"

Armstrong looked up at them. "It's a letter to his parents. He says in the note to us, 'Goodbye chaps. Sorry I can't be with you for the party'…" His voice tailed off.

A Flight looked around. The envelopes from the lost aircrew usually contained cheerful messages, scrawled in happier times when immortality seemed obvious and life was all a joke. Somehow Bunny's message seemed solemn, even macabre.

Armstrong sensed the mood. "I'll write to his parents tonight and send the letter on." He raised his glass, gathering his audience.

"Gentlemen. *THE* Flight. And absent friends!"

In the 'A' Flight ritual his audience responded "*THE* Flight! And absent friends!"

They drank and a dozen glasses crashed against the wall.

Further down the hut the other flight commanders and the Adjutant looked up at 'A' Flight's noisy ritual send off to its lost airmen.

Armstrong ran a hand through his hair again. "Come on chaps... let's have one more for the road. We ain't flying tomorrow." Suddenly he laughed. "And I hope you lot have written better messages than those two! Steward – Drinks please!"

"Why not a boat race?" said a voice.

"Observers against drivers, airframes?"

"No contest!"

"Good idea. Six against..." The voice tailed off

Roberts, silent up to now, spoke up. "What's to happen to me, Jack? Now that Jimmy's gone? I still haven't got a regular observer..."

From the other end of the hut the Adjutant looked up.

"Ah yes, Roberts. We've got something for you, my friend. Never mind sitting around feeling sorry for yourself. That was just bad luck with young Cartwright, but don't blame yourself. Think yourself lucky it wasn't you. Anyway, the skipper wants you back in the saddle tomorrow. You're to go up on your own. You're to take the new chap, Higgins, with you. Put him in the back seat and show him the sights. Any time after 10 a.m. So don't go overboard tonight."

"But Higgin's a pilot, not an observer," cut in the whisky drinker.

"New policy, old man. Major Duffus wants all newly joined aircrew to be given a couple of familiarisation trips in clear daylight before being attached to an operational flight. Steer clear of trouble. Just sightseeing. Young Roberts here could do with the practice and he's waiting for a new observer. Just the man."

"I say," said a voice, "Now that's my kind of flying. Joy rides round the Salient. Trips round the bay, half a crown a time. No Huns. Cushy number, what? You can swap duties with me, Robbie, any time."

A cushion sailed through the air. Roberts stood up. Were they ragging him? "Where do I go? Sir,' he added uncertainly.

Coachman smiled at the younger man. 'Don't call me "Sir", in the mess, Roberts. Save that for the squadron commander. We're a friendly squadron. Not like some. Briefing in the morning. Find Higgins and you can both report to me at ten ack emma. But no risks, no tangling with Brother Boche. Stay strictly behind our lines. Brigade wants every new aircrew to be given the chance to learn the ropes."

"Good scheme," said a voice. "I'm all for it."

"I'm so glad you approve," purred the Adjutant, with heavy sarcasm. "The CO will be delighted by A Flight's unstinting support. And do try not to crash your machine, Roberts, like some of these ham-fisted hooligans you're drinking with. When the Hun push comes, we're going to need every pilot and every observer, believe you me. Goodnight, Gentlemen."

Shaking his head, Captain Peter Coachman, '*Cauchemar*' – 'Nightmare' - to his young pilots, stumped off to his endless work, leaving 'A' Flight to mourn its dead.

*   *   *

The 'Hun Push' was absorbing the attention of more than 25 Squadron's rowdy young airmen and the German High Command.

As a frozen January drifted into an even colder February, an anxious group scraped noisy chairs to sit round a polished table at Montreuil, not twenty miles from Roberts as he clambered heavily into the DH4 to show Higgins the ropes.

It was a cold, clear day. The wind had died down and clouds and bright winter sunlight alternated. It was very cold. As the DH4 swung into the wind, the speaker at the far-away Montreuil meeting looked down the gleaming table. The cold light outside was reflected off the mirrors on the walls.

The Intelligence Staff of General Headquarters, British Expeditionary Forces France & Belgium were meeting in the Blue Mirror room of the BEF headquarters to discuss the 'Big Push'.

The man at the end of the table was a tall, pink-faced officer with thinning hair. The scarlet tabs on his collar and the two stars and a crown on his shoulders proclaimed him a colonel on the British General Staff. He was a worried man.

For weeks now his staff had been bringing him daily reports of German troop movements. All were in one direction. As the Colonel Int 1(A) of the British Expeditionary Force GHQ stood at his map every day he was watching an inexorable draining of German divisions from east to west. It was an alarming pattern. From Luxembourg in the South to Ostend in the North, reports had flooded in of new German units identified settling in on the Western Front. And as the little black pins proliferated on his wall map, it became ominously clear that most of them were clustering in the North, facing the British Expeditionary Force.

There could be no doubt for Colonel Jeremy Mackenzie and the staff of Int 1(A). The BEF was to be the Huns' next target. The only question was, when?

"So, we're all agreed, then?"

The men round the table nodded. Everyone knew what they were seeing; and everyone knew what it meant. Over the past three months, the intelligence staff of GHQ had watched with growing concern as the cards were slowly stacked up on the table against them.

It was a constant struggle for the Int Staff.

A sceptical operations staff and a stubborn commander in chief had not paid much attention at first to Int's warnings. They never did. Officers had even been prevented from briefing the C-in-C the previous summer. "We don't want to upset the Chief," Charteris, the Brigadier General, responsible for Intelligence, had murmured to an officer on one occasion the previous autumn, taking the damning file from his concerned subordinate.

"But, Sir!" an anxious Captain James Marshall-Cornwall had exclaimed, "We can't not warn the Commander in Chief."

"My dear boy," said Charteris, smoothly, "you don't understand the sort of pressures the Chief is under. We don't need to worry him with these kinds of details. He's got enough on his plate at the moment."

And with that, Brigadier General John Charteris had locked the report of the real German losses in Flanders firmly in his desk drawer, leaving another 100,000 men to die, or be maimed, in the mud around Ypres, as the slaughter of Passchendaele went on for another three months.

Now Charteris had long gone.

Like some ghost at the feast, he was still seen dining occasionally in the senior officer's mess at Montreuil, but his post was now some non-job, an ill-defined liaison officer with the Transport Directorate. Intelligence was now firmly in the hands of Brigadier General Edgar Cox, and the door marked "Secret - No Admittance" securely bolted against its former leader. Rumour had it that Charteris had gone because the politicians were angry about Passchendaele. There were even stories that the Prime Minister, Lloyd George, had tried to get rid of the C-in-C, Sir Douglas Haig himself, but, thwarted, had had to settle for lesser scalps.

Looking round the table, Mackenzie knew that his junior staff were only too aware of the political machinations and in-fighting swirling around the court of GHQ. His problem was to ensure that G (Int) brought the Holy Grail of Intelligence to the C-in-C of the BEF, and as soon as possible: just where would the Germans attack? And, more importantly, exactly when?

Failure to get the right answer would not only mean that Mackenzie would lose his job overnight; it would also mean that thousands of British soldiers would lose their lives as they were caught by surprise.

"Well, gentlemen, we have a clear task," be began. "The Commander in Chief called me to his office with the Chief of Staff this morning, as you know."

He cleared his throat – this was a difficult area.

"He now accepts – completely – G Int's thesis that the Huns are going to come for us as, the BEF, soon as they are ready."

Glances were exchanged round the table.

Everyone round the table knew only too well that Mackenzie had been arguing for nearly a month about the inevitability of a German spring offensive against the BEF. Equally they knew that G (Ops) had refused to accept G Int's warnings and were even rumoured to be planning some daft new push of their own. Even when they had accepted Int's warnings, the Operations staff had shrugged them off.

"So what?" ran Operations' reply in a hundred memoranda and meetings. "If we and the French haven't been able to break through in three years, why should the Germans suddenly solve the problem? It isn't as if the Germans have got some magic wand to solve the problems of trench warfare. They don't even have tanks."

There was some truth in this. The rules were the same for both sides.

The only way to break through the defensive trench lines was to have a massive bombardment that went on for days. That lost surprise; so even where you got into the enemy's shattered trenches, fresh reserves would always be waiting to seal off the breach and to counter-attack. Trench warfare was as formal and inevitable as a deadly quadrille.

The only thing that might work was tanks, as Byng and his 3rd Army had proved at Cambrai three months before. But the Germans hadn't got any tanks to break through, and even at Cambrai, after four days, the Germans had smashed the British back in the inevitable counter-attack. So even that was out. Breakthrough was impossible.

Operations agreed with their dour and stubborn C-in-C. The only way to win the war now was attrition: attrition to wear down the Germans and win the numbers game until the hundreds of thousands of new American reinforcements arrived. Killing the Germans was the policy; and if the Germans wanted to attack, well, more fool them. Everyone knew that the attackers always suffered more casualties. You only had to look at Loos, the Somme and Passchendaele. As Lloyd of G Ops had so succinctly put it at the last GHQ Staff meeting, "Mac, if the Hun is stupid enough to attack, it'll only bring about a quicker collapse. Q.E.D., eh?"

Mackenzie wasn't so sure.

Disturbing reports were reaching him of hurricane bombardments on the Eastern Front; new German units, trained in "special tactics", whatever they were. German prisoners reported a rise in morale, better rations, new weapons. Above all, the G Int map showed more and more infantry divisions, more and more artillery batteries.

"So the question the C-in-C wants answering is: where will the Hun attack? In what strength? And, most important for the Chief, exactly when?" Mackenzie looked down the two rows of faces.

"That's our task, gentlemen. We need answers, and quickly. It's now the second of February. There were 160 German divisions in the line this morning and 30 more on the move. I don't have to tell you about our problems. Fifth Army are to take over another twenty miles of French trenches, south of Peronne next week…" A ripple ran round the table. "I know," went on Mackenzie, "our gallant allies are still sorting themselves out."

A few smiles greeted this. 'Our gallant Allies' had become a GHQ shorthand for 'our incompetent French colleagues who refuse to fight…' Every officer round the table knew that the French Army had mutinied the previous summer and were still refusing to attack, only manning defensive trenches. It was the biggest secret in France.

"You mean, they're still workin' to rule, Colonel? Like the dockers and miners back home?" a languid cavalry voice floated up the table. Laughter greeted this sally.

"Well, yes, you could say that. But it's their country that's been invaded, and they did hold the ring for us to get ready for over two years, so I'm not too hard on the Frenchies." Mackenzie looked down, re-arranged his pens. "We can't be too careful ourselves. That Etaples nonsense proves it ain't just the French, y'know."

The group stirred uncomfortably. The 'Great Etaples Mutiny' of September 1917 had shaken the BEF to its core. Thousands of bored and angry soldiers had rampaged through the coastal bases at Etaples and le Touquet, refusing to soldier and forcing the Base Depot Commander to call in loyal troops to quell the disturbances. After a week of trouble it had all simmered down. The Base Commander had been quietly posted and the troops in the base camps hastily despatched back to their regiments at the Front; but it had been an ugly couple of weeks last September.

"What are these French trenches like?" said the cavalry voice. "I mean, are they good positions?"

"No," said Mackenzie. "Gough's people tell me that there's only one line of trenches and it'll take weeks of work to bring them up to standard. Fifth Army are going to have their work cut out, gentlemen… "

More glances were exchanged. Of all the British Armies in France, Sir Hubert Gough's headquarters staff was known to be the slackest, with sloppy staff work and a casual attitude to detail.

"Fifth Army must get on with it," said Mackenzie, "bad trenches or not.

Our problem is to find out what the Hun is up to." He stood up and went over to a blanket-covered blackboard on an easel. Throwing the blanket back he pointed to a list.

"Here are our sources of intelligence. You all know them. And here," he stabbed at a second column, "are the best answers we can expect."

The group stared at the blackboard. Someone started writing on a pad.

"Now, here are our traditional sources. First, photo recce and arty observation. Aeroplanes and pictures. Second, there's the Secret Service. They're getting better and better agents' reports; not always accurate, sometimes late, but good – provided the Belgians don't eat the carrier pigeons. Third, the railway reporting system. Solid, accurate and well able to be checked."

He gestured at the blackboard. "What this tells us is how many divisions Jerry had and, pretty well, where they are. What it doesn't tell us is when he's going to attack, and exactly where." He banged the blackboard. "That's our real problem, gentlemen."

"What about prisoners, Colonel? Surely they can help?"

"Yes, of course. But Brother Hun isn't even telling his own chaps. We got two good prisoners last week, south of Arras. One was an Alsatian and spoke French better than German, acording to the interrogator. Wanted to talk. No, they sang like canaries, thanks to James and his people. But not a word of any help to us. Oh yes, there's going to be an attack, but of when, not a word. The fact is, even they don't know."

Down the end of the table the two captains were whispering. "Excuse me, Sir," said one. "What about the telephone tapping? Wireless? Are R.E. Signals picking up any hints?"

Mackenzie shook his head. "'Fraid not, Teddy. Not a whisper from the Engineers. Lots of background stuff, but nothing on dates."

"It's really intentions," the sharp cavalry voice brayed. "What you're looking for, Colonel, is the Hun's intentions. We know what they've got and where they are, but we don't know what they're going to do. Ain't that it?"

Mackenzie smiled. Captain Sir Robert Purfitt, Baronet, of the Dragoon Guards might pretend to be an ass sometimes, but he was far from stupid, however hard he tried to hide his undoubted brains from his fellow cavalry officers.

"Exactly, Bobby. That's our real problem. The Hun's intentions."

"But that's really Secret Service stuff, surely?" said an earnest Sapper Captain. "Can't *they* tell us?"

The cavalry voice brayed again. "Ask 'em. Can't do any harm. After all, they're supposed to be on our side, too."

Bobby Purfitt's sally was greeted with laughter. Even Mackenzie grinned.

"Well, yes, strictly speaking you're right, Bobby. But do I have to draw your attention to the fact that our esteemed Secret Service couldn't even be bothered to attend this meeting? They really are a bit of a law unto themselves."

"Squeeze them, Colonel," growled a blue-jawed major sitting on Mackenzie's right. Major Horace Cuffe DSO, was head of the Order of Battle office. His dislike of the Germans was closely followed by is dislike of the "funnies", as the Secret Service in France and Belgium was known.

"Squeeze 'em," he repeated. "After all, they can hardly refuse to help in the present situation, can they?"

Mackenzie grimaced.

"Horace, you're absolutely right. But I can't force them. We can only ask nicely. And they're not helping. Everything they get goes straight back to London. When we see it – *if* we see it – it's usually three weeks old, or more sometimes. They don't even answer to the Brigadier General, and if we put too much pressure on them, they just go running to the Chief of Staff, or even worse, to London, saying we're being difficult. Frankly, there's not a lot I can do with Special Int."

"They may be able to help in another way." The voice came from halfway down the table. The speaker was a shortish, square-faced young major who had been silent up to now.

Captain, acting-Major, James Marshall-Cornwall, DSO, MC, was one of the longest serving officers in G-Int. Speaking five languages and "out since 1914" he had applied to go back to his regiment on numerous occasions. But his services to the BEF Intelligence Staff were too important to be left to the Royal Regiment of Artillery and the hazards of the front line with its unpredictable shells and bullets. So Marshall-Cornwall stayed firmly in GHQ Int, chafing at the lack of action, but the most experienced and respected officer on the int staff.

"Go on, James."

"Well, there are TWO secret services, correct? That funny bureau in London and our own GHQ set-up out here. As I understand it, the arrangement now is that Cumming's Secret Service lot in London do all the high level foreign stuff with the War Office, but GHQ out here has a responsibility for the stuff from the occupied zones in France and Belgium. That's what I understand."

He went on, "Well, if you look at the fine print of the Kirke agreement, it says that our own GHQ Secret Service is responsible for all special operations in the German occupied zones, too. Special operations," he emphasised.

Marshall-Cornwall had the whole table's attention.

"So?"

"So, why don't we task them to run some of these mythical 'special operations' for us? After all, they're supposed to be supporting the BEF. Not London"

Mackenzie shook his head. "Good idea, James; but since Cameron's gone they're even more uncooperative. Who's going to order them?"

Two weeks before, in a messy shake up, Colonel Cameron, the head of GHQ 'Special Intelligence' had been sacked in a welter of recriminations, after Cumming's Secret Service in London, the War Office, and the Allied Intelligence Liaison Office at Folkestone had finally ganged up to remove the stubborn and secretive head of Secret Services in the BEF. The order from London still rankled in the more secret corridors of GHQ.

"The Chief. The Chief'll order them all right." Horace Cuffe looked up at Mackenzie. "Quote the C-in-C, Colonel." A rumble of assent greeted his words.

"Colonel, he's right." Bobby Purfitt was leaning forward down the table.

"If Haig demands action, even Special Int can't say no. They'll have to chip in and help. If they don't, they're finished."

"Bobby's right," added Marshall-Cornwall, "But collection isn't just my point. Of course we need information. Spies, pigeons, burglaries, whatever," he waved a dismissive hand. "That'll give us intentions. But what I'm suggesting is something else: *disruption*. *Real* special operations behind the Hun lines to slow him down. Attack behind their lines. Choke off the blood supply. Maybe even stop any offensive before it gets going."

Marshall-Cornwall had the meeting again.

"What are you suggesting, James? Mass sabotage? The Huns will take terrible reprisals against the civilians. We'd never get the Chief to agree to that."

Heads nodded round the table. The German policy of *schrechlichkeit* – literally "frightfulness" – in the occupied territories was savage. Just before Christmas, two Belgians had been shot near Mons for the crime of possessing carrier pigeons; and only last week at Lille, ten Frenchmen had been executed as a reprisal for the murder of two German officers.

Marshall-Cornwall persisted. "No, no, I don't mean that. Not big stuff. What I'm suggesting is something much more precise." He looked up at the puzzled faces round the table. "What would be the effect if the big German Headquarters was blown up? With its entire staff? Or even Rupprecht's HQ – at a key moment just before the big attack?"

There was a long silence, broken only by the distant buzzing of a far off aeroplane.

Cuffe broke the silence. "Are you suggesting some kind of bombing, James?"

"Yes, exactly." Marshall-Cornwall waved a hand at the Chateau windows where the aeroplane noise was getting louder. "Imagine that's a Hun. Think what one well-placed big bomb, here in this building now, would do." His listeners stirred uneasily.

"Steady on, old man," a gunner captain said. "Why, that would be assassination, murder, surely?"

Marshall-Cornwall rounded on the speaker. "Murder? When over 300 men are being killed or wounded on average every day in the BEF.

Dammit, this is a war we're fighting, not a game of cricket! What is all this if it's not just organised killing on a grand scale?"

Mackenzie intervened hastily. "I see your point, James. So what you're suggesting is disrupt the attack by killing their key generals?"

"At the right moment, yes."

Eyebrows went up round the table. "Pretty unorthodox, what?" said a voice.

The gunner captain scowled. "Why not go the whole hog, then? Why don't you just try and kill Hindenburg and Ludendorff," he added sarcastically. "That should fix it." A few laughs greeted this. Emboldened, the gunner went on, looking round for support: "Hang it all, why not just kill the Kaiser and be done with it, eh? That should win the war!" The laughter grew louder. Two spots burned on Marshall Cornwall's cheeks.

Bobby Purfitt broke into the guffaws. "And why not?" The room fell silent. "Why not?" he repeated. "After all, he's the chap responsible for this whole stinkin' mess, ain't he? It's the Kaiser what started it."

The cavalry officer stared round the room.

"I agree with Marshall-Cornwall. If we can, why not try and kill a few generals? And the Kaiser too. If that saves lives and helps us to win this beastly war, then I'm all for it. And I'll wager the fellows fighting at the Front would agree with us, eh?"

A silence greeted this intervention. Traditionally, generals did not war on generals. Deep in the psyche of the fourteen men round the table was the notion of 'fair play', playing the game, fighting fair. To a group of men raised on the English public school tenets of muscular Christianity, blowing up unprotected headquarters behind the lines seemed underhand: somehow both fanciful and ungentlemanly.

The gunner captain voiced the thought. "I can't see the Chief approving any plan to murder the Kaiser ..." He paused, then saw a trump card. "Hang it all, if we do things like this, what's to stop the Huns then pooping off at the King?"

Mackenzie stepped forward to stop the debate, but Purfitt was too quick. "Nothing at all," he said. "And if they could, I'll wager the Huns wouldn't hesitate for a moment to kill the King, if they thought it would help them to win the war. Their Zeppelins are bombin' London ain't they? But it isn't in their interest. But Generals and HQs, well they're fair targets, surely? Didn't we bag a couple of divisional HQs at Cambrai, generals and all?"

The meeting absorbed this truth. In the great tank raid at Cambrai the previous November, nearly 400 British tanks had scrunched through the German wire, taking the enemy completely by surprise. For a few glorious hours, British cavalry and light tanks had run amok behind the German front lines, shooting up horse lines, artillery batteries, and even two divisional HQs. It had been a triumph until the Germans counter attacked and sent the Byng's men scuttling back to their own front lines. But there was no denying that German generals and their staff had been killed or captured.

In the silence that followed, the droning of the aeroplane outside grew more insistent. Mackenzie cleared his throat.

"So what you're suggesting is that we not only ask GHQ Secret Services to step up their collection service to the C-in-C out here, but also to pinpoint the key enemy headquarters for any attack and … and kill them? Put a bomb under them?"

"Pretty well," Marshall-Cornwall nodded.

The Gunner captain returned to his argument. "But how? With those?" He waved a hand at the buzzing of the invisible aeroplane. "They couldn't blow up a whole HQ. They might kill a few chaps and frighten the horses, but you're not going to stop a Hun offensive with a few kites sprinkling 25lb Cooper bombs from the air."

"That's true. But there are plenty of other ways of planting a bomb."

The whole table looked aghast at Marshall-Cornwall, and the Gunner captain said triumphantly, "Ah-ha! So you do mean murder, then!"

Purfitt rolled his eyes at Mackenzie. "Of course we don't mean murder. But going for the enemy's commander is as legitimate an act of civilised warfare as any other combatant." Mackenzie was acutely conscious of the irony of Purfitt's phrase "civilised warfare".

"You mean it would be legal under the Hague Convention, Bobby?"

"Exactly, Colonel," said a grateful Purfitt. It's a legitimate act of war.

And if it works it could even end the war. That's worth a shot, surely? Winning the war?"

"Well," said Cuffe, "then I, for one, would recommend it. It's a bit unorthodox, but a sound scheme. Anything that helps end this bloody war gets my vote!"

Reluctant nods followed round the table. A flat northern voice came from the end as the most junior officer present spoke up. "Well I don't see anything wrong in trying to bump off Germans, however exalted they are. After all, is there a war on or not?"

Several faces turned to the speaker and tut-tutted.

Mackenzie tried to suppress a smile. Charles Powell, Cuffe's junior staff offficer was not a regular soldier and sometimes it showed. Undeterred, Lt Powell went on, appealing for support round the room. "Well coom on; are we trying to win this war or not? I can't think of anything better than knockin' off a few generals… I can think of a few generals I'd like to bump off for a start. And they're not all German either." A mixture of shock and hilarity rippled round his audience. "If it gets us all home sooner, I'm for it. A top secret job to shoot a few senior officers and end the war. Great scheme."

Bobby Purfitt clapped his hands in silent applause. Lt Powell stared defiantly round the table. "Anyway, that's what I think."

Mackenzie's smile was now unconstrained as he shook his head. "I think you've summed it up beautifully, Charles. A secret operation to neutralise the German High Command." He looked round the table. Most heads nodded, although the gunner captain who had argued against Bobby Purfitt looked down and refused to catch his eye.

"A secret operation it is then. Now, any more ideas…?"

Down the table the two captains were whispering.

"Excuse me, Sir…"

"Yes?" said Mackenzie.

"Surely if we're going to do something really secret like this, then nobody ought to know about it? Apart from those who need to."

"Quite right. Let's close this particular subject now. I think we have quite enough ideas to be going on with. I'll brief the Chief. Now let's look at some of the other ways we might be able to make an impact…"

*   *   *

Two thousand feet above the meeting, Roberts gently banked his DH4 and headed back for St Omer.

"So that's GHQ – Montreuil. Quite a good landmark really. Walled town and so on. Easy to recognise." He was shouting down a lashed up speaking sysytem, comprising a petrol-filling funnel connected by a rubber tube to the metal tube linking pilot and observer. In the rear, the new boy, Higgins, was listening intently through the improvised voice pipe, picking out Roberts' words above the bellow of the engine.

"If you see Montreuil," went on Roberts, "You're too far west – unless you're going back to Blighty."

Higgins glanced over his left shoulder at the coast of England, tantalisingly close from 2,000 feet. Boulogne drifted below the left wing, Napoleon on his column staring hopelessly across the Channel.

"What's at GHQ?"

"Oh, not much. Bunch of red tabs, lots of talk. Bin there once on a binge when I first came out." My God, he thought… that was only six weeks ago. He felt quite the old soldier in front of Higgins. "Saw the C-in-C drive by… at least someone said it was Haig. We all had to stand up. Lots of cafés and restaurants. Some of 'em reserved for senior officers only. A bit stuffy, really. Bit of a waste of time, Montreuil …"

And having delivered his considered opinion of General Headquarters, British Expeditionary Force, Second Lieutenant Roberts, Royal Flying Corps, banked to his right, south east for St Omer and a late lunch. Little did he know that he just flown over the birth of an idea that would have momentous consequences.

CHAPTER 4

Haig's Office, GHQ Montreuil

4 February 1918

"What?!"

General Sir Douglas Haig was angry. In fact, for a self-controlled, quiet-spoken man, very angry indeed.

"You stand here in my office and seriously suggest that I should sanction the ..." He stumbled for words, inarticulate as ever. "The assassination – no, the *murder* of my German counterparts?"

Mackenzie stood his ground.

In the last twenty seconds the Intelligence Colonel had decided that now he was definitely going to be sacked, so he might as well see it through and fight his corner.

"No, Commander in Chief. I am only responding to your request this morning for information on the Hun push and any ideas I might have for slowing it down. That I have done. I am only doing my duty. Sir." he added slightly plaintively.

Haig calmed down. Over three years of war had sapped even his legendary self-control and patience. A fair man, overworked, lacking sleep and under pressure from both the government at home and the French, he knew his temper was getting shorter. It wasn't Mackenzie's fault, even if it was a damned silly idea. He glanced up at Lawrence, his new Chief of Staff.

"Well?"

Lawrence rubbed his moustache. "Mackenzie's proposal is unorthodox, No doubt about it, Chief. But I feel that he's right about the first part: getting GHQ Secret Services to work more to you and a little less to London." General Sir Herbert Lawrence, like most of the general staff, had strong views on the rabble of civilians in uniform, prima donnas and disgraced ex-officers who lurked behind the 'Secret Service – Special Intelligence' door down the hall.

Haig grunted. "No difficulties with that, Lawrence. After all, they are supposed to be part of the BEF."

"Yes, sir."

"It's this other thing." He glowered at Mackenzie who returned his gaze. Haig's lips compressed under the moustache. "It's not – well – it's just not <u>British</u>, is it?"

"Colonel Mackenzie's idea is sound enough, Sir."

Mackenzie realised cynically that suddenly it was all 'Mackenzie's idea'. If the Chief bought the plan then it would not take long for it to become GHQ's - and thus Sir Herbert Lawrence's – plan. He had few illusions about the new Chief of Staff.

The other occupant of the room, Brigadier General General Edgar Cox, spoke up for the first time.

He had only been Brigadier General, General Staff (Intelligence) for a month, and was still feeling his way in the minefield of strong personalities that made up GHQ. His first briefing on the German threat to the Army Commanders' conference in February had not been an unqualified success, with raised eyebrows of disbelief from some quarters when he'd told them that G Int had confirmed that a major German attack would definitely fall on the BEF.

He'd seen the superior smiles at the new BGGS Int's expense.

He didn't want to appear alarmist, so soon in a new job. His feelings were mixed. He knew that the C-in-C resented his arrival in the HQ and his usurping the post of the C-in-C's old friend, John Charteris. Equally he knew "*bugger all about this intelligence business*", as he had put it so succinctly to the senior Int Staff on his arrival. He could ill afford to lose Mackenzie's expertise and command of his Int branch. But if his best subordinate upset Haig…

He cleared his throat.

"Excuse me, C-in-C, but it's not just Mackenzie's scheme. I was fully briefed before we came in; if it hadn't been worth listening to I wouldn't have proposed he brief you, Sir. G Int's my branch; it's my responsibility; not just Mackenzie's"

Haig stared at his new Intelligence Chief. He knew exactly what was going on. He didn't much like Cox, whose briefing at Doullens only two days before had been hesitant. A hundred and eighty two German divisions…

Even if that ridiculously inflated figure were true, John Charteris would have handled it better. He would have got the Army Commanders on his side, convinced and laughing, and he would certainly never have brought him a disgraceful murder scheme like this one Cox had brought him, even if it did have some merit…

The silence lengthened. Mackenzie could distinctly hear the clock by the chimney ticking.

"Look, we all know that some kind of German attack is going to come once the weather turns." Haig cleared his throat in turn. "And I understand from Gough that he needs every day God can send to get ready down south. This manpower nonsense doesn't help either."

It was common knowledge that Lloyd George was holding over a hundred thousand trained men back in Britain rather than risk releasing them to Sir Douglas Haig for yet another fruitless and bloody offensive. As a result, BEF divisions had just been forced to reduce its brigades from four battalions to three, which meant that all British divisions were overnight cut back to 75% strength. The BEF's manpower crisis was a real one.

"But I'm not going to authorise attacking the enemy's higher command. God knows, we're not reduced to that yet. Let the Germans be the ruthless killers. We're not murderers."

"Oh, yes," thought Mackenzie. "You're only ruthless sacking your own colonels and generals who don't meet your standards. And your soldiers too", he thought cynically.

Haig glanced at him. "I'm not saying you're wrong to recommend such an ungentlemanly proposal, Mackenzie. This war's a desperate business, I know." He paused, irresolute for a second.

"May I respectfully propose a solution, sir?" broke in Mackenzie.

Lawrence frowned.

Haig stared. "Well, yes, of course…"

"If going for the Hun staff saves lives or delays their offensive, then it's our duty to do it, Sir. If we can."

Haig's eyebrows knitted. He didn't like lessons in duty from his staff.

Even full colonels.

"But just because it's our duty to examine all ways of beating the Hun, it doesn't mean it's always *our job*, here in the BEF, to carry them out."

Cox looked at his subordinate with new respect. He saw immediately what Mackenzie was up to. The man had brains. "...I therefore suggest that we pass the idea as a request *to London* to examine and carry it out, Sir. After all, it's more their cup of tea. Secret operations behind enemy lines and so forth... I mean, it's not really the BEF's type of soldiering. Surely this is the Secret Service Bureau's responsibility, Commander in Chief..."

Haig face cleared. He nodded.

Lawrence smiled to himself. Clever. At a stroke Mackenzie had won acceptance for an unpalatable idea, saved his own skin with the C-in-C, and made sure that someone else would be responsible for any of the dirty work. Or the repercussions if it went wrong. And if it doesn't come off, well, let Cockerill and his shifty crew in London take the blame.

"Clever," thought the Chief of Staff, watching his Commander's face. "Very clever." Yes, Mackenzie of Int was sometimes too clever by half. And quick on his feet. But Douglas Haig would say yes now. Lawrence knew his man.

"Well, that puts a different character on things, Mackenzie," said Haig. He glanced at his new Chief of Staff. "What do you think, Lawrence?"

"Oh, it's a good idea, Chief, no doubt about it. But I think Mackenzie's right. This is London's job, not ours. And this sort of unorthodox thing is much more Cockerill's area. But we should definitely ask them." Cox was nodding. As the new BGGS [Intelligence] he was not going to disagree with his boss, particularly one who had been the temporary Chief of Intelligence in GHQ after Charteris had been sacked.

Brigadier General Cockerill's Directorate of Special Intelligence in the War Office was a long-standing thorn in GHQ's side. Supposedly there to help the BEF in France, Cockerill and his DSI 'funnies' had long ago given up any pretence at soldiering and 'gone political' in Whitehall. "Let bloody Cockerill get his fingers burned," thought Lawrence. "And when it goes wrong, GHQ BEF can blame London." He liked that idea. "I support Mackenzie's proposal."

Haig nodded. Once he made his mind up, no one could argue that he was not a decisive and tough-minded commander with a highly developed moral sense of responsibility and duty. True, there were some who whispered that a little less sense of responsibility by Sir Douglas Haig and perhaps a little less willingness to shoulder the burdens of duty and command might actually benefit the BEF sometimes, but they were in a minority. Douglas Haig – even his enemies agreed – was a man of firm beliefs and strong character.

"Well, that's settled, then. Well done, Mackenzie. I agree. We'll pass this on to the special operations people in London. This sort of thing is much more their cup of tea. And our own Secret Services out here can get on with collecting information on this Hun push. It's about time Drake's people were reminded that they're supposed to be working for us, not just Whitehall. Especially now that Cameron's gone. Never did really trust the feller," he added in a rare flash of candour.

Haig tugged at his moustache.

"That jewel thieving business with his wife before the war…" Cameron had resigned from the Army in 1913 following a highly publicised court case about his wife stealing jewellery. Some said that it was a ploy to give him secret cover. Rubbish!

"Anyway, that's settled. Good. Anything else, Lawrence?"

"No, Sir."

"Good. Give the orders, will you? Let's get a letter drafted to the War Office, whatever. Let's ask London to sort out the Huns in the rear areas and we'll get the Secret Service out here to do some work for us for a change. Tell the new man in charge, what's his name… Drake? to come and see me tomorrow."

"Sir."

"And Mackenzie, Cox. Well done, well done. Good to see G Int thinking ahead. But just get me the date and place of this Hun offensive, eh? Vital we know; vital."

Haig moved to his desk, already thinking to his next problem, his next decision.

A stack of court martial files was piled on the side, flagged up by the

Adjutant General as capital cases. Only the Commander in Chief had the Royal Warrant, the power to overturn the death sentences imposed by court martial in France. Douglas Haig alone had the responsibility of deciding whether courts martials decisions were correct.

And with over a million men under arms overseas in a strange country with women, drink and guns freely available, there was no shortage of courts martials. Or death sentences.

Even with the Suspended Sentence scheme, and though he resolutely refused to confirm nine out of ten executions, sometimes, in a few really bad cases he saw no option but to make an example and allow the hard path of military discipline and duty to take its ultimate course: execution by firing squad. But only a tiny handful. Douglas Haig was proud of the good behaviour and solid discipline of his army.

Duty and responsibility.

Douglas Haig knew he was no stranger to duty: hard decisions, military duty and discipline. That was what command, real soldiering, was all about. And now those damned civilians in the House of Commons were making trouble about the way he had to enforce discipline too. What did a dishonest, lying, greedy, bunch of cowardly civilians know of war, duty, and the demands of discipline? Useless, idle, wafflers, the lot.

Damned radicals! As if he didn't have a war to fight. He smoothed his moustache and pulled a file towards him. He became aware of the three men staring at him, waiting to be dismissed.

"Thank you, gentlemen, thank you."

The door closed and General Sir Douglas Haig, Commander in Chief of the British Expeditionary Forces in France and Belgium returned to his ever-present burden of deciding on matters of life and death of the men under his command.

CHAPTER 5

ST OMER, FRANCE

10ᵗʰ February 1918

"It's a matter of life and death, isn't it?" said Charley Markham as the Crossley one-ton tender accelerated away from the airfield in a slurry of rain and mud. Outside it was dark, and a raw gale slapped icy sleet in showers against the canvas sides of the lorry.

"What's a matter of life and death?" said a voice from the darkness, where a dozen aircrew huddled in the back, clinging to their seats.

"The weather. If it's fine, we fly. When it's bad we can't. So it's the weather that really decides our lives,"

The lorry slid on a corner then straightened up.

"Not with Corporal Guard driving, it doesn't," said another voice.

Corporal Guard's voice rose in protest from the cab. "Now come along, gentlemen, I'm doing you a favour running you into St Omer. 'Specially on a night like this."

"Anyway," said another voice, "Cpl Guard drives a damn sight better than most of you characters can fly. Take it from me. We backseaters know all about bad driving, don't we chaps?"

"Observer's cheek!" someone shouted and the truck swayed as the dozen high spirited young men wrestled with each other in the back.

It might be blowing the worst gale of the year outside but every one of them knew that it provided the perfect excuse to escape the airfield and head for town. No plane could fly in winds like this. Every DH4's wings had been tentpegged to the earth, and even the canvas hangars had been double lashed down. Squadron binges could only take place if there was no flying, and that came round infrequently. For Johnny Roberts the mid February gale was a double celebration; only that morning he had shot down his first enemy aeroplane. So the rowdy aircrew of 'A' Flight, 25 Squadron were anticipating a big party, a great letting off of steam.

They needed it.

Even to young men confident that it would never happen to them, the deaths of their friends produced a curious schizophrenia among RFC aircrew. Despite their outwardly casual air and affectations of immortality, they behaved like men who were only too well aware that tomorrow they really might die. Tonight, however, they could blot out the fear and the tension in a drunken binge.

As Dalrymple, the observer who had pointed out the flying shortcomings of his colleagues, put it so clearly, "Tonight I am going to get very, very drunk!"

And get drunk they did. The *Arche de Soleil* café off the town square became a roistering, noisy 25 Squadron party. Stories were told, legs were pulled, and long dead aircrews' reputations destroyed or remade in myth. But the constant was drink. Wine, whisky, gin and cognac flowed.

Finally, as the clutter of plates was cleared away, Armstrong stood up to make his Flight Commander's speech. If Jack Armstrong was mildly drunk, then his audience was more so. A chorus of drunken cheers rocked the windows, as 'A' Flight acknowledged their youthful leader.

Outside, hearing the commotion, a couple of military policemen looked in through the café windows at the noise.

"Pilots," said the older man, a Serjeant with a waxed moustache, pulling a face. "Bloody pilots."

He gazed dispassionately at the spectacle of acting Captain Jack Armstrong standing on a chair pouring white wine over an observer's upturned face. The observer eventually opened his mouth and pretended to drink before falling backwards off his chair.

The RMP Corporal's lip curled. "Shall I break it up, Sarge?"

"No point, son. Officers. Just high spirits. Not worth the trouble."

He looked on sardonically as Armstrong pointed at Roberts, to deafening cheers.

"Anyway, chances are most of this lot will be dead in a couple of months."

The Corporal raised his eyebrows. He was new in France.

"Dead? What, all of them?"

"It's true, lad. Pilots, Royal Flying Corps; they don't last. Here today, gone tomorrow. Most of them don't last three months. You should ave bin out here last spring. 'Black April' they called it for the Flying Corps: Black April. Slaughtered, they were," he observed with relish. "Slaughtered."

The Serjeant stared with interest as wild cheers greeted the arrival of an attractive dark-haired woman carrying a large coffee pot. He shook his head.

"They say that it's a bad way to go, too. Burn to death in the air, or jump. Not my idea of soldiering, flying in bleeding kites up there."

The Corporal looked at him.

"No, don't bother them, lad. They'll all be dead in three months." He shook his head as Armstrong clutched at the dark-haired waitress's bottom, and was rewarded with a solid clonk on the head with the coffee pot for his temerity. Tight lipped with fury, she poured. Roars of laughter drifted through the steamy windows.

The Corporal stared back at the party with renewed interest at the young woman. He'd heard about French women. This one looked better than most. Tasty bint. Filled that blouse very nicely.

"Oi, you!" bellowed the MP Serjeant suddenly, seeing two kilted Highlanders lurching cheerfully along on the other side of the road, hats under their shoulder straps, tunics unbuttoned.

"Put your bleeding caps on and get those jackets buttoned up. Where do you think you are, Sauchihall Street? Nah look like soldiers and cut abaht!"

Hastily the two Jocks, men from Rosshire, neither of whom had been near Glasgow in their lives, pulled their Glengarries on straight and slunk into the darkness.

*　　　　　*　　　　　*

Inside the Arche de Soleil, the party had calmed down. Groups sat drinking at the bar; two pilots had passed out and were sleeping in the corners, one clutching a crudely pencilled sign proclaiming,

Y AM A DORMOUSE'.

At the bar, Armstrong was telling some implausible story to an admiring audience. Further down, a cheerfully drunk Doc Josh Moon was trying to explain the mysteries of American football to a sceptical group of RFC aircrew. He suddenly started drawing with his finger on the top of the bar. "No, it's tougher than your Rugby football, ahm tellin' you....' His audience smiled disbelievingly.

Roberts and another officer, older than the rest were still sat at the table, smoking and drinking coffee.

"I see Doc Josh is on good form," said Charles Barton. "He's a good man, Robbie. We're lucky to have a quack, even if he is only a Yank on secondment."

"He doesn't like being called a Yank."

Barton looked up, enquiring.

"It's something to do with coming from the South. The Civil War. They hate being called Yankees..."

Barton nodded. "What does he call himself then?"

Robbie shrugged." I haven't asked; I heard the Brigade Major call them 'Sammies' once."

"*Sammies?*"

Robbie shrugged again."After Uncle Sam, I suppose..."

Barton grunted. "That'll never stick." He eyed his younger companion, relaxed, collar open, legs sprawled out, stroking a coffeee cup.

"So," he said. "Just how did you get that Hun?"

Roberts looked embarrassed.

"Bit of a fluke really, Charley. It's all in the report."

The observer smiled and recited in a mock-official voice, "*At eight ack emma I saw three enemy aircraft. I followed the E.A. down and fired a 3-second burst from my forward Vickers m.g. One of the E.A. fell in flames and was seen to crash near map reference Q12345.*"

Charley Barton drew on his cigarette. "Oh yes, I can just see the report."

Roberts smiled wryly. "Well, the report was a bit like that, true, but it didn't happen like that." He looked down at his coffee. "The truth is, they jumped us on the home straight."

"On the way back?"

"Right. We'd got rid of our bombs the other side of Peronne. We were climbing to get underneath the cloud base when suddenly there were these three Albatri coming from nowhere. Straight out of the cloud, dead in front and coming down at us …"

"Three against three?"

"That's it. I would have put the nose down and run for it, but Jack signalled keep climbing. You know Jack. So we went nose to nose. Jack opened fire; so did I. It all happened so fast. I could see the flashes of my chap's guns, then suddenly it was over and Jack put the nose down and we all sent downhill for home. Pretty damn fast I can tell you. But I was a bit slow diving so we were tail end Charlie."

Roberts took a mouthful of cold coffee and pulled a face. "Well, as you know the old DH4 is probably the fastest thing at the front, so imagine my surprise when Timmy suddenly shouts out and I can hear him banging away behind me."

"More Huns?"

"No, Timmy said that our Albatros had whip-turned after we'd crossed over, gained some height and was following us down." He shook his head. "I looked back, saw him and just pulled up – hard. I did it once before, the first time I got in a show. Anyway, the Albatross skidded by below, I dropped the nose and there he was dead in front. He was bright green."

Roberts paused, reflection and memory crowding in to accelerate the end of his story.

"So I gave him a good burst and down he went."

"Flamer?"

"Timmy saw him go down behind us. Not much fire. But he definitely crashed."

Charley Barton regarded his friend thoughtfully.

Roberts looked round for more coffee. He couldn't tell Barton about the way the startled Albatross pilot had looked back over his shoulder as the bullets from Roberts' .303 Vickers machine gun had walked up the fuselage to smash into the German's back. He couldn't tell him how he had felt a mixture of exultation and horror as the German's arms had spread-eagled like the crucified Christ and the head had jerked backwards as the DH4's bullets found their mark. Maybe he was dead before the plume of blue and white vapour from the ruptured petrol tank ignited. Maybe he was already dead as the blowtorch of the petrol fire, fanned at over a hundred miles an hour, had crisped the canvas and wooden frames and flesh and blood that made up a modern scouting fighter into a blazing comet arcing to earth. Maybe.

Roberts shuddered involuntarily and pulled a face.

"Well, it was him or me," he concluded lamely. The noise of the party suddenly roared out behind them, filling the silence.

Barton leant back in his chair and regarded the young pilot. He himself was one of the oldest members of the squadron and certainly the oldest aircrew. At 30 he was older than the Squadron Commander: even Major Duffus was only 26. But observers could be older, he reflected. In fact, it was better if they were.

Charles Barton, 'CB' to his friends, had volunteered to join the Royal Artillery in 1915, despite his new wife's misgivings. By 1916 he had been blooded as a Forward Observation Officer on the Somme. Literally blooded, in his case. A chunk of German 5.9" shell had sliced open his left buttock as he lay in the open near Delleville Wood, controlling a shoot to support the Scottish division. Barton hadn't even realised he was wounded until his signaller had looked up from their field telephone.

"Blimey, that was close," Bombadier Townsend had said, watching the black smoke cloud drift away. Then he had noticed the bloody rent in his officer's breeches.

"Coo! Them bastards 'ave got you, sir, in the bum. A nice Blighty one, as ever I saw," he added enviously.

So 2Lt Charles Barton, Royal Artillery, had spent six glorious months back in England, in hospitals and then convalescing, able to see his wife and baby daughter and to review his future. By the beginning of 1917, it had not looked good. A medical board had passed him fit for duty and fit to go back to the Front.

The question of his next posting had come up.

"Truth is, Barton," the elderly major in charge of gunner subalterns' assignments at the Larkhill Depot had said, "The truth is we'd almost have to completely retrain you as a Forward Observation Officer, now. A lot's changed over there for the gunners since the Somme show last year. There's new ideas, new guns, lots of new fangled kit. Hmm – how about the Training Regiment at Oswestry? They can always use a young officer as a troop commander who's got a bit of experience at the Front.'

He picked at his papers, "Or you could go as an observer with the RFC – they're screaming out for gunner officers as flying artillery observers." The major had a quota to fill. "You'd have to volunteer for that, though. Flying."

He noticed something in the Officer's Record of Service in front of him. "You're married, aren't you?" Unusual in a second lieutenant. He looked harder at Barton. Older than most.

"Any children?"

"Yes, sir. A daughter. Nearly a year old now."

"Hmm." The major paused, then looked up: "Where d'you live, Barton?"

"West London, sir. Hounslow."

"Hmm." Another pause. The gunner postings major was a wily student of human nature. He had to be. "Well, if it's any help to you, the RFC training takes place here, on Salisbury Plain. Only just over an hour by train to London, and the course lasts for four months. Might rather suit a married chap like you livin' in London, eh?"

And, as the elderly postings major had so shrewdly calculated, 2Lt Charles Barton had promptly volunteered to become yet another gunner observer in the fledgling Royal Flying Corps

Now, a year later, he was an acting captain, and the most experienced observer in the squadron. He had seen pilots come and go. Every day he marvelled that he himself was still alive. He put it down to caution, not taking risks, and knowing when to order stupid young pilots to turn for home. He liked Roberts. Of all the pilots he had seen, Roberts was the best. Not a great flyer, but an unusual combination of skill, caution and a genuine diffidence in his own abilities. Not a man to take unnecessary risks, but brave enough to fight it out if need be. He'd go far – if he survived. Charley Barton badly wanted to survive and wanted only to fly with natural survivors, not the kids with the haunted face of fear and death on them before their first patrol. He leaned back and blew smoke at the ceiling.

"Well it's always him or you, old chap. Better it's him, eh?"

Roberts looked up, "Have you ever….?" He tailed off, embarrassed.

"Shot a Hun? Oh yes," Barton smiled reminiscently. "Once, when our beloved Jack was just a pilot, before he became Flight Commander,was backseating for him over Arras. We popped out of clouds and flew smack alongside a Halberstadt. Two seater. Straight and level. I don't know who was more surprised. You should have seen the look on the Jerry's faces! 'Well, go on, then,' shouts Jack, 'Shoot the bugger! I'll hold it steady.' So I let him have a whole Lewis drum at about 25 yards."

"What happened?"

"Dunno – he just disappeared. Jack was laughing fit to bust. Apparently the Australians saw the Hun crash and Jack got another one to his score."

His eyes strayed to his flight commander, jabbing a finger into a pilot's chest at the bar. "Armstrong's quite a character, you know. Likes to think of himself as Mad Jack. Told me afterwards that he liked to know that the chap in the back had the guts to kill a man in cold blood. Said it made him feel safer in a two seater. Odd chap. Not my favourite officer. But understandable. In a way…"

Roberts absorbed this insight into his flight commander in silence.

Barton stood up. "Do excuse me for a bit old chap. Got to pop upstairs. This French food, y'know." He disappeared inside the door to the kitchen, nearly knocking over the French waitress as she emerged with another jug of coffee. Roberts noticed how they avoided each other's eyes and looked away, embarrassed.

*   *   *

Later, noticing Roberts was on his own, Armstrong called him over.

"Robbie! Come and join the party. This lot'll all be unconscious soon, the way they're going. Where's CB gone?"

"Upstairs. Tummy trouble; about half an hour ago."

Armstrong guffawed. "Too rich, old bean; that's the trouble with this Froggy muck. Kills you next morning at 15,000 feet. Bloody agony in the guts. Decent, straightforward, English stuff. Bacon and eggs, milk and brandy with an egg in it. That's the ticket. Not Raggoo or Booeybays. Fish stew - I ask you!" He slurped his cognac. "So tell us about your Hun."

Roberts paused. "Not much to tell, skipper. I roared up, he came by, and I got him in the back."

Armstrong looked at him hard. Roberts noticed the dark rings below the cold blue eyes and the fingernails bitten to the quick on the hand that clutched the drink.

"Well?" said Armstrong. "That's it? Did he jump? Did he burn?" He turned to the circle of young pilots. "I like to watch 'em burn, y'see. Sizzle, sizzle, sizzle, wonk; fry in Hell all the way down. That's the way to deal with Brother Boche, eh, Robbie? Ain't I right?" He appealed to the sycophantic group of young pilots around, who grinned nervously.

Roberts paused, irresolute. Armstrong's bloodthirstiness was legendary. He sometimes wondered now how much of it was really bravado to mask the pilot's own fear. He was saved from committing himself as the café door crashed open and Peter Coachman limped in, his good eye blinking in the lamplight.

"Ah – at last! I've been looking for you lot all round the square. Bad news, I'm afraid, Jack. The whole squadron's been put on standby for first light."

A collective groan went up. A voice said, 'In this weather?' The adjutant looked round, sympathetic for once.

"Sorry, boys, that's the way it is. Corps HQ have ordered the whole of 9 Brigade to stand by for ops the minute it's flyable. Big flap. Someone's got the wind up."

"Even in this weather?"

"'Fraid so, Jack. Everyone's got to be back on the aerodrome. So stir your stumps and let's get these sleeping beauties into the tender. Black coffee for them, I think." He looked round. "Everyone here?"

Roberts suddenly remembered Charles Barton. "I'll just go and find CB. He's upstairs. Plumbing problems," he added as the knot of aircrew began to drift towards the doors, sobering up rapidly.

He walked through the swing door, looking for the lavatory. The kitchen was dark and smelled of stale food. Laughter and French voices came from the scullery where the washing up was being done. Outside a WC stood open, door swinging in the wind. Odd.

He walked upstairs.

"Charley," he called. "Charley! Time to go back. We've been recalled. Nightmare's here."

There was no answer, but a scuffling noise along the landing led him towards a door. He banged on it. "Charley! CB! Is that you? Time to go. The adjutant's here. We've got to go. Are you all right?"

A muffled voice came from inside. "Robbie, I'm fine. I'll be right down. Just give me a minute."

"Well done, Charley. I'll see you downstairs," and he walked off down the landing.

Back at the lorry, 'A' Flight's sullen aircrew were being shepherded into the back by Armstrong. Peter Coachman greeted Roberts amiably. "Well done, Robbie. You found him all right?"

"Yes, Peter. Upstairs in the thunderbox."

"Good man. Well, chivvy him up, will you? We want to get back as soon as possible."

Roberts walked back into the now darkened café. The dining room was empty. From the kitchen came shouting in French. Light spilled from the hatch, leaving a sharp yellow square on the floor. He stopped, eyes straining in the gloom. There was no sign of Charley. Puzzled, he walked to the door to the stairs.

As he came round the corner, lit by the glow from the street, he froze. The shadowy figure of Charles Barton was locked in a passionate kiss with the dark-haired waitress. They hadn't seen him. As his eyes grew accustomed to the dark, he could see a hand fondling the back of his friend's neck. The front of the woman's white blouse was in disarray and even in the gloom it was obvious that Charley's hand was inside, on her breast. He saw a flash of pale skin.

Irresolute, he stared. He had never seen a woman's breast. The lovers broke off and she said something tender in French. Roberts saw his fellow airman button her blouse as the dark-haired woman stroked his face. Her teeth gleamed white in the dark.

Roberts knew little of women and nothing of sex. Like all his generation and class, his single-sex boarding school had elevated women into mysterious creatures and messing around with other boys, the height of 'beastliness'. Sex was something illicit; something for which boys had been occasionally and swiftly expelled from school. His own knowledge of love was confined to kissing his cousin, Amelia, at Christmas. She had seemed cool and distant but had kissed him back. He had felt nothing. Women were objects of crude jokes by the older officers and soldiers and of the pictures from lurid French magazines pinned on the mess wall.

Last summer, on leave, he had kissed a girl he had met in a pub in London during a drunken evening, cheered on by a couple of other young officers on leave. The kiss had been wet and sloppy and he had pulled away; but afterwards he remembered her breasts, heavy soft against his chest and wanted to do it again. He had noticed how her hair curled and how she laughed as she went off with her boyfriend. He had felt a throb of jealous longing before he returned to the bar.

Of married love and grown-up sex he knew nothing. He knew Barton was married – the only aircrew on the squadron who was. The discovery of his friend 'messing about' with a French waitress shocked him profoundly. His first feeling was of astonishment that his friend could betray his marriage, closely followed by a pang of regret that he was also deceiving his friends. How could he?

Stunned, not knowing what to do, he backed away unseen in the shadows, moving towards the street door.

Just as he got there, it burst open and Coachman stumped into the café.

"Charley!" he bellowed, cannoning into Roberts' back. "Damn! Sorry about that, Robbie. Didn't see you there in the dark. Where's Charley?"

Roberts, still shocked, burbled.

"What?" said Coachman. "Where's CB? He peered into the gloom. "Charley?"

Suddenly Charles Barton appeared. Not from the alcove by the stairs where Roberts had seen him seconds before, but through the swinging door that led to the kitchen. Bright light flooded into the room. He was buttoning his tunic.

"Hello, Peter! Here I am. Sorry about that – call of nature, y'know. What's the flap, then?"

He looked at Roberts, who was standing by, a mixture of emotions flooding across his face. The two men stared at each other.

Coachman, broke the silence. "Right. Let's be having you. All aboard."

Stunned, Roberts followed them out. Of the waitress there was no sign. Charley seemed his usual cool cheerful self. Had he imagined the embrace? He shook his head and heaved himself into the back of the Crossley. He must have made a mistake. He shook his head again.

"You all right, old chap?"

"Yes, Charley, it's just ….." He looked round the back of the lorry. Most of the 25 Squadron aircrew were either talking in low voices or snoring. Roberts look a deep breath and dropped his voice, "Well, it's just that I ……" he paused, "I saw you back there in the café. I didn't mean to. But there you were; with that girl. I'm sorry, but I was looking for you, and then …" He broke off.

"Ah."

In the glow of a passing lorry's lights, Roberts saw his friend nodding thoughtfully. "How could you, Charley?" he hissed. "You're a married man with a little girl."

"Ah."

"Is that all you can say?"

"Well, there's not a lot I can say, Robbie. I'm sorry you saw us."

"Sorry?" Roberts voice rose. "I should jolly well think so."

"Oh, for goodness' sake!" snapped Barton, "Stop being such a prig."

"Why's he a pig?" a drunken voice came through the darkness.

"Just a joke, just a joke," reassured Charley. To Roberts he said, "Keep your voice down."

The ride back to St Omer was cold and bumpy. Barton and Roberts didn't speak, wrapped in their own thoughts. At the mess huts the aircrew clambered stiffly down, the more drunken being escorted to their cubicles by their only slightly more sober friends.

Soon only Roberts and Barton were left behind as Cpl Guard's lorry whined away into the night. The wind, though still gusting, had dropped.

"I'll turn in then, Robbie."

"No, Charley. Don't go. I don't understand. You and that French girl. You're married."

Wearily, Charles Barton turned to his friend, "Robbie, I'm older than you. These things are very complicated. I know I've got Victoria back home, and I adore little Betsy. But – well, they're back home and we're out here. It's not the same. Françine's been in the wars herself …"

"Françine?"

"The girl in the café. She lost her husband. She's lonely. I'm lonely." He ran his hand over his face. "Christ, we're all bloody lonely. It's not natural stuck out here, living in these stupid huts, not knowing whether you're going to be next, I mean, is it?"

"But it's wrong!"

Charley Barton took a pace back and eyed his young friend. "You're right, Robbie. It is wrong. But this whole damned mess is wrong. Flying, drinking, living in these stupid huts on some stupid bloody field in France." He paused. "Dying. Or wondering if you're going to be next or the man next to you. Don't you even get the wind up, old man?"

Robbie's mouth opened, then shut. "Sometimes," he admitted, surprised at his own honesty.

"Well, Françine's someone who can make me forget that Slugs and

Bunny got killed. She can make me forget that that maniac Armstrong could get us all killed at any moment. Did you hear what he said at dinner?" he added with sudden vehemence. "'*Sizzle, sizzle, wonk! I like to see 'em burn.*' I ask you…" In the glow from the mess hut window Robbie saw a look of disgust on Barton's face. "He got that from Mick Mannock, I know he did. Mannock's his bloody hero. The trouble with Armstrong is that he wishes he was a scout pilot, like Mannock and Ball. Well he isn't and the silly fool'll get us all killed if he goes on this way…."

Charley Barton ran a hand despairingly over his head.

"But don't you see, Robbie? It could be us burning next, or him." He remembered something else Armstrong had said, to drunken cheers and imitated his drunken belligerence, "'*We don't need parachutes, chaps, do we?*' What a load of… I wouldn't mind a bloody parachute sometimes, I can tell you." He paused and glared belligerently at Roberts. "And did you see the way he behaved towards Francine back at the café? Eh? Grabbing at her. The man's a bloody oik, I tell you, even if he does think he's Jack the Lad or Mad Jack, or whatever he calls himself. He's no bloody gentleman, that's for sure."

He broke off. "I'm going to bed, Robbie. If this wind drops any more, we will be up tomorrow. Then we'll need all the sleep we can get. I'm off to my hole. It's all rot, anyway. Good night!"

With a muttered "goodnight" Charles Barton turned on his heel and disappeared into the darkness.

Roberts heard a hut door bang. A sudden gust of wind made him shiver as he squelched through the mud to his own hut, an empty maze of tiny cubicles, with its leaking tin roof, iron cots and candle light. Somehow he felt that he had lost a friend in a friendless place: and he didn't quite know how.

*　　　　　　　*　　　　　　　*

Elsewhere that wild night the wind was affecting other men's lives too. As the Channel Packet SS Astoria pitched and rolled her way heavily across the forty miles from Boulogne to Folkestone, James Marshall-Cornwall clambered on deck, leant across the rail and heaved his dinner up, to be whipped away into the blackness of the night.

Wiping his mouth, he staggered back into the warmth and smell of the saloon with its prostrate company of equally sea-sick inhabitants, mostly members of the BEF going back on leave.

Marshall-Cornwall was not going back on leave. For the hundredth time he checked the courier briefcase locked on a chain to his left wrist, to ensure that General Sir Douglas Haig's 'personal and secret' letter to the War Office was safe from prying eyes. He could afford to lose a steak and a bottle of red wine, he thought wryly. But if he lost a personal and secret letter from the C.inC. BEF to the Director of Military Operations at the War Office, then he might as well follow his dinner into the heaving black water of the English Channel.

*   *   *

A hundred miles to Astoria's south, near Peronne, a puzzled Serjeant and ten frightened soldiers of the Lancashire Fusiliers lay shivering on their bellies, listening to the gale. They were lying in a circle within yards of the German front line, every nerve raw, every ear cocked. The freezing wet mud soaked slowly into their uniforms. Somewhere, close by in the blackness, were hundreds of well-armed German soldiers.

More important, somewhere in that blackness was one of Mackenzie's G Int Royal Engineer officers. And they had lost him.

Serjeant Arkwright and his Fusiliers had strict orders to ensure that the GHQ officer did not fall into German hands. In fact, Lieutenant Colonel Ramsbottom, CO of the Lancashires had been quite clear at the briefing in the battalion HQ dug out before they had set out.

"This Sapper Officer. He's some kind of specialist, Serjeant Arkwright. He's got a little box of tricks and can tap into the German's telephone wires. Your job is to get him behind the Hun trenches. He'll do his stuff and then you bring him straight back, safe and sound. He's done this kind of thing before, apparently."

He looked at the grim vision of Serjeant Arkwright, face blackened, trench club in hand and festooned with hand grenades.

"There's one other thing, Serjeant Arkwright."

"Sir?"

Colonel Ramsbottom paused. "You're not to lose this officer."

"Sir?"

"If there's any chance that Captain Wright should fall into the Hun's hands, you are to make sure he doesn't."

The Adjutant's head came up from his writing table in the corner of the dug out as he stared at his CO.

Ramsbottom ploughed on, embarrassed.

"You understand what I'm saying, Serjeant Arkwright? The General's orders are quite clear. We can't afford Captain Wright being captured by the Germans. He's some kind of GHQ signals specialist. He knows too much. So we can't allow him to be captured. Alive."

The Adjutant's mouth was now wide open.

Arkwright seemed unmoved.

"Very good, sir. If necessary I'll deal with the gentleman myself." He patted an officers' pattern revolver on his hip. "I understand, Colonel."

The Adjutant shook his head in disbelief; Ramsbottom looked relieved.

"One other thing, Serjeant Arkwright. This is a fairly chancy thing. Going behind the Hun trenches. Oh, I know you've done it before; that's why I selected you. I've talked to Brigade. General Cruikshank knows you're our most experienced patrol NCO. Pull this one off and there's a medal in it for you. I'll see to that. You deserve it."

"Sir."

With his Colonel's promise ringing in his ears, Serjeant Len Arkwright had led out the special GHQ raid to tap into the German telephone wires in the Vth Army Sector.

Now, with his belly pressed into the soaking mud, Arkwright was wishing that he'd stayed closer to the cheerful young engineer captain with his two Military Crosses. Even with the buffeting wind to mask the noise he could hardly stand up and whisper "Captain Wright – where the hell are you?" The bastard had disappeared.

Around them in the blackness, like a star pointing outwards, lay Corporal Phillips and the rest of the patrol, blackened faces flat to the ground. The wind gusted on their backs.

Somewhere to their right a German flare shot up to burst with a pop and shed its cold wobbly light on the battlefield. Immediately, the wind pulled it away behind the German lines. But, even as the shadows lengthened and distorted into blackness, every member of the patrol could clearly see the metallic gleam of a German steel helmet not twenty yards away, a sentry staring blankly into the night.

Cursing silently, the Fusiliers pressed themselves even deeper into the mud.

"Damn!" thought Arkwright. "Where the bloody hell was that officer?"

Corporal Phillips' fingers suddenly tightened slowly on his bicep. He pointed into the darkness. Arkwright eased back the hammer of the Webley as a darker patch of blackness rustled and then resolved into the mud-smeared face of Captain Wright. His teeth gleamed in the dark and Arkwright could smell the whisky on his breath.

"All done," the apparition whispered. "Let's get to hell out of here." And infinitely slowly, inch by inch, the patrol slithered back to the secret rabbit tunnel cut through the German wire that led to safety and a warm dug out with a stiff tot of rum.

It took them over two hours to cover a hundred yards. As they pulled back, a signals lineman carefully smeared mud over the telephone cable he was unreeling behind them. That wire, thanks to Wright's nerveless fingers in the dark, was now tapped into the secrets of the Germans' frontline field telephone system.

Mackenzie and G Int at GHQ were not going to be accused of not trying their best, however dangerous the task.

*   *   *

Two days later and out of the line, the Lancashire Fusiliers' Adjutant collared Arkwright, ostensibly to tell him that he had been recommended for a Military Medal. In strict confidence, of course.

"By the way, Sjt Arkwright. That business the other night. When the CO told you to make sure that the Sapper officer wasn't captured. Do you really think you could have done it?"

The NCO had grinned at young Captain Willis.

"No, no, sir. I'd never 'ave shot him, don't fret."

The adjutant smiled, relieved.

Misunderstanding the look on the officer's face, Arkwright added to reassure him, "No, don't bother thi'ssen, Sir. It'd given t'game away. No, I'd have smacked him quiet like over t'head. wi' a club. Less noise thi'see? I'd not give patrol away sir. Oh aye, I know my duty, Sir, never fear."

And with that Len Arkwright had saluted and gone to get a well-deserved beer in the Serjeants' Mess, leaving an open-mouthed adjutant behind him.

CHAPTER 6

THE WAR OFFICE, WHITEHALL

13 February 1918

"So this is Sir Douglas's famous hush-hush letter, is it?"

The Director of Military Operations took the envelope from Marshall-Cornwall, busy unlocking the courier briefcase from a rather chafed wrist. He hadn't expected that. General Sir Frederick Maurice weighed the slim blue package in his hand, inspecting the wax seals curiously.

His confidential clerk opened normally secret correspondence. He dinged the brass dome of a bell and a smartly dressed Serjeant appeared soundlessly at a side door.

"Ah, S'arnt Briggs. Better open this and register it in the Confidential Correspondence book."

"Very good, Sir."

"Erm, excuse me, Sir." Marshall-Cornwall looked embarrassed. "I think the letter is addressed to you personally; for your eyes only."

Maurice re-read the address. "Good God. Yes, you're quite right, James. Most unusual. Oh well, let's see what Sir Douglas is up to, shall we?"

He nodded to Briggs. "Thank you S'arnt Briggs."

"Sir." His curiosity aroused, Briggs silently backed out of the room.

Before the war he had been the confidential clerk for a large firm of City stockbrokers. Along with his friends he had rushed to the Central London Recruiting Depot in August 1914 and enlisted. By Christmas 1914, discreet and bookish Edward Briggs realised that he'd made the biggest mistake of his life. The way of the warrior was not for him. The discomforts of bad Army food, cold wet tents, and endless marches across the frozen bleakness of Salisbury plain in winter withered any dreams of glory.

Any final traces of martial enthusiasm had been destroyed at Loos in September 1915. He'd only been in France two weeks.

His battalion had tramped endlessly in the rain-soaked dark for two nights, slept on open muddy fields and then suddenly been ordered to advance. No-one, least of all the officers, knew what was going on. All he knew was that the Division had been ordered to advance and consolidate the victories of the Scottish division the previous day.

They had lain out all night among dead Highlanders and been shelled most of the morning. No-one knew what was going on.

"God damn and blast it!" the Colonel had raved. "I need clear orders!" And still the shells had crashed down.

Eventually a runner from Brigade had appeared, bareheaded and panting. Colonel Sewell had read the grubby slip of paper, perplexity and fury chasing across his face. "Right!" He had shouted. "General advance. Forward! All companies advance!"

They had watched from battalion headquarters on a small rise as his friends lined up and began to walk across a flat open plain into the German machine gun bullets. One by one he had watched them sink to their knees in slow motion then fall forward face down. Line after line of sleeping, lifeless khaki bodies. The adjutant ran forward to speak to a company commander and Briggs had watched in amazement as Captain Gascoigne suddenly spun round like a top, then collapse like a drunk. But not before Briggs had seen the scarlet mask of blood where Captain Gascoigne's face had once been…

The Colonel had been raging with frustration and impotent fury into the battalion's only field telephone. Finally he slammed down the handset, shouted to the dozen or so officers and clerks around him, "Come on then!" and charged down the slope after his attacking companies, waving his cane. In a daze, Briggs had followed his CO, until he tripped and sprawled headlong into a furrow.

It saved his life. Recovering he breath, he looked around. Of Colonel Sewell and the rest of battalion headquarters there was no sign. He could hear the crack of bullets all around and the steady tak-tak-tak of machine guns. It started to rain and German shells began to thunder down in the gathering dusk. A falling clod of earth hit him on the head and he remembered nothing.

For two days Briggs had cowered in the field at Loos, surrounded by the corpses of his friends. He never saw Colonel Sewell again. He remembered crawling into a big shell hole and weeping with fear. When the battalion was relieved he found that he was the only survivor from battalion HQ and the abortive attack. Somehow, in those two days, he had collected a ripped arm from a shell splinter, and a dead officer of the Surreys was sharing his shell hole. When they found him he was lying on top of the body as if to cover it. They said he was a hero. Edward Briggs remembered not a thing, but had the wit not to let on.

From that day on the ex-stock broker's clerk had used every means at his disposal to wangle a cushy clerk's billet as far from the front line as possible. Now, over two years later, as the confidential clerk to the DMO at the War Office in London, he had exceeded his wildest hopes.

As Briggs discreetly closed the green baize door he smiled. He'd see that letter by the end of the day. The likes of General Sir Frederick Maurice CB, didn't ink his fingers writing out lists of secret correspondence, let alone filing them.

Serjeant Briggs leant back in his chair.

"Olive, I wonder if I could trouble you for a cup of tea, please?" he enquired politely of the typist.

Army Serjeant or not, it was the clerkly manners of Leadenhall Street and the City of London that had brought him here to the War Office, after all. "No letters, Serjeant Briggs?" Olive admired Serjeant Briggs enormously. Yet again she glanced at his medal ribbons. Such a gentleman; and a real hero, too.

"Not yet, my dear. It's all a bit confidential apparently. But I'll get it registered and in the safe before we lock up for the night. Can't leave anything to chance, can we? Anyway, I expect we'll find out what it's all about before we're done"

Olive smiled. She, like the rest of the staff, knew who really ran the Directorate of Military Operations.

*   *   *

Inside the office, General Maurice was frowning. "Have you seen this?" He waved the single sheet of typed blue paper at Marshall-Cornwall.

"No, sir."

"Damned odd. Says 'the courier of this letter, Major James Marshall-Cornwall of my intelligence staff, will be able to brief you on the details'.

Don't see how you can if you don't know what's in it, do you?"

Marshall-Cornwall said nothing. The room fell silent as the DMO re-read the letter. From Whitehall came a rumble of traffic and the slow clip-clop of horses' hooves.

"Well, suppose you'd best read it yourself and explain what your C-in-C has in mind." Maurice pushed the letter across the desk. He had a pretty shrewd idea of exactly what General Sir Douglas Haig had in mind. But the tone of the letter screamed caution.

He'd known Haig for over twenty-five years. He could almost see him holding his nose as he signed the letter. It didn't seem like Douglas's style, but desperate times, desperate remedies. The DMO took off his reading pince-nez and pinched the bridge of his nose, watching Marshall-Cornwall reading his commander's letter:

MOST SECRET - PERSONAL & CONFIDENTIAL

Field Marshal Sir Douglas Haig, KT, GCB, GCVO,
British Expeditionary Force France and
Flanders
General Headquarters
MONTREUIL
Forces Post Office 101

12th February 1918

DO(S)/C-in-C/GHQ/G Ops 1a/021/18

Dear Maurice,

As you are aware, the likelihood of an impending German attack remains my prime concern. The preparations to resist any assault are taking up the greater part of our energies at present. Gough assures me that his 5th Army is ready for anything, but the state of the old French line he has inherited is lamentable for modern defensive purposes.

In the circumstances, I feel that we should now consider any measures that could buy us time or even disrupt German planning for an attack. We out here are naturally making every effort both to determine the date and place of any offensive and also doing all we can to hinder the enemy's build up.

It occurs to my intelligence advisors, however, that your people in London may be able to render particular service in this latter by striking at specific strategic targets. Such targets would be those beyond my reach as Commander of the BEF, whose loss might prove a grievous blow to any German enterprise against ourselves or the French. The courier of this letter, Major James Marshall-Cornwall of my intelligence staff will be able to brief you more fully on the details.

The timings of such an intervention would, of course, be crucial; but without such assistance I fear our task will be rendered even more difficult than it is already, given the present serious shortfalls in the BEF. The manpower situation is most unsatisfactory and unless we do something to redress it within the next three months I fear we may face real problems after the enemy has started his attack.

I do not have to remind you, I consider these shortfalls to be completely unnecessary. The need for your extra help is thus rendered even more necessary to assist us in resisting any future onslaught.

Yours aye,

Douglas

Maj Gen Sir Frederick Maurice KCMG,CB
Director of Military Operations,
The War Office
Whitehall, London

The "you" was heavily underlined.

The DMO fixed Marshall-Cornwall with a sharp eye. "What on earth is this all about?" He took back the letter and smoothed it onto his blotter.

"What 'strategic targets'? What '*intervention*'? Eh?"

Marshall-Cornwall looked uncomfortable. He hadn't seen the letter before and certainly hadn't expected the explanation for the whole enterprise to be dumped onto his shoulders by Lawrence, the BEF's new Chief of Staff. Typical.

"Well, Sir, I think what the Chief means are targets whose loss would cripple the German war effort."

"Strategic targets beyond my reach….?" The DMO's eyebrows went up. "What's he mean? Factories? Railways? Krupps? Berlin?"

"No." Marshall-Cornwall swallowed. "He's talking about individuals, Sir."

"Individuals? Is he, by God?" Maurice rubbed his chin and stared at the young major seated in front of him. "Who, for instance? Which individuals?"

Marshall-Cornwall wriggled in his chair. There was no other word to describe it.

"Well?"

"Well, Sir, I think we're talking about the German High Command here Sir: Senior Officers, Generals, … people like that."

Maurice leaned back in his chair and smiled grimly.

"Generals, eh?" He tapped his pince-nez on his teeth and stared at the uncomfortable young major. "Any particular general in mind as a target?"

"Well - Army commanders. Rupprecht. Maybe even Ludendorff and

Hindenburg. Really where London can best help us, Sir."

"By 'intervening'" Maurice looked down again at the letter. By God, no wonder Dougie Haig was being so damned careful on paper. This really was explosive. He tapped the offending words with the pince-nez.

"Intervening? What does intervening mean?"

"Neutralising the key enemy commanders, Sir. It means capturing or killing them."

Marshall-Corwall's reply was suddenly crisp and determined. He'd got over the shock of finding himself having to outline G Int's idea in person to the DMO in London. Believing totally in the scheme, he was now perfectly prepared to advocate it with all his might.

"So your C-in-C wants London to bump off the German High Command? Is that it?"

"Yes, Sir, that's it exactly."

The DMO got up and stared out of the window at Whitehall. There was a pause that lasted for half a minute.

Maurice was no fool. He knew it was a good idea; but equally he saw the repercussions would be serious if an assassination attempt on the German High Command went wrong. The Germans would undoubtedly retaliate in kind if they knew it was a British-inspired attack. They would scream blue bloody murder to the neutrals. And those high-minded Americans too, he thought. Now, that would be a disaster. Especially after 1916 in Dublin.

He tapped his pince nez on his teeth. And ... and if the attempt failed and it all came out, then the soldier who ordered such a political attack would be crucified by the press and politicians. There was all kinds of mayhem going on in Whitehall already, what with Haig suddenly dashing back to see the Cabinet two days ago, Robertson being fired as Chief of the Imperial General Staff by the Prime Minister, and rumours that Henry Wilson was going to take over as CIGS. All part of LG's new scheme to exert greater control over the Army, and Haig in particular....

Like everyone else in Whitehall, Freddy Maurice had no faith in Lloyd George's trustworthiness. He thought that the Liberal Prime Minister was "*a slippery, untrustworthy little shit*" in the words of a distinguished Tory politican who had dined at his club two nights ago. Most of Whitehall agreed. Indeed, some thought that was a generous tribute to the Welsh Goat. … The truth was that the Prime Minister's reliability as a backer when things didn't go his way was as bad as that Churchill fellow and the rest of the gang. Bloody useless slippery lying politicians in their frock coats and with their false smiles….

But as DMO he couldn't ignore a direct plea from Haig, however vaguely couched. Especially with a major German attack pending and the BEF short of manpower. But if he said "yes" then it would have to be something that he had passed on for action. And … he'd have to spread the responsibility, to cover his own department. Yes … that made sense.

Maurice nodded to himself and came to a decision.

He turned and said, "I like it. In theory it's a good scheme. First rate. But damned difficult to do, y'know, political attacks. Assassinations can go horribly wrong. Look at that fellow Cabrinović for example."

"Cabrinović, Sir?"

Maurice smiled. "You've never heard of him, have you young man?"

Marshall-Cornwall shook his head.

Maurice turned to the window. "Not many people have. He was the chap who chucked the bomb at Franz Ferdinand back in '14 at Sarajevo."

"But I thought that was …" interrupted Marshall Cornwall.

"Prinçip. Quite so. But friend Prinçip was *second*. The *first* assassination attempt failed. Jumped in the river – Cabrinović, I mean. Tried to get away. Of course the Austrian police hauled him out. Friend Prinçip was actually brooding round the corner an hour later about the failed attempt when the Archduke's car suddenly pops up in front of him. Taken a wrong turning. Pure chance, you see."

He turned back towards the younger man. "So there you have it. Friend Prinçip pulls out his pistol, shoots the Austrian Archduke to free Servia. And ends up now with every country in Europe at each other's throats, and Servia in ruins. War everywhere. Chancy business, assassinations."

"Yes, Sir."

"Hmm. Did Sir Douglas have any of these fellows in baulk? Or is it open season as far as he's concerned on the whole of the German High command?"

Again Marshall-Cornwall wriggled. He had not expected to be personally selecting the targets for his scheme.

"I think the C-in-C and Chief of Staff felt that we should avoid members of the Imperial Household, Sir. But apart from that – OHL and their Western Army Commanders. Sir."

Maurice grunted. "Well, that makes sense. We can't go around shooting the crowned heads of Europe, can we? Leave that to those bandits in the Balkans. That's what got us into this mess in the first place," he grumbled. "Anyway, that lets Little Willie off the hook."

The German Crown Prince, Commander of the Northern Army Group, was universally caricatured as 'Little Willie' in the Allied press.

The DMO came to a decision.

"Right. Well, there's not a lot we can do about this here. I'll need to take advice on this. This sort of stuff is more for Cockerill's lot and that feller Cumming and his Secret Service people. You push off now and come back at 3 o'clock tomorrow. I expect you could use a night on the town, eh? I'll fix the meeting and if we need you, we'll call you in, all right?"

"Sir." Gratefully, Marshall-Cornwall left the DMO's office. As the door closed, General Maurice called, "Serjeant Briggs!"

Instantly the green baize side door opened and Serjeant Briggs appeared, a large ledger in his hand. He had the air of a discreet butler.

"I've brought the Confidential Correspondence book, Sir."

"Oh, I can't be doing with that." Maurice thrust the letter at his confidential clerk. "You take it. Just do the necessary and bring it back to me by lunchtime."

"Very good, Sir." And with a quiet smile – carefully concealed – Serjeant Briggs disappeared back into his private kingdom of secret paper.

"There you are, Olive," he said triumphantly. "Told you we'd know what C-in-C BEF wanted by lunchtime."

But try as they might, neither Edward Briggs nor Olive the typist could make head nor tail of exactly what Sir Douglas Haig's 'personal and confidential' letter really meant.

CHAPTER 7

GHQ BEF, ST OMER

14 February 1918

"Stollen? What on earth are stollen?!" Mackenzie waved an intercepted flimsy carefully transcribed and translated by his Signals Section. He looked round the Intelligence Staff office.

"Well, Colonel," the bespectacled, rather serious young man wearing the badges of a lieutenant in the Intelligence Corps badges rose from his seat, "I seem to recollect it means a kind of cake the Germans eat before Christmas."

Mackenzie frowned. His own German was barely adequate. To be teased, however gently, by Doctor, now Lieutenant, Charles Powell, a 28-year-old Cambridge Don in uniform, was difficult for him, despite the fact that the young man in question had been Reader in German Studies at Corpus Christi College before the war. However, Mackenzie was no fool and he knew only too well how much he depended on his Intelligence Corps 'experts' for his branch's success. Powell's contribution to the January intelligence conference had been a classic: the whole idea of a secret attempt to kill the German generals had been a brilliant idea, gift wrapped in trouble. A bit like young Charles Powell, he reflected.

As a regular officer of the pre-war army Mackenzie was keenly aware of the mild contempt in which many of his senior colleagues held these newer officers, brought in for hostilities only. *"Temporary gentleman"* was one of the kinder descriptions meted out to the new breed of officers. Young Powell personified the type perfectly. With his grammar school background, bookish air, and slightly flat northern vowels, he would never have gained an officer's commisssion before 1914.

However, four years of war had taught MacKenzie not to be over concerned with the way in which some of the newer officers behaved in the mess, or which school they had been to. Two years in the front line, a Blighty wound, and now eighteen months on the staff had ensured that he knew the harsh demands of the soldier's brutal trade from end to end.

As a professional soldier thrust into the world of intelligence he had quickly realised that Charles Powell was a brilliantly perceptive analyst of the Germans and their military. He knew only too well that his own survival, let alone promotion, depended on the skills and commitment of the rather earnest academic before him now. Mackenzie may have been an old-fashioned pre-war soldier at heart, but he knew talent when he saw it. Unlike many of his stuffier brethren, he neither resented nor was he intimidated by the clever young civilians with their mocking disdain for 'brass hats', the military and very things he had once held so dear. On the contrary, he was prepared to use these new men and exploit their skills to the hilt.

"I know it means marzipan cake; '*Weinachtstorte*' (he pronounced it badly), but what the hell are stollen doing in the German front lines? That's the question, my young friend."

The younger man smiled. "If you would care to read our translations of the Verdun attacks, Colonel, I think you may have your answer. We know all about stollen … "

He pulled out a file. "Ah, yes, here we are. The after-action analysis of the original attack; '*Zwei-und-funfzig Stollen, jeder mit einem Stosskompanie*' …" The pronunciation was flawless *HochDeutsch*, the manner an almost boyish enthusiasm. "That's twenty five bunkers each with an assault company," he went on. "So I think we can presume that these *Stollen* – your *Weinachtskuchen*, Colonel – mentioned in the German signals are in fact the underground concrete bunkers for these new stormtroops we've been hearing so much about. Probably because the bunkers are *stollen*-shaped …rounded at the ends, you know…" he tailed off. "And *stuffed full of good things*. Good gracious, I'd never thought of that before…. How very unoriginal of the Germans…*Stollen*…. Of course!"

"Good. Well thank you for that lesson in German, *Doctor* Powell. He emphasised the 'Doctor'. "Well done." Mackenzies's manner was gently mocking. "I knew I could rely on a clever feller like you. The good news is that Wright's little wire-tap on the Hun cables appears to be working perfectly."

He looked down at the translated intercept. "And the bad news is that your German friends have apparently emplaced thirty-four of these 'Christmas stollen' opposite 16 Division in the last month." He put the flimsy onto the table. "Let's hope they're not too stuffed full of 'good things', eh? Otherwise I think we have a serious problem, Powell. Don't you?"

Charles Powell looked down at the flimsy. It confirmed all his own worries over the Germans' preparations. For weeks the younger man had been trying to prove that the Germans were massing opposite 5th Army. Now the concrete – in every sense – proof lay on the table in front of his eyes. He brightened visibly. "Good Lord: this is really important, isn't it Colonel? It proves we were right all along, doesn't it?"

Mackenzie smiled at the young man's innocent enthusiasm for a piece of news that could spell death and destruction to thousands. "Yes, Powell, it is. Really important. Now I want you to get a report out to Fifth Army. Right away. Warn them. Now!"

*   *   *

"That's our job, chaps. Warn them!" Major Christopher Duffus, CO of 25 Squadron's final briefing was strong in Roberts' mind as his DH4 suddenly broke out of cloud into dazzling sunlight, 15,000 feet above the Douai plain. Timmy, his new observer, whooped and pointed. Fifteen thousand feet below, the white plumes of at least three steam engines were clearly visible, crawling west toward the front line. Timmy bent to his task of slotting glass plates into the side-mounted camera and Roberts concentrated on holding the aircraft steady. He scoured the sky. This was where photographic flights were at their most vulnerable; straight and level, doing their job.

His eye took in the half dozen other two seaters surrounding him. They were Bristol Fighters, 'Brisfits' of 62 Squadron, large, two-seat fighters, deliberately selected by HQ 9 Wing as escorts to confuse the Germans. At nearly forty miles behind the lines, they were almost certain to be intercepted, and the two-seater Bristols could handle the longer-range escort work.

Even as he looked up, he saw the Brisfits' leader waggle his wings and point. Far off to the right, out of the low afternoon sun, a gaggle of black dots began to grow larger. Huns. "Finished yet, Timmy?" The lashed-up speaking tube was working well.

"Nearly, Robby. Just two more."

"We've got company."

"So I see. One more now."

Three of the Bristol fighters suddenly broke hard into the looming Germans. They scattered like a flock of pigeons, not expecting aggressive head-on attacks from two seaters. Roberts saw the smoke whips of de Wilde bullets and a German fighter began to go down, a minute jewel of flame beginning to flicker against its side. Oh well, another flamer. Down he went. One less…..

Then, to Roberts' astonishment, a tiny black bundle fell from the doomed German. The pilot had jumped. Poor devil. His astonishment turned to disbelief as a flutter of grey silk suddenly pulled the black dot up short and cracked open into an umbrella canopy, "My God. A parachute!"

"With you in a mo', skipper. Just clearing the last plate."

"No, Timmy, look. Down there," he pointed. He'd never seen a parachute before.

"Good God, a parachute! Just like the balloonatics!" Only observers in static observation balloons normally had parachutes on the British side. Rumour had it that the High Command was nervous that, if they issued them to the RFC, aircrew would jump at the first sign of danger.

Suddenly their attention was arrested by a red Verey light curling across their nose, the emergency signal to turn for home. He looked up. The Brisfits leader waved a 'get out of it' sign and pulled viciously into the path of an oncoming attacker. In a flash the German fighters were all over them. A glowing network of smoke trails and tracer bullets filled the air around the DH4 as the Bristols fought desperately to protect their charge.

"Time to go, Timmy" and with its sixteen precious glass plates now safe in their darkened pouches, Roberts rolled the DH4 hard to port, dropped its nose and turned hard for home. A lone German scout broke off from the melee and followed them down; but from 15,000 feet and accelerating away at over 150 miles per hour, nothing on the Western Front could catch the DH4 in a shallow dive. Timmy fired a long-range burst, then raised two derisive fingers at the disappearing enemy.

Twenty Five Squadron, GHQ's special strategic reconnaissance unit, had got Mackenzie and G Int their perfect pictures of the logistic build up in the German's rear area on the Belgian French border.

Two of the escorting Bristol Fighters failed to return.

CHAPTER 8

DIRECTOR OF MILITARY OPERATIONS' OFFICE, WHITEHALL

15 February 1918

"As you so rightly say, my dear Cockerill, this is a 'rum do'."

The speaker was a small, neatly-dressed civilian, looking strangely out of place among the other four khaki-clad occupants of the DMO's office. His name was Hubert Neville and his brief in Whitehall was still not really clear either to Hubert Neville or to his military colleagues in the War Office.

Three months before, while quietly reading a rather bad essay on German linguistics and philology, he had received an urgent letter written on Cabinet Office paper. Unusually, the letter had been hand delivered to his rooms by a college porter, with the muttered excuse that it had been brought by motorcycle courier from London. Intrigued, Neville had sliced open the envelope and read its contents.

As he did so, the porter, a pensioned-off old soldier called Mulligan, eyed Dr Neville and his lair. He didn't often get to see inside the Dons' rooms. The room smelled of sweet tobacco smoke and a pipe smouldered alongside a glass of what looked like pale dry sherry. The walls of the room were covered in bookcases. Mulligan could see most of them were in German. The red wallpaper made the room look dark, despite the bright autumn sunshine outside. Across the quad Mulligan could see Tom Tower, over the entrance to the college.

Neville suddenly grunted with surprise and leaned forward to re-read the single page. Mulligan looked around, noting the dark oak desk and its carefully stacked papers. Not like some of the Fellows' rooms. Doctor Neville had the reputation of being a fastidious and friendly soul, more given to the intricacies of German literature than the day-to-day doings of Christ Church, better known to its population as "The House". His bedder described him as a "lovely man" and "a real treasure, no bother at all."

"They told me to wait sir, in case there was a reply." Mulligan explained to Dr Neville's neatly brushed hair.

"Quite, quite," muttered Neville absently, now reading the blue sheet of paper yet again. Eventually he looked up, seeming to take in the figure of the burly porter for the first time.

"You'd better take a seat, my dear fellow. They need a reply. I'll scribble off a quick note." He waved at a leather upholstered armchair. He looked at the porter closely. "It's Mulligan, isn't it?"

"Yessir."

"Good man, good man." Neville heaved himself out of his armchair and moved to his desk. While he scratched away with his pen Mulligan examined him carefully. Tidy looking man. Decent feller for a don, he thought. Half of the buggers didn't know his name, let alone treat him civil. But Doctor Neville was different. Organised, quiet; a proper gentleman. Rumour was he'd turned down a professorship last year because he didn't want all the fuss and administration work. Now, that was unusual. Normally the Fellows fought like Kilkenny cats in a sack to become a prof. Ambitious bastards most of them.

Neville blotted his note and wrote an address on the envelope, handing it to Mulligan. "You'd best take that back to your motorcyclist, Mulligan. It's a long ride back to London." The Porter noted the address with surprise;

> *Personal for:*
>
> *The Principal Private Secretary,*
>
> *The Cabinet Office,*
>
> *Whitehall, SW 1.*

He raised his eyebrows.

"Quite," said Neville. "Quite. We're mixing in exalted company now, Mulligan."

"Visiting London are we, sir?"

"Yes. But not for a visit. I'm afraid I've been conscripted."

Mulligan's eyes opened in genuine surprise. "Conscripted, sir? You?"

Neville stood up and laughed. "In a way. It seems that our esteemed masters want my expertise on Germany. Foolishly, I offered, back

90

in fourteen. They turned me down. Said the war would be over by Christmas. Now, a couple of years on, they still haven't worked out *which* Christmas. So I am now to serve in London as some sort of advisor to the Committee on Imperial Defence on matters German, it seems."

Mulligan was stunned. "Does that mean you'll be leaving us, sir?"

"It would appear so. I'm going to become a temporary civil servant, it seems, to help the war effort. Now, be a good fellow and get that letter back to your man on a motorcycle. I'd better go and tell the Vice Chancellor."

The memory of that afternoon came flooding back as Hubert Neville surveyed the four soldiers. He nodded reminiscently; whatever he'd expected when he was uprooted from Oxford, it hadn't been this - trying to offer advice to military planners.

They had all read Haig's letter and heard Maurice's explanation of its implications. Marshall-Cornwall had been called in, questioned closely on his Commander's wishes, and dispatched back to wait in the corridor.

Maurice passed the now well-thumbed letter back to Neville. "I thought you'd have a view on this, Neville. That's why I asked you to join us, you being a professor on Germany. Having a go at the Hun High Command. That sort of stuff. I'm not even sure it's legal."

Neville smiled a thin smile. Although he had no chair in Oxford, in his short time in Whitehall he had become universally known as "The Prof." "Gentlemen, I can assure you that what C-in-C BEF proposes – no, requests – is perfectly legal. The Hague Conventions on the subject are quite clear. In war, any soldier in uniform is a legitimate target."

Neville smiled at the assembled array of scarlet tabs. "And that, you will be sorry to learn – or maybe not? – includes general officers too. Even those many miles behind the front lines."

"Well, that's a new one."

"Not really." Neville, now confident in his role of advisor from the Committee of Imperial Defence to the armed forces and secret services, leant forward on his silver-topped cane.

"It's really no different from the Germans' Zeppelins and Gothas sprinkling their wretched bombs across London. After all, they do justify it by saying that they are attacking legitimate military targets. Sadly, that includes you, gentlemen," he added maliciously.

The four soldiers glanced at each other.

Personally brave, they had never considered themselves at risk here in London. And yet, here was Haig seriously suggesting – no, demanding – that they open what was effectively a new front against the Germans. Moreover, if the Germans retaliated in kind, every senior officer could well be back in the firing line again – even here in London. They digested the implications in silence.

"I see the point," said Cockerill of War Office Special Intelligence, "but couldn't it blow back in our faces?"

"Indeed it could. That's why I don't think we should make an advertisement of any scheme we might concoct – should we indeed agree with Haig's request." Neville pronounced it *advert-eyes-ment*

"When you say don't advertise, what do you mean, exactly?" Browning, Cumming's Deputy Head of the Secret Service, spoke up for the first time.

Neville sighed and jabbed the floor with his cane. Really; soldiers could be so stupid sometimes. Even the urbane and clever Browning.

"What I am saying, my dear Browning, is that if we send a platoon of Grenadier Guardsmen with fixed bayonets marching up *Unter den Linden* to attack the next weekly meeting of the *ReichsOberKriegsLeitung*, or the *Oberste Heeresleitung* . . ."

"Say that again," interrupted Browning. "The what?"

"It's their Supreme Army Command or OHL," replied Neville. He went on, "We will be indicating fairly clearly to the German War Cabinet that His Majesty's Government is responsible. And it probably wouldn't work anyway," he added.

"However," he leant back and looked at the ceiling, "if something particularly unpleasant were to happen to that War Cabinet in Berlin, but no one knew who was responsible, then it makes direct retaliation against ourselves less likely. And it would probably be more effective than a platoon of Guardsmen, too."

"Aha! Got you! You mean we could deny it? Pretend it wasn't us? Let 'em think it's someone else: is that it?"

"Exactly, Browning. A *deniable operation*."

The meeting digested the idea. The DMO broke the silence. "So what you're suggesting is some kind of secret operation. Nothing to do with soldiers?"

"My dear DMO, that is precisely what I'm suggesting. Indeed it is what I am recommending. But the decision is yours."

Maurice's brow cleared. "Well, that's more in Cockerill's area – yours, too, Browning. Secret Service Bureau stuff. Not War Office business, strictly speaking." The DMO looked relieved.

The two Secret Service officers concerned looked at each other. It was hard to fathom their reaction; but it wasn't unalloyed enthusiasm.

Cockerill cleared his throat. "But hang it all Neville, what about the political implications?"

Neville smiled with undisguised pleasure, "But that is precisely why we must not, on any account, have our fingerprints on any plan to attack the Germans at this level." He poked his stick on the floor to emphasise each point.

"It must absolutely *not* be attributable to His Majesty's Government. Absolutely not. That way there are no political implications. And we would – in strictest confidence, of course – indicate our condemnation of any outrage directly to Berlin; sympathise with them even, through the usual channels. They might suspect," he pursed his lips judiciously, "but they couldn't prove a thing. They would probably blame the French. And we could always suggest it was some Balkan plot. Berlin would believe that. They usually do."

He smiled benignly at the meeting.

There was another silence as his audience digested the duplicities that lay behind this speech.

The DMO addressed the Secret Service man directly. "Could you organise something like that?"

Browning considered the factors. And his boss, Cumming, Head of the

Secret Service's likely reaction. "It depends."

"On what?"

"First the target; who? Second the location; third," Browning struggled to think, ticking the points off on his fingers. "Third, can we get access? Fourth, what we're planning to do exactly. And last," he struggled, then went on, "well, do we all agree that we should do this? Do we need to do this?"

The soldiers looked at each other. Neville barely concealed an air of quiet amusement.

"Strictly your business, gentlemen; but should you not accede to C-in-C BEF's request, might I suggest that he might subsequently be able to claim that we in London had not given him wholehearted support in his hour of need. In the circumstances of an impending German attack in the West, I think the Prime Minister and your new Chief of the Imperial General Staff would find that an unhelpful development. But the decision is entirely yours, of course."

He banged his cane on the floor and leant back, eyes half shut.

The DMO cleared his throat, tapping his *pince nez* on the offending letter on his desk. He wished he'd never seen the damned thing. There was strained silence.

Neville suddenly sat straight up. "But it might help shorten the war, gentlemen."

"That's all very well for you to say, Neville." Browning's irritation was plain to all. "But you're pre-supposing we've got people to do this kind of job. Hang it all, this isn't just another shifty piece of political manoeuvring, y'know. This means finding real men to do a real job behind German lines. Not easy. Not easy at all. The Secret Service doesn't have unlimited resources. We don't even know what the job is yet. And it could be damned dangerous and damned difficult."

Cockerill nodded in support of his colleague. "That's true, Neville. We haven't even decided who – or what – we're after. It could be all a busted flush…"

"You are absolutely correct." Neville nodded and raised a pacifying hand. "DMO. Could you oblige us by reminding me exactly - precisely -

what General Haig requested, please?"

The DMO read out the paragraph and looked up.

"So," Neville spoke to the ceiling, "Sir Douglas requests us to strike at specific strategic targets, beyond his reach, whose loss *might* prove a grievous blow to any German attack. Am I correct?"

"And Marshall-Cornwall tells us that he means senior commanders, not gun parks in Essen," added Cockerill.

"Or Krupps."

"Nor Krupps." Neville stirred the carpet with his cane. "So who – after the all Highest, the Kaiser, of course – who are the key German commanders, gentlemen?"

"*Ludendorff.*" "*Hindenburg.*" The answers were simultaneous.

Neville embraced them warmly with his smile.

"Exactly, gentlemen. The so-called Duo. May I suggest that there are your targets? You have said it yourselves. The whole German war effort now rests on those two men. *General officers*: soldiers. Military targets? Certainly. Ludendorff more than Hindenburg, I suspect. They are the real obstacles to peace. Berlin is already full of political ferment. We know that there are strikes all over Germany; 400,000 workers are thought to be on strike in Berlin area alone. They have food riots; unrest in every major town. Only these two warlords – there's no other word for them – are holding the Germans to this war now. Knock out those two pit-props and politically, the whole roof could come crashing down about their ears."

The DMO leant forward. "I have to say, Neville, that the picture you paint isn't exactly the view from War Office intelligence: Haig's people and MacDonogh tell me that they're expecting the biggest Hun push since 1914. They're pretty clear that they are facing more divisions on the Western Front than ever before."

"Hardly what we'd expect from a country on the verge of defeat, eh? A big successful attack?" Cockerill chuckled.

Neville nodded. "Quite, quite." He looked round at the meeting, holding their attention. "But let us be equally clear, gentlemen: if Germany attacks and fails then she will be ruined. She is gambling for the highest stakes. Should this attack fail, than for Germany the war is lost. And one man – one surgical thrust at the heart of the German war effort - could make all the difference. Haig's request – if it works - could finally win the war, gentlemen; let us not be in any doubt on that."

He swung to the Secret Service man. "But do you have anyone who could accomplish such a task, Browning?"

Taken by surprise, Browning looked down at his hands. "Well, I'd have to speak to 'C' of course; but, well, er, yes, I do think the Service might have certain assets – an agent – who might be able to help. Get at Ludendorff. Perhaps. But I can't commit 'C' to anything, you understand."

"Hmm. Pity Cumming couldn't find time to come himself this afternoon," grunted the DMO. He and Neville exchanged glances

Browning looked uncomfortable. Captain Manfield Cumming, RN, Head of the Secret Service, better known as 'C',-was well known for his reluctance to cooperate with the War Office. Gossip had it that he was too busy trying to build up his own personal Secret Service empire in Whitehall, and as a sailor he instinctively looked to his Admiralty contacts for his activities.

"Yes, you're right DMO", mused Neville. "It is a pity he couldn't spare the time: but I don't think Cumming will find it too difficult to agree: even if he can't spare us the time."

He looked directly at the Deputy Chief of the Secret Service. "I'd be awfully grateful if you'd advise *Captain* Cumming if he's got any problems about co-operating, I'll be happy to arrange a personal interview with the Prime Minister," he cooed. "That should help him to make up his mind."

Browning blinked. The message was obvious. So was the threat.

"I don't think that will be necessary, Mr Neville. I'm sure I can recommend to 'C' that we take this on. Study it at least. Perhaps with Cockerill's people?" Cockerill nodded a hasty assent.

"I'm sure you can," beamed Neville. "But you'll need to do more than just study Haig's request, I suspect." His eye swept the room. "Much more."

"So we're decided, then gentlemen? Might I suggest that our answer to Sir Douglas Haig is '*delighted to be of assistance to the BEF in your hour of need*?' That should please your new leadership in this building. Henry Wilson has a reputation of not tolerating those who don't come on board with his views, has he not?" General Sir Henry Wilson, arch-intriguer, Francophile, and firebrand had just taken over as Chief of the Imperial General Staff at the War Office. His ambition – and ruthlessness – were legendary.

"May I advise Number Ten that Cumming will take on the task with his Secret Service agents, assisted by General Cockerill and his Intelligence people? And the targets are Generals Ludendorff and Hindenburg, perhaps keeping us all informed through DMO's office. In strict secrecy of course. Are we agreed?"

The meeting was agreed.

"Splendid, splendid," said Neville, rising to his feet. "I do so like meetings with a clear decision."

He suddenly addressed himself to the fourth red-tabbed occupant of the room, DMO's Chief of Staff, who had said not a word throughout the proceedings, but who had been busily scribbling notes in the corner. The silver ferrule tip of Neville's cane reached out to rest gently on the notebook.

Their eyes met.

"And I don't think we need to keep a record of this meeting, do we? We all know what we've got to do, yes?"

He removed his cane.

Colonel Sir Walter St. G. Kirke closed his notebook. "Security. Yes, sir, I understand."

"Good man; good man," said the Cabinet's Liaison Officer to the Committee for Imperial Defence as he walked to the door. "What a useful meeting. Good of you all to spare the time. Such a shame about Cumming. I'll brief the PM when you get back to me, DMO. Perhaps you'd oblige me with a copy of your reply to Haig? Good, good… So kind. Thank you. Good afternoon!"

And with a cheery wave of his cane, "Professor" Hubert Neville left his military colleagues considering just what they had let themselves in for.

From the window the DMO watched the civil servant's hat bob across a foggy Whitehall.

With a slight sense of unease he noted that he was accompanied by, and deep in conversation with, Major James Marshall-Cornwall. Freddie Maurice watched the civil servant and the soldier with a sense of foreboding. Both of them were nodding. Haig's intelligence courier was smiling as they shook hands, before he saluted and turned back into the War Office.

"Sometimes," said DMO, turning back to the room, "I just wish I knew what that feller Neville did – exactly." The others looked at him. "Oh well, at least we can tell Sir Douglas that we tried, eh? I'll get Marshall-Cornwall a letter to take back"

"I'll better see that our reply doesn't commit anyone too obviously, Sir."

The three others turned to the speaker.

Colonel Sir Walter Kirke was busy ripping pages out of his little notebook.

CHAPTER 9

OHL, *OBERSTE HEERESLEITUNG*
ARMY WEST HQ, SPA, BELGIUM

16 February 1918

"We've got to nail these spying flights!"

The speaker was a short, blonde General Staff major. Apart from the empty left sleeve, the feldgrau uniform was immaculate. "It's just not acceptable the way these Englishmen sail across our skies. They must be stopped."

Major Rheinhold Wendel flipped the file on his desk. "Over five flights in the last week. One of them as far as Soignies – halfway to Berlin! And last week they bombed a Rhine bridge! And every time the Englishmen get away. Well?"

Standing rigidly to attention in front of the desk *Leutnant*, Acting *Hauptmann* Hermann Goering of the German Air Service said nothing.

"Herr Goering, I need hardly remind you that the responsibility for stopping these flights lies with the German Air Service and your squadron in particular. You were leader of the interception flight yesterday. Your squadron is the security cover squadron for OHL. You let the Tommies get away. As security officer for OHL I have to tell the C-in-C something. He seeks explanations." He eyed the young officer standing rigidly to attention before him. "So this is no time for *Kadavergerhorsam*, corpse obedience. Come; we are not drill corporals on the parade ground. There must be a reason. What is it?"

The flyer shifted uneasily.

"Well, man? Say something!"

Herman Goering eyed Major Wendel's stocky form, taking in the missing left arm, the black eye patch and the blue cross of the *Pour le Mérite* medal gleaming at his throat. He wondered what the Bavarian major had won it for. The single blue eye blazed at him. "Well?"

"The truth is, *Herr* Major, that the Tommies are using new tactics and new machines. We shot down two of their escort fighters but the photo plane escaped. It is not easy. These longer-range spy flights are at over five thousand metres. That's high. And the warning time is less for us because they are using DH4 machines. They are very quick. Over 200 kilometres an hour …"

"So?"

"Well, by the time we are warned, take off and climb to altitude, the Tommies are gone. We need to be in the air before they arrive in order to catch them."

Wendel considered this. No airman himself, he couldn't see the problem.

"So get up there earlier."

Goering relaxed. "*Ja, Herr* Major. Easily said - but where? Which sector? It takes us over twenty minutes to get to 5 thousand metres – climbing hard. By then the DH4s could be 50 kilometres away."

Wendel shook his head. "So, get up there first; be waiting for them."

Goering stiffened to attention again. "*Jawohl, Herr* Major. Standing air patrols. Will you be ordering *Flieger Kommandeur* West of this change in Command policy?"

Wendel was wary. "*Herr* Goering, are you telling me that flying standing patrols are NOT our air security policy?"

"Absolutely, *Herr* Major."

"Why?"

"Expensive in wear and tear on machines. Pilots get exhausted. Accidents go up. And you never know where to mount them." Goering looked hard at the General Staff Security Chief. "The sky is a big place, Herr Major. Believe me. That's why the Flieger Kommandeur avoids standing patrols. They are wasteful for our men and our machines. With respect, we cannot have machines in the sky everywhere, every hour of the day. Sir."

Wendel nodded.

Seizing his advantage, the young pilot said, "Would you like me to advise that you see General Marcks about your new policy, *Herr* Major?"

Wendel realised that General Heinz Marcks, Commander of the German Air Service aircraft on the Western Front might not take kindly to his questioning one of his pilots about the deficiencies of his service.

"No, that will not be necessary. There is no new policy. Now I have heard your specialist explanation as a fighting airman, I can brief the *Luftstreitkräfte* Staff. And I will discuss this with General Marcks myself. You may go."

As Goering left, Wendel sat down heavily.

As Chief Security Officer for German Headquarters it was his main task to ensure that the HQ was secure from attack at all times. But he was also responsible for the security of all major operations. The Kaiserschlacht plan had made his job a nightmare. Now it was proving more so than ever. As fast as the Operations staff moved divisions and batteries secretly into position at night, they were photographed by the British Royal Flying Corps the next day: and the following day the inevitable artillery barrage or bombers arrived. How could he guarantee security to the Chief of Staff while the Air Service was unable to stop the Tommies' photographic reconnaissance flights?

He sighed heavily.

It has seemed a good idea to interview the flight commander of yesterday's thwarted battle flight personally. Now he wasn't so sure. He hadn't realised that the unit responsible was Jasta 11: von Richthofen's own squadron, no less. The aggrieved pilot was sure to complain to his *Staffel Kommander*, he mused. And Freiherr von Richthofen, High Command's darling of the media, and virtually a law unto himself, would be sure to raise it with the Air Staff. There'd be trouble now. He swore at the window.

"*Scheisse!*"

The door opened and *Gefreiter* Weissmüller came in. "You called, *Herr* Major?"

"No, no Weissmüller. I was just cursing."

"Can I get the *Herr* Major something?"

Wendel considered. It was gone 16.00 hours and light outside was fading.

At 19.00 he faced a difficult meeting with the Chief of Staff and the operations staff to discuss Security. Oh well, he needed a drink. "*Ja, eine cognac, bitte.*"

"From the *Herr* Major's bottle, Sir?"

Wendel grinned. As a semi-cripple he alone was allowed a personal servant inside the HQ building. It was the only real advantage of having lost an eye and an arm and still being allowed to serve on the General Staff. It was common knowledge that Corporal Weissmüller kept him going.

"Ja, unless you've already drunk it all."

Weissmüller tutted in reproach, and came back with a bottle. He poured a glass. Wendel drank it in one. "Ah, that's better."

"Still painful?"

"*Ja*; bad today. Sometimes it feels like the damned arm's still there. How can my hand hurt when I haven't got a hand?" He wagged the empty sleeve of his jacket and held out his glass for a refill.

Weissmüller splashed in more brandy. "Don't have any more before the Staff meeting, Major."

"You're right. It'll be bad enough without them accusing me of being drunk on parade."

"Why bad?" Weissmüller had been with Wendel for nearly a year now and their relationship was relaxed and informal to a degree impossible in the Prussian-dominated Imperial German Army before the war.

"Security. No one takes it seriously round here. We're sitting on the biggest build up and battle the world has known and no one gives a shit. We're wide open. It's impossible to hide the preparations for the big attack and the Tommies sail overhead every day without any interference. Yesterday they located and bombed 18 of the new ammo dumps – and I get the blame." Wendel gulped his brandy.

Weissmüller nodded. "So that pilot fellow can't stop them?"

"*Ja*. Sure. But only if they're there in time. The sky's a very big place, *Herr* Major," mimicked Wendel and shook his head.

Weissmüller took the empty glass and corked the bottle.

"Well, the good news is that I've discovered what your nickname is among the staff clerks."

"Oh, really? What?"

"Nelson. They call you Nelson. One arm, one eye…"

Both men laughed. The door swung open.

"What, pray, is the joke?"

Immediately they sprang to parade attention as *Oberst* Ernst von Zelle, Chief of Staff Coordination strode into the office. Senior Staff Colonel, a stickler for protocol, von Zelle was the bane of the staff. A Prussian officer of the old school, von Zelle could spot an undone tunic button quicker than a drill Serjeant and regarded even the most minor breach of discipline or a mis-placed full stop as being as dangerous as any Allied breakthrough.

He took in the convivial scene.

"Brandy, in the office, *Herr* Wendel?"

"*Jawohl, Herr* Oberst. For the pain." Wendel wagged his empty sleeve. "Prescribed by the doctors. It's medicinal."

Von Zelle signalled his dismissal of *Gefreiter* Weissmüller.

"Maybe you should go back home, Wendel. Are you sure you're really fit for active service?"

"Absolutely, *Herr* Oberst. At least my task here sitting in a staff chair frees another able-bodied Bavarian for the real fighting."

Von Zelle compressed his lips.

He didn't like Bavarians, whom he regarded as casual, ill-disciplined and frivolous; and for Wendel to remind him of the "real fighting" was either a carefully concealed insult or just plain tactless. Alone of the General Staff officers in the OHL HQ, von Zelle had seen no front line fighting throughout the war, a fact well known to the other officers, and a point on which he was very sensitive. Behind his back, the junior staff officers joked that von Zelle had "*Gnickeschmertz*", a "pain in the throat" - because he didn't have an Iron Cross to hang there.

The staff co-ordinator breathed hard through his nose.

"You are right, Wendel. But we cannot all enjoy the privilege of serving the Reich on the field of honour as you have done. You have paid heavily; but you have also been well rewarded for your sacrifice." He flapped a dismissive hand at the "Blue Max", the PLM at Wendel's throat.

Wendel stared at the Staff Colonel.

"Was there something, *Herr* Oberst?"

"Yes." Von Zelle was crisp. "The meeting with the Chief of Security is now brought forward to 18.00. You will attend, but the Head of the Frontal Aviation and the Chief of Military Police will also be in attendance. The Chief needs to know how you intend to tighten up operational security." He looked round the office, his eye resting on the piles of disordered files, the bottle of brandy and the glass. "Which I have to tell you, *Herr* Wendel, is like your office, too lax. Too lax by far."

"As you direct, *Herr* Oberst. I will get Weissmüller to tidy up while I'm at the meeting."

Von Zelle nodded. "Why did you interview that young pilot?"

"Because I need to know the real reason why we seem to be unable to stop the Tommies flying overhead and photographing our build up. I could have sent a formal memorandum to the *Luftstreitkräfte* staff, but we need answers now, not in three weeks' time in beautiful staff papers. The British fliers need stopping now."
"And can the Air Service stop them?"

"Not unless they are already in the air, according to *Leutnant* Goering. He was the flight commander of yesterday's air patrol".

Von Zelle nodded. "Understood, Wendel. You did right, even if cutting across the chain of command is irregular. I will deal with General Marcks. He will not be happy."

"Thank you, *Herr* Oberst."

"Nothing to thank, Wendel. We must all pull together at these critical times. Staff officers and wounded heroes alike, *nicht wahr?*" he added, in a clumsy attempt at humour.

Wendel smiled. "So, should we ask General Marcks for standing air patrols, *Herr* Oberst?"

"That I do not know. But someone must secure our preparations from prying eyes, that is for sure, Wendel; and the responsibility, I need hardly remind you, is yours."

With a final disdainful look round the office, *Oberst* Ritter von Zelle swept out.

"Pompous Prussian prick!" thought Wendel and began to shuffle files with his good hand.

A few seconds later the door opened and Weissmüller's head poked round. "Is the coast clear, *Herr* Major?"

"Yes, yes," said Wendel, testily. "You've got me into trouble again. Can't you keep this damned office tidy?"

"Oh dear, old von Zelle was touchy, was he?"

Wendel's single blue eye took in the slightly rumpled form of his batman-clerk. The unlikely combination of the cheerful Jew from the Rhineland and the Bavarian major shared a bond of common amusement at the antics of the Prussians. Both of them had been wounded in frontline units, and as a result, Weissmüller, like Wendel, was a category 4 soldier – medically downgraded for combat duties. Both had volunteered to stay at the Front for headquarters duties to free up an able-bodied man. Together they shared a bond of experience and outlook that transcended rank.

But sometimes, thought Wendel angrily, sometimes, even for a badly gassed veteran of Verdun with the Iron Cross and the man who helped him to pull his boots and breeches on and off every day, Weissmüller was just too damned familiar and took too many liberties

He regarded his batman coldly. "Can't you get a decent uniform, Weissmüller? You look a sight."

"Love to, *Herr* Major, but the HQ staff QM tells me that all the new tunics are being issued to the assault troops. There are shortages. Shall I switch to my old combat uniform? That will look the part, perhaps. And that should really piss off old *HausFrau* von Zelle," he added mischievously.

"Weissmüller! You forget yourself!"

"Sorry, *Herr* Major!"

Weissmüller drew himself up and crashed to full parade attention in front of Wendel's desk, clicked his heels and stared stonily at a point three feet above Wendel's head.

"*Gefreiter* Weissmüller reports and respectfully awaits the *Herr* Major's orders!" he intoned loudly in a parade ground bellow to the wall in a mock Prussian accent. "Does the *Herr* Major need help with his trousers? Or may the Corporal respectfully have your leave to go about his duties? Sir!"

Both men burst out laughing.

CHAPTER 10

25 SQUADRON, ST OMER

17ᵗʰ February 1918

A roar of laughter greeted the punchline of Armstrong's joke.

The briefing room of 25 Squadron's wooden huts was packed with forty pilots and observers and the key support staff.

The squeal of scraping chairs replaced the noise as the door opened and their Squadron Commander came in, followed by the limping figure of Peter Coachman. The assembled aircrew sprang to their feet.

Major Christopher Duffus, Military Cross, surveyed his squadron's officers and waited for them to settle down. As quiet fell, he began to speak without histrionics. His Canadian accent was mild but there all the same.

"Well, I'm glad you're all here this evening. I'm sorry for dragging you out of your various messes." This remark was addressed to a knot of a dozen or so Serjeants sitting together towards the front. "I know how Serjeant Pickthall enjoys his pink gin before dinner." This raised a laugh as Dave Pickthall, one of the four Serjeant pilots on the squadron, was known as a strict teetotaller and member of the Methodist Chapel. Pickthall smiled ruefully.

Duffus went on, "But I wanted to let you all know what's happening before the orderly room gossip went round the cookhouse. From 9 ack emma tomorrow, 25 Squadron is going to be split to become GHQ's Special Duties Squadron – full time. That means that although we still come under 9 Brigade for admin, spare parts, etc, etc, operationally we come directly under the Commander in Chief's orders direct from GHQ. What that means I don't exactly know at present, although the Adjutant may be more up to date than I am. He's just come off the telephone to GHQ at Montreuil and can add his information to what I have to say."

He paused and took in the aircrew, rapt and attentive. "What I do know is that we are going to have to move…" A groan went up. Duffus raised a hand for silence. "We will have to move to wherever GHQ wants us. It's a great honour. The SD flight has always been part of 25 Squadron.

Now, the whole squadron is to become special duties."

A buzz went round the room. The two black painted SD aircraft in the hangar in the farthest corner of the airfield were rarely used. The pilots who occasionally flew them never spoke of their flights, which always took place at night.

The room quietened again as Duffus raised his hand. "What I do know are three things. One, only bits of the Squadron may have to move." A bubble of talk greeted this. "As some of you know already, we've been reccying aerodromes further south and the advance party at Serny is operating already. Secondly, we'll do more photographic flights than bombing in future." The hubbub rose again. "And lastly," Duffus raised his voice, "Everyone – pilots that is – must qualify for night flying." The babble of talk rose. Night flying was dangerous and unpopular.

Duffus looked across at his adjutant. Peter Coachman banged his stick on the floor for quiet.

"Quiet, you rabble! Everything the squadron commander has told you will be briefed to the whole squadron on parade tomorrow morning at 9 o'clock. The Brigade Commander is coming down to address all ranks. He'll probably have new orders for us." The fire-ravaged face surveyed the room. "But for the moment we are stood down for twenty-four hours." The babble of voices rose again.

"Quiet!" shouted Coachman. "There's one other important piece of news for you. From now on, all DH4 operations are to be at 15,000 feet or above. GHQ orders." The room fell quiet. "It's not just us, gentlemen; it's all DH4 flights from now on. Don't come below 15,000 feet unless you absolutely have to. That's a General Command Order from now on."

He looked at the Squadron Commander.

"Right!" shouted Duffus. "Any questions?"

A hand shot up. "Where could we move to, Skipper?"

"Don't know for sure, but probably Serny to join the advance party."

"What sort of Special Duties could we do?" asked another voice.

Duffus looked at Coachman, who looked down at a slip of paper. "Night bombing," – a groan went up, "long-range photographic flights" – a bigger groan – "and dropping agents behind enemy lines."

A hubbub of conversation broke like waves on the shore.

Duffus held up a hand again and the room fell silent.

"I want you to know that we have been specially selected for this. We are the only squadron in France to come under GHQ's orders direct. I expect every man-jack of you to do your best. And I want you to know that I will personally fly the first night mission! Right, gentlemen!" he shouted above the noise, "That's it! Let go and have a drink."

*   *   *   *

As the aircrew streamed away from the hut, Peter Coachman stumped across to Roberts and Charles Barton.

"A word with you two, please. You two will not be moving to Serny if the whole squadron goes. You're staying here."

"Why?" asked Barton.

The Adjutant ignored him.

"You," he nodded to Roberts, "Are to get ready for night flying as quickly as possible. You're up in two night's time. And you," he waved his stick at Barton, "are the best navigator on the Squadron. The CO wants you to stay behind and amalgamate as one team."

Roberts and Barton looked at each other, horrified.

"But I have told him that would be a mistake." Coachman went on. "Never break up teams. And we'll need more than one top-flight crew. So you, Robbie, will keep Timmy in the back seat; but on Special Duties you're to fly with Charley's aeroplane to act as a lead navigator in future."

"Why, Peter?"

"Because, young Roberts, you will probably have an empty back seat, so you'll need navigating. CB will be your guide. You probably need one."

"Why will I fly without an observer?" asked Roberts, puzzled.

"Because you'll probably have a passenger, young Robbie."

Barton and Roberts looked at each other.

"Does that give you a problem, gentlemen?" Coachman's single savage eye stared at them.

"No, no," the two airmen mumbled.

"Good, because from tomorrow you are the lead SD crews. CO's orders. Congratulations. Don't let us down."

Peter Coachman banged his stick on the path and walked away. Deep down he was filled with a fury of blind impotence. He wanted to fly again, to avenge his dead brothers, to hear the wind in the wires and smash every Hun he could see … But; but: he would never fly in battle again. Even if he tried, Duffy would stop him. He could hear him now: "This Squadron needs a good Adjutant, Peter, more than most. Kid pilots are two a penny. But an experienced Adjutant and Recording officer… now that really is important… and you're the guy who's for it…." Deep down, as a regular officer, Coachman actually agreed with his CO. So it was up to the younger men now, especially the ones who could be trusted to make it, to do the fighting.

He sighed and went back to his office.

Roberts and Barton walked silently through the evening towards the Mess Hut. The younger man broke the silence. "Coachie's fierce."

Barton nodded. "I think he'd rather be flying than than sitting at a desk, Robbie."

A silence fell between them.

Robby stopped and turned to Barton. "Look, I wouldn't mind flying you, Charley. It's just that – well – Timmy's settled in as my backseater. And after Jimmy Cartright, well…. We understand each other."

Barton nodded. "I know. Anyway, swapping from kite to kite lets me look at all the pilots. I expect that's what the skipper wants."

Roberts was awkward. They hadn't spoken much since that night in St Omer and the argument over the girl in the café. "I meant to ask you…" He was going to say, "how are things at home?" but realised that it would be supremely tactless. Covering his confusion, he said, "How long have you known Nightmare?"

Barton smiled. "Peter? Ever since I got out here, last summer."

"How did he get smashed up?"

"Ah, well, he was in the original 26 Squadron, with Bob Cherry, back in '16. They had Fees then. One day he got shot up. The story is that he landed all right but the undercart collapsed and his kite folded up." The frail, rear-engined pusher FE2's were notorious in a crash for depositing half a ton of hot whirling metal on the unfortunate crew in front. "Well, the petrol tank exploded and that was the end of Cauchmar's flying days. The observer was burnt to death. They didn't think that Coachie would live. Dreadful burns."

Roberts shuddered. Of all the deaths, burning to death was the airman's greatest fear. Not for nothing did the mechanics call petrol 'witches brew'".

"Why's he still serving? He could be out of it, surely?"

"He's a regular; the Army's all he knows. And his two brothers were both killed, I heard. One at Ypres, the other on the Somme. So he pleaded to be sent back to the front." Roberts shook his head.

The two airmen walked up the steps of the mess. "Robbie, have you ever seen him with his shirt off?"

"No."

"Well, it's a total mess: solid scar tissue, back and front. Frankly, I don't know how he survived." Barton pulled a face: "I'd hate to go that way: fire, I mean."

Roberts shook his head again, slowly.

They stopped at the Mess door.

"Look, Charley, about the other night. Well, I know I was a bit – well, pompous or whatever – but I don't want us not to be chums. I mean, whatever you do, it's all right by me. 'Specially if we've got to team up for ops."

Charles Barton stroked the wooden wall of the mess hut. "I know. It's not easy for me either, Robbie. Life's too short. Who know's how long we'll be here? There's nothing to argue about. Let's just try and make it through this wretched show, shall we? 'Cos you can be sure that this Special Duties lark is going to be pretty tricky." He stuck out his hand.

"Chums?"

Robbie smiled and shook the proferred hand.

"Chums, CB. Chums"

The pilot and the observer, arm in arm, walked into the Mess.

Jack Armstrong, glass in hand, was telling a joke. Only the punchline greeted them: "So the actress says to the Bishop, '*Bugger that, my Lord!*'"

His audience rocked with laughter.

CHAPTER II

SECRET SERVICE, LONDON

25th February 1918

"Bugger!"

The Head of the Secret Service, Captain Manfield Cumming, RN stabbed the paper knife deep into his right leg. The blade sank in deep and jammed.

Even though his audience knew it was a wooden artificial limb, they still winced.

"Bugger!" The knife plunged in again.

At moments of high stress, Cumming was prone to absently stabbing his cork and wooden artificial leg. Whether it was deliberately to shock or just a vague expression of anxiety, it always startled his watchers. Some said that he did it when interviewing potential recruits for the Secret Service to gauge their reactions.

And, thought Cockerill, the Assistant Director of Special Military Intelligence, cynically, it all added to the legend of Cumming the Great Secret Service chief, and his mystique.

Everyone knew the story of how C, driving around the French lines in 1914 with his son, a second lieutenant in the Highlanders in the car, had crashed at speed in the dark. The boy had been killed outright, and the trapped Cumming had supposedly sawn his own ruined leg off with a penknife to escape, so the story went. Frankly, thought Cockerill, it smacked of another of Cumming's tall tales, but who would ever know the truth?

He gazed out of the window at the top of the Whitehall Court building in which Cumming had his offices. Rumour had it that Cumming had paid for it himself. But then, rumour had it that C had access to huge sums of money and didn't have to account for any of it. Cockerill doubted that. Cockerill tried to imagine not having to account for public money. He snorted.

"Something up, old boy?" Cumming looked up. His monocle gleamed.

Cockerill shook his head.

"There's not a lot we can do about this," Cumming said gloomily. Freddie Browning, his indispensable number two, and Cockerill nodded.

"We can say 'no', but if we do we'd be crucified in Whitehall. That damn' Neville and his lot would make our life hell. And if we say 'yes', then it's one hell of a job."

He turned over the pages of Browning's report. "And those damn' frocks will hammer if it goes wrong." "Frocks" was the soldiers' universal label of contempt for the politicians and civil servants of Whitehall.

"The trouble is we can actually do it, C."

Cumming glanced up at his deputy. He liked Browning, whose urbane charm and network of contacts had made his life so much easier since someone had wangled the posting for him two months back. "So you say, Freddie; but it's actually a *bugger* of a job. We need the right men for work like this."

Cockerill, who had spent the previous week preparing a joint study with Browning, gestured at the report. "But you do have an asset – what's his name? 'A34 ?' He's got everything, C, access, he knows the scene and good cover."

C looked at the Special Int man from the War Office suspiciously. "What do you know about A34? How d'you find out about him?"

"Nothing C, except that he can get at the Duo in their HQ and that he's done good work in the past. That's all Browning would say."

"Too damn much already." C glowered at his number two. "Biggest secret we've got."

"Well, if he can get close to the duo; if he can smuggle in a bomb, then we've got a plan."

"Too damn many 'ifs' for my liking," snorted Cumming.

"Well, the biggest one seems to be if we can talk to him," said Cockerill. "We need to give him his orders."

"And get him the bomb," added Browning.

"That's easy," grunted C. "Good timing device, you chaps in the War

Office can do that; he can find his own explosives – not a big problem. The big problem is making contact in time. Can we organise that in time?"

Browning nodded. "We'll have to send someone to talk to him. It's the only way we can brief him in time we've got. We'll have to send a courier."

"That's true. But who? Who've we've got?"

Browning pointed at the report. "Two suggestions; at the back, C."

Cumming flipped over pages.

"Hmm. 'Jim' and 'Charley'" C drummed his fingers and toyed with the paper knife, idly prodding his leg.

Cockerill raised his eyebrows. "Agents' code names," explained Browning. "These two are trusted couriers. Both been to Germany before."

"Who'd you recommend?" snapped Cumming.

"Jim's more experienced, C, but he's only just got back. He's tired."

"I remember," said C. "The 'Q' ship man; sailed round the world before the war?" He nodded, remembering. "Lawyer. Sound chap. Naval reserve officer. Had to run for it from Flensburg. Germans challenged him to a duel or something"

"That's the man, C. Back in '15, '16, I think."

C nodded, leaning forward, reading the brief. "So … in through Norway, then down through Denmark and into Germany. Then into Holland – how long will all this take?"

"A week, at least, Chief; maybe more."

"Hmm." C stared at the calendar. "Assume he starts in, say, three days? That means half way through March at the earliest to actually do something. Might not be quick enough for Haig?"

"Best we can do, Chief."

C nodded. "You people at the War Office go along with this scheme, Cockerill?"

"Absolutely C. It's a good plan – provided your A34 chap can do his stuff at the other end."

C stared at the uniformed soldier.

"Oh it's a good scheme all right, Cockerill. Gets the War Office off the hook, too. Our pigeon, eh?"

"Not entirely C. We're providing the wherewithal and fixing the Q side of things for you. I guarantee we can get you a device that works. We're doing our bit, too. And we are co-operating – that should please the Whitehall Weasels for once."

C nodded morosely and jabbed the knife deep into his leg again.

Cockerill winced.

Cumming came to a decision.

"Right! Let's get cracking. Get me Jim as soon as you can brief him. We'll do it. Browning, tell that feller Neville and the rest of his slippery gang across the street that that the Secret Service will do his dirty work for him, will you?"

C plunged the knife deep into his leg again

The point snapped. "Bugger!"

*   *   *

Two days later, on the 27th of February, Cockerill and Cumming met again, this time not in the airy splendour of Whitehall Court but in the Assistant DMI's pokey little office in the War Office building on Whitehall. The view of the Thames had been replaced by a drab print of a pale, waiflike pre-Raphaelite woman, who looked, thought Browning, as if she could do with a damn good meal.

Cockerill was acutely aware of the lack of space but Cumming had insisted that the final meeting "took place on War Office territory", as he put it.

MacDonogh, Cockerill's own chief, had the Director of Military Intelligence's grand office upstairs. However the DMI had suddenly found himself far too busy to chair the meeting. Moreover, he had insisted that the discussions with the Secret Service took place well away from the prying eyes of the rest of the building. So the four men were squashed together, the three visitors almost knee to knee in an office in the cellar. A fug of tobacco smoke added to the claustrophobic air in the cramped basement office.

Mansfield Cumming had brought Freddie Browning, who would oversee the operation. The fourth member of the group looked like a scruffy merchant seaman trying hard to appear respectable.

C tried to stretch his artificial leg without much success. He grunted.

"The chap you've got to watch out for is that Bavarian. Freddie.... Whatsisname?"

Freddie Browning read from a red crossed file.

"He's called Wendel, C.... Rheinhold Wendel, born 1881 in Bad Murnau, Bavaria. Good horseman, cavalryman, 4th Royal Bavarian Dragoons. Major at the last report. Started as a student on the General Staff Course 1914, then sent out to join old von Lettow-Vorbeck in Africa when the war broke out. Lost an eye and an arm in East Africa. Got a medal... *Pour le Mérite*." His eyebrows went up. "That's their VC. Next seen late 1916, identified on security duties in War Ministry in Munich. 1917, Berlin. Early 1918 identified as security officer OHL West. He's obviously been medically downgraded but they can still use him on HQ duties. Security... makes sense."

He handed the file to his Chief.

Cumming read the file and grimaced. "Caught two of our chaps in 1917 apparently. Saw through their Dutch cover. Both executed."

Nicky Everitt, the seaman, raised an eyebrow. "A problem for me, C?"

Cumming shook his head decisively. "No, they were War Office types. BEF people. Not ours. That idiot Cameron playing spies. Serve him right. We didn't even know they were out there." He shot a hard glance at Cockerill, who studiously avoided his eye. Little love, and even less cooperation, was lost between the Secret Service and the War Office over who ran spies in German territory. "You shouldn't be anywhere near this Major Wendel character. He lives at their HQ, OHL or whatever you call it. But A34 will be watching Wendel like a hawk, depend on it. He has to live with the bugger, day in, day out. And Wendel's no fool. All you have to do, Everitt, is get the package to A34."

He sat back. "Just run through it again for me. We can't get it wrong."

Everitt nodded. "Right, C., I catch the boat from Hull to Norway, Norwegian papers, Norwegian ticket, leaving on the 4th. That's Monday. Dock in Oslo by Wednesday. Then on to Denmark, Copenhagen, by Thursday: that's the 7th. Then train from Denmark to Rotterdam: through Hunland. Should get there by Saturday or Sunday next week."

"That's the 9th and 10th," said Cockerill looking at his 1918 calendar for March.

Everitt grimaced. "Once I'm in Rotterdam go to the Café Argus in Groote Hafenweg. Starting on Sunday next week. That's the 10th. Wait for a contact at nine minutes past the hour, at nine o'clock every morning and nine o'clock every evening until A34 identifies himself. As I don't know him, it's up to him to initiate the meeting." He looked at Browning; "Correct sir?"

"Absolutely correct. For his security it is essential that you never know his true identity. You'll see his face; we can't help that. Just pass him the clock."

C grunted. "Got the clock all right?"

Everitt nodded. "Yes. Carriage clock. Ready for collection at Garrards from tomorrow morning. Nice smart French make, pre-war. Your Q chap has already given me all the supporting documents to prove I bought it in Germany." He tapped his pocket.

"How will you know our man? A34?"

"Very tall, carrying a worn brown leather music case with a metal bar. He'll ask me if I know where you can buy the Dutch cigars with a straw down the middle?"

"And?"

"I reply, 'Yes. I've got a box with me that I bought at the station'."

"Hmm." C contemplated Everitt.

The naval officer bore the inspection with equanimity. Cumming took in the shabby boots, old tweed suit and scruffy ginger beard. The dusty bowler hat on Everitt's knee was suitably distressed and completed the deception. Lieutenant Commander Nicholas Everitt, Royal Navy, looked like a merchant seaman, down on his luck.

"*Sprechen Sie Deutsch?*" Cumming snapped.

"*Naturlich, mein Herr. Was wollen Sie?*"

C grunted again and switched back to English.

"Name?"

"Nils Petersen."

"Occupation?"

"Third officer, SS Lurline, Crown Shipping Line, sailing out of Oslo. Sunk by torpedo, 14th December last year, off Scarborough. Rescued by English. Now returning to Norway. Sir." The real Nils Pedersen's body had fed the fishes months ago

C continued his stare, then switched to look at Everitt's Admiralty file. Royal Naval Reservist, Norwegian mother, 'Q' ships, special duties. Recommended twice for a medal. Speaks Norwegian, Danish, German. Should be all right, he thought. Experienced, five missions, mainly Scandinavia. Still…

"You've drawn funds?"

"Two hundred, C: gold and notes".

C grunted again, reading on. He noticed a footnote.

"What's this 2,500 Marks on your head, Everitt?"

"Ah, well." Everitt looked embarrassed. "The point is, C, that when one goes into places like Lübeck and Kiel, the German frontier guards are a bit aggressive. Very Teutonic. Even to their Scandinavian brethren. That's why everyone tries to avoid the regular ferry boat services. They really are, well, Prussian. Even the honest travellers try and go in by the back routes. It's easier. Even for Danes and Norwegians. And Swedes."

C was a patient man. "So?"

"Well, back in '15, autumn, I went ashore in Schleswig and was in a Kro, just north of a place called Ribe, when …"

"Kro? What's a *Kro*?"

"It's a kind of small Danish pub, C. Sometimes not even licensed. Like a shebeen, but with good beer."

C wrote on the file. "Go on."

"Well, the waiter was gossiping. He told me that there were two Germans looking for an English spy who kept creeping into Jutland to cross the frontier. Red hair, blue eyes, 5'10". Well it was me, wasn't it?"

Everitt had C's attention. "And?"

"And they were sitting in the corner."

At the desk Cockerill put down his pencil and leaned forward, eyebrows raised in astonishment.

"Go on."

Everitt swallowed and looked at Cockerill before glancing back at Cumming. "Well, I looked round and sure enough there were a couple of bounty hunters in an alcove. Huns to a T. You could have spotted them a mile off. Drinking Karlsberg Porter." Everitt looked down at his fingers, twisting like snakes, hand to hand.

"So I went up to them and asked them straight, were they looking for the English spy who crossed the border? In really heavy Danish. They were a bit surprised, but said 'yes'. So I asked them what the reward was, as the blockade had forced me to sell my fishing boat. I made that bit up," he added unnecessarily. "They said a thousand gold *Krøner*." Everitt smiled at the memory. "So I told them I would show them the English spy at Ribe pier at 6 o'clock next evening."

Everitt was smiling beatifically.

"So I said, 'bring the *Krøner* and he's yours.'" He paused and looked at his hands writhing in his lap.

"And they did. So I shot them. I took the money."

"You killed them?" interrupted Cockerill. "How?"

The spy looked up at C, who nodded.

Everitt looked directly at Cockerill and for the first time, the Intelligence Officer saw the anguish in his eyes.

"I shot them. One in the head. Well, the face really," he mumbled. "There was a lot of blood. The other one started to run, so I shot him too."

"And?" said Cockerill.

Cumming was about to stop him but Everitt went on.

"I got him. In the back. He was running away. He was on the ground so I finished him off…Well, I couldn't afford to let him get away and talk could I? And we're all soldiers. It's the war, I suppose."

Cockerill stared at C's agent, now staring down at his writhing hands as the memory of the screaming German on the cobbles flooded into his mind once more. The terrified face of the wounded man begging for mercy had haunted Everitt's nightmares ever since. He had put the gun to the German's head and seen the look of horror dawning on the downed agent in the split second before he fired. He remembered the final pleading in the eyes as he pulled the trigger. He'd closed his eyes and looked away, he remembered, and the wounded man's shrieking of "*Nein! Nein!*" had ended abruptly with the pistol's bang. When he looked down, the head lay on the ground in a spreading pool of blood and the pleading eyes stared up at him. But the light behind the eyes had gone out.

There was a very long pause. Everitt went on

"So I took their money and finished the job, just as C wanted. Hamburg, Bremen, Hannover and then out through Venlo and Rotterdam. Usual run. That's when I saw the reward. It was a poster at the Venlo crossing. 2,500 Marks for my arrest as an English spy. And a murderer."

Everitt smiled shyly down at his hands.

"I wouldn't mind, but I'm half Norwegian, half South African. I'm not really English at all …" He smiled, a little private smile to himself.

Cockerill stared hard at C, trying hard to signal his concern.

Browning began to tap his pencil unconsciously, watching Everitt's obvious tension. The man was on the edge of a breakdown. Anyone could see that.

Cumming's voice was surprisingly gentle. He had already decided that this was Everitt's last mission. The man was burnt out.

"Everitt. Can you do this? Can you deliver the clock and a message to A34?"

Slowly Everitt came back to reality. "Oh yes, C. I'll get the clock to Rotterdam."

He looked around helplessly, seeming to see Cumming, Cockerill's cramped office and the picture of the pale-faced woman on the wall for the first time. He focussed on it and addressed his reply to the picture.

"Oh yes, I can do this. It's not hard." He paused. "But what do I do, when I've finished?"

Cumming paused, taking in the brittle creature before him. The silence dragged on as Everitt played with his writhing fingers.

"Just come home, Nicholas. Just come home." Cumming's voice was surprisingly gentle. "Then you can have a rest. A long leave. How does that suit you, old man?"

Everitt bowed his head. "I'd like that, Sir. I really would."

"Good. Go now and God speed. The Empire depends on men like you. One last time, eh? And then a rest, eh?" He rose and they all shook hands.

"Good luck, old man," said Cockerill. "That clock's more important than you know. We've had it specially rigged as a precise timer: almost to the second. There's a message concealed inside. Less you know the better. Don't let anyone else get their hands on it, mind". He patted the smaller man on the shoulder. Browning never took his eyes off Everitt's face.

Again the shy little smile. "I won't, Sir. Thank you Sir," and with a nervous nod, Nicky Everitt left the office, eyes downcast, twisting the battered hat between writhing fingers.

Cockerill looked hard at Cumming after the agent had gone.

"Were cutting it a little fine, don't you think? Those timings only give your chap a week or so at best."

C shrugged. "Best we can do. Anything else, Cockerill?"

"Well, yes... that fellow, Everitt. D'ye think he's really up to this, Cumming? He looked a little... well, fraught, if you take my meaning."

"Oh yes," said C firmly. "He'll do us fine. Everyone gets the wind up a little before these jobs. Even the toughest."

Freddie Browning wasn't so sure.

He could have sworn that C's chosen agent was swallowing hard and fighting back tears as he went out.

CHAPTER 12

SD NIGHT FLIGHT

ST OMER, FRANCE

1ˢᵗ March 1918

"This sort of thing would give anyone the wind up, old boy."

Major Duffus stepped back from the DH4. "I know. I did the first two SD flights. Scared the hell out of me, the first time; but if you concentrate, night flying's just a matter of taking care … ah, here comes your passenger."

Roberts turned to look at the strange figure approaching out of the darkness. A French peasant clad in the unmistakable *travail bleu* of the working man limped heavily into the lamplight, walking awkwardly as the heavy parachute sack bumped against his thigh. In his hand the figure clutched a large square picnic basket.

A cheerful young face, split by a large moustache, revealed a gleaming white smile, and loomed close. The unmistakable odour of red wine, French tobacco and garlic wafted over Roberts as the apparition spoke. "What ho, old man. Permission to come aboard, Sir?"

"Good God!"

Duffus laughed as he helped the 'peasant' clamber into the back seat of the DH4. "Sorry to give you a shock, Robbie. Need to know, I'm afraid. Just fly to point Toc Emma, watch for the three red flashes from the ground and let your observer jump."

"My observer?"

"Your passenger. One of GHQ's agents. Special delivery. Here you are, old boy."

Duffus handed up the picnic hamper to the agent, busy strapping in.

"Why the hamper, sir?"

"Pigeons. But you don't know that. Less you know the better, Robbie. Safer, if you have to land behind the Hun lines. Don't know nothing, eh?"

"Pigeons?"

"Don't laugh, Robbie. If your man's caught with these pigeons, the Boche will shoot him. It's a capital offence to own carrier pigeons in the occupied zone. Sure mark of the spy …"

Duffus addressed the backseat passenger, now strapped in. "Good luck to you, then." They shook hands. "Robbie's our best Special Duties pilot. You're in good hands."

He stepped up to the pilot's seat. Now remember; watch the electric lamps on Charley's kite to keep station. Keep your distance; and when he gives you the three flashes, look down for the three reds on the ground. That's your jump signal. Just keep Charley's plane in sight. He'll guide you in. You're just the delivery driver."

Robbie looked across at the shadow of the second DH4, its engine already roaring. An electric torch winked from the observer's seat.

Duffus slapped him on the shoulder, and stepped back. "Good luck Robbie. See you about two ack emma."

"Start engine, Sir?" came a voice from the mechanic in the darkness.

"Right-oh. Suck in? Contact!" And with a throaty roar the 250 horsepower Rolls Royce engine clattered into life.

*   *   *   *   *

Once off the ground, Robert's eyes grew accustomed to the dark. A cold moon lit the night sky, glinting off the rivers and railway lines a thousand feet below. Slightly ahead and to starboard, the dark shape of Armitage's DH4 flitted across the sky, the electric lamp on its struts gleaming like a pale star. Roberts saw Charles Barton in the back seat wave his electric torch in a circle once and settled down to follow the navigation aircraft. From the backseat came no sound. The compass read 110 degrees as the two DH4s sailed across a silvery clear sky, heading for the East.

After ten minutes, a series of yellow and red flashes on the ground far off to their right caught his attention. "Crossing the front line now!" he bellowed to his passenger. A grunt was the only answer as the DH4 lurched in an air pocket. A burst of silver and red tracer sailed up, slowly arcing astern. "Flaming onions!" Robbie called again. Even at night it seemed that the German 'archy' -anti aircraft guns - on the frontline were alert. "Definitely Hunland now." Then the front line slid behind them and the two dark shadows flitted across the sky, the only sound the bellow of the engine.

The horizon was quite clear now in the moonlight, and far off to his left front, Roberts could see the yellow lights of a large town. Somewhere, far below, the red glare of a locomotive's fire box was reflected off the pale glow of its steam as it raced across the darkened countryside, Roberts decided that, on nights like this at least, nocturnal flying was for him.

Suddenly, bright as a star, Charley's torch flashed twice, twice, and twice again. He fumbled for the heavy torch and flashed back two flashes. The DH4 lurched as he acknowledged the signal. "Five minutes," he shouted.

"All right, old man," came a muffled shout from the back. "Ready when you are." The DH4 rocked as the agent prepared to drop.

Roberts scanned the ground ahead. The moon silvered off a lake to his left. An "etang" he thought. Funny language, French. Straight ahead were flat fields, just visible, while to the right was the dark mass of a wood. Charley's aeroplane began to loom higher to his right. He realised that unconsciously he was losing height. The dark wood slid behind his right shoulder. The lights of Lille gleamed yellow to his front. Suddenly Charley's torch flashed. Three flashes. Three flashes. He flashed back. The DH4 lurched. Desperately Roberts scanned the fields ahead. The altimeter read 800 feet. He trimmed back and slowly began to rise, throttling back. Where were the red lights? They should be near. The seconds ticked·by like hours. Nine hundred feet. Where the blazes .... There, three red lights gleamed off to his left front about half a mile ahead.

"All right," he shouted. "Here's your spot."

"Right ho, old man." The DH4 lurched.

"Stand by!"

In the middle of the three red lights a fourth torch suddenly gleamed, three red flashes from the ground. "That's it! Go for that."

The aeroplane swayed to the left and Roberts corrected. The agent must be clambering down the ladder on the port side. He cut the throttle right back and pulled the nose slowly above the horizon. The airspeed began to fall off. The engine noise dropped. "*Go!*," he shouted. "Go now." The three red lamps slid beneath his wings and disappeared.

Like a startled racehorse the aeroplane suddenly jerked upwards. Freed from its load, the DH4 soared a hundred feet. Roberts banked hard to his left and looked below. The three red lamps tracked into view from behind his left shoulder. He pushed the nose down and swung round until they were straight head, hoping for a glimpse of the parachute. But as the lights drifted gently below, he saw nothing apart from a momentary blackness as something obscured one for a split second. He checked the compass, steadied on course 290 degrees and looked back. The ground was black. The three red lamps had gone out. He searched the dark side of the sky to the west. Of Charley's navigation DH4 there was no sign. Suddenly Roberts felt very alone. He checked his compass and began to climb for home.

*　　　　　*　　　　　*

Captain David Craig hit the ground with an almighty thud. Winded, he sprawled in the cow pasture as the pale billows of silk settled around him. Lying perfectly still, he looked at the stars and tried to think. For a moment he saw the dark shadow of an aeroplane flit across the moon, then he was alone, the drone of the engine receding. In the silence, he felt for anything broken. Since his wound, that leg was always suspect. He was all right, alive and safely in occupied France. Thank God for that. The cooing of his agitated pigeons attracted him. Dragging the parachute, he found the pigeon basket and limped across the moonlit field to a clump of trees. A match flared in the darkness where the copse fronted on to a small lane.

"Armand?" he called. "*C'est Monsieur Armand?*"

"*Ouai. C'est Martel?*" The Artois accent was strong.

Martel was his cover name. A cigarette glowed only feet away. In the faint light he could see an old man's face with a heavy grey moustache beneath a black workman's cap. "*Bien sur; ç'est Martel.*"

The old man grinned in the darkness and embraced him. "Ah my friend, I am very happy to see you. You are safe and content? The flight went well?"

"Good, I am good. Even the pigeons are good."

"That's well done," said the old man. "Now listen, we don't have much time; you are at Escobeques. You have your papers?"

"Yes. Charles Martel, factory worker, resident of Englos. I am a wounded ex-POW, now a gateman at Wattignies. I report to Jacques Rykenbosch at the Wattignies works at ten o'clock tomorrow morning. *D'accord?*"

"Good. Rykenbosch. His address is Rue Haubourdin 28. You could not have a better contact. Not a German General farts round Lille but Rykenbosch knows about it. It is now 6 hours to dawn. If you walk towards the lights you cannot go wrong. It is only a few kilometres."

The old man produced a bottle of cognac. "Take this. If anyone stops you, splash it on your clothes and take a good swig. Pretend you are drunk. If Rykenbosch is not at the Rue Haubourdin, then go to the house of Madame Lagrange at Rue Carnot 60, in Wattignies. She will give you lodgings. She will say you have lived there." The old man's bird-like eyes gleamed as he flicked the cigarette to the ground. Normally he smoked a pipe. "You have understood everything?"

"Yes. Rykenbosch at 10 am; if Rykenbosch is not there, then Madame Lagrange at 60 Rue Carnot. It is all understood."

"Then good luck, my friend." The Frenchman shook his hand. In the darkness David Craig could smell the brandy. The old man had sampled the bottle first, he guessed. Still, who could blame him? It was dangerous under the occupation to be out after curfew, even in the countryside.

The old man wrapped the torches into the parachute and pressed then into a fallen tree, scrabbling earth and leaves on top, shadowy in the moonlight. "I will return in the morning with the dogs and the gun. Then I will hide them in the barn." He looked hard at David Craig. The pigeons cooed.

"One word of warning, my friend. The Germans have no mercy for *Colombiers*, pigeon fanciers, these days. Be very careful. To possess one pigeon is to invite a special Military Court. To be caught with a box of pigeons is to invite a sentence of death. These military courts: they have no mercy. Be very careful. The *Boche* sometimes they have night patrols, roadblocks. Be vigilant, I implore you. If anyone asks where you have been after curfew, say you went to collect a bottle from your cache at Brulle." He gestured down the dark lane. "That's the village there.

There are three other cognacs underneath the pulpit should anyone look. Remember that. Your story will hold up, believe me. But not with pigeons, *tu compris*?"

"I understand, Monsieur Armand. And thank you for all your help. It must be a great danger to you."

The Frenchman grunted and they shook hands again. Then the old man threw his leg over an ancient bicycle hidden in the shadows. "Go then. Go in the direction east, a little north east, towards Lille; towards the lights. I will return to the village. *Et bonne chance, mon ami, bonne chance.*" With a creaking of pedals the old man pedalled off down the lane, gleaming pale in the moonlight.

In the stillness the pigeons cooed. "You'd better stay quiet, *mes enfants*" David Craig chuckled to himself. "Otherwise we'll all end up in a pie". Hefting the basket and clutching the brandy bottle, he set off in the opposite direction towards the glow of lights.

*   *   *

Eighteen miles to the north-west, Roberts had decided on three things: one, on mature reflection he did not like night flying after all; two, he much preferred the company of a navigator, and three – he was completely lost. There was no sign of the other DH4. Desperately he peered into the blackness ahead and for the umpteenth time checked his compass: 290 degrees. Damn! Where the hell was Charley? And where the hell was he?

Suddenly a sparkle of pink flashes appeared on the ground off to the north in the direction of Ypres. To his astonishment they began to spread like a rash in a line towards him, across the darkened countryside below. Even over the engine he could hear the faint crump of shells. The wind-up! The front line sailed below him, a red ribbon of flashes as both sides pounded each other's lines in a sudden panic, neither side knowing quite why. He could even see tracers whipping to and fro. Maybe a trench raid had sparked it off; maybe a nervous sentry firing at a shadow. But like a river of flame, the red rash spread along the front. From the shape of the line, Roberts guessed he was near Hazebrouck. Sure enough, off to his right was the unmistakable shadow of Mount Cassel; well, at least he was on course. The DH4 droned on. He could see the glint of moonlight on the railway lines below, and ahead the dark shape that must be St Omer.

Nearly there. Where was that bloody airfield?

Suddenly, as if in answer to his prayers a light began to burn, miles ahead and slightly right; then another, and another. A dim flarepath emerged.

He put the nose down and headed for the glow, pushing the speed up. The Forest of Clairmarais flashed below, a dark shadow on the ground. The airfield lights drew invitingly near. For a second he panicked as two lights went black, then sighed with relief as he realised it was another aeroplane landing ahead of him. Armitage and Charley's DH4! In his haste, he pushed the nose down further, letting the airspeed build up as he swooped dangerously low.

Suddenly the flickering lights were very near. He was going much too fast. Chopping the engine, he pulled the nose up. Of course! He had no observer as ballast: the DH4 was flying unbalanced. The aeroplane wallowed and he pushed the nose back down, speed now 70 mph. Still fast, but the flares on top of the lights were zipping by and he could see the aerodrome buildings. Too high!

He cut the throttle and the engine quietened to a whisper. As he ran out of airfield lights he flared and let the ground come up. With a crash and a bounce he was down. The last flares whipped by and he thought he saw a startled face in the light as he rumbled into the blackness. The aeroplane began to bump as it ran off the flat airfield and hit the rough pasture, slowing all the time. Just as it stopped, the wheels suddenly dropped and very slowly the DH4 tipped on its nose. Roberts pitched forward against the straps, cracking his head on the dashboard and seeing stars. Out of the darkness came running figures and torches.

"Mr Roberts? You all right, sir?"

Roberts smiled. Serjeant Doughty's voice was like coming home.

"Yes, I'm OK. But I'm afraid the old kite's on her nose."

Doughty was alongside, flashing the torch. Others arrived. "I've seen worse, sir. Can you get down all right?"

"Oh yes," and with a sigh of relief, Roberts clambered out of the DH4, its tail canted darkly at 45 degrees to the stars and slid off the wing. Leaving the cluster of ground crews and hand torches fussing round the stricken DH4, he began to trudge towards the squadron office.

By the time he got there he was sweating under the thick flying suit. Major Duffus, glass in hand, was sprawled in a wicker chair accompanied by two red tabbed staff colonels. Armitage and Charles Barton appeared, now out of their flying suits and clutching a whisky bottle and glasses.

"I'll have one of those," announced Roberts. "And I bloody well need it!"

Charley poured a generous measure and Roberts seized the glass. Armitage collapsed in an armchair and exhaled sharply through puffed out cheeks.

"Well?" said Major Duffus. "How'd it go?"

Roberts slurped the neat whisky. "Alright, sir. No problems. He jumped at point Toc Emma. The three red lights were all there. I couldn't see how he got on. Then I lost Armitage's kite. Came back by myself. Lost really. Bit of a wind-up over the Front. Saw the flares and came straight in."

He took another pull of the scotch and pulled a face. He didn't really like whisky. Funny, at school he'd have been punished for drinking. Was it only just two years ago? "Overshot, I'm afraid Skipper. She's on her nose half way to the hedge."

Duffus nodded. The strain showed in the young pilot's face. He understood. He'd only expected one of the two aeroplanes to return home safely, if he was honest. The first time he'd landed at night the previous week he'd nearly screamed in fright as he wrestled the big DH4 down cross wind between the flickering lights. But Majors commanding squadrons in the Royal Flying Corps weren't allowed to scream, he thought wryly. Let alone admit to being frightened . . .

"These things happen, Robbie. How about you two?"

Armitage replied. "It's a bit scary, Skipper. But with a clear night and the flarepath it's possible."

Charley nodded. "Navigation's no problem with a clear moon."

Duffus nodded, then looked quizzically at the two Colonels. The pink faced one leaned forward and spoke directly to the aircrew.

"My name's Mackenzie, from GHQ. This is Colonel Drake. Just two things; what we need to know are just two things: did it go all right, and could you do it again?"

Armitage spoke first.

Despite his nickname of the Dormouse from his heavy eyelids, and his episode of lapsing into snoring unconsciousness at the Arche de Soleil in St Omer last month, he was a deeply serious young man. Rumour had it that he had been studying to be a priest before he had joined the Army. "The flying's straightforward, provided the weather's clear, Sir. You couldn't do it in bad weather. The navigation is the really tricky bit."

Charley Barton chipped in. "Even the navigation's not too difficult provided you concentrate and stick to the planned route. But once you lose your place, it's jolly hard to check where you are." He looked at Robbie, who nodded and added, "I could do it again, Sir. But you do need to either have a navigator or a guaranteed way of keeping station on the guide plane."

"But it can be done?"

"Oh yes." they chorused. Duffus smiled. Drake, the shorter, dark-haired Colonel, spoke. His brilliantined hair was parted in the middle and gleamed as he leant forward in his chair.

"You see, I'm giving away no secrets, here, but we have done this before. Then we had to stop it. We used to use FE2s, but it all started to go wrong about autumn last year. Two reasons: the pilots said they couldn't do it and we started to lose our chaps on the ground." He looked up at the three aircrew. "If we're going to continue to do this kind of op, I need to be sure that you can do it and that whoever's on the ground is doing their bit."

Mackenzie nodded, swilling his glass. The three RFC officers looked at each other.

Roberts shrugged and spoke up. "Yes, we can do it, Sir. Provided the weather's clear and the lights on the ground are there, it's perfectly feasible. Right, fellows?"

Armitage and Barton nodded.

The two Colonels exchanged glances and rose. "Thank you, gentlemen. We won't detain you any longer." Mackenzie looked at Duffus. "Shall we …?"

"Of course." Duffus rose and banged down his glass.

"Right. Get to bed, you chaps. That's an order. And I don't need to remind you that this is highly confidential. Not a word, not a cheep, even to your best chum. You'll note that even the Adjutant isn't here. No-one else is to know what's gone on. And definitely not to the ground crew. What have you written in your log books?"

The three aircrew looked at each other, embarrassed. Log books were supposed to be filed in immediately after a flight but rarely were. They were the subject of much testy comment from Peter Coachman, who as Adjutant had to review them every month.

"Er, not yet, Sir," muttered Armitage, like a naughty schoolboy.

"Good; then don't. Put it down as a 'night training flight'. I'll sign your logbooks off for you. Understand?"

"Yes, Sir," they chorused as Duffus led the two GHQ officers off to their car in the dark.

"Good work, Duffus," said Mackenzie. "Good young men. Absolutely. I think we're back in business. Sorry about splitting up your squadron, but it's important that we have a special ops facility near GHQ. If you can keep this up, Duffus, we've got more business for you."

"Thank you, Sir. Twenty Five squadron won't let you down." Duffus held the car door as the GHQ driver saluted in the darkness.

Duffus was suspicious of the whole evening.

Like many of the men in the line, Duffus thought that the staff was a bloated and incompetent bunch of red-tabbed careerists and grasping military shits. He was particularly unhappy about having been forced to send the majority of his command down south to Serny near the French sector, leaving just the newly revived Special Duties flight behind. Splitting the squadron was making his job difficult if not impossible. But there was definitely something odd about this mission. He spoke up:

"One thing puzzles me Colonel: I was a bit surprised when you said that the FE2s weren't up to it. I've flown Fees. I'd have thought they would be ideal for this kind of flying. I could land a Fee on a football pitch."

Drake stopped, running his hand along the metalwork of the car. In the dark his expression was unfathomable.

"Truth is, Duffus, that wasn't the reason. The real thing is that we were losing too many of the Fees, trying to land in the dark; and every time we lost a Fee, we lost another of our special agents. And they're damned hard to find, I can tell you." He snorted in disgust. "Take young Craig there. The fellow your people dropped tonight. Excellent young man. Good family. Royal Naval Division, wounded on the Ancre back of '16. Got a French father, English mother. Travelled round Lille with his old man before the war. Commercial traveller or some such. Speaks it like a local. We've given him papers as a *'grande mutilié de la Guerre.'*"

"A what, Sir?"

"Seriously wounded by the war. Can't soldier any more. It's a French thing. They get special discharged veteran's papers; lets them move around freely, even in the Huns' zone. Craig's got all the qualifications; even to getting his arse shot off." Drake shook his head.

"What!?"

The other two officers stared at the Special Int Colonel. Even the driver drew closer in the darkness to listen.

"Feller's got no backside, left side. Took a bullet through the front of the hip. Tumbled inside him apparently and exited through the left buttock. Pretty well blew his arse off. That's why he limps. Didn't you notice?" Drake went on. "Could've been invalided out. Should've been. Chooses to soldier on though. Transferred to the Army; Intelligence Corps. Special Intelligence. Brave man. But how many chaps are there around like that, eh? That's why this sort of thing is so important, Duffus. We can't find and train that many Craigs. They just don't exist."

He climbed into the car. "But not a word to those pilots of yours, Duffus. Secret stuff. What they don't know they can't blab should Brother Hun ever get his paws on one of them. The Craigs of this world can fend for themselves; they're trained for it."

The car ground off into the night.

Duffus walked slowly back to the squadron hut. It was two a.m. He pulled a hand across his unshaven face. He'd been up since four that morning.

The dawn patrol was due for about six, and then there were the squadron admin returns for the last month: they were late – again. The move to Serny hadn't helped…. Should have gone off yesterday. You can't run a squadron from two locations… Petrol was mysteriously missing again – probably being sold off by someone working a racket with the bloody Frenchies at the petrol point. Talk to the serjeant major about that… A new observer and two new NCOs to interview, two airmen absent on leave back in Blighty – probably overstaying their leave – who could blame them? Explain to the Brigade Commander why he couldn't possibly release Josh Moon, his seconded Yankee doctor, to go back to the American Expeditionary Force until he'd been replaced by a British one, even though he had finished his experience training… He liked Josh… a good man…. Doc Moon was a damn fine squadron doctor too…the boys liked him. That report on airframe modifications needed a careful look, too…some new modifications there…inspect the armoury… and – Goddammit! He'd forgotten – that bloody airfield evacuation plan, which was a week overdue already. And then he had to move down to Serny to join the rest of the squadron before tomorrow evening. Good job Peter Coachman was staying behind at St Omer as Officer Commanding Rear Party…. Oh well, Coachie would just have to deal with things….

Christ, he was tired.

Thank God for Peter Coachman….

*   *   *

"Well?" Mackenzie enquired as the car sped away into the night. "Didn't I say we could deliver him safely?"

Drake, known to his friends as DeeDee, nodded in the blackness of the car. "Yes, and those RFC boys are as good as we'll get, Mac. No, I think we couldn't ask for better."

"So, will you be sending more agents?"

"Yes. As many as I can safely risk on the other side. But we don't have a lot, as I said back there." He mused out of the window at the darkened countryside flashing by. "It's all very well for the Chief to demand action, Mac. And for MacDonogh and the rest of the London end. But it's not easy. If we don't have the men, the French speakers, then we can't do the job, however much he insists we cooperate."

"Did you see DMO's reply to Haig's letter?"

Drake snorted. "That could have meant anything: *'Be assured that we at this end are doing our very best to ensure that all avenues are being explored to delay any impending attack'* …What the hell does that mean in plain English, eh? Load of tripe. Civil service drivel. I'm surprised at Maurice: thought better of him."

"Marshall-Cornwall told me that he was pretty certain that Neville, the chap from the Cabinet, had fixed it so that Cumming and his Secret Service people would definitely do something."

Drake absorbed this. "Well, let's hope so. Maybe London doesn't think it's important…"

"*Balls!*" Mackenzie was angry. "What could be more important than crippling the Hun war effort? It could win the war! Come *on*, Dee Dee."

"Well, I agree," said Drake, anxious to mollify his colleague. "But London may see things differently. When's the Hun attack due, by the way?" He added, anxious to change the subject.

"Cuffe's people reckon between the 19th and the 26th."

"You agree?"

"Yes. Cuffe and his order of battle boys have been spot on so far. Young Powell's been doing nothing else but tracking this Hun offensive for weeks. The difficulty is getting the Chief to agree. There was a row about it yesterday."

Drake turned in the darkness to stare at Mackenzie. "Why?"

Mackenzie glowered out of the car window. "Because we're sure we are right, but Coxie won't push it with Haig. Apparently Gough says that '*Fifth Army has a different evaluation*'. He doesn't agree, if you please! As if Gough were an expert on what the Huns are up to. Gough's a bloody menace, take my word for it…."

Drake sniffed in sympathy. "You can't really blame him. After all he has got to dig about fifty miles of new trenches. And how the hell he's supposed to do that in the next month is beyond me."

"Yes, that's all very well. But the bloody man won't listen to the intelligence. Keeps insisting that the attack's going to come in the north, and Haig'll back him".

"Gough and Haig go back a long way. It's the Cavalry Club again, Mac…"

"And if Goughie doesn't like it then, '*the Chief ain't going to interfere with the views of the senior officer responsible on the ground*'. Un-bloody-quote. Sometimes I don't know why I bother."

The car drove on in silence.

Mackenzie didn't tell Drake that secretly he was ashamed that he hadn't pushed his case further in the Chief of Staff's office. But he knew better to risk an argument that he couldn't win with a senior officer. It would only prejudice good relations in the jungle of competing egos and rivalries that made up the BEF headquarters, even when he knew he was in the right. Everyone knew that Haig favoured his protégé, "the darling of the cavalry," General Sir Hubert Gough. He consoled himself with the thought that he had done it for the good of his G Int Branch: but deep down, he knew he had funked a scrap. Then again, he mused, maybe he was being practical.

"So Fifth Army's in for trouble?" Drake's voice intruded on his thoughts.

"I have no doubt about that whatsoever, DeeDee. Fifth Army and brother Gough are sitting right in the path of a tornado. But getting that arrogant shit to agree is another matter."

Drake digested this in silence as the car slowed for a crossroads. "Well, we're doing our bit for G Int, Mac. Special Int is virtually working for you chaps now. Young Craig's been put in for one reason and one reason only: and that's to try and back your lot over this big offensive. If a chap like that can't find out for us, no one can. If I know Craig, he'll probably be telling us the Hun zero hour down to the second."

Mackenzie nodded. "I know you're doing your best, Dickie. And I appreciate it. We never got this kind of cooperation with Cameron, I can tell you."

Drake grinned mirthlessly as the car swung towards Montreuil and GHQ. "Well, they don't come any better than young Craig. He's our best."

If he survives, he thought to himself: if he survives. But even as he spoke, fifty miles away Captain Craig of the Intelligence Corps, attached Special Int 1B of the BEF, was rolling down the bank lifeless, a German bullet in his spine.

CHAPTER 13

NEAR LILLE

2ⁿᵈ March 1918

Serjeant Dietrich Lutz was bored and irritated.

After eight month's service at the Front he was only too happy for his division to be pulled back into Army reserve, well behind the lines. But for the battle hardened veterans of 63 Infantry Regiment to be ordered to mount night security patrols around Lille was, in his opinion, a waste of time and energy. Moreover, his platoon thought so too and the lanky ex-school-teacher from Bremen had had to speak very firmly to them; especially young Hartmann, eighteen years old, large, red-faced, blond, loud-mouthed and stupid. Worse, he was cocky and arrogant, and a natural bully of the barrack room. Only last week he had blacked young Rosenberg's eye. Definitely one to keep an eye on.

Hartmann had been sampling the girls and wine of Lille for the past week, and to be ordered to do night roadblocks was, as he so ringingly announced at the platoon orders group, "just another shitty extra guard duty." Serjeant Lutz, ever mindful of good order and military discipline, had rebuked Hartmann and put him as outer sentry in a hedge all night as a punishment.

A hundred metres down the lane the rest of the platoon had mounted a temporary roadblock with a coil of barbed wire across the road. Here they dozed, drank dreadful coffee and smoked. Hartmann, shivering and wet, looked back longingly back at his comrades and tried to stay awake in the dark. Just his luck if he dozed off and Lutz caught him. It would be straight in front of the major and field punishment if he knew Lutz. *Scheiss'* NCOs! One day, he thought, in some trench, when Lutz's back was turned he would fix the Serjeant once and for all and no-one would ever know

Hartmann stared into the darkness, sucking a boiled sweet and reminiscing about the French girl he'd bedded two nights ago. Now she really was something. Karl-Heinz and Jacob had questioned him closely the next day when he had boasted of his conquest in the barrack room. "I'll bet she's got the clap!" Jacob had said.

"You're just jealous," he'd answered. "That's bollocks!"

"*Ja*, I'd keep checking those as well," Karl-Heinz had replied, "you might need to!"

Very funny. But what if she was poxed up? A lot of these French girls were … Hartmann's reverie was broken.

Someone was coming down the lane towards him. He could hear footsteps and a dark shape formed against the paler darkness of the lane. He pushed his rifle forward, then remembered Serjeant Lutz's orders: "*Warn the platoon. Don't challenge. Do you think that you can remember that, Hartmann?*"

So he lay in the cold hedge as a Frenchman limped past him in the lane, carrying a suitcase. When he had passed, Hartmann pulled hard on the string that led back to the road block.

"Aha!" said Lutz as the tin can clattered in the wire. "Hartmann is still awake. We've got company. He remembered to pull the string."

"He's probably got the string caught in his fly buttons, Sarge!"

"Enough! Müller, Sorge, stand to and check." Grinning, the two soldiers moved into the road, slinging their rifles onto their shoulders.

*   *   *   *   *

Despite his assurances, David Craig's walk had been painful. His hip was playing up, and he'd already taken a slug of the brandy when he saw the glow of the fire as he rounded the bend. He stopped and saw the unmistakable helmets. Then he heard boots clattering in the road and shadowy figures ahead. He stopped but the pigeons rustled and cooed. Damn birds!

Quietly he stepped to the hedge at the side of the lane and thrust the incriminating basket deep into the shadow. He could always come back for it. If not – well, too bad.

"*Wer ist da?*" A voice challenged ahead. And then in dreadful French, "Advance so we can see you."

A bloody German roadblock. Just his luck. He gulped brandy and shouted back, "It's only me!"

"Step forward."

Craig wandered down the lane, taking care to weave, the brandy bottle in his hand. A bulls-eye lantern suddenly burst into light, and he stopped, shielding his eyes.

"What's the problem?" He waved the bottle. "Anyone want a drink?"

Lutz sighed. Another stupid, half-pissed Frenchman, out after curfew. Why the hell couldn't they just obey regulations like normal people?

He stepped forward, flashing the lamp on Craig. "Papers, Jacques. And you're breaking the law."

"Oh my God, it's our victorious conquerors. Don't shoot me, I beg you! Have a drink, my friends. As one old soldier to another. And it's Charles, not Jacques …"

Lutz looked closely at the Frenchman. He was young enough to be a soldier. Odd.

"Who are you?"

David Craig pulled himself to a swaying semblance of attention. "Me, I am Charles Jean Martel, of Englos. Sir!"

Lutz studied the French ID documents. They were normal. He could understand the French card for '*grand blessé*'.

"Where were you wounded?"

"Notre Dame de Lorrette. 1915. Shot in the hip. I was captured. And then a prison camp. Near Friedrichshafen."

Lutz stared at the Frenchman. "So how are you free?"

"Released, *Herr Feldwebel*. Too badly injured to be a soldier any more. Courtesy of his Imperial Majesty Kaiser Wilhelm and the Red Cross..."

"But still you can walk the night, eh? Haven't you ever heard of the curfew?"

Craig tapped his nose. "Curfew. Got to be careful. Germansh y'know." He waved the brandy bottle at Müller and Sorge, both vastly entertained by the cabaret of the drunken Frenchman.

"Have a drink. Reminds me of Friedrichshafen. Nice Germans."

Back up the lane Hartmann could hear the voices at the road block, but couldn't make out the words. He was mystified by the case in the hedge. He'd seen the Frenchman hide it. It was probably something valuable he was trying to keep secret.

He glanced down the road. That bastard Lutz was engrossed in his questioning. The group was concentrating on the drunk. He heard someone laugh. No-one was watching him. Good! Very slowly he stole across the lane, his rifle at the trail. No-one could see him in the dark and if that Frenchy had something good to hide, well, then Hartmann wanted some. Probably black market stuff; real coffee? Maybe even hams or booze. He could sell them...there was always a sucker in the new recruits.

He rummaged under the hedge and pulled the wicker basket towards him and opened it. Something squawked and pecked his hand.

With an explosion of noise, their wings a sudden clatter round his startled face in the dark, birds suddenly rocketed round him like missiles in the night, taking to the air, free. He reared back in shock, his heart hammering.

Then the realisation hit him. Pigeons! Spies, saboteurs!

Hartmann didn't stop to think.

"Serjeant! He's a spy. Pigeons! In the hedge. He's hiding pigeons! Stop him! He dumped his pigeons here!"

Lutz and David Craig reacted simultaneously.

Lutz and the two soldiers spun towards the shouting voice, peering into the darkness. At the same time, Craig pushed the German NCO hard in the chest and ran as fast as he could back up the dark lane. Sorge and Muller looked on open-mouthed in astonishment as Serjeant Lutz sprawled at their feet, his lantern clattering to the ground, nearly knocking them over. The drunken Frenchman disappeared into the shadows.

A bedlam of shouting broke out.

"Stop him, you idiots!" bellowed Lutz. "Get him!"

Sorge loosed off a shot into the night. "No! Get him, you idiots! After him! *Schnell!*"

Lutz scrambled to his feet, swinging the lantern's beam up the lane. "Get him!"

The two soldiers began to sprint up the lane: but the Frenchman had disappeared into the night.

Craig made good progress. His sudden dash had taken him about thirty yards into the darkness. The place where he'd hidden the pigeons was on his left. To hell with them.

He dived through the hedge on his right and began to run hard across the field, bad leg forgotten. Behind him he could hear pounding feet in the lane and shouting. Another shot rang out but not at him. He grinned as he ran. Provided he could get across the bank and hedge twenty yards ahead in the moonlight he would escape into the dark shadows of the wood behind. This bunch of clodhopping jackboots milling around would never catch a platoon in the dark, let alone one man.

He sprang up the bank. Funny, he didn't feel frightened at all. In fact, he thought as he got to the top, it was all a bit of a lark and his bum and hip seemed to be working a damn sight better than he ever expected.

*   *   *

Private Hartmann was puzzled.

He'd shouted a warning, the lamp had gone down on the ground down by the checkpoint and then Serjeant Lutz had ordered them to stop someone. A man had run towards him, then disappeared as if by magic. Then a shot had been fired up the lane in his direction, followed by Sorge and Muller running past him up the lane. What the hell was going on?

He peered through the hedge to his left where the fugitive had disappeared. In the last of the moonlight he could see a vague shape of a man disappearing across the field.

"Stop him, you fools!" Lutz shouted as he ran up the lane, lantern swinging. "Stop him!"

Hartmann needed no encouragement. He chambered a round, swung the Mauser 7.92mm rifle to his shoulder, and fired at the dark shadow of the fleeing Frenchman just as he was silhouetted against the bank, fifty metres away.

It is hard to hit a running man with a snap shot at night, particularly for a half-trained *ländser* like Hartmann, who only that morning had been scathingly described by Serjeant Lutz to the rest of 9 Platoon as "the worst soldier, the worst shot and the laziest man in the whole of the German army," adding for good measure, "And the most stupid too!"

Lutz, who was sprinting up the lane after the fleeing Briton, nearly jumped out of his skin at the sudden flash and bang of a gunshot almost under his nose. He skidded to a halt. "What in hell...? Who fired that?"

"It's me, Serjeant." Hartmann swung round, recocking his rifle.

"Hartmann, you idiot! What the hell are you shooting at?" They cannoned into each other in the dark.

Hartmann's rifle went off, the bullet striking sparks off the road as they both sat heavily on the ground. The lamp flew into the hedge and went out.

"Hartmann! I might have known! You fool! Get out of the bloody way." Serjeant Lutz sat up, his right leg buzzing from the collision, where that moron Hartmann had given him a dead leg. "You idiot! Get the Frenchman."

Lutz stood up and lurched. Instinctively he clutched at his leg and rubbed it. A stab of pain shot up his thigh and his hand came away wet and sticky. What the hell? The realisation hit him slowly. He stared at his hand in the dark. Blood. He'd been shot. That half-witted bastard Hartmann had actually shot him! For a second he was speechless with incredulity and rage.

"You imbecile, Hartmann! You're the biggest clown I have ever seen in my life! You've shot me, you...!"

The rest of the platoon began to gather round them in the dark, nervous and excited.

"What's going on, Serjeant?" asked *Gefreiter* Schneider, cocking his rifle. Lutz stared amazed at the blood on his hand, dark in the night.

"This mental pygmy Hartmann has just shot me. That's all! Never mind standing round like a damned old wives' coffee morning! It's only a flesh wound! Get the Frenchman!"

Only too glad to escape their shocked leader's wrath, the platoon streamed through the hedge and scattered across the field.

"And try not to shoot each other in the dark, you idiots!" bellowed their infuriated platoon leader at their retreating backs. Lutz peered disbelievingly at the dark rent in his uniform trousers. Two years in France without a scratch and then this from some half-trained, half-witted *dumkopf* of a half-albino loud-mouthed farmer's boy from Ostfriesen…!

*   *   *

Hartmann ran to the spot where the Frenchman had disappeared up the bank on the far side. He was only too happy to get away from the enraged Lutz. A vision of a penal battalion flitted into his mind. Maybe he'd better run away like the mysterious Frenchman…

He tripped over a lump on the ground, dark in the moonlight, crashing to earth.

Captain David Craig lay peacefully face down by the hedgebank. His arms were sprawled sideways.

Hartmann's bullet had hit him smack between the 8th and 9th thoracic vertebrae and stopped abruptly, lodged in the bony mass of his spine. The 7.5 grammes of lead and copper travelling at nearly 1,500 miles per hour had promptly transferred their 3,000 pounds of kinetic energy directly to the delicate animal mechanism that was David Craig's body. A hydrostatic shockwave had roared through his soft tissues like an earthquake, rupturing blood vessels, collapsing the lungs and reducing the spleen to a splattered jelly. At the same time, the impact had torn up the spinal column and then stopped dead, driving the brain hard against his skull.

Craig had died instantly.

He never knew he'd been shot.

His last thought was that he had eluded his pursuers and was free. As Hartmann rolled the body over over, the German was astonished to see that the dead man was grinning from ear to ear.

The body had a strange rubbery quality. After nearly six months' front line service, Hartmann knew exactly what to do with the dead.   Rob them: fast.

Quickly he searched the Frenchman's pockets, then stopped. The dead man wore a heavy bandolier round his waist. Odd. Pulling open the shirt, Hartmann saw that it wasn't a bandolier at all but a white canvas money belt. He ripped it off and tore it open, frantic as a hyena at a kill that some one else might arrive and steal his booty.

Golden coins spilled out, glinting in the darkness.

"Shit!" He exclaimed. Hartmann was a man of limited vocabulary.

Quickly he stuffed his find into his tunic. It was heavy.

"Serjeant," he called out. "Serjeant! I've got him. He's over here. He's dead."

*   *   *

Fifteen minutes later, 9 platoon had gathered back at the road block.

The lamp had been re-lit and Serjeant Lutz's thigh was being bandaged by Roth, the platoon medic. David Craig's now stiffening body lay face up in the lane, an empty sandbag hiding the eternal ghastly grin. Alongside Lutz was the empty pigeon basket, the spy's false papers and a small Swiss automatic pistol found in his pocket.

Serjeant Lutz had the twelve gold coins found on the ground by the body in his pocket. In the lamplight they had proved to be English sovereigns. He would pass ten of them to Major Winzinger when he saw the battalion commander. He had a strong suspicion that Hartmann may have pocketed a couple too, but that would be hard to prove, short of ordering the wretched idiot to turn out his pack and pockets. A runner had been despatched to Regiment to bring back an ambulance and the major.

When the bandaging was finished, it was Serjeant Lutz who delivered the verdict on 9 Platoon's evening's work.

"What a God-awful shambles!"

He shook his head. "What a *bescheissener* shambles. Hartmann, I must congratulate you, soldier. You've managed to shoot your platoon leader and a French spy – all in the dark. Even for a *dummi Ostfriesen* that is some kind of record."

He looked round the assembled platoon in the firelight as Cpl Schneider helped him to his feet. Several half grins were hastily suppressed. "Hartmann – you are an idiot. What are you?"

"I am an idiot, Serjeant!"

"Do you know the penalty for shooting your superior officer, idiot?"

"Court martial, Serjeant. But it was an accident."

"Oh, ja. So you say. An accident. Attempted murder of your platoon leader. What kind of sentence do you think that a *Kriegsgericht* would give you, idiot?"

"I dunno, Serjeant," pleaded Hartmann. "But a court martial? It really was an accident, Serjeant!"

"Lucky your first shot was better, eh?"

"Yes Serjeant."

"Yes Serjeant," mocked Lutz. "But it was one hell of a shot; that I must admit. A running man in the dark. Lucky, eh? And it looks like you got us a spy too. Unbelievable." He shook his head. "Hartmann, I don't know whether to recommend you for a court martial or an Iron Cross."

Lutz winced as his leg took his weight. His leg was beginning to send sizzling sparks of pain up his thigh.

"Let's say you're a hero, shall we?" He grinned, his teeth gleaming in the dark. "Nine platoon needs all the heroes it can get. That should please the Major. He'll probably recommend you for an Iron Cross. That will look good for the *Herr* Oberst and his beloved regiment. Oh sure. And all down to Hartmann, our big, dumb Ostfriesen farm boy. Well, well, well."

He shook his head, disbelievingly.

"I give up." The pain was coming in solid waves now. He gritted his jaw. "As for the other," he looked down at his leg. "Well. Let's just say that's an accident, eh?"

He looked round the ring of cheerful young faces in the firelight.

He had been *Zugführer* of "lucky 9" for over a year; the oldest surviving platoon leader in the whole battalion, since Peter Schroeder fell over and broke his arm at Christmas, half pissed at Christmas. Lucky bastard…

He knew these boys better than their own mothers; and now he was to desert them and go to the hospital; wounded, and by one of his own, as well. Unbelievable. Again he shook his head. Still, he was out of the war at last. He felt a surge of relief, cut short by the realisation that he was now about to leave the closest family he had ever known: or would ever know. He loved these men, his boys. And now he was abandoning them to the war. What would become of them? He choked.

He recovered himself. The leg was throbbing now with regular hot drum beats of pain. They were all staring at him. He must leave like a man. He was still their platoon commander.

"So, Hartmann, for the platoon, and for getting me out of this damned war, thank you: idiot. If you survive this war, which I doubt, then you can go back to your wretched dungheap of a farm secure in the knowledge that you have behaved in the fiinest traditions of OstFriesland. Like a bumbling *VOLLIDIOT!*"

"Yes Serjeant!" shouted Hartmann. "Thank you, Serjeant!"

"Hartmann, you are a big, heroic idiot. Let's leave it at that. What are you?"

"A big, heroic idiot, Serjeant!" shouted Hartmann into the night.

The money belt with its 188 remaining gold sovereigns was warm and heavy against his belly. With a windfall like that he could afford to buy his own farm – two farms! - once the war was over. And get the best girls in Lille once they got back to the Kaserne. Happy in the sudden realisation, he grinned his stupid cheerful grin at the faces of the rest of the platoon, glowing in the firelight.

Lutz stared at him. His leg felt on fire. He grunted disbelievingly, "It's your lucky night, Hartmann. What is it?"

"My lucky night! Thank you, Serjeant!"

*   *   *

Four kilometres to the south west, in his run down farmhouse at Brulle, Joseph Eschalier heard the brief rattle of gun shots blown on the breeze.

He swung his legs into bed alongside his sleeping wife.

"That's your doing, I take it?" she said sourly. "One day the *Boche*'ll catch you, Joseph: or Armand, or whatever you pretend to call yourself when you go out playing at spies. And then where will that leave me, you selfish pig, if you get caught like those two from Gondecourt? They were executed. I hope that you've hidden that stupid bike."

"Shut your mouth woman. And don't forget that I've not left the house all evening, if you value the roof over your head!"

Sometimes the Germans burnt houses of those who were caught helping the Allies as a warning to others.

"Why?" She snuffled. "*Why?*"

"For Anton. And his cherry tree. Now go to sleep and forget, wife."

With a grunt, Eschalier settled down to sleep. Behind him his wife cried silently, remembering their only son, Anton, *mort pour la Patrie* in that blazing late summer of 1914, and the cherry tree they had planted the last spring before he went away, and which was just beginning to come into bloom again.

CHAPTER 14

THE NORTH SEA, DAWN

5th March 1918

It was the sudden realisation that the thump, thump of the steamer's engines had stopped that roused Everitt. Bleary with sleep and with a headache from the drinks in the saloon the night before, slowly he took in the pale grey light filtering in through the porthole.

Six forty five said his watch: "Made in USA" he read, waking up to the sudden silence. Voices shouted on the upper deck. He could have sworn one was German. "Shit!" He swung his legs out of the bunk.

Coming on the deck he shivered in the grey dawn and pulled the heavy overcoat closer over his pyjamas. The sea was flat calm. The SS Christiniana was stopped, rolling gently on the North Sea. The Norwegian Captain was remonstrating with somebody over the starboard wing of the open bridge. His eyes followed the gesticulating arm of the angry skipper.

Fifty yards off, a German U boat rocked gently on the oily sea. Halfway between, a tiny rowing boat was pulling towards them, water splashing from its oars.

Everitt's first reaction was of total shock.

In five undercover wartime crossings of the North Sea on neutral ships he had never once been stopped and boarded. His brain rapidly took in the grey mist; the extraordinary pale grey of the U boat's paint; the chipped white "U53" on the side of the conning tower; the fact that the little boat contained four rowers and an officer; the way the Christiana's other passengers were slowly emerging on deck to see why their ship had stopped; and the furious argument going on between the Norwegian skipper and the German officer in the boat. It stopped when the officer pointed back to the submarine. The U boat's gun was now trained on them and at fifty yards they could all see the guncrew ramming a shell into the breech.

"All right," shouted the skipper in Norwegian. "I cannot stop you searching my vessel. But I will lodge a serious protest when we dock. We are a neutral ship."

The German lieutenant scrambled aboard and waved a perfunctory salute to the bridge. Three armed sailors clambered after him.

"*Ja, Kapitän*, I hear you," he called back in a curious mixture of Danish and Norwegian, "but we are within our rights to search for spies and contraband. There is a war on, you know!"

At the mention of spies Everitt's brain snapped back into life. Shivering, he went below to his cabin and started to dress. He was just buttoning his jacket when there was a knock at the door and the purser appeared, followed by the German officer and a sailor with a rifle.

"Sorry to disturb you, Mr Pedersen. The Germans want to search. They are checking all the ship's papers. Passengers too."

Everitt took in the young naval officer. He was tall and very blonde. He snapped his fingers impatiently. "Papers!" the German demanded in his strange accent.

"Warum? Why?" snapped Everitt back in German.

The German was nonplussed. Everitt pressed his advantage. "I'm a torpedoed Norwegian ship's officer, on a Norwegian ship, going home to Norway. And you, a German, demand my papers. We are not at war with Germany. Who the hell do you think you are?"

The Purser sucked his breath in and grimaced.

An angry flush flooded the young German's face and he stepped into the cabin.

"This vessel is being officially searched by the Imperial German Navy for contraband and prohibited individuals. I demand to see your papers – now!" The fingers snapped again.

Grumbling, Everitt turned his back and pulled out his temporary passport and the letters from the Norwegian Consul in Hull. The German peered at them, suspiciously. "Where are your real papers?"

Everitt stared at him, simulating an anger he found surprisingly easy to summon up.

"You sank them *Lieber* Fritz, along with my ship. My Norwegian ship, the Lurline. Now they lie with my ship, at the bottom of the sea. With many of my friends. So I had to ask for more papers to get back home to Norway. All right? Or are you going to sink this neutral ship, too?"

He snatched his papers back and turned his back to stuff them into his sailor's duffel bag. At the bottom he could feel the gift-wrapped box with its timer rigged clock. When he looked back he saw that the German was still standing, an embarrassed look on his face.

"You are a sailor?"

"That's right, Fritz. Yes. Third officer, SS Lurline, registered Oslo. Sunk off Flamborough Head, 15th December 1917, by a German U boat. Pulled out of the sea by the English. No thanks to you."

The German's embarrassment increased. "The fortunes of war. It is regrettable *Herr* Pedersen…"

Everitt stared him down until the German dropped his eyes. "Regrettable! You call it regrettable? You might tell that to my Captain and the fourteen innocent neutral Norwegian sailors who were killed, my young friend." He turned away again, yanking viciously on the duffel bag's drawstring. "Fortunes of war …"

The German officer looked at the Purser, who shrugged.

"I regret the inconvenience Herr Pedersen. It is my duty to check, you understand. We all have our orders. Perhaps one day we will meet again when this unpleasantness is over, yes?" He put out his hand. Everitt regarded it until the exact moment the German's shoulders began to move, preparatory to pulling it away in embarrassment.

"Oh what the hell," he said. "We're all sailors, Fritz." He shook the German's hand. "Good luck to you, too. We're all seamen. Blame the war, eh?"

The young officer clicked his heels and bowed. "Thank you, *Herr* Pedersen. And my name is Lothar, Oskar: not Fritz." He smiled. "May I wish you too, a successful homecoming." He went out.

The Purser raised his eyebrows, glared at Everitt and blew out his cheeks then followed. Their boots clumped down the gang-way.

When they had gone, Everitt sat on the bed and ran his hand over his beard. For a long time he stared at the bulkhead opposite. He could feel the sweat dribbling down his armpits and back. He looked at his hands, trembling like birch leaves in the breeze. The shaking started to quiver his whole body. Standing up, he took a bottle of whisky from the luggage rack, uncorked it and took a long pull. Through the porthole he could see the *KriegsMarine* search crew scramble aboard their submarine, the tiny boat collapsed and taken below.

Jets of blue grey smoke suddenly puffed from the rear of the hull and U53 slowly slid away, smooth as a shark on the oily grey sea into the grey morning.

Nicky Everitt took a deep breath and shook his head. "I'm getting too windy for much more of this lark," he announced to no-one in particular – in English.

He took another long pull of whisky.

CHAPTER 15

ARMSTRONG'S DIVE BOMBING

THE WESTERN FRONT

8th March 1918

Jack Armstrong drained the last of his late breakfast. The rest of his flight looked on, fascinated, as the strange mixture of coffee, milk, brandy, and a raw egg disappeared from the pint glass.

"Right," he said, wiping his lips with the back of his hand and handing the glass to a stony-faced mess waiter, holding a silver tray. "That's the ticket! Let's go!"

He caught Barton's eye. "Good of you to join us, CB. Thought that you'd be pleased to see your old chums from A Flight back up here at St Omer. Bet you're glad you didn't have to move down to Serny, eh? Missed you in the mess last night. Still on the nest down the village are we?" He sniggered.

Barton stared at him but said nothing, his jaw tightening. Robbie noticed his fists were bunched.

Armstrong shrugged and began to walk. The aircrew of A Flight glanced at each other then followed him out of the mess and straggled towards the waiting aeroplanes. Suddenly Armstrong ducked back into the lavatories, leaving Roberts, Barton and the rest of A flight waddling on in the thick flying suits.

"Unusual breakfast," observed Roberts.

"Unusual fellow, our Jack," responded Barton. "And he'll be a damn sight more unusual if he comes out with any more witty cracks like that, I can tell you."

He squinted into the rising sun. "This could be awkward. No cloud. We'll have to stay up high. Mind you, at 15,000 feet we should be well up on the Jerries"

"Well, the Dolphins should do us all right." Roberts waved towards six smaller biplanes, their wings strangely staggered back and seemingly bolted on top of the fuselage. "They say they can get up to 22,000 feet."

"Funny looking brutes."

Timmy Turner-Tompkins, Roberts' observer chipped in excitedly: "They say they can see better with the top wing below the pilot's head; and once Dolphins're up really high they never need to look above them. The only problem is that they can go funny. The pilots, I mean. Because the air's thin. Their Flight Leader said that they're even experimenting with bottles of oxygen. So that they've got something to breathe. He said that they had new tactics, because they can go up so high. The Dolphins swoop down like hawks then zoom up again. Nothing can catch them …" He broke off, breathless.

"You seem to know a lot about Dolphins, Timmy. Goin' for a scout pilot are we?" Armstrong broke in, rejoining the group.

"No, Jack." Timmy was embarrassed. "I just talked to them. The Dolphin people. At breakfast. Their flight was in last night. We went into the village. Nice lot of chaps."

Armstrong grunted dismissively and pulled on his gloves. "Well, gather round."

He spread a map on the wing of his DH4.

"Here's what we do. It's a straightforward bombing job. Two 112 pounders each. Heavy stuff." He traced the route on the map. "St Omer to Commines. Straight over Hazebrouck, Bailleuil and Messines. Then here," He jabbed the map hard, "Here at the Commines canal, we turn hard right and head south east, course 135 degrees. Follow the Deule canal to Lille and then here. The rail junction at Lesquin." He pronounced it "Less-kwin." "Bomb the rail junction, then head back west as fast as we can."

The group peered at the map with its thickly crayoned line heading east into the German lines then abruptly doglegging to the south. "Odd sort of route," said a voice from the back.

"It is; that's the point. GHQ say there's a big build up of Boche trains at Lesquin. Something to do with their big offensive. The aim is to look as if we're heading for the usual stuff south of Ypres. By the time the local Hun scouts are up to altitude round the salient, ready to intercept us, we'll have turned right and scooted off to the south. So we take everyone by surprise."

"How do we drop the bombs, Jack?"

Armstrong looked at the speaker. It was a young ginger-haired pilot, Halloran, who was one of his principal admirers. "What do you mean, Hal?"

"Well, do we drop on your signal, all together – or do we bomb individually?"

For a split-second A Flight's leader seemed non-plussed. Halloran persisted. "The point is, Skipper, from 15,000 feet it's going to be hard to do it right. If you give the signal, at least we all blanket the target together." He tailed off. "If you see what I mean…"

Armstrong waved a dismissive hand. "Don't you worry about that 15,000 foot nonsense. If A Flight gets a mission, we hit the target. Just follow me and watch for my signals. All right?" He turned to go.

Barton raised his eyebrows and caught Roberts' eye. "Er, right oh, skipper…but what about the escort formation?"

Armstrong looked irritated. "Now what?"

"What about the Dolphins?"

Armstrong looked impatient, and glanced at his wrist watch. "They'll take off after us, to save petrol. They'll climb faster that our kites. No bombs, less weight. By the time we get to the turning point, they'll be at 20,000; well above us. All right?" He looked up. "Ah, at last. Here comes Mr Dolphin himself."

A burly figure muffled in a leather flying suit joined the group. He was over six feet tall and broad, with a big moustache. Armstrong held out his hand. "A Flight. Hello Clive."

"Good to meet you again, Armstrong. Sorry to have missed you last night. How d'ye do chaps. All set then?" The muffled apparition banged his hands hard together. "Clive Sinclair, Leader B Flight, 79 Squadron." He nodded to the DH4 crews. "We'll see you all right. Once we're above you, we'll conform to your moves. I'll try and stay up sun from you. If you do get bounced, we'll send down three Dolphins."

"Only three?" asked Armstrong. He seemed unsettled and impatient.

Sinclair grinned, a huge cheerful beam. "That's it. Just three. And when they've hit Brother Hun, then down'll come the other three. So there's always three above the German planes. Three diving, three zooming. Works like a charm." He looked round at the doubtful faces. "You mark my words. If anything comes near you, watch 'em scatter like partridge on a shoot, once the Diving Dolphins get among 'em. Works every time!" He roared with laughter. "Provided you stay close at 15,000 feet and keep close to us, you'll be safe as houses. Mark my words, chaps!"

Sinclair turned to Armstrong and clapped him on the back, "Ready, old man? Good to see you again. Let's go then." He grinned genially at the DH 4 aircrew.

Barton noticed that Armstrong looked distinctly out of sorts.

*   *   *

As the DH4s lifted off, Roberts glanced back.

The six bullet-nosed Dolphins were racing across the field in formation and began to climb slowly after them. With the bombs on, and full petrol loads, the DH4s climbed at rather less than a thousand feet a minute. Roberts' mental arithmetic told him that climbing at about eighty miles an hour, they would reach 15,000 feet somewhere around twenty miles to the East. Good! That would mean that they would cross the front line, twenty-five miles away at fifteen thousand feet. With luck, nothing would be waiting above them.

Satisfied, he settled down and concentrated on tucking his machine in closely under Armstrong's port wing. It was a beautiful spring morning. Off to starboard he could see Halloran's aircraft making the third member of the leading Vee formation. It rose and fell slowly as the little formation droned upwards, the other three DH4s of A flight forming a second Vee a hundred yards behind.

A dark shadow flitted over his face. Alarmed, he looked up, squinting into the sun. A hundred feet above, the black silhouettes of 79 Squadron's Dolphins were now climbing above them gradually getting higher even as he watched. He checked his intruments.

Eight thousand feet.

From the back seat of Halloran's DH4 the cheerful figure of his backseater waved across. It was Dalrymple, the observer who had started the scuffle on the way to St Omer by his wisecrack about "We observers know about bad drivers, don't we chaps?" Roberts grinned back and I raised a gloved hand in reply.

"Nice morning, Robbie." Timmy's voice was muffled by the noise of the engine but clearly audible through the newly installed Gosport speaking tube. "Can you hear me?"

"Yes. Loud and clear. D'you need to test your gun?"

The muffled voice came out of the ear trumpet by his right ear, "When we get to the other side of the line, Robbie. I'll shoot a burst down to port."

"All right, Timmy. Loaded your own drums?"

There was no reply. Robbie grinned. Two flights before Timmy's Lewis gun had jammed in a fight. None of his efforts would free it, and on examination back at the airfield a horribly mangled .303 bullet was found jammed solidly in the barrel. The armourer had needed a special extraction tool to unblock the breech. A shame-faced Timmy had admitted that he hadn't checked each bullet and loaded the Lewis gun drums himself, preferring to leave it to the armourers. Now he had found out the hard way why most Royal Flying Corps observers insisted on loading and cleaning their own guns. Robbie smiled at the memory. Live and learn, eh?

Ten thousand feet.

The Dolphins were far above them now and well up sun. Robbie could clearly see the dark scar of the front line ahead, smears of smoke drifting downwind from the occasional shell. He tried to imagine the life of an infantryman, stuck in a cold muddy trench being shelled at any time, night or day. Thank God he was in the RFC! At least he could sleep secure in a warm dry bed, have a bath and a good dinner and the risks were pretty much the same. He mused on these thoughts as the altimeter crept slowly round t0 15,000 feet and the front slid far below. It was bitterly cold. All the time his eyes automatically searched the sky ahead and around, his hands and feet unthinkingly adjusting the every rise and fall of his aeroplane to stay in close to Armstrong.

16,000 feet. Christ, it was cold!

As they crossed the line, a distinct tightening of the DH4s' formation betrayed the increased in tension that always accompanied entering enemy airspace. Observers tested their guns, the brief banging lost in the roar of the engines. Far above and ahead the six Dolphins were tiny black dots.

Roberts scoured the sky around, searching for the tell-tale specks of other aircraft. The mild March air was gin clear, not a cloud in the sky. At 17,000 feet they could see for fifty miles. Nothing.

Far, far below the morning sun glinted briefly on the unmistakable junction of the Lys and Deule river, the Deule leading south east to the industrial heart of Lille. Roberts became aware that Armstrong's machine was slowly tilting to the right, and the whole formation gently banked to the south, the sun now way off to their left.

The shadows on the wing changed place.

Roberts noticed that the Dolphins continued to the East for a full minute before banking sharply to their right to follow the DH4s. Ahead, to the South, lay the sprawling roofs and streets of Lille and, coming into view, the distant railway lines running to the junction at Lesquin. Roberts scanned the sky above and below for the thousandth time.

Nothing.

Suddenly, to his surprise, Jack Armstrong's machine began to crowd in on him from above. Adjusting the formation, he realised that the Flight Leader was losing altitude. The DH4s were in a shallow dive. He glanced at the altimeter: 14,000 feet and unwinding. Across to his right, Halloran's aircraft was floating higher, then falling. Halloran kept looking to his left, but Robbie couldn't see any reaction from the flight leader as Armstrong steepened his dive.

"What the hell's going on?" Timmy suddenly squawked in his ear, a note of rising tension in his voice. "I thought orders were to stay at 15,000 feet? GHQ?"

"Search me." Robbie began to nose down. Armstrong was now below him and well in front. Roberts saw the flight leader's hand raised in the air, a vertical slice, the signal for "follow me in line astern". Obediently he slid in behind his leader's aircraft. What on earth was going on? Halloran followed suit astern and behind them the other three DH4s straggled in a line. Their airspeed was rising; 140 mph; 13,000 feet. What the hell was Armstrong up to?

The dive steepened still further. Robbie was having a job keeping up with the flight leader. He risked a quick search of the sky above. Of the Dolphin escort he could see no sign. The airspeed built up, the wind screaming in the wires. Suddenly he was scared. Ten thousand feet. This was madness. The DH4s were well below their operational height and still diving. Eight thousand feet. Too fast. The airframe started to buffet as he struggled to keep up with Armstrong, now in a 45 degree dive. Somewhere ahead he saw a white puff of archie as a German anti-aircraft gun opened up. Ahead of that, and well past the bucketing shape of Armstrong's DH4 was a railway yard with trucks and sidings.

Six thousand feet!

The DH4s were rocketing down in line astern, their speed now well up to 160 mph. Jesus! This was stupid. The aeroplane's controls were stiff as boards and the railway yard was dead ahead. He had to glance up to see the line of the horizon. Somewhere ahead another AA shell burst but they were going so fast he was through the smoke puff almost as soon as he saw it. 3,000 feet! The DH4 bucketed and bounced as it hit the turbulent airflow behind Armstrong's aeroplane. Behind, the rest of A Flight was strung out in a long straggling line. The roar of the engine was now almost a scream. That silly bastard would rip their wings off if he went any faster. Robbie's mouth was dry with fright and the ground a blur as the DH4s rocketed down.

At about 1,000 feet Armstrong began to level off, flattening out to streak across the suburbs of Lille. Robbie followed him, the stick hard and unresponsive, the airframe rigid and unforgiving as a plank. Timmy's voice echoed in his ear, "Oh my God!"

Then trains were flashing beneath and the two black eggs of Armstrong's bombs suddenly hung above the horizon for a split second as they fell away. Desperately, Roberts pulled the release toggle and felt his DH4 jerk upwards with relief as the two 112 pound bombs dropped off. He was dimly aware of an explosion, the DH4 bucking against the controls and pitching, a red glare and smoke then they were through, 800 feet on the clock and rocketing in a steady bank to the right and the safety of the British lines twenty miles to the west. Only five minutes at worst. He could see Armstrong's machine ahead and below, and he dropped the nose to catch up with its header. Their shallow dive increased the airspeed still further. His aircraft felt like a rocketing uncontrollable missile.

Behind them was a mayhem of smoke and explosions with DH4s bursting through all over the place. Ahead was a stretch of green fields, roads and woods blurring past below. The thicker air at low level buffeted the DH4 and Roberts fought to hold her straight and level as A Flight roared for home at less than three hundred feet and nearly 150 mph. Straight ahead a German soldier stood in the road, futilely raising his rifle but the DH4 was flashing by too fast.

A line of field guns appeared spread out in a field with white faces and men pointing. Horses stampeded. Then they were roaring over trenches, mud, wire, a burst of tracer pullets whipped past and then a balloon. Suddenly they were over the British lines and slowly pulling up. Roberts' heart hammered in his chest. He became aware that he had been holding his breath. His breathing hissed in his ears. Then he became aware that Timmy was speaking, " … do that again. Nearly tore the bloody wings off. Stupid trick. And God knows what happened to the Dolphins. Have you seen our tail?"

Roberts glanced over his shoulder and focussed on the DH4's tailplane. Bare struts and the rags of ripped canvas fluttered on the port stabiliser. "Nasty. How did it happen?"

"Over the yard. Must have picked up the blast from Jack's bombs. Gave me a hell of a fright, I can tell you, Robbie. Surprised you didn't rip the tailplane off completely, at that speed."

Roberts stared ahead, watching the shape of Armstrong's DH4 rising above to climb to the North-West and head for home. He pondered Timmy's implicit rebuke, realising the justice of it.

"You're right. Jack was mad to pull a stunt like that. Sorry, Timmy. Just following our leader."

"Well, he's damn crazy, I say. Man's a maniac. Fifteen thousand feet's the orders. Have you seen Hal's kite? Can't see it anywhere."

Robbie swivelled round, searching for the third member of the first Vee. Halloran was nowhere to be seen. A couple of DH4s straggled a long way behind, too far off to be identified. He looked up. The Dolphins were nowhere in sight – hardly surprising after such a stunt, he thought.

As they flew into St Omer, Jack Armstrong's DH4 was already landing, plumes of dust or dew rising from its wheels. They followed and nosed up to the ground crew.

"Hello, Sir! Been in the wars again, I see." Serjeant Doughty's face was a picture of surprise as he inspected the aeroplane.

Roberts swung out of the cockpit. The engine, now still, began to give cooling off, clonking noices. "Yes. Something hit the tailplane."

"It's not just the tail, Sir. Have you seen your rigging?" Doughty pointed to the rigging wires bracing the wing struts. Normally taut as a violin string, they now hung slack and loose. One seemed to be missing completely. The lower wing's canvas sagged.

"And look at your canvas, Sir. Top wing."

Roberts looked up and suddenly felt cold. He swallowed. The dark green canvas of the wings was supposed to be tight as a drum. Instead it was sagging and wrinkled. Even as he watched, the wind actually rippled the fabric. The plummeting dive had strained the airframe to the limit.

A long whistle from Timmy brought him back to reality. "No wonder she was hard to fly, Robbie. This tailplane's almost gone. Look!" He indicated the bare ash struts and shreds of green doped canvas that had once been a tailplane, pushing his arm to the elbow through the hole.

"Bloody 'ell, Sir! 'Ave you seen your engine?" Serjeant Doughty's brow knitted as Cooper's cockney whine came from the nose of the aeroplane. They joined him. An engine panel lay on the turf as a drip tray. A steady splash, splash of dark oil dropped from the engine. Cooper's thin pale face peered in at the Rolls Royce. "I dunno wot you dun, Sir, but it's gorn an' blown a gasket. See 'ere. These seals. All bleedin' gone. You've over-stressed it good an' proper, Sir. Careful!" he added as Roberts reached up a hand to touch the smear of oil running down the block. "It's red 'ot, Sir. Take the 'and orf yer."

Cooper dashed a nervous glance at Serjeant Doughty. "It's buggered Sarge – Serjeant, beggin' your pardon, Sir. But it'll need stripping down and new seals. "Onest Sir, you've over-revved it."

Doughty nodded and made a show of inspecting the engine. The truth was, he knew little about the big 250 and 375 horse power Rolls Royces that powered his charges. When he'd transferred to the Royal Flying Corps, all the motors were rotary; big simple things that clattered round, spewing castor oil everywhere. He'd specialised as a rigger, tightening and balancing the big box kite airframes of 1916. These modern planes were technically beyond him, the engines particularly so. He suspected Corporal Cooper was aware of this, but couldn't be sure. He might, thought Jack Doughty, be a whining, miserable little sod, but Cooper seemed to know his way around engines. No doubt about it.

Aircrew and ground team morosely surveyed their sagging DH4.

Roberts began to realise they were not alone. Wails of dismay came from the other aircraft. He counted. Six. All back. Halloran broke away from the grumbling knot around his aircraft and came striding towards him. His cheeks were pale, with cold or rage it was hard to tell. "Robbie! What the hell was that about?"

"God only knows," answered Timmy. "About the only thing airworthy on our kite now are the guns."

Halloran surveyed Roberts' DH4. "Good God! It's come unglued."

"Jack was going down like a maniac," said Roberts. "It was all I could do to keep up with him."

"We didn't bother," said Halloran, walking round and inspecting the damage. "I left you two to get on with it and flattened out. So did the rest of the boys. We couldn't have kept up." He fingered the smashed left tailplane, shaking his head. "Anyway, it was a stupid stunt. I thought you and Timmy were goners when you flew into Jack's bomb bursts."

Comprehension dawned on Roberts' face. "So that's what threw us around!"

"Didn't you realise?" asked Timmy. That's what blew a bloody great hole in our tail. I told you."

"Where's Armstrong?" said Roberts. He could feel the anger rising in his chest. Where's bloody Armstrong!" He suddenly shouted.

The chattering crews around the other DH4s fell silent at his shout. Throwing his leather flying hat on the ground and ripping off his gloves, he began to tread purposefully towards the flight leader's aircraft.

"Where's Captain Armstrong?" he demanded of the crew chief, a grizzled little Scotsman called MacNaughty. Roberts' eye took in the alarmed faces of the other ground crew and how they faded from his wrath.

Slowly wiping his hands on a cloth, Serjeant MacNaughty eyed the angry young officer, "He's not here, Sir. He went straight to the CO's office. Urgent message, so they said."

He took in the compressed fury in Roberts' face and the knot of leather-suited aircrew gathering behind. "You'll no doubt be wanting to tell him that he's been a wee bit reckless, Sir?"

Roberts controlled himself. "Something like that, Sarn't Mac. Have you seen my plane?"

"Aye, ah have, Sir." MacNaughty jerked a thumb over his shoulder. "And have you seen what he's done to oors?" Roberts took in the same sagging wings, the loose canvas, the broken rigging wires. He calmed down.

McNaughty put his head on one side and looked Roberts straight in the eye. "It'll take two days to sort this lot our, Mr Roberts. Even if we work all night, Sir. She's not battle worthy. Any more than yours is either, from the look of her rigging. Half the flight's oot of action by the look of it. It'll no' do, Sir, I'm tellin' ye." MacNaughty cocked his head on one side. "I'm thinkin' that mebbe ye'll be having a wee word wi' Captain Armstrong?"

Roberts breathed hard through his nose. "Yes. Don't be in any doubt that I'll speak to the Flight Leader, Serjeant MacNaughty. Thank you."

MacNaughty stiffened to attention as the angry knot of aircrew grumbled and muttered away towards the Squadron huts.

"Well," he said to no-one in particular, the Scots accent broad and clear "Armstrong's a mad bastard and he's had it coming. I've said for a long time, that if the Germans don't get him, that lot will. "Mad Jack" indeed. That man's a fule. A bloody fule."

He noticed Serjeant Doughty standing watching the aircrew going up the steps of the Squadron hut. "Hello, Jack." He jerked his head at Roberts striding angrily away. "Now there's trouble, I'm thinking."

"Yer bloody right." Doughty and McNaughty were old friends and drinking companions in the Serjeants' Mess. "Is yours buggered, too Mac?"

"Och aye, she's a right mess. Saggy as a whore's drawers on a Glasgow Saturday night. I tell ye, Jack, it'll tek two days at least to get her up again." The Scotsman contemplated the front of his DH4 gloomily. "It's bad enough having to operate from two airfields without havin' to work bloody miracles as well…" He sighed. "Ah cannae see us flyin' this wee lot back to Serny in a hurry."

He looked at Doughty.

"Ah wonder if ye'd do me a favour, Jack? Can ye ask young Cooper to take a look at the engine." Misunderstanding Doughty's startled look, he added hastily, "Ah know ye're busy with y're own, but he's an absolute whizz on these Rolls Royces. All the fitters say so. Is that not right, Corporal Henries?"

MacNaughty's mechanic nodded vigorously. "Right Serjeant. Corporal Cooper's got a real nose for it. "Specially with the American built ones. They don't tighten them up properly like the English ones. Bloody Yankee rubbish, I say."

Doughty absorbed this insight into his new subordinate slowly. Rubbing his chin, he nodded. "Oh aye, I'll get 'im to come and look yours over Mac. No problem." He jerked his chin at the Squadron huts. "I'll bet those officers are giving Captain Armstrong a right goin' over there."

He looked up at a sudden roar of engines.

"Look lively now," shouted an NCO's voice. "Here come 79's Dolphins. Park them in the lee of the hangars. Corporal James! Get a bloody move on with that petrol lorry. They'll want refuelling …"

*   *   *

Twenty Five Squadron's surprise raid on the Lesquin railway yards did however have some unexpected side effects.

Jack Armstrong's bombs hit a key set of points and stopped all rail traffic in the sector for nearly a whole day. It would delay the Kaiserschlacht by a vital twenty-four hours, although no-one but the Germans would ever know that.

Roberts' two bombs landed either side of a hospital train bound for Düsseldorf and Hamburg. Thirteen of the wounded men were killed and over twenty injured still further.

Among the mangled bodies was a Serjeant Lutz of 63 Infantry Regiment heading for Hamburg with a thigh wound. Now he was almost unrecognisable, his stomach and entrails blown across the ruined compartment. Going through the dead man's pockets the medical orderly found four golden English sovereigns. He pocketed them. After all, what use were gold coins to a dead NCO?

And anyway, how come a German infantry serjeant was carrying English gold?

CHAPTER 16

A MEDAL CELEBRATION

8th March

The crowd of aircrew, led by an angry Roberts, surged towards the Squadron office.

"What're you going to do?" asked Halloran.

"I'm damned well going to give our great flight commander a piece of my mind, that's what!" snapped Roberts. "The man's bloody dangerous." He wrenched at the collar of his Sidcot flying suit.

As they mounted the steps a roar of laughter greeted the angry crews. Puzzled, Roberts paused. The hut door flew open and the lanky figure of Major Duffus, brandishing a glass of champagne in his hand, stopped in the doorway. He beamed at the crowd.

"Well done, boys! I guess you didn't realise that I was back up at St Omer? So you haven't heard then?" He waved the glass at the men in the office behind him. "Jack's got his Military Cross. It's just come through. Some of the boys came back up to celebrate."

The group stopped, thunderstruck.

"Well, c'mon then," added Duffus, his Canadian drawl more pronounced then usual. "Come and join the party. No more flying today. The shampoo is getting warm."

No-one moved. Duffus looked puzzled. "Say, are you boys all right?"

Roberts and Barton looked at each other and then at Halloran. Like water coming off the boil, they felt their rage cooling. Roberts shrugged and shook his head. "Yes, we're fine, skipper. Aren't we?" He saw the aircrews' baffled looks, sensing that this wasn't the time or the place to take their Flight Commander to task.

"Well, come on in and have a drink. The General's here from brigade and so's Maurice Baring."

"Baring?" Colonel Sir Maurice Baring was the eyes and ears of the Commander of the Royal Flying Corps in France. As personal aide to

General Trenchard he had wielded both power and influence in the RFC well beyond a mere Colonel's status. The catchphrase, "*Take a note, Baring*," was a long standing RFC joke as Trenchard had stumped round the airfields of France on his inspections, cajoling, encouraging and occasionally reprimanding air crews on the Squadrons, and always accompanied by the shadowy figure of his Senior Military Aide, the ex-banker, Baring.

The packed squadron office bulged with cheerful faces. Behind a desk now covered by a white cloth and bottles, Corporal Guard pushed a glass of champagne into Roberts' hand while the Mess steward popped more corks. In the centre of the crowd a flushed and excited Jack Armstrong held court, legs apart, glass in hand. Roberts took a mouthful of wine and caught Barton's eye.

Slowly the observer shook his head, pulling a face. "I think we missed our moment, Robbie."

Their conversation was interrupted by the Squadron Commander calling for silence. "Now, I'm not one for making a speech," he began, "but it isn't every day that 25 Squadron gets a Military Cross. And it isn't every day that we can celebrate the daring and pluck of our pilots – and observers, too. I'm going to ask the General to say a few words, but first, gentlemen, may I ask you to raise your glasses and toast A Flight's leader and one of the Squadron's great characters: Captain Jack ARMSTRONG!"

A cheer greeted the announcement, and cries of "Good old Jack!" and "Speech!"

Speechless, Roberts drank, exchanging glances with Barton.

Armstrong stepped forward. An air of cocky self-confidence came off him like waves. The centre-parted brilliantined dark hair bobbed as he took a mouthful of champagne.

"Well, like the Major, I ain't one for speechifying. But I want to say it's an honour. Not just for me, but for the whole Squadron." He saw his flight-crews crowded near the door. "I can't say I've done more than any other fellow to deserve it, but it's really an award for A flight; my crews. All of us. The best damned fellows in the best damned squadron in the whole of France!" He raised his glass and beamed at the company.

A mighty cheer greeted his words, fading as Brigadier General Hogg stepped forward.

Smoothing his moustache, he waited for quiet. "Well, I've little to add to that," he began. The voice was low and controlled. "Except perhaps that I consider Nine Wing to be the best damned wing in France, too." He looked round the room, gauging the mood.

"I came down here today for something else. As you know, the idea of putting all the flying units together has now been approved at the highest levels. Parliament no less. What I really came down for today was to tell your CO that from the first of April, you're definitely all going to be members of a new Royal Air Force. The Royal Flying Corps and the Royal Naval Air Service are going to be combined at last into one new service. You – we - will be the Royal Air Force."

A hubbub of noise greeted his remarks. It was common knowledge that for over a year there had been intense political activity back in London to create a separate Air Force. But all attempts by Lord Derby and Lord Curzon had fallen at the fences of political intrigue, Whitehall bureaucracy and the bitter back-biting and inter-service rivalry between the Army and the Navy.

General Hogg, Commander of the RFC's 9th Air Wing, held up his hand for quiet. "Now I don't know all the details, yet, although I expect Colonel Baring from London might have a better grasp than I have: but I just wanted to add that 9 Wing and 25 Squadron's role will remain unchanged, as GHQ's special duties squadron. For you fellows, things won't change much at all." He stopped abruptly, smoothing his moustache again. "That's all I have to say. Except, of course, to add my voice to the congratulations for Jack Armstrong here."

He drank to Armstrong, then turned to say something to Colonel Baring. The crowd started talking again. Fresh drinks were poured.

"Well," muttered Roberts to Barton, as they refilled their glasses. "Captain Jack Armstrong, MC. What a load of tosh!" He drank deep. "I could have punched the stupid sod, but now ..." He looked round, despairingly. "Well, it's all such a load of balls."

"And why should your flight commander's MC be a load of balls, young Roberts?" murmured a quiet voice behind them.

Shocked, Roberts and Barton whipped round to meet the single beady eye of Peter Coachman, leaning in the corner.

Close up, the scar tissue of the ravaged face gleamed shiny pink. The twisted mouth smiled as "Cauchemar" drank. "Well, don't you think he deserves it?"

Roberts and Barton were wrong-footed. "No, sir, I mean, Peter. It's just that…" Roberts spluttered, embarrassed.

"It's just that you think the stupid sod takes stupid and unnecessary risks?"

Coachman's single good eye bored into them as he echoed Roberts' comment. He drank again, surveying the crowd. "I think I agree with you." The Adjutant swilled his champagne, catching their surprise.

"Oh, I agree with you. There's not a lot escapes me on this squadron, y'know. I may not be able to fly any more but I know what's going on." He looked down at his glass. "I've known a few Jack Armstrongs in my time. They're quite common, in fact. There were chaps in the original 25 Squadron – and 32 - who were just like him. It's got a lot to do with how chaps cope with it all. The flying, I mean. For RFC flyers it's better and worse than the other fellows in the trenches. My brothers used to envy me when I transferred to the RFC. They'd pull my leg about being able to have a bath and getting a decent bed to sleep in every night; being warm and dry, that sort of thing. Compared with their life in the trenches it was a pretty good way for a chap to go to war."

He glanced out of the window, noticing a straggle of pilots headed their way.

"Ah, here come the Dolphin boys. Anyway, what they never knew is just how bloody it can be. Up there. *You* know. The cold; never knowing if the engine will last the whole trip; tangling with brother Hun; wondering if you'll ever make it; seeing your friends burn to death before your eyes." He stared down at his drink. "The empty chairs in the mess every day." Roberts and Barton were spell-bound. They'd never heard Peter Coachman talk like this before.

"Well," he went on reminiscently, "it gets different chaps in different ways. Some turn to God – not many in my experience; quite a few turn to booze: they don't last long. You need a clear head up there on a dawn patrol. Some go into themselves, become loners."

He drank.

"Ball was like that, y'know. Lived in a little hut on the edge of the airfield, all by himself towards the end; never spoke to anyone in the mess; grew flowers and walked around playing the violin in the dark on his own. S'true, y'know," he added, catching the raised eyebrows of his listeners.

"Strange chap – but damn brave. If ever a man deserved his VC it was Albert Ball. Well, the point is," he went on, "lots of fellows deal with it all like Jack Armstrong. Drink, party, hail-fellow-well-met sort of nonsense. Loud, a bit cocky. It's the fear, you see. Drives it away. You show me a fellow who says he's never had the wind up, and I'll show you a liar." He finished his glass, looking round at the rowdy throng. "That's why Jack's the way he is. It's his way of keeping himself going, driving himself on; but damn risky for anyone round him."

"Like that stunt today?" Roberts ventured. He was curious to see just how much the Adjutant knew.

Coachman grinned, if the strange twisted writhing of the bloodless lips could be interpreted as a grin. "Like today. Oh, yes, I heard," he said noting their surprise. "As I told you, not much escapes me. Blair's already complained to me." David Blair was Armstrong's regular observer, a thin quiet, dark-haired lowland Scot with an ability to be Armstrong's acolyte without ever being a sycophant. Roberts noticed that he was, unusually, not standing close to his flight leader.

"Blair's told me all about what Jack did today. I suspect if his MC hadn't come through your esteemed flight commander might have been tapping the boards in the squadron commander's office in a completely different way.

He looked grim. "But take my word for it, he'll not take A Flight dive bombing from 15,000 feet again; or if he does, he'll be doing it on his own. Fifteen thousand's the GHQ order and fifteen thousand it'll stay. So next time he pulls a stunt like that, don't follow him down. Now, that is an order!"

Roberts and Barton looked at each other.

"But the truth is," Coachman went on, "he's a good fighter. He did exactly what he had to do today. It's just that it's too expensive to knock out half of A Flight for the sake of just one raid. He was lucky not to lose kites, and all for no good purpose. Now A Flight won't be battle worthy for at least forty eight hours, and with the Huns' big push coming, that's a problem the CO doesn't need. We're going to need every aeroplane we can get before the end of the month, believe you me. All it has done is push more work onto B and C Flight."

The door burst open and a group of Dolphin pilots crowded in. They looked angry and surprised. "I see we've got guests," said the Adjutant. "Do excuse me." He stumped away, using his stick to prod his way through the throng.

"Well," said Barton, as they were left alone in the corner. "What do you make of that?"

Roberts considered the question carefully. "I think," he said slowly, "I think that Nightmare is a wily old bird. A very wily old bird indeed."

Barton nodded. "I agree," he said, "and I think," he added, equally deliberately, "that we both need another drink."

Pushing their way to the bottle-laden table they joined Sinclair, the Dolphin flight leader and his pilots. Roberts noticed their air of suppressed anger.

"Sorry about that nonsense earlier," Robbie greeted the 79 Squadron visitors. "If it's any consolation we were as surprised as you. 'specially as we virtually wrecked our kites."

Sinclair stared at him.

"The fact is," Robbie went on, "We all came in here to make a fuss about it, too, but he's just got his MC and the general's here, so there was nothing we could say about it."

Sinclair's face relaxed and he exchanged looks with the other Dolphin pilots.

One raised his eyebrows; another shook his head. "Damn fool stunt," growled Sinclair. "And if it wasn't for the General and old Duffy here, I'd make a row about it too, I can tell you. A bloody big row. We lost you completely over Lille. You just dropped down and disappeared. We hadn't got a clue what was going on and couldn't have done a damn' thing to protect you if we had. First thing we knew about it was the bombs going off at the railway yard – miles away. We saw the puffs and just came home. It's lucky for you that there were no Boche low down waiting for you. We couldn't have done a damned thing to help you."

He drank and thrust his glass out for a refill, followed by most of his Dolphin pilots. A stony-faced Corporal Guard refilled the glasses.

The roar of the party swelled up around them. Sinclair seized his glass and seemed to come to a decision. "Well, I suppose I'd better go and congratulate our medal winner." He sniffed. "It's not too often that your fag gets to be a great hero."

"Fag?" Barton was surprised.

"Yes. Didn't you know? Armstrong was my fag at Uppingham. Cleaning rugger boots, making toast. He was useless. Frightful little tick he was in those days. Cocky, lazy, always with some excuse … Still." He walked away, leaving Roberts and Barton stunned.

"I thought Jack was uncomfortable this morning." Barton shook his head. "Seeing Sinclair must have come as a bit of a shock."

Robbie grinned. "No wonder he looked so damn jumpy. Sinclair must have been quite a character."

"Still is, old boy," one of the Dolphin pilots turned towards them.

The speaker had discarded his thick flying suit and opened the double-breasted maternity jacket of his RFC uniform. He unwound a silk scarf from his neck. "Clive Sinclair is the best damn officer I've ever met. The chaps worship him. If it wasn't that he was so much on the side of the boys he'd probably be a colonel by now." A couple of the Dolphin pilots nodded in agreement. One of them, an intense dark-haired RFC lieutenant, older than the rest, said, "You're goddamn right there, Bullseye!" in an American accent.

"Mind you," said one, a fair-haired Lieutenant wearing Royal Scots badges, "telling Dowding that he was a pompous, stuffy ass probably didn't help matters."

"Dowding?" asked Roberts.

"Oh yes. Clive was a pilot when Dowding was commanding 16

Squadron. He formed up for a CO's interview with Dowding. Asked for it. The story is that when he was in there, he told Dowding that he was a useless CO. "Pernickity old woman" was what he's supposed to have called him."

"What did Dowding do?" asked Barton, fascinated. Dowding's reputation as a grumpy disciplinarian and a stickler for formality had made his squadron one of the gloomiest in the RFC. His nickname, "Stuffy," said it all.

"Oh, Stuffy's supposed to have gone red and said that Clive was an insubordinate young pup and if he was a Regular Officer he'd be sent back to England and court-martialled." The Royal Scot drained his glass and nodded to Corporal Guard.

"Anyway, story goes that Clive said he wasn't a regular looking for his pension, thank God, he was a real soldier who'd enlisted in 1914 to fight for King and country and that if Dowding sent him back to England the Germans would be the only ones to benefit. He'd shot down a Hun that morning, apparently," he explained. "Asked Dowding which was more important, putting a tie on for dinner or killing Germans?

"Anyway, Dowding threw him out, but Trenchard transferred him to Scouts. That's when Clive began shooting down all the Huns; 24 Squadron. Hawker loved him before he was killed. Clive's a hell of a pilot and Hawker taught him everything he knew. You know he was back in Blighty as an instructor for most of last year?"

Robbie shook his head.

"Well, anyway, he was a damned good instructor apparently. None of your 'Go round the field and see if you can do it too', stuff. Didn't lose a single pupil in eight months, so they say." His 25 squadron listeners' eyebrows shot up. Nearly as many RFC men were killed by accidents in training as on operations.

"Oh, yes. Clive's a safe pair of hands, I can tell you. He does exactly the same with us. Joined the squadron when we were forming as a flight leader. Trained every single pilot in his flight individually. When we got out here last month…"

"Nearly two now," the American corrected him.

"You're right, Leggit. It is nearly two months now. When we got out here he led every single patrol himself. No risks, careful flying and worked out exactly what the Dolphins can do. Never lets a chap fly on a show until he's satisfied he's ready. Always hangs back and lets the new boy make the kill. He's not greedy like that Canadian chap, whats-'is-name."

"Bishop. Billy Bishop," supplied one of the 79 Squadron pilots. "Cocky little fellow who came to that Mess Night...showing off. Always writes his own citations, they say!"

"I remember. Well, Clive Sinclair could have had twenty Huns since I've known him, but he lets the new boys do the business. Great man."

A murmur of agreement went round the 79 Squadron group. The American pilot started to say, "He gave me my first Hun. On a plate. Cornered him then let me shoot..."

Roberts eased away from them and went to congratulate Armstrong on his award.

His Flight Commander was flushed with alcohol, talkative and over-confident. "...Well, it seems to me," he was saying to Colonel Sir Maurice Baring, "that this new Air Force is the way of the future. Get a good medal out here," he patted his left shoulder vaguely, "and lead the troops well, and then after the war good chaps'll probably be promoted and run things. They'll need top men after the war to run any RAF."

Baring nodded gravely. "And do you believe that these ideas of a new Royal Airforce Service will survive the war?"

"Oh yes," slurred Armstrong. "Absolutely, Colonel. Way of the future. New men, new ideas, new service. S'only way for airmen. After the war. Here's to a Royal Air Force." He waved his glass drunkenly; "To the new RAF that starts in April!"

Baring nodded again. "Well, you may be right," he added smoothly. "Sadly, however, we must take our leave of you. But such interesting views. Goodbye, Armstrong, and congratulations on your Military Cross." They shook hands and Baring gathered Brigadier General General Hogg and departed, escorted by Duffus.

When they had gone, Jack Armstrong turned to Roberts. "Well then, young Robbie. What happened to you this morning? Couldn't keep up with me then?" He sniggered.

Roberts felt a wave of anger swelling up. Remembering Peter Coachman's words, he controlled it. "Oh yes, Jack. Right behind you. Nearly blew me and Timmy up, we were so close."

Armstrong guffawed. "Well, if the Hun doesn't get you, the Cooper bombs will." He clapped an arm round Roberts' shoulder. "But we showed 'em this morning, didn't we Robbie? Talk about the whites of their eyes, what? Right down their gun barrels. Now that's A Flight flying!"

Roberts realised that Armstrong was drunk. "Well, the other thing I wanted to say, Jack, is that, well, congrats on your MC. I'm sure it's well deserved," he added, lamely.

"Deserved! I should jolly well say so," said Armstrong. "Nearly a year out here and…"

He looked up, noticed Sinclair standing watching. "And here's the mighty Sinclair. Head of School, Captain of the First XV." He peered blearily at Sinclair's chest. "But you haven't got an MC, have you Clive?" He spilled his drink. "I have. I've got an MC. What d'you think of that, eh? MC, 'For bravery and leadership'", he slurred.

Sinclair smiled good-naturedly. "Well done, Jack. Every MC tells a story. I'm sure yours will tell *lots* of stories." He stuck out his hand. "We've got to go now, so forgive me if we leave the party. Champagne and flying don't really mix. But congratulations, old man. Well done, 25 Squadron."

Armstrong surveyed the outstretched hand.

For one awful moment Roberts thought that he was about to say something rude or even knock Sinclair's hand aside, but then realised that in his drunken state, Armstrong was merely trying to focus on the outstretched hand. We over-precise articulation, he said, "Thanksh, Shinclair. It was frightfully good of you to come by. Good to see you after so long." He swayed dangerously. "Do pop in and see us another time."

Roberts realised that Sinclair was trying hard not to laugh.

"Not at all, my dear fellow. Such a privilege. So kind." With equal formality, Sinclair bowed his head slightly and took his leave with his own pilots.

From the window, Roberts could see them laughing as they made their way across the field to their waiting aeroplanes. At one point he saw Clive Sinclair make a formal bow, like an eighteenth century courtier, with much bowing and scraping, which elicited roars of silent laughter from his flight. Turning from the window, he sighed.

"Well then Robbie, are you fit?" Peter Coachman stood in front of him leaning on his stick.

"Oh yes, Peter. Just watching 79's chaps leaving."

Coachman's eyes drifted to the window. They watched the Dolphins take off and roar over the hut before climbing towards their own base. When the roar faded, Coachman said in a low voice, "I've got a job for you tomorrow. A special: using one of the SD flight's aeroplanes."

"Not a night show?" Roberts felt his stomach tighten.

"No." Coachman glanced at Armstrong, now singing a drunken song with his cronies in the corner.

"No. This is something that the Major would normally have asked Jack Armstrong to do."

He took in Armstrong's collapse onto the floor and being helped up. "But I think our Jack's off flying for the next 24 hours. So you can do it. Come and see me after dinner for your orders."

He looked across the room at Charles Barton. "And let's have CB as your observer, not Timmy. Let's put the first eleven in to bat, shall we?"

CHAPTER 17

GHQ AND OHL, FRANCE

Saturday 9th March 1918

To say that Colonel Mackenzie of GHQ was angry was an understatement.

He was beside himself with suppressed anger, made worse by the realisation that he had to keep up some appearance of respectful military deference to a very senior officer.

The source of his fury was sitting opposite, drinking coffee, and talking. General Sir Hubert Gough, Commander 5th Army, was explaining precisely why he personally disagreed with Mackenzie and the rest of General Headquarters Intelligence Staff over their assessment of the forthcoming German attack and, in particular, its timing.

The patronising tone of the braying cavalry voice grated on Mackenzie's ears almost as much as the speaker's words. Brigadier General Edgar Cox, Mackenzie's immediate boss, after a worried glance at his subordinate's infuriated face, had glared him into silence and was trying to defend GHQ's assessment without alienating Fifth Army's Commander.

Lieutenant General Herbert Lawrence, the BEF Chief of Staff, listened intently to the argument, his brows beetling, occasionally frowning at a point.

"The truth is," opined Gough, banging his cup down in its saucer, "the Boche could attack anywhere. My only fret is that we're the thinnest manned Army on the Front. My Army. My chaps are diggin' trenches like niggers, night and day; 200 miles of them and all over the place too. Fifth Army needs manpower, not intelligence."

MacKenzie broke in; "But we do have some very good intelligence indications, General, that it's your 5th Army that's most at risk." He waved an arm at the junior occupant of the room, sitting mute in the corner. "Young Powell here has been tracking the Huns' build up for weeks. What's the latest, Powell?"

Gough looked the lieutenant up and down and sniffed. Powell was nervous of the exalted company in which he found himself and it showed. He tapped the pile of files on the table in front of him.

"Well sir, there's a German called Bruchmüller: one of their top gunners. We hear reports that he's heading for Peronne. That's smack opposite your Army."

"I know where Peronne is. And we've all heard of this gunner chappie. So?"

Powell persisted. "Well, Sir, where Bruchmüller goes trouble usually follows. He's their top artillery man. Plans all their big attacks."

Gough shrugged and pulled a face. "So? I know that. I've been hearing warnin' about him ever since February. Miracle bombardments, etcetera. But I don't see any barrage."

"Barrage?" Powell looked puzzled.

"Yes, *barrage*. You can't have an attack without a barrage. Even a shortish one. Surely even you intelligence chaps know that. Thought you chaps were supposed to be clever? That's the trouble with you ex-civilian types; all theory and no knowledge of real war."

Powell flushed.

Gough put his cup down. With the patient air of someone explaining something to a child he said, "Look, young man, as I have no doubt that Brigadier General Cox and Colonel Mackenzie will explain to you, we bombarded brother Hun for a week on the Somme in '16 and couldn't break through. We hammered 'em for *months* at Ypres at Passchendaele last year and still couldn't get through all their defences. So how on earth do you think the Huns are going to break through *our* lines now? Magic?"

Powell swallowed hard and persisted, the slightly flat Northern vowels in stark contrast to the cavalry general's patronising aristocratic bray. "Well Sir, they are doing really short barrages now, from what we can tell. They might just open fire and attack at the same time…"

Gough wiped his moustache dismissively. "Of course they can do quick barrages. We all know that. That's what they did when they counterattacked at Cambrai in November. But that can't work against *properly prepared* lines. If we can't break through, then I'm damned sure *they* can't."

MacKenzie and Cox exchanged glances. Mackenzie wasn't so sure. Young Powell had shown him some disturbing French reports about a hurricane bombardment at Riga in the Baltic back in September. Apparently the Germans had attacked after only a short bombardment and burst through the Russian defences with storm troops. A general called Hutier had been in charge. Bruchmüller had been there too, he remembered. He thought he should intervene, but, noticing Lawrence's frown, he decided to keep his counsel. Gough's long, horsey face was still braying on.

"...so when we see the barrage then I'll start to fret. Not before. It's not as if this Brookmiller fellow has some secret weapon, eh? Well? Is it?" Powell was silent.

Gough turned dismissively from the young officer and spoke to Mackenzie. "Are we really wasting our time on details like this? Haven't you int chappies got something really new to tell me apart from the travel arrangements of Hun generals, eh?"

"That's precisely my point, General." Cox's voice was controlled and reasonable. "They may have got some new tactics. Our intelligence indicates that you ought to go on full alert now."

Gough pulled a face. "Couldn't stay like that for long. We need time to dig and wire, to build up the position; not be standing-to all the time and exhausting the men. Dammitall, my chaps are workin', not loafin' around, y'know. It's time we need, and more men. I'm desperately short of good divisions."

He pounded the table gently. "It's *manpower* I'm short of, not intelligence, dammit. Fifth Army needs first call on some of those precious divisions you've got tucked away in GHQ reserve. What I need is more Flying Corps - another squadron of reconnaissance aeroplanes, at least. I need more RE railways behind the lines."

He banged the flat of his hand gently on the table as he emphasised his points.

"I need first call on all those engineer stores, some of those US engineer units just out, lookin' for experience. Well I'll give 'em experience! I need more labour companies to help dig us in. And I need a couple of reserve divisions if I'm really in the firing line. Give me *those* and in a couple of weeks my chaps will see this Hootier chappie and his magic gunner off, with their tail between their legs. By the time we've finished Fifth Army'll be like the Rock of Gibraltar."

Gough smacked his hand hard down. "But I need *men* and I need those defence stores you've got squirrelled away." He glanced at the Chief of Staff, who remained silent. "When's the Commander in Chief due back?" Gough addressed his question to the table in general.

Glances were exchanged. Everyone present knew that Haig favoured Gough. Both were cavalrymen, and both went back a long way. Gough was obviously trying to get his hands on their precious GHQ reserves.

Lawrence stepped in. He had called the meeting at G Int's insistence. Cox and Mackenzie had sold it to him as one last chance to inject some sense into Fifth Army's Commander. As Chief of Staff, Lawrence was now effectively acting as the mediator in the discussion between his own intelligence staff and one of Haig's senior Army Commanders. It had gone wrong. Bringing young Powell in had seemed a good idea at the time but Gough clearly wasn't in the mood to listen to experts, however bright.

He nodded to Powell. "Thank you for your help, Powell. You can go."

The young lieutenant left the room cheeks burning with embarrassment. Gough didn't even acknowledge the junior officer's departure. When he had gone, Lawrence turned to Gough.

"The Chief's been called away to London. He should be back here by the 18th." He drummed his fingers on the table.

Gough sniffed. Without his protector, his own influence, even as an Army Commander, was limited over the General Staff at GHQ. And Lorenzo as Chief of Staff was too powerful to tangle with. "Well, that's a week away. Surely he wouldn't be back home if he thought the attack was imminent? Eh?"

"He was called back to the Cabinet. By the Prime Minister," said Lawrence shortly. "And his wife's due to have the baby any day now."

Mackenzie broke in. "Sir, all our evidence points to a Hun attack on the 19th or 20th of March. All the divisional identifications point to a build up right opposite you in the St Quentin area. Our assessment is that Fifth

Army will be smack in the middle of the Germans' main axis of attack." He looked to Cox for support. "And that's MacDonogh's view in London, too, General. All our intelligence sources point to that conclusion, Sir."

Gough stared out of the window. "Well, mine don't and it isn't my view, although I'm at risk, I grant you. All this activity across from my chaps at Peronne could be a bluff; designed to fool us. Fifth Army Int tell me that the real attack'll fall to the North, around Ypres. And," he added triumphantly, "so does the C-in-C. Told me himself before he went off that he thought it could be around Ypres. Or even against the French in the Champagne."

Mackenzie sighed and sat back. Brigadier General Cox looked out of the window at the trees outside the Chateau of Montreuil. He noticed that the first green buds of spring were beginning to show. Further off, a cherry tree was coming into blossom. "Why do we bother?" he thought.

Lawrence let the silence run. As Chief of Staff it was his job to adjudicate in Haig's absence.

Gough suddenly broke the reverie. "Anyway, what about all this Secret Service stuff? Thought you Int chaps had been put onto some special scheme to spike the Jerry's guns and stop the attack?"

Mackenzie sat forward, but it was Lawrence, the senior man who spoke. He picked his words with care. "Well now, General, that's true. What exactly have you heard?"

Gough pulled a dismissive face. "Oh, the usual rubbish. That Mackenzie here had some Int plan or other to stop the Hun offensive before it started." He waved a vague hand. "Chief mentioned it at the last Army Commanders" conference."

Cox and Mackenzie glared at Lawrence, but the Chief of Staff looked puzzled. "I don't seem to recall that in the Army Commanders' Conference minutes, General," he said, cautiously.

Again the vague hand wave. "Oh, really? Sir Douglas must have mentioned it over lunch, then. Anyway, nothing in it, I suppose?" Gough stood up, taking a large scarlet handkerchief from his cuff and wiping his mouth. "Don't see how anyone could do much at this stage, anyway." He laughed. "Bit late, if what you say is true, eh?" He cocked his head and looked at the two Intelligence Staff officers who in turn looked to their

Chief of Staff.

Lawrence pulled at his moustache. He didn't want to tell Gough too much. He didn't like him and didn't trust his backstairs access to Haig. The blasted man talked as if he ran the BEF sometimes. "Truth is, we did have some ideas, General, but we passed them to London and we haven't heard anything solid since. Probably the best thing; secrecy and so forth. We'll just have to hope that the Secret Service people back in London have got something up their sleeve. We haven't heard anything more here, have we?"

He looked at Cox and Mackenzie, who both shook their heads.

"Oh well." Gough reached for his red-banded general's cap and looked round for the door of the small conference room. "Probably wouldn't have made much difference anyway. It's hard-nosed soldiering and manpower, lots of it, as'll win this war, not sneakin' round with spies, eh, gentlemen?" He eyed the two Intelligence officers. "So you reckon it's the 19th or 20th?"

Cox nodded. "And opposite your Army, Sir."

Gough clapped his hat on his head and sniffed hard. "Well, we'll see who's right, shall we?"

He chuckled. "Spies, eh?"

CHAPTER 18

OHL AVESNES OHL
The Need for Public Relations
9ᵗʰ March 1918

A hundred miles to the east in the Belgian holiday town of Spa, a surprisingly similar conversation was taking place. Major Wendel of OHL was settling down to a quiet cup of coffee in the hotel annex that provided extra accommodation for the officers' mess of Germany's Western Front HQ. The soldier steward withdrew and the other occupant of the small smoking room leaned forward to pour. The liquid steamed.

Wendel's nose wrinkled. "*Ersatz.*" One armed, he took the proffered cup. "It's hard to get real coffee, even for a Kaiser visit."

His companion smiled. "I can get you coffee, *Herr* Wendel. Would you like some? Real Dutch coffee."

Wendel laughed. "Ah, *Herr* Stube, what it must be to be able to soar over the frontiers like a bird." He drank and pulled a face. "Disgusting. They say it's made out of acorns."

"It is."

Wendel surveyed the man opposite.

He'd met Stube before but never had any real dealings with him. Security and the press made for poor bedfellows. He sipped the foul black coffee substitute, taking in the figure before him. Stube was tall and spare. His long legs and thin arms gave him the air of a daddy-long-legs. Or an undertaker in his black suit, strange among the uniforms of a military headquarters. The cheeks were pock-marked with the craters of long dead acne. An unusual man, thought Wendel.

Stube caught his eye. "So, *Herr* Wendel, how can I help? You asked to see me. Spies and secrets, I think was the note?"

"Can you really get proper coffee?"

Stube laughed, his face crinkling into a surprisingly boyish grin. "Ja, naturally. I'll buy you some in Rotterdam on Friday."

"Rotterdam?"

Stube nodded. "*Natürlich*. As part of my duties I go to see the Consulate and the Embassy in Den Haag every month. I can bring back anything you like; provided I can carry it, of course."

Wendel was puzzled. "But how -" he began.

Stube interrupted. "I can't get back to Berlin to check up on things as often as I should. But the press has a big international corps in Holland. So in order to get at them all, enemy, neutrals, everyone, I have to go to the Netherlands. We have a formal meeting at the embassy, I issue the official *communiqué* approved by Berlin, answer their questions and tell the people who really matter our side of the tale." Seeing Wendel's dubious look, he added "Usually in a bar over a few drinks. And it works, believe me, *Herr* Wendel. Remember the *Skaggerak Schlacht?*"

Wendel nodded. The great naval battle of 1916, known to the British and the world as the Battle of Jutland, had been a press triumph for the German Reich.

"Well, I got our official *communiqué* out first. Of course, that was before America came into the war, but I knew where my loyalties lay. I was giving out the Berliner Tageblatt's story in Rotterdam before the English fleet had even got home to Scapa Flow."

Wendel was fascinated.

Stube was a man of mystery to most of the German Headquarters staff. A few - behind his back – said that he was a renegade, an object of suspicion and no "pure German". But to the rest of the inhabitants of the hothouse atmosphere of OHL, Stube was quite simply the German from America who could talk to the world's newspapers and put Germany's side of the war better than they dared hope. And, thought Wendel grimly, pouring himself another cup of "coffee", in this spring of 1918 the German Reich needed all the good publicity it could get.

"Can I ask you a question, *Herr* Stube?"

"Naturally."

"You know I'm the Security Officer for OHL …"

"I know that. So?"

" … and I wondered just how an American journalist becomes Head of the OHL Press Office?"

Stube grinned again. "My God, *Herr* Major! Are you worried whose side I'm on?"

"No." Wendel shook his head. "I have your personal security dossier in my own safe. You are cleared by Berlin. Count Nicolai himself, no less." Colonel Count Wilhelm Nicolai was the Head of the German Secret Service. There was no higher clearance. "I just wondered how it happened, that's all."

"Ah, that." Stube put his cup down. "Look, this so-called coffee is disgusting muck. Really." He pulled a face. "Why don't we have a cognac to sweeten it?" He rang for the steward who appeared instantly. "Cognac, *bitte*. A bottle and two glasses."

Noiselessly the mess steward obliged.

Wendel drained his glass at a gulp and leaned forward for a refill. "So, just what is the story, *Herr* Stube?"

Stube watched the second glass being lowered. So it was true. Wendel really did need alcohol to dull the pain of a botched arm amputation. "Let's do a deal, Major Wendel. I'll tell you my tale if you'll tell me yours." He waved a hand at the Bavarian. "The Blue Max, the arm, the eye. That has to be quite a story. You have a reputation as a great war hero in the Headquarters, you know. Maybe I should write a story about you, like the ace pilots? 'Heroes of the Reich'… You know the kind of stuff."

It was Wendel's turn to laugh. "Not at all. The *Pour le Mérite*," he fingered the blue enamel Maltese Cross of the medal at his throat, "was for East Africa. I was dragged off the Staff course when the war started and sent out to be a General Staff officer for old von Lettow-Vorbeck in Dar es Salaam. He didn't have any proper staff. Just a bunch of native Asakaris in Schutztruppen units and some dead beat drunks as officers. I was pissed off, believe me. I thought I'd miss the war, going out there on that damned slowboat. When the English tried to land at Tanga, Lettow-Vorbeck sent me forward to the beach to report. A place called Ras Konone, just outside the town. What a shambles!" He shook his head reminiscently.

"What happened?" asked Stube.

"I went forward to see what the hell was going on. It was case of everyone for himself at first when they landed, I can tell you. No place for an officer on the General Staff! Our battalions were all over the place. There was a lot of firing in the mangroves, confusion, the askaris were running back, shouting. I pushed on; I could see a clearing ahead. Then suddenly they weren't our askaris, but some kind of English troops – Indians, I think. I was in the middle of the swine!"

"And?"

"Well they weren't paying much attention among the trees: it was all chaotic. Then I saw two niggers with bayonets about to do for Rudi von Arlsberg. He was on the ground. So I shot one, pulled the other one off who tried to stick me instead and gave him a bullet in the guts for his pains. Big niggers dripping with sweat and wild eyes." He swilled the brandy. He'd shot them with a wooden handled pistol and dragged Rudi back into the bushes. He hadn't had time to be scared; he just remembered the sense of frantic urgency and the terrible noise. And how damned heavy von Arlsberg had been.

"Of course in those days it was all heroes of the Greater German Empire stuff. I wouldn't do it now."

Stube said quietly. "And the arm and the eye? Did you lose those in the battle?"

Wendel laughed, a genuine bellow of amusement. "We took cover in the cemetery. It was full of dead men. Above and below ground," he added sardonically, seeing Stube's look. "We took cover in some bushes. An English bullet hit the bush I had dragged Rudy under. It blew a thorn into my eye."

"A thorn?"

Seeing Stube's look of surprise, he added. "This was a five centimetre wooden spike, my friend, not some little rose prick off a Munich florist's flower arrangement, you understand. The bastard thing was sticking out of my eye like a bolt." He shrugged. "Of course, the eye was gone."

"And the arm?"

"I was shipped out to the Field Hospital up the railway at Usumbura for the eye wound. That was a shithole, I can tell you. While I was there a mosquito bite on the arm turned septic. Suddenly it was blood poisoning and gangrene. Then one night the doctor came and told me it was lose the arm - or die of gangrene." He smiled ruefully. "What a choice! Of course I said, 'take the arm'. I was half out of my head with fever, anyway. What I didn't realise was that dear old von Lettow-Vorbeck's force didn't have any anaesthetics left. So that was the night I was introduced to real pain."

Stube noted the far away look in Wendel's eyes.

"You see, Stube, they have to do it quickly. Something to do with shock. They gave me a skinful of English whisky, two big blacks held me down and then it was off. The surgeon said it was only two minutes." He looked down and refilled his glass. "It seemed like two years. I couldn't scream. Not with all those wounded niggers lying only metres away. I was an Imperial German officer, after all. A Hauptmann on the German General Staff, the great white chief from the Fatherland. So I nearly bit my God-damned tongue through trying not to shout. And I shat myself. And then I screamed. *Lieber Gott*, how I screamed!"

Stube stared at Wendel.

The Bavarian gazed down at his glass, swilling his brandy round.

Into his head floated again the nightmare memory of the hot darkness of that dreadful night in that muddy little Tanganyikan jungle camp. The smell of the antiseptic mixed with rotting vegetation; the groans of the wounded African soldiers in the dark; the dreadful grinding scrape of the saw on bone - his bone - and the indescribable red hot pain that seared his memory for ever. Above all, the oily stink of the kerosene lamps.

He looked up and caught Stube's appalled gaze.

"And do you know, I haven't liked whisky ever since!" He drained his glass, smiling a twisted smile. "They gave me this when they'd shipped me home." He fingered the blue cross at his throat. "For saving Rudy. Apparently some *OberstLeutnant* of the *Schutztruppen* saw me being heroic. I wonder where he was skulking, eh, watching while I was wrestling with the niggers? But I'd rather have my arm and eye back though." He sighed.

A long silence fell as Stube digested Wendel's tale.

"So what about you, Herr Stube? What's your war story, my friend?"

Stube swallowed. "Well, it doesn't match yours, that's for sure."

He poured the brandy from his glass into the coffee cup and began to stir it absent-mindedly. "My story's very simple. I was born in Bremen. My father was a tailor. A good one, but not a fashionable one. Money was tight. He always wanted to do better, so in 1890 we all got on the steamer and emigrated to New York. That came as a surprise, I can tell you. My mother didn't want to go. I used to lie awake and listen to them arguing. He was a hard man. A real old fashioned German." He drank the coffee and pulled a face before pouring more cognac. "But we went. I don't know if you know what it's like to be a 13-year-old in a strange land and a place like New York, not speaking a word of English?"

Wendel shook his head.

"It was tough, believe me. I had to go to school. My father insisted; 'You must learn to be a real American'. There were lots of real Americans there, right enough: Irish, Jews, Italians; just boys, but bullies, crooks already. By God, I learned English quickly!" Stube wrapped his hands round his knees and leaned forward. "I hated it. I hated America, New York, everything. I hated my father for dragging us there. Most of all I hated Americans. The funny thing is, my sister loved it. But Mama and I hated it."

"How come you're here?" asked Wendel.

"Oh, that's easy. *Mutti* died when I was sixteen. It was a bad time. Father and I fought. Really fought. He wanted me to be a tailor, but I got a job as an office boy with the New York Times - I left home. Then in 1900 the paper needed someone to go out to the Cape quickly to help George Adams cover the English war with the Dutch. Adams got sick on the march to Pretoria, so I filed some stories using his name. Adams was their big name reporter out in South Africa." He drank the coffee/brandy mixture and pulled a face. "They liked my stuff, so suddenly I was a writer, too, not just the office boy."

He grinned again. "And I didn't like what the English were doing, so I said so. That went down well back in New York. Then the *Allgemeine* asked me to telegraph some stories in German, so suddenly I was the *wunderkind* reporter of the brave little Boers' war against the mighty English. The

English tolerated me because thet thought I was American. So when I got back to New York I was rich, I was successful. When the Berliner Tageblatt asked me to join their staff in '04, I jumped. Back to Germany, back to my homeland. I was a happy man, believe me. Back home." He grinned and sat back. "Nice apartment in Berlin; girls in Unter den Linden, money in the bank. So I didn't have any problems, believe me."

"What happened to your family?" asked Wendel.

"They're still in America. Ilse – that's my sister – got pregnant by some idiot Italian stud. She's married now; calls herself 'Elsie' apparently. Elsie Paravacini. I ask you! Father's still a tailor in Queens. Drinks a lot, they say. I've only had two letters since America came into the war last year."

"You're not married?"

Stube looked serious. "No. It's hard, doing what I did. Travelling; London, Paris, back to London again. I did the Morocco crisis, you know; and Agadir in 1911. It's not easy to settle down. When the war broke out I had actually been sent to Vienna to get a story about unrest in the Austrian Empire. I was in Vienna the evening the news came through that Franz Ferdinand had been shot at Sarajevo. You should have seen that town! Lights going out; silence in the cafes; women weeping. It was like a morgue, I tell you. Even the Viennese whores stopped work as a mark of respect," he added sardonically. "And you?" He poured more brandy. "Are you married?"

"No. No wife. In my regiment, only the Colonel and the Senior Majors had wives. We Bavarian Cavalry officers tended to live more – ah – colourful lives before the war. After all, a certain lively standard of behaviour is usual for people like me; it was rather expected of us," he added with mock solemnity.

Stube laughed. "I'll bet."

Wendel, he thought, the image of the tough young Bavarian aristocrat with his blond hair and uniform, must have gone down big with the ladies in Munich café society before the war.

"But you, *Herr* Stube, how did you get to be the OHL press man? Didn't you have problems once the Amis joined the war?"

"Oh, that's easy. Remember I had been back in the Fatherland since

1904. I was never an American citizen. I'm German through and through - wherever my stupid father chooses to live. I covered the Eastern Front for Berliner Tageblatt until autumn '15. Then I was pulled back to Berlin – Head Office. So in '16, when Ludendorff and Hindenburg came back to Berlin, when Falkenhayn was fired as C-in-C, the Government set up a War Ministry Press Office and asked me to help on their staff. They knew that I'd done some special work for the *ReichsKanzellerei* and they trusted me to tell Germany's side of the story for them. "And," he added, "God knows, we need to see that Germany's message does get across."

Wendel pondered this in silence. Eventually he said, "Well, that's really why I need to talk to you." He glanced keenly at the journalist. The eyepatch and the one good eye gave him a cheerfully piratical, surprisingly youthful air.

"You said spies and secrets," prompted Stube.

"You know about the big offensive?"

"Of course." Stube shrugged. "The *Kaiserschlacht*. Germany's last hope. Is there anyone who doesn't know?"

"The English, I hope," said Wendel quickly. "They'd better not know too much about it otherwise we're all in the shitpit." He drank, slowly. "What I need from you, Herr Stube, are two things; and I am speaking as OHL Security Officer for General Ludendorff himself. One, I need to know what the International Press is really saying about our attack, and not just what the Propaganda Office in Berlin says they are saying. We cannot afford a leak, any breach of security at this final stage in the game. Tell me what the press is saying or going to say; the neutrals, the English, even the Americans. We need to know. Secondly - and I don't know if you can do this - we need to make a big splash once the attack starts; a very big splash in the World's press. Germany's great offensive to finally win this war!" He didn't add, "and it's Germany's last chance to win this war," but he thought it. He looked hard at Stube. "That's what the Chief wants. Can you do this?"

"Of course," said Stube, automatically. "No problem with either. But it all depends on the level of information you want and your timing. When is *der Tag*?"

Der Tag, "The Day", had a wider meaning in German headquarters.

It didn't just mean zero hour for the attack: it also meant the "Day of Reckoning".

Wendel answered easily. "The 19th or 20th."

Stube's eyebrows shot up. "Of March? Of this month? So soon? *Grusse Gott, Herr* Major, today's the 9th already!"

Wendel smiled at the use of *"Gruss Gott!"*, a peculiarly Bavarian dialect exclamation. "Well, if it takes a *SauPreussen* from Bremen by surprise, my dear Stube, let us hope that it takes the French and the British equally by storm. This attack will win us the war."

Stube laughed in turn. "Prussian Sow" was a new one to him. In landlocked Bavaria, inhabitants of the old northern Hanseatic ports were often referred to as "fishheads". He considered the case. "The 19th. That's only ten days time. Hmmm... I go to the Netherlands as normal tomorrow – entry through the Venlo rail crossing. So I'll be in Rotterdam by Sunday night and Den Haag the day after." He thought for a moment. "More cognac?"

"No. Better not."

The pause lengthened. "Today's Saturday," mused Stube. "Travel to the Netherlands tomorrow... I'll meet the Rotterdam press corps on Monday morning as usual. They're crawling with Allied agents and spies. All sorts, and happy to gab and booze for hours. Yes; I'll find out whose saying what, who's expecting something big. Especially the London Times correspondent. He always asks lots of questions..."

Wendel's eyebrows shot up.

"Oh yes, *Herr* Wendel: I only mix with the most exalted company." Stube grinned, a cheerful infectious grin that made Wendel shake his head and smile back. "And Reuters?"

"Ah, yes." Stube smiled. "And what do you know about Reuters News Service in Rotterdam and den Haag, *Herr* Security Officer Wendel?

"Only that they are nothing but a complete front for the British Secret Service, *Herr* Stube..." mocked Wendel.

"*Ja:* you are right. My God, but don't give the game away: let them stay that way. The stupid idiots think they are really secret!"

Both men burst out laughing. Stube went on, "I can let you have a telegram for Monday night – midnight. That should give you a flavour of what they are saying. And a proper answer 24 hours later, on Tuesday. I'll code it from the German Consulate in Rotterdam. Is that all right?"

Wendel nodded. "I'll warn the Consulate to expect you. That should let us know just what the Allies expect, and with a week in hand. That'll please Ludendorff."

"And once the attack is launched, *Herr* Wendel? What do you want me to say?"

"Ludendorff will talk to you separately I'm sure. But he'll tell you to trumpet our triumph from the tallest building, Stube. Because it will be, believe me: a triumph. We'll drive the English back to their Channel."

Stube said nothing, and stretched. "Good. Then I must see the official *communiqué* from both OHL and Berlin while it is still in draft. Then we'll really have something to say, my friend. I'll enjoy that."

He stood up. "Now, I have to be going. Would you like some real coffee bringing back from the fleshpots of Holland?"

Wendel grinned. "But of course. And also a Dutch cheese."

"*Ja*, I can fetch you a cheese; a nice big round one? Or the roly-poly sort. The Netherlands has them all. They like them big and round in den Haag."

"Plump, like a nice girl," Wendel nodded emphatically. "Well rounded."

Stube entered into it. "Wendel, my friend, a big Dutch girl I cannot do, even for an officer of the Bavarian Cavalry with a Blue Max and a wooden-handled pistol in your belt. But for you, I can bring a big round Dutch cheese. Sadly without nipples, but a good round cheese is a cheese, eh? And coffee, too? It's a deal!"

Stube stuck out his hand. "Until the next time, my friend."

Major Wendel shook the hand. He liked this spindly, dry-humoured man. "*Ja*, hopefully. When are you back?"

Stube scrubbed his face. "The 13th. That's next Wednesday. Von Zelle told me to either join the OHL train at Aachen or move forward with the H.Q. when it goes forward to Avesnes or wherever. Now I know at least why we keep moving the damned Headquarters." He glanced down at the bottle of Hine, now a third gone. "Keep the cognac, Wendel. Drink it for luck. See you on Wednesday?"

"*Ja*, Stube. Until Wednesday *mein freund. Auf wiedersehen, Stube: Gruss Gott.* And good luck; watch out for those spies. Especially that Times man from London!"

Stube laughed, a good-natured chuckle. "Ja. Spies. They're all bloody gathering information. It's called being a journalist."

As Stube left, Wendel poured himself another large brandy and sat back.

He liked Stube.

CHAPTER 19

EVERITT AT THE BORDER

Sunday 10th March 1918

As the train stopped at the Venlo border crossing, Everitt woke with a start, feeling the familiar symptoms of fear clawing deep in his belly. It was almost as if his body reacted automatically to the mere sight of uniformed guards with their coal scuttle helmets, rifles and dogs. The German shouts of "papers!" "border police!" and the slamming doors after the train had squealed to a stop, made his mouth dry and his bowels churn.

"*GrenzePolizei!*" a voice shouted and someone banged on the side of the carriage.

He got out and stood on the platform with the other passengers, trying to look unconcerned, surveying the bustle of security men guarding the German border with neutral Holland.

It was a cold, clear morning, with traces of frost on the roofs, rapidly disappearing as a blood-red sun warmed them. The engine panted steam like some great iron beast and platoons of uniformed border police marched around. With much shouting and clonking, the engines were changed, a shiny blue Dutch engine backing up to replace the black German *Reichsbahn* locomotive.

"Your papers!"

The demand made him jump. He had been looking forward at the engines, and the green uniformed *Zollamt* man had approached from behind. Two bored-looking *Landser*, both well into the forties, rifles slung over their shoulders watched the routine without interest. Everitt noticed that their uniforms were old and worn.

Interesting, he thought.

Normally, the border crossings were manned by good troops, not second echelon *Heimwehr*. Where were the active divisions, then? That would make for an interesting report. He noticed the Regimental numbers on the soldiers' collars. *HiemWehr*, over-age Regional Home Defence troops based around Aachen, he seemed to recall. Now that was…

"I said show me your papers!" snapped the voice. "Don't you speak German?"

Everitt's reverie was broken. "*Ja, natürlich.* I was just…" He patted his pockets. "Ah-ha, here we are." He produced his now well-creased set of papers. The little Customs man scanned them closely, a sour expression on his face.

"So, you are a Norwegian seaman. Why are you in Germany? Why are you going to the Netherlands?"

With practised ease, Everitt ran through his story. It must have been the twentieth time he had been checked since he started the train journey at Flensburg three days earlier, he reflected.

The little Customs man's brows knitted. "So what ship are you intending to join at Rotterdam, Herr Pedersen?"

"I don't know. It will be the next Krone Line ship that docks in the harbour. I berth where the company ships me."

The little man looked dissatisfied. "And where have you been in Germany?"

Everitt sighed. "It's all in those papers. They're stamped – you can see."

The Customs man searched the papers. Further down the platform Everitt could see similar groups going through the same routine. People began to get back on the train.

"Can I go now?" asked Everitt.

"No," said the little man. "First I must ask you some questions."

Fear made Everitt bold.

"Why?" He pointed further down the platform to a tall man who was being ushered into a first class carriage, with much heel-clicking and saluting. "Why me? No-one's asking him questions."

The Customs man smiled a superior smile. "But naturally. That is a distinguished representative of our High Command. He travels frequently on this train; and Herr Stube is a German citizen; whereas you, Herr Pedersen, are not. Now then." The little man sniffed and rubbed his little black toothbrush moustache. "And what are you taking out of Germany?"

"Nothing."

"Any letters?"

"Letters?" Everitt was dumbfounded.

"Yes, letters."

"Why letters?"

"Because that's what the people in Belgium try to smuggle out to Holland." Baffled, Everitt shook his head. "I haven't been in Belgium. I've come from Denmark."

The customs man sniffed again and stared at Everitt. "Your bags?"

Everitt jerked his chin at the train. "In there."

"Search them!" ordered the little man imperiously, waving the soldiers into the compartment. Everitt's valise and duffel bag were dumped unceremoniously on the platform.

"Empty them!"

Slowly Everitt began to pull his possessions into the daylight. Impatient, the little man joined in. "Are you taking anything prohibited out of the Reich?" He demanded.

Everitt thought of the booby-trapped carriage clock. "I don't think so, *mein Herr.*" He swallowed.

"Hmph!" The little man pulled a face. "Let us see," and to Everitt's horror he began to rummage inside the duffel bag.

"Ah-ha!" he cried triumphantly. "What have we here, eh?" He pulled out a blue woollen jumper and unwrapped it to reveal a tiny gleaming carriage clock. "And what is this?"

"A clock."

"Ja, a clock." The little man began to inspect the clock closely. "It's yours?"

"No, it's a present." Everitt could feel the sweat dripping from his armpits. "It's just a clock. It's a present."

"For whom?"

"My mother."

"Where?"

"Oslo."

"And where did you buy this clock?"

"Hamburg. See, I have the receipt. Lippe und Sohn, Marktplatz. I bought it on Wednesday. It's a good clock."

"Oh, *ja*, it's a good clock, all right." The little man looked at Everitt and sneered. "But you don't get away with this so easily, my friend. Are you telling me that you don't know what this is?"

Everitt's bowels turned to ice. He pulled his buttocks hard together. "It's just a clock."

"*Nein, nein.*" The little man wagged an admonishing finger. "You don't get a clock like this out of Germany just like that. This is no ordinary clock, my friend. As you can clearly see, this is a very special clock."

He produced a little black notebook and opened it, officiously taking out a pencil. Everitt glanced around, considering whether to make a run for it. He could hear his pulse thundering in his ears. He wouldn't get twenty yards, he reckoned. The place was crawling with armed guards, police and officials. Shit! He swallowed hard, his mouth dry with fright.

"So, let us record this special clock, *Herr* Pedersen." The little man was writing. "You realise what you are doing is illegal?"

Everitt was baffled. What the hell was he talking about? Of course the clock was illegal. It was a bloody bomb timer, for God's sake. He felt the blood roaring in his ears but force himself to stay calm. "Illegal?"

"Naturally. This is a no ordinary clock, *Herr* Pedersen. You could be arrested." He scribbled away. "It is a serious offence."

"Arrested?" Everitts bafflement increased. "For possessing a clock? That's a serious offence?" How did the little bastard know that the clock was rigged as a switch, just by looking at it?

"Of course. Smuggling. Contraband. Trying to take it out of the Reich. This is a very valuable clock."

Smuggling? Everitt gasped. "Valuable?"

The little man waved Everitt's forged receipt from Lippe & Sohn dated two days earlier and which had been carefully hidden, sewn into the lining of his jacket ever since he had collected it from Q in Cockerill's office. "Did you really only pay 25 marks for this clock?"

"Yes, of course," gabbled Everitt. "It says so, for Christ's sake. Why, what's wrong with that?"

The little man smiled a superior smile. "Because, Herr Pedersen, this is a very valuable clock. Its export is theoretically prohibited by law."

"Valuable?"

"This clock is by l'Epée, Paris. It is a very fine example of a minature carriage clock. Its case is solid gold, Herr Pedersen. Solid gold."

"What?" Everitt's startled exclamation brought a reaction from the two soldiers and the bystander standing near.

The little man smiled his smile. "Of course. The case is gold and the uprights are gold, too. It's a very valuable clock. See?" He tapped the clock, pointing to markings on its base. "You honestly try to tell me that you didn't realise you had bought a golden clock?"

"My God. No, I didn't. Gold?" Everitt began to babble. Christ, he thought, if I could get my hands on those bastards in London now. His heart rose in his chest to choke him.

"I thought it was brass, plated. You know… Anyway, it only cost twenty-five marks. Gold would be much more…"

The little man laughed a self-satisfied laugh. "No, no. It's gold, all right. Good quality." He studied the crumpled receipt carefully. "I think you have got yourself a bargain for 25 Reichsmarks, neh? So." He eyed Everitt up and down. "What are we to do, Herr Pedersen? Brass indeed!" He laughed again. One of the soldiers yawned and looked idly down the platform.

Everitt was stunned to silence. His mind was working furiously. The clock's role was as a timer. Those idiots in the War Office had given him too valuable a clock. Whoever heard of a gold bomb timer, for God's sake? He became aware that the little man was still talking.

" ... a serious offence, of course, *Herr* Pedersen. Contraband and smuggling precious metals out of the Reich is a most serious charge, punishable by a prison term and confiscation of the goods."

Everitt gulped with fright. "But," said the little man, "the rules are unclear for your case. You are a neutral citizen, clearly acting in good faith, as your receipt proves. I believe you did not understand the value of your purchase. In such cases I can invoke the normal customs rules for this border. A clock is, after all, hardly a 'precious object' by the rules." He tapped his pencil on his pad.

"Get on with it," thought Everitt. One of the guards walked off and began to to talk to one of the other passengers getting back onto the train.

"However, you must pay. While the clock is not contraband, the value of the gold means that an exportation duty must be levied." He looked hard at Everitt. "Fifty Reichsmarks, I think. You must pay and then you can go!"

Everitt's knees went weak. "Fifty marks?" he gasped. He sagged with relief.

The little man misunderstood his reaction for disbelief. "*Jawohl!* There is a 100% duty payable. And you are exporting valuable gold – a restricted commodity - out of the Reich. For that there is a special export tax, too. I know it is a lot, but there can be no exemptions. Otherwise I will have to confiscate the clock. That is the law."

Everitt thought of the two hundred gold marks sewn into his valise, the base of the duffel bag and on his body. Fifty marks was nothing.

He pulled out a handful of notes from his coat. The little man's eyes bulged.

"It's my pay for last year," explained Everitt. "When I was torpedoed they paid me off, in full." He counted out the marks into the official's palm, receiving a carefully stamped receipt in return. The little man handed it over with a flourish and a smile, "*Vielen dank, Herr* Pedersen!"

As Everitt boarded the train, the two sentries helped to hand his two bags up. The little Customs man saluted. "May I wish you a good trip, *Herr* Pedersen. And may I hope that your mother appreciates her fine present?" He beamed.

"Thank you," answered Everitt mechanically.

As the train pulled away he collapsed back onto his seat, weak with relief. He could smell his own sweat: the sweat of fear. The train slowly inched forward into the Netherlands through the barbed wire, blockhouses, gates and electric fences that separated neutral Holland from war-torn Germany, before coming to a hissing stop to let the Dutch customs and immigration men board in their turn.

Everitt was in shock, rudely thrusting his papers at the Dutch official when he was asked for them; but his heart was still hammering in his chest and choking his breathing even as the train finally inched away from the border for the run north five minutes later.

As it picked up speed, he pulled a flask from his pocket and drank deep of the schnapps. The liquor burnt like fire in his belly, and with the Dutch countryside whipping by the windows, now safe and secure from danger, Everitt stumbled down the corridor to the safety of the lavatory, where he vomited his heart out.

Trembling with shock, he wiped his lips and looked at himself in the mirror. The face that stared back was pale, the ginger beard bright against the white skin. His eyes were dark shadowed and red-rimmed. It was the face of a stranger.

"Christ," he thought, "I look ghastly."

Then a bright thought burst in his mind: it was over, he was finally safe in neutral Holland. All he had to do was hand over the clock to the mystery agent A-34 and then he was free.

The fear and tension of the last week drained away from him.

He was safe.

"Never again," he intoned solemnly in English to the apparition in the mirror, before draining the last of the schnapps. His hands were shaking. He had never felt so frightened and alone in his life.

Now, thank God, it was over.

"That damned clock! Never, ever, bloody again. Ever!"

Everitt would have felt more reassured if he had realised that the man he was to meet in the bar in Rotterdam and to whom he was to hand over "that damned clock" was sitting only two carriages away, studying a sheaf of papers. A leather music bag with its long metal bar lay on the seat by his side.

*   *   *

At nine o'clock on the Monday morning, Everitt sat in a café on Markt Weg nursing a coffee and with a glass of *oude Jenever* for company. He was wearing a suit with a clean shirt and tie to look respectable. The duffel bag was at his feet with the clock and the box of cigars well wrapped. He scanned the other occupants of the room, mainly prosperous Dutch burgers in smart suits, contentedly puffing their cigars and reading *De Telegraf.* He looked round the room, feeling out of place.

It was a smart, expensive café, all brass and mahogany and not at all the sort of establishment that a beached merchant officer would normally frequent. A plump matron waddled in, wrapped in furs and with a small dog on her arm. She caught his eye then looked away quickly. A white-aproned waiter led her away to a table laden with cream cakes by the window. Everitt began to feel uncomfortable. At eleven o'clock, two cups of coffee later, no-one had turned up, so he paid his bill, shouldered the duffel bag and headed for the Krone Line offices off *Groothafenlaan.*

There, as instructed, he asked for a Nils Pedersen, third officer of the SS Moldanger, saying he was supposed to meet him. The motherly Dutch secretary consulted her lists, looked puzzled and opened a big ledger with columns of neat copper plate names and entries. Her brow cleared as she smiled and said the *Mijnheer* Pedersen was on his way from Oslo to report for duty, and would probably be arriving in the next day or two. "He's due in by train from Head Office; but you know what the train service from Copenhagen is like nowadays," she added helpfully. She glanced down at the ledger, "and he was torpedoed too, poor man, when we lost the Lurline." She tutted. "This stupid war. Such a waste."

Everitt agreed with her, made his excuses, and promised to come back next day. He would try and meet A34 again at the planned fall-back that evening.

Until then all he had to do was to get back to his hotel, lock the door and while away the hours until nine minutes past nine. He thought he would sleep. A couple of drinks and a good sleep – that's what he needed. He must make sure he was awake and alert for the evening rendezvous. He smiled as he walked into the lobby of the Hotel Surabaya.

At least he had the most expensive and most precise alarm clock in Western Europe, he thought wryly.

CHAPTER 20

PHOTOGRAPHING BRUCHMÜLLER'S TRAIN

12th March

"This is Colonel McKenzie... You remember him from the other evening?" Duffus waved the four 25 Squadron aircrew back to their seats as they sprang to their feet.

"Sit down, gentlemen. Relax."

McKenzie sat heavily at the table in the squadron commander's office, taking off his red-banded hat and running a hand over his thinning hair. He surveyed the four aircrew sitting opposite in the sagging armchairs. Peter Coachman sat in the corner, knees crossed, pencil poised.

"Gentlemen, we need your help," he began. "Truth is, we have a problem. You'll know, I suppose, about this big Hun push?"

The aircrew nodded. The expected German offensive had become a regular topic of conversation in BEF messes by March 1918. "Well, it's true enough. It's no secret that the Germans are going to have a crack at us before long. We think it'll definitely fall on the BEF. I don't think that is much argument about that. The key point is where? And when? When and where - that's all we need to know. That's GHQ's problem."

He got up and began to pace the floor. "We've got all sorts of answers coming in, but we can't see too clearly behind the Hun lines at short notice. That's where you come in. We need you to get some vital information for us and we need it today. I'm not going to go into the reasons why. That wouldn't be fair on you. You fly over enemy lines every day, you risk your lives and you could fall into Jerry's hands. So I'll say is that we need photographs of a train, just one train and I need it at 4 p.m. tomorrow afternoon. Can you do that?"

The aircrew looked baffled. Barton looked at Roberts and then the pair of them looked at the hung-over Armstrong, who yawned, open-mouthed.

Only David Blair, Armstrong's observer, spoke up. "Where's the train, sir?"

Mackenzie tore his gaze from Armstrong's cavernous yawn. "In a siding near Wassigny junction between Cambrai and St Quentin. Or it will be, by four o'clock, either today or tomorrow afternoon, if our information's correct."

"Surely that's a job for the RE8s?" interrupted Armstrong rudely. "Sir." The slow and heavy RE8 two seater observation planes were the mainstay of the RFC's reconnaissance squadrons.

"Normally, yes, but I need special pictures and I need then as soon as that train hoves into view. An RE8 wouldn't do."

Blair nodded. The RE8 was notoriously vulnerable deep into Hunland. "What sort of pictures, sir? What height?"

"I only need two, both low-level obliques."

"Low level? Obliques?"

"Yes, taken from the side, not straight overhead. This isn't like normal arty-obs trench photography. We need to identify the carriages." Mackenzie stopped abruptly. He'd said enough already.

"What height?" persisted Blair.

"Low as possible, I'm afraid. Well below 15,000 feet. Ground level."

Blair's eyebrows shot up as the aircrew exchanged glances. Armstrong's dive-bombing 'stunt' was still the talking point of the squadron. Rumour had it that Major Duffus had been delayed going back to rejoin the rest of the squadron down at Serny. The gossip was that he had been summoned to Nine Brigade HQ to explain why four of his squadron's airframes were unflyable because one of his flight leaders had dive bombed from 15,000 feet. To be ordered suddenly now to fly low-level missions came as a surprise. Only Armstrong, nursing his hangover, seemed oblivious. He shrugged. "Suits me, sir. We'll get your pictures, don't worry. A Flight to the rescue again, eh?"

Duffus intervened. "No," he said emphatically. After yesterday he didn't trust Armstrong. His behaviour was getting wilder by the day. He was beginning to regret selecting him for the mission. "This isn't an A Flight show, Jack. I want you to look on this as a Special Duties flight show. And that's why I'm splitting up the crews."

He'd taken the decision on the spur of the moment. He raised a hand to stifle the protests. "I want you, Charley, to go as Jack's back seater, and I want you, Robbie, to take David."

"But, sir…"

Again he raised his hand, "Oh, I know you boys don't like it, but that's the way it's going to be, and no arguing. The fact is, I'd personally send only one 'plane, but Colonel Mackenzie here tells me that he needs to be sure. So we're going to have to send two. Just in case. We need those pictures. Right, Colonel?"

MacKenzie nodded.

The squadron commander surveyed the four aircrew. "Now you boys do your preparation, get out there, run up both sides of the train, then get the hell out of it back home, without any fuss. GHQ needs the pictures. You heard the Colonel."

He began to unroll a large-scale map. "And here, courtesy of Colonel Mackenzie and GHQ is exactly what you have to do and where you have to go. Gather round."

The four crowded forward, Armstrong suppressing another massive yawn.

*   *   *

By three o'clock, the two DH4s were airborne. Mackenzie and Duffus watched them take off and walked back to the Squadron office.

"Good chaps," said Mackenzie. "I thought that your captain – what's his name?"

"Armstrong," answered Duffus shortly.

"Armstrong, that's right. I thought he seemed a bit, well… tired?"

Duffus grunted. "Yes, I suppose he is." The Canadian accent was strong. "To relate it honestly, Colonel, he's tired all right. Fact is, Master Jack got an MC yesterday and he kinda binged it up last night. Big party. But he's tired anyway; needs to go home now and have a rest."

He gazed at the departing aeroplanes, now silent specks on the horizon. "But they're all tired, Colonel. Flying exhausts a man; Jack's been out for nearly a year. I guess he's due some leave. But with the big push coming there'll be no leave without a GHQ order and that's the long and short of it. Anyway," he added, turning away, "I don't reckon as the boys in the trenches are getting much rest or leave at the moment."

"Actually, they are," said Mackenzie. Duffus looked him. "GHQ policy has been to get as many men back as possible for Blighty leave over the winter. There's still lots back home." Mackenzie was more right than he knew. In addition to nearly a fifth of the BEF taking home leave, Lloyd George had over a million men under arms bottled up in Britain, refusing to let them be posted overseas to a desperately under strength BEF. The Prime Minister didn't trust Haig, and Haig didn't trust his Prime Minister. Everyone in GHQ knew that.

Duffus nodded as the two men walked on in silence.

"Is this train really important, Colonel?"

"Oh yes." Mackenzie nodded emphatically. "Obviously I couldn't tell your men everything, Duffus. They might be captured, and what they don't know, they can't tell, eh?"

"Absolutely."

"And you don't fly over German lines as a Squadron CO?"

"Not often," lied Duffus, "It's against Royal Flying Corps regulations".

"Well, the train they're going to look at is the German's artillery train. No, I don"t mean the guns. It's the carriages – a kind of travelling office - they've given to Colonel Bruchmüller. You ever heard of him?"

"No, Colonel, can't say that I have."

"Bruchmüller is the German's artillery top man. He's the man that orchestrates all their artillery. We've had our eye on him for some time. He's a bit of a genius, according to the Gunners. He was the man who planned the counter attack at Cambrai last November that caught Byng and his men so badly. At least, we think he was. But he definitely was the planner for Riga on the Russian Front, last autumn. Hurricane bombardment; then an attack in just four hours. Amazing! Apparently he's full of bright ideas. And now he's heading for France, and a specific place at that, we think." Mackenzie shook his head. "And do you know, he's only a Colonel?"

Duffus was puzzled. "It's true, Duffus. It's as if a full Colonel, and a Territorial one at that, was advising Haig on all Gunner preparations in the BEF. The man's a bloody amateur, for Christ's sake! But where friend Bruchmüller goes, German attacks go. That's a fact. They don't call him *DurchBruchmüller* for nothing."

"*DurchBruchmüller?*"

It's a joke in German; "It means 'Breakthrough' Muller."

Duffus absorbed this in silence. "So knowing where he is is important, right?"

Mackenzie looked at 25 Squadron's CO intently. "Oh yes. Very. Where Bruchmüller goes, Duffus, that's where the attack will fall. It's as important as that. And my people, my other sources, tell me his train will be at Wassigny station at 4 pm this afternoon, heading for OHL. That's why your men are flying this show for me. It's important. We need to identify the two railway carriages he uses as his Gunner HQ. If we spot Bruchmüller's Artillery HQ train heading south, then that will confirm all our assessments, and the attack will fall on Fifth Army. Those carriages are as clear as a signature. If your boys confirm them, that is."

"Could he be heading further south? For the French?"

"No." Mackenzie shook his head emphatically. "No, we know that the Germans have realised that the only way they're going to win this war is to knock Britain out of the fight. They're coming for us all right."

He stared at the horizon.

"And your boys can tell us where, and probably a pretty good idea of when as well. Bruchmüller's almost the last piece of the jigsaw. All we have to do is wait."

CHAPTER 21

A QUIET LUNCH AT THE RAC

13th March

The two men who glanced warily at each other up over the lunch table could not have been more different. Captain Manfield Smith-Cumming Royal Navy was a tall, cheerful extrovert, with a firm jaw, and a monocle screwed tight into his right eye. He looked every inch the ex-naval officer and man of action. His guest, short, plump and donnish, looked equally the civil servant he now was.

"So what'll you have then? The turbot's pretty good today, so they tell me." Cumming's voice was bluff, commanding.

His guest, Hubert Neville, glanced briefly at the handwritten menu and nodded politely. "The turbot sounds splendid." The Club waiter glided away.

The Chief of the Secret Service gulped at his Sancerre, looked round conspiratorially and leaned forward. "So, what's this all about, eh? You said it was important."

Neville seemed not to hear, gazing round at the dining room. "Thank you for inviting me here, Cumming. Most civilised. Makes the Reform look rather old-fashioned."

Diverted, "C" followed his gaze. The Royal Automobile Club was Pall Mall's newest club and its décor reflected the modernity of a new century and a new reign. As one of the privileged rich and an enthusiastic pre-war motorist he had been almost a founder member.

"Didn't know you were a Reform man, Neville?"

"Oh yes. One needs a bolthole from the ceaseless chatter of the politicians. Your RAC would seem to be an admirable place. And I hear that you have a swimming pool, no less?"

Cumming nodded proudly. "Every modern convenience in the RAC." He returned to his theme as the meal was served. "You said it was important," he prompted. They waited while the silent servant put down two plates and served them boiled potatoes.

"Yes." The civil servant tasted his turbot and raised appreciative eyebrows. "You were right. It really is quite delicious."

Cumming ground his teeth. Getting a straight answer out of these blasted civil servants was, as he had exasperatedly explained to Freddie Browning, "*Like getting a broken cork out of a wine bottle*". He persisted. "Jolly good. Glad you like it. Now, what's this all about?"

Neville tasted the wine. "Excellent. What a good choice." He put his glass down slowly. "Well, it's really just a progress report. Just to see how you're getting on. We like to keep an eye on things, and this must be a very busy time for you."

C was baffled. When Neville had telephoned him the day before, suggesting they had lunch to talk over a couple of things, the Cabinet Office man had insisted that it was "*really* rather important." He rubbed his jaw.

"So, how are things?" said Neville.

"Well, the usual nonsense, I suppose. Same old problems: too little money and too much War Office. And Morton's trying to interfere, even though the bloody man has only been doing the job for a couple of months."

Neville's eyebrows rose interrogatively. "Morton?"

"Desmond Morton. This chap that MacDonogh's foisted off on me as our administrative officer."

Neville looked blank.

Cumming ploughed on. "The trouble is, I like MacDonogh. I mean, as a friend. He's a good man. Probably the best Director of Military Intelligence we've ever had. But he thinks he owns me. He's dumped this Morton character on me, and he knows perfectly well that I'd rather choose my own staff. He's forever sticking his blasted nose in: giving orders, that sort of thing. And MacDonogh still keeps insisting we're a Branch of the War Office. M.I. One or some such. I mean, he even suggested that he come on a tour of inspection, for God's sake."

Neville smiled. "An inspection? Of the Secret Service? By MacDonogh? A formal Army *inspection*?"

"That's right. It's not funny, Neville. Imagine it. The War Office wants to inspect the Secret Service in the middle of a war. Lot of smartarse army officers stamping around in shiny uniforms, takin' notes. Damn' silly, I call it. Admiralty will go mad. What d'you think?"

"What did you say?" asked Neville, who, like all good civil servants, strove to be all things to all men.

"Told him that it was impossible; quite impossible. I'm afraid that the Army just doesn't understand what we're about as a service. We're nothing to do with the damned War Office ..."

Neville nodded sympathetically and applied himself to his lunch. "And the Navy?"

"Well, that's just it, Neville. It's not just the Army. I've got Blinker Hall on to me as well, complaining that the Admiralty isn't getting enough intelligence from the Secret Service. Virtually threatening to sack me if I don't work to him and get everyone doing exactly what the Navy wants. Very difficult for me: y'see, theoretically I'm still a Royal Naval officer. On the books. Damned trying, I can tell you." He speared a chunk of fish and gazed at it moodily. "I'd like to tell them to go to hell sometimes, I can tell you."

Neville patted his lips with a napkin. "It always seemed to me that your organisation would have a difficult time serving two masters..."

"Three," interrupted Cumming glumly. "Don't forget that the Foreign Office wants to get in on the act, too. They're setting up some new FO Intelligence outfit under Tyrell, apparently."

"Oh that. Yes. I know all about Sir William Tyrell's new group. But I wouldn't worry about that if I were you, Cumming. It's only an assessment staff. Set up, dare I say it, mainly to assess your reports. It's not a threat. Not at all. No; I'd take it as a compliment to your service, to the quality of your chaps' reports."

Cumming looked relieved.

"And your work out there - in the field? Going well, I trust?" Neville fixed a quizzical eye on the ex-sailor.

"C" shrugged. "Well, yes. We've never had so many agents." He caught Neville's enquiring look. "Six hundred and forty nine at the last count", he said proudly. "Lots of reports. Of course, I've got the usual squabbles with the Army over our networks in Holland…"

"And how's that network of yours in Belgium?"

"The *Dame Blanche*?" Cumming brightened. "Top hole. Really good stuff. Landau and his people have reported every Hun train going to the Front. Haig's people are delighted, I hear."

"Quite so. Your White Ladies have been a great success, Cumming. All credit to you and to your people." He reflected. "When this nonsense is over we really must see that they're well rewarded. Medals and so on …" Neville waved an airy hand. "And the rest? The other networks going well?"

Cumming nodded emphatically. He could trust Neville not to blab, unlike most of the other residents of Whitehall. "Oh yes. All going well. Grohman's still doing brilliantly from Hamburg - mainly naval material - and Romulus still does its stuff inside Germany."

Neville's brow furrowed. "Romulus?"

"The Romulus group."

Puzzled, Neville shook his head.

"Ah," explained Cumming. "Thought you knew about them. Started, let's see. . . 1916, before you were seconded to the Cabinet Office. Romulus is the network that looks after industrial disputes: strikes and so-forth inside Hunland. Set 'em up last year after we got that directive about political warfare…"

Neville's brow cleared. "Ah yes, I remember. He stared at the ceiling and quoted: "*To hasten political crises and to accentuate internal dissensions…*" Yes. I remember now. Last year."

"Well," Cumming went on, "They're doin' a damn' good job," he said proudly. He was proud of the Romulus network. The secret group was doing better than he had dared expect when he had first set up his chain of disaffected trade unionists, Socialist politicians and militant workers in the major industrial cities of Germany. Now they were rapidly gathering strength and influence as the Royal Navy's blockade increasingly choked off economic life inside the Kaiser's Reich. With a little discreet encouragement and gold from mysterious - and anonymous – "benefactors", the anti-capitalist and Imperialist groups had already managed to set up secret worker's Soviets in Hamburg and Kiel; even Potsdam itself, at the heart of Berlin, was calling for an end to the war...

He grinned with satisfaction. "Oh yes. Things are goin' well enough on the ground." But this was more than even Neville needed to know. Far too secret to discusss. Cumming tried to change the subject. "And you?"

"Me?" Neville smiled. "I go my jolly way pretending to be a civil servant. Not like Oxford, I must admit. Downing Street's intrigues makes Christ Church high table politics look gracious and helpful. I sympathise with you sometimes – too many masters."

Cumming looked shrewdly at the civil servant. "*Hankey*?"

Maurice Hankey had started the war as an obscure Royal Marine Colonel and Secretary to the Committee of Imperial Defence. Now, nearly four years later, he was effectively Secretary to the War Cabinet itself and, if Whitehall gossip was true, working hard to make himself indispensable to Lloyd George, Britain's unscrupulous wartime Prime Minister. Neville's dislike of his power hungry colleague was no secret.

Neville twirled his glass. "Yes. Hankey." He swallowed the wine. "Yes, there's something particularly unedifying about an ambitious Royal Marine Gunner on the make."

C smiled. "Wouldn't worry about it, Neville. He"ll retire once the war's over. I expect we all will."

"I'm not so sure." Neville trailed a finger round the rim of his wineglass, deep in thought. "I think this war's changed everything."

He marshalled his thoughts.

"There is an old Arab saying, *'Once the jug is broken, you can't put the spilled water back'*. We won't be able to put the genie back in the bottle. I think that a lot of the things we've invented for the war will stay on. We can't put the clock back to 1914. In fact, I'd go so far as to say that a lot of Whitehall won't want to. That's why I wouldn't worry too much about the War Office if I were you. Oh, I know that you and Kell's people were originally established as sections of Military Intelligence, but no-one realistically expects you to go back to being part of some obscure Army Department funded by the soldiers. You're far too useful. The politicians positively lap up your reports. Believe me, old chap."

Cumming glowed.

"The point is," continued Neville, "A lot of the things we've invented to run the war will be just too attractive to discard when it's all over. Take amalgamating all those little railway companies into the Railway Operating Department, for example – and then there's rationing, licensing hours for alehouses, control of civil labour… Lots of things we've had to bring in to run the war."

He waved a hand.

"Whole new ministries, telling people what to do and how to live their lives. Rules, regulations, all that sort of sort of nonsense in the Defence of the Realm Act. The Government loves it. And what the PM and the Cabinet likes, Whitehall exploits. They love it too." Cumming noted the "they". "It gives Whitehall control, you see. New power. The politicos need civil servants to run the things they want, so it pays the civil servants to make the politicians feel powerful, efficient – in control."

He smiled. "Of course, it's a total illusion. The politicians aren't really in control. It's my fellow civil servants, and we've invented a whole new army of them to run the country. No, these new ministries are loving it. They're running everything. It's all so modern: planning, efficiency, that sort of nonsense. Trying to control things. Every blessed thing if some folk had their way." He paused and looked away. "Did you know that the government actually owns breweries?"

Cumming choked. "Breweries? The government?"

Neville eyed his companion with a kind of savage satisfaction. "In Carlisle. They're running breweries. Have been since '16. They bought up four breweries on the quiet. So now His Majesty's government sells beer to the workers through a whole clutch of public houses… It's actually called 'the Carlisle Experiment'."

"But *why*?" expostulated Cumming.

"Control, my dear chap. Control. This way Whitehall can control the drinking in Carlisle. It's a big munitions manufacturing area, the workers are paid far too much and they need to be protected from the evils of the demon drink. Oh it's wonderful," he beamed, "And it's all done in the name of temperance and good social order."

Neville smiled beatifically. "Every parson and old maid busybody in the Borders is rallying to the cause of temperance and controlling the evils of alcohol. It's very popular with the non-conformists and the Chapel, I believe... May I?" he enquired with deliberate irony, pouring himself more Sancerre.

Cumming raised his eyebrows in disbelief and shook his head.

"I can't believe it... The Government owns ale houses; *public houses*?"

"Oh yes, "smiled Neville. "The planned economy, socialism, planning: we're all Socialists now, don't forget. Efficiency, planning. That's the ticket these days."

Cumming shook his head in a kind of bemused daze. "I had no idea..."

"Oh, Cumming. Look around you. This war has been the most wonderful opportunity for all the do-gooders, cranks, academics and and busybodies who want to run everybody else's lives. All in the name of doing good and improving the lot of the common man, you understand. After all, we're all supposed to be democrats now, are we not? Socialists, even. It's the rule of the man in the street, the common man, so they tell me. Well let me tell you, Cumming, that some of our new masters are very common men indeed. But still we must feed them, pay them and educate them. Bribe them with political sweetmeats. And all that takes plans, efficiency drives, offices full of 'your humble servants', all being paid a nice steady stipend at the taxpayer's expense." Neville shovelled in a mouthful of food. "No, we've opened Pandora's box, I fear. We can never go back to what it was before. Never. We've invented a whole new oligarchy as our rulers."

Cumming wasn't exactly sure what an oligarchy was. "Oligarchy?"

Neville laughed. "Where's your classical eductation, Cumming?"

"I went to Dartmouth," said Cumming as if that explained everything. "Don't think we had much call for oligarchy in the Navy..."

"Ah," said Neville. He had read Classics at Christ Church, and never failed to marvel at the ignorance of others. "Well, oligarchy is the rule by an exclusive few..."

Cumming guffawed. "Well, we've certainly got that, Neville."

"Quite," Neville conceded the point. "Quite. But what we are in danger of doing now is exchanging our present rule by about two hundred great families; historic families – plus our new horny-handed sons of toil from the labouring classes, of course – with a completely new ruling class of civil servants. Clever men who've done very nicely out of Whitehall during the war, thank you. Men with subtle minds and an appetite for power. Men who positively relish controlling their fellow citizens and telling them what to do. Ambitious men. Men who won't like yielding up their cosy powerful jobs easily when this is all over, you mark my words." He laid down his knife and fork and wiped his lips on his napkin. "So we've invented a new oligarchy. A new ruling class of ambitious civil service mandarins, just like the Chinese."

Cumming looked at his lunch companion and grinned. "People like you, eh Neville?"

Neville smiled, acknowledging the sailor's thrust. "Yes; people like me, Cumming. People like me." He picked up his knife and fork and looked Cumming straight in the face. "But I'm only temporary, don't forget. When this war is over, unlike many of my more ambitious collegues, I will go back to the House at Oxford. With pleasure. Take my word upon it. And to tell you the truth I'll be damn glad to do so, believe me."

Cumming raised his eyebrows. He had never heard Neville swear before. There was a long pause.

C shook his head and sighed.

"So where does Hankey sit in all this?"

"The good Colonel Hankey is the prime example. He proves my point. He starts off as the Secretary to some inconspicuous little committee on defence planning, then he's secretary to the War Cabinet. What next? I think Brother Hankey has wormed himself in rather cleverly; made himself a permanent fixture in Number Ten. Like an industrious bed bug."

He shook his head. "He was even sent out by Lloyd George to spy on Haig last month. Imagine that! A mere colonel of Marines. A 'fact-finding mission' if you please!" He snorted. "Absolute rot; the man might as well be Lloyd George's poodle dog, sniffing around the BEF to see if Haig's up to his job and then reporting back to the Cabinet in secret. A colonel of Marines! Imagine…"

Cumming shook his head.

Neville continued. "I think brother Hankey's bent on turning the War Cabinet's Secretary post into something that's going to be very hard to do away with after the war. Just like all the other jumped-up placemen in Whitehall. No, I suspect Hankey and his like will be around for a long time. The politicians love him: it's hard to believe he's just a soldier. He organises them, you see; drafts skillful compromise documents overnight, makes things work while they're blathering over lunch, that sort of thing… makes them look organised, powerful. In charge. Takes all their little decisions for them. He's gets total access to power by helping them." Suddenly it was Neville's turn to look gloomy. "And I expect he'll be taking big decisions soon."

"Does it bother you? Surely Hankey doesn't tell you what to do?"

Neville nodded, acknowledging the point. "No, but one day he will. I can see it coming. He'll ask for something to be done in the PM's name."

"So?"

"So, how will we ever know if Lloyd George really asked for it? I can hardly march in and cross-examine that randy old goat on his orders now, can I? Most of the time we're just taking Hankey's word for it. Or LG's signature on a memorandum. Drafted by Hankey, of course…"

It was Cumming's turn to nod. "See your point. Damned tricky, what?"

"For example," Neville turned the conversation to his real agenda, "this request by Haig to have a pot shot at the German High Command. Does Lloyd George really know all about it? It's hardly the sort of thing they're going to discuss in Cabinet, now, is it? "Let's try and kill off the German High Command gentlemen. That should win the war, what?" Far too sensitive to be discussed by that lot of old gossipy old women. It would leak to every dining room in London inside twelve hours. You might as well publish it in the Berliner Tageblatt."

He waved a despairing hand.

"So how can we prove that the Prime Minister has authorised this idea? Or is Hankey just covering for the PM in case it all goes wrong, so he can deny it? Does LG *really* know about the scheme to have a pot shot at the Duo? Or is it Hankey just *saying* that LG knows? LG is as slippery as an eel and a well-proven liar to boot. So who *really* approved it? And how do we know? The whole thing's so secret: in every aspect. You see the dilemma?"

He accepted the cheeseboard from the silent steward.

When he had gone, Neville went on, "How is that getting along, by the way? The special job for Haig?"

"Oh that," said Cumming, cramming a mouthful of Stilton. "All right. Got a man contacting my chap inside their HQ." He looked around furtively. "Under control. Bomb, y'know."

Neville nodded absently. "Jolly good. Any idea about timing?"

"Soon, I should think; in the next week. It's got to be before the 20th."

"Oh, why's that?"

Cumming tapped his nose and beamed. Neville thought that C's pink face and prominent nose made him look like Mr Punch.

"Let's just say I know, eh, Neville?"

"Hindenburg and Ludendorff?"

"C" looked around again and nodded. "The Duo."

"Good." Neville seemed satisfied. "Will it work?"

"C" shrugged. "Who can tell, old boy? It's all in the lap of the Gods."

Neville fell silent, contemplating the fingerprints on his glass. For the first time the enormity of the scheme really struck him. With Hindenburg and Ludendorf dead, Germany wouldn't last three months. He was sure of that. It really could win the war...

He sighed.

"At least we can tell Haig we tried. And the PM, if he ever asks. Which I suspect he won't…"

The lunch rolled on. Neville declined C's offer of splitting some port and making an afternoon of it, pleading pressure of work. Cumming looked disappointed, so Neville relented, taking one glass.

"Nice port. You chaps do yourself well at the RAC."

C grunted. His thoughts were on future problems. Money, as always, was foremost in his mind. He glanced up at Neville.

"How do I get more money?" he asked abruptly.

Neville was unsurprised. Cumming was always asking for money. "For the Service?"

"Of course."

"Ask the FO. They're your paymasters. That's why you don't need to get too fussed about the War Office and the Admiralty. They don't pay for you. We do. Or the FO, I should say."

He smiled beatifically. "Tell the FO that you're running secret networks against the Bolshevists in Russia. You've got some good chaps there. You did brilliantly with Hoare and that dreadful salesman chappy – what was his name?"

"Reilly. Sydney Reilly. Frightful bounder."

Neville nodded, remembering. "That's it. Sydney Reilly. Well, they did a sound enough job over getting rid of Rasputin. Kept the Russians in the war for most of last year, until Lenin and his Bolsheviks grabbed the throne. And the people who matter are no friends of the Reds, believe me. And they'll back you, too, Cumming. Get Sam Hoare – he's still your man in Moscow, is he not? – to order Reilly or some of your agents to blow up a couple of those arms factories that the Reds have taken over in Russia. Kharkhov, Smolensk. Omsk, Tomsk. It doesn't matter. Places like that. Pretend that the Whites did it." The White Russians were the rump of the old Czarist regime and sworn enemies of the Bolsheviks. "The FO will pay for anything to avert the Red Menace."

C was baffled. "Why? These Bolshies are just a rabble, surely?"

Neville's eyebrows shot up. "Oh no. They're dangerous, my dear Cumming, very dangerous." He saw C's puzzlement. "You see, Trotsky, Lenin and his lot, they're a threat to the 'established order;' a mortal threat. If the Reds succeed in Russia, then where next? Germany? France? Liverpool? Clydeside? The East End? They're Red enough already, God knows. Where will it all stop? Oh no, the Red menace scares most of Whitehall silly. There are some very nervous fellows out there. Ask the House of Lords," he gave a thin smile. "People who really believe that we could have a revolution too, when the war's over."

Cumming scoffed.

"No, I'm serious, Cumming. You should hear Winston on the subject. He's positively obsessed with the Bolsheviks: truly. Sees the Red Flag of revolution everywhere."

Cumming smiled. Young Churchill's reputation as an erratic enthusiast for lost causes was a constant source of amusement around the smart dining tables of London.

"And not just Whitehall, either," continued Neville. "I don't think that the Palace is particularly pleased about Cousin Nicky, languishing in some ghastly Red prison in the Urals or wherever. The PM and the King are already arguing about what we're going to do with the Czar of not quite all the Russians now." He nodded emphatically. "No, go for the Reds, C. There's lots of money in the Revolution – for Secret Services especially. For an anti-Bolshevist crusade, the politicos will give you anything."

He beamed at Cumming, who nodded, understanding. 'so, if I pitch for funding to keep an eye on the Reds, Neville, I"ll get it from the FO Vote; is that what you're saying?" Cumming tipped his head to one side.

"That's exactly what I"m saying, Cumming. Talk to Kell about it over at MI5 or whatever name he's calling himself these days. And if you play your cards well, you'll both keep your jobs after the war. And your service, too." He smiled maliciously. "Why don't you get some reports to Hankey? That should do the trick. Frighten them a little, eh? Hankey'll like that. Bolshevist cells. Reds under the bed. Revolution brewing, what? That sort of stuff. Grist to his mill."

Cumming looked thoughtful.

As Neville took his leave to stroll back down Pall Mall towards The Horse Guards, Cumming's mind was turning over possibilities and plans for the future. He was too absorbed to notice Neville's seemingly casual questioning about Everitt, and it never, even for a second, crossed his mind to enquire who really had ordered him to make the Bolshevists a prime target for Britain's intelligence services.

CHAPTER 22

The Crash

ST OMER

13ᵗʰ March

Serjeants Doughty and McNaughty stood to one side of the Special Duties hanger waiting for the return of the two SD DH4s.

The wind was beginning to gust, billowing the windsock. The rest of the groundcrews were huddled behind the hangar, Corporal Cooper concealing a crafty smoke in the palm of his hand and keeping a wary eye on the two senior NCOs. Sjt. Doughty was fanatical about smoking anywhere near the aeroplanes.

Two specks on the horizon slowly grew into the spindly silhouettes of biplanes. Rocking slightly, they began to turn into wind, preparatory to landing.

*   *   *

The day of the photographic flight had gone well. The previous day had been a complete washout, with the crews roaring past a Wattignies station tantalisingly empty of any trains. They queried the orders from 9 Wing but Wing said nothing. Even they were in the dark. Only Mackenzie and his Intelligence Staff knew that the Belgian train-spotting network had alerted them that Bruchmüller was delayed by a day. Even they didn't know that this was as a direct result of Armstrong's hare-brained dive-bombing on the Lille railyards two days before.

Today, however, everything was going smoothly. The two DH4s had crossed the line at ten thousand feet to avoid the anti-aircraft fire and headed east for five minutes. Armstrong had then let down to treetop height to avoid observation before turning sharply south and setting course for Wassignies.

Despite his misgivings about the hangover of the day before, Armstrong's flying impressed Barton. His control was smooth and fluid, and the DH4 responded like a thoroughbred to his touch. Whatever else Armstrong was, mused Barton as he watched the French countryside flash by two hundred feet below, he was a good pilot. He returned to scanning the empty sky for sign of German scouts.

A hundred yards away, Robbie's DH4 rose and fell as it kept station off their starboard wing. He could see David Blair fiddling with the camera. The two aircraft roared on above the trees and fields of occupied France.

Armstrong's warning shout to get ready alerted him. As the two aircraft came up to the line of a railway, they banked hard right and split up, one on each of the tracks about 400 yards out from the line of telegraph poles that marked the line. At the briefing they had agreed that this plan would ensure the best pictures at the safest distance; and by following the railway lines on both sides towards the station, they would take the Germans by surprise. Yesterday had been a valuable practice run and they had turned too late. Today they were spot on.

Barton took a last look at the empty sky, put his Lewis gun to "safe" and made ready with the camera. His was pointed out to the right of the aircraft. On the dark shape of Robbie's DH4, half a mile away, Blair's camera was pointing left. With one sweeping pass on both sides of the line, they should both get their pictures. Everything now depended on a slow, smooth flypast and the observers' skill at changing the cameras' plates quickly. Barton took his gloves off and checked that the glass plates were loose in their leather pockets. Armstrong shouted again and pointed. Dead ahead, a plume of white steam could be seen above a cluster of dark buildings and trees.

Barton's pulse began to race and he swallowed hard.

The DH4 wallowed for a second as it slowed and settled down to a rock-solid straight approach, boring in parallel to the railway line off to their right. A train, no, two trains, were in the station, one blowing off steam. Barton's eyes took in the rapidly growing cluster of vehicles, the station buildings, a long goods train with army wagons on low loaders heading north: and facing south, a train of passenger coaches. He began taking pictures automatically as the trains came level with them, Armstrong flying a gentle arc, right wing slightly down to help the photography. With well-practised ease, Barton got six plates exposed then suddenly the train was past, disappearing far behind, and the two DH4s were banking hard to the right and for home, sweeping low over the treetops. Not a shot had been fired at them and Barton even waved at the white blob of an upturned face as the DH4s, now back in close formation, thundered over a herd of cows, stampeding them across the field.

"Got your happy snaps?" shouted Armstrong.

"Yes," he bellowed back. "Nice flying, Jack."

Across to starboard, David Blair raised a hand in triumphant salute, holding up five fingers. Well, thought Barton, they'd got their pictures, too. That should keep GHQ happy. He settled down to watching the sky above and thinking about Francine in the café as the DH4s set course north-west for St Omer. He took the Lewis gun and scanned the sky for trouble: nothing.

*   *   *

As the two returning aeroplanes turned into wind to land, Jack Doughty shouted to his crew to fall in. Adjusting their caps and stamping their feet, the groundcrew lined up to await their charges. The squadron photographic officer and his assistant came out to join them.

The two aircraft droned in for a formation landing, dropping steadily. Suddenly one of the DH4s swooped up like a lift as it crossed the boundary hedge. As Robby's aircraft landed to bounce and bucket across the grass, Armstrong's split off, climbing hard to a thousand feet, before standing on its tail for a second to do a slow, deliberate wing over and dive across the airfield.

"What the bloody hell ?" muttered Doughty aloud.

"A good question, Serjeant Doughty."

The NCOs jerked round to see a grim faced Major Duffus standing hatless behind them. The CO looked angry. Nervous ground crew backed off. The CO's Canadian temper was legendary if he was crossed.

They returned to staring at Armstrong's DH4, now doing a smooth loop overhead, then thundering across the airfield and the hangars, its wheels just feet above them. As it gained height, the aircraft banked into the circuit, throttling back to come in to land.

" 'E's just showin' orf." Cooper's cockney whine drew a venomous look from Serjeant Doughty. Major Duffus said nothing. His face spoke legions. The little knot of men stared at the DH4 coming towards them ready to land.

Suddenly the plane began a slow roll. "What the..." muttered Cooper.

"The goddamn stupid bugger. He's too low for a roll", voiced Duffus, unaware that he had even spoken. "The stupid bugger. I'll have him for breakfast." The Newfoundland accent was strong.

The DH4 was now standing on its wing tip, vertical in the sky, only a hundred feet up. Slowly it inverted, to hang upside down for a second before beginning the slow roll back up to the vertical. Painfully slowly, the DH4 began to right itself.

" 'E ain't goin' to myke it." Cooper's observation went unheeded.

Armstrong's aeroplane was very low and sinking.

The slow roll had cleared the wing tip from the ground, but the speed was insufficient to maintain height. Even as the aeroplane began to right itself, with a dreadful inevitability, the watching group saw the wingtip of the approaching aircraft touch the ground and begin to disintegrate into a splinter trail of white wood and ripped canvas as the DH4, with horrifying slowness, flew into the ground.

"Oh my God!"

The wreckage settled. Like a broken bird, the DH4 stopped abruptly, the wings folding forward like tissue paper as the fuselage stood on its nose, tail in the air. A cloud of dust and bits of canvas blew away in the wind. For a split second there was silence.

Then men began to run.

*   *   *

The great danger with aircraft wrecks is always fire.

Every member of the group panting across the turf knew that, somewhere in the wreckage, petrol was dripping onto doped canvas, dry wood and a red-hot engine. A more inflammable mixture would be hard to find. They also knew that somewhere in the wreckage two of their friends were trapped.

Holmes and Cooper, the two junior NCOs, were first to arrive at the crash.

The intact fuselage of the DH4 were canted forward, tail high in the air. The remains of the wings and struts were strewn forwards across the grass, shredded into firewood. Of the pilot nothing was to be seen. The observer was slumped forward in the rear seat. A reek of petrol filled the air. The two men skidded to a halt, then ploughed forward, Holmes to the backseat, Cooper to the front.

As Holmes looked in, he saw the limp figure of Charley Barton slumped head down against his straps. At the front, Cooper found the front cockpit empty. Baffled, he looked round.

Like a ghost rising, Jack Armstrong stood up ten yards in front of the aeroplane. He had been thrown clear by the impact, clean over the engine. His face was a red mask of blood, and the apparition clawed at his eyes. "I can't see!" he shrieked.

The rest of the party ran to help, stumbling over the broken wings strewn on the turf. Only Holmes was standing on the side of the fuselage six feet up in the air, clawing at the trapped Barton's straps when the fog of petrol vapour ignited with a solid *whump!*

Men scattered out from the fireball.

Armstrong was led rapidly away cursing and shouting. Holmes leapt off and sprinted for safety through the fire, flames licking round him. As he jumped down, the DH4's fuselage crashed back to the ground, sending a gust of flames outwards. In the middle of the fire the dark unconscious shape of Charley Barton could be clearly seen slumped forward.

For a second, the horrified ring of watchers stared at the flames.

Jack Doughty started towards the burning plane, then stopped, helpless at the edge of the burning grass, his hand shielding his face from the roaring heat. Not ten feet away, a man was burning to death before their eyes. Doughty clutched his head in frustration. He wanted to move, to save Captain Barton but, frozen with fear of the fire, he stood impotent and indecisive.

Suddenly the wind gusted hard and the inferno billowed forward, pulling the plume of flame and black smoke away from the aircraft. To everyone's astonishment, Barton, clothes smoldering, stood up in the rear cockpit. It was like seeing a dead man walking. The roar of the fire filled their senses. No-one moved, rooted with shock at the horror at the spectacle.

Serjeant Doughty stood paralysed, not daring to plunge into the gap in the fire.

Someone said, "Oh my God…"

To everyone's astonishment, Corporal Cooper suddenly pushed Doughty aside, sprinting past him to snatch the blackened figure of the observer and tip him over the rim of the cockpit. As the body crashed to the ground, the wind veered and the flames began to lick back as suddenly as they had flared forward. The whole incident lasted no more than five seconds.

For a split second the pair were engulfed by fire. Then Cooper appeared, clothes smoking, dragging Barton's smouldering body away from the ring of flames before collapsing onto the grass. Willing hands rushed to help.

Doughty remained stock still, staring at the drama, as desperate fingers pulled open Barton's leather flying suit. The metal buckles were hot enough to burn. The figure of Josh Moon sprinted across the grass, medical bag in hand, to skid to his knees beside the recumbent blackened form. His southern drawl was now a bellow. "Git outta ma way!" as he pushed the helpers aside and began to pulled at Barton's clothes. "Fetch some water! Lots of water, Goddammit! Move, you bastards!"

Men ran from all directions.

Corporal Cooper sat apart on the turf, staring blankly at his burnt hands. The fire crackled in the background, hissing as foam extinguishers were gradually brought into play. He felt sick and weak. A shadow fell over him.

It was Serjeant Doughty. "Well," he said, "'ere's a fine to-do Cooper, and no mistake. I've not seen "owt so brave since I've been out 'ere, and I've been 'ere too bloody long, I can tell thee. I'm proud to shake your 'and, lad." The Serjeant stuck out a massive hand and Cooper, open mouthed, took it. As he did, he screwed his face up in agony.

"Wassoop, lad?"

"It's me 'ands, Sarge. They're bleedin' burnt to buggery."

Carefully Doughty let go, and Cooper inspected his scorched fingers.

A yell drew their attention. Fifty yards away someone was pouring water over Jack Armstrong's face to wash the blood off. Armstrong was yelling and cursing as his sight cleared. He'd cut his forehead. Nearby, Doc Moon was inspecting Charley Barton as he carefully poured water from a jug onto the silent, blackened form. It steamed off the leather flying suit. Whitefaced men stood, watching helplessly. The fire crackled in the background. Bullets began to explode from the heat, scattering the spectators.

Doughty shook his head and looked around at the chaos.

A grim-faced Major Duffus stood, hands on hips. "Well at least we've got one set of those bloody photographs. Now get them back to GHQ!" he announced to no-one in particular. No one moved.

"Now!" he bellowed in sudden fury. The Canadian accent rang out above the fire. "We've still got one set. Now, you goddammed sons of bitches! Now!"

Frightened soldiers ran to unload the camera from the other DH4. Alongside it, bareheaded, Roberts and David Blair stood aghast as the fire and medical teams went to work busy around the crash.

Doughty took Cooper by the elbow and helped him up. An anxious Corporal Holmes joined them. "We'd best get thee fixed oop, lad," said Doughty. "Corporal Holmes, see as Corporal Cooper gets properly looked after at the Medical Hut." He looked up as more men rushed to join the rescue party.

They were bringing a stretcher for the smoking body of Charley Barton.

CHAPTER 23

The Handover

ROTTERDAM

Wednesday 13th March 1918

Everitt finally got lucky at ten past nine on the Wednesday evening.

 After two abortive visits to the café, he had become resigned to a long wait for "agent A34". He didn't mind.

The hotel was comfortable, he was safe in Holland and he was quite beginning to enjoy his war. The terrors of the previous week and the passage through enemy Germany were largely forgotten, extinguished in a warm glow of security heightened by alcohol. With sufficient funds, he reasoned, he could stand this for a month; and God knows he deserved a holiday, he thought. He ordered another *Oude Jenever* liqueur gin with a beer chaser, and settled back in the booth at the back of the case.

The door burst open, spilling a cheerful, talkative crowd into the bar. Everitt looked up at the commotion and was startled to see the tall dark-suited figure of the German on the train in their midst. What the hell was he doing here? The familiar knot of fear suddenly clamped its talons in his stomach.

Then he relaxed. This was Holland. No one would dare to touch him here. Not even a German from their OHL. With a detached amusement, he watched the group at the bar, faces flushed in the lamplight. This wasn't the first café they'd visited tonight, he guessed. The tall German was the life and soul of the party, it seemed.

Everitt smiled. "Oh, if only you knew, my German friend!" safely relaxed on his third drink, safe and warm, drawing deeply on the Dutch cigar. He could even remember the Hun's name, thanks to that yappy little Hun border official: Stube – that was it. Herr Stube; "a distinguished official of OHL."

Well, you don't know me, Stube, but I certainly know you. Everitt smiled to himself and buried his nose in his drink.

He looked up with at start as a shadow fell across his table. The tall figure of the German loomed over him, serious and forbidding. Everitt glanced at the door, momentarily panicked, ready to run. Then he noticed the briefcase – except it wasn't. It was a worn, brown music case, with a long metal bar. His mouth dropped open.

"*Entschuldigung* – excuse me," said the tall German. "But I couldn't help noticing your cigar." He pointed to Everitt's half smoked cigar smoldering in the ashtray. "I wonder if you could tell me where I can buy them. The cigars with a straw down the middle. I'm only visiting."

Everitt's mouth worked. This was him! This was A34. It was Stube. "The distinguished German at OHL." Oh my God...

"It's *Herr* Stube, isn't it?" said Everitt.

Stube's face was impassive in the shadow.

Everitt gabbled. "I saw you at the border crossing point. Venlo. Couple of days ago. The customs man pointed you out to me."

"Really?" Stube's expression was unfathomable, his German precise. "Did he, now?"

"It was you – I would never have guessed – I mean, recognising – " Everitt was babbling. "Oh yes, the cigars..."

"*Bitte?*" The German was staring down at him.

"Ah, *ja; gern...* yes, gladly." Everitt's mind raced, remembering. He collected himself. "*Ja, natürlich.* I've got a box with me that I bought at the station."

Stube sighed and reached out a hand. "May I see them, please?" Everitt hesitated. "I would like to take back a box as a present," explained Stube. Everitt's eyes over Stube's shoulder flicked at the group at the bar.

"Relax, it's all right," Stube said very quietly in English. Everitt came out of his shock and pulled himself together. "Are you all right?" asked Stube, reverting to German. Everitt's nervous eyes flicked again to the group at the bar.

"It's all right," said Stube impatiently, then added loudly, "Can I see the brand? Of the cigars?" The German accent was strong with a nasal twang.

Everitt hauled the box of cigars out of his duffel bag and handed it to Stube, who examined it. "Hey," called an American voice from the bar. "Your beer's getting warm!"

"*Ja, ja,*" replied the tall German. "*Ich komme gleich!*"

He handed the box back to Everitt. "Well, pop it in my music case." Everitt suddenly realised that Stube's case was open, sitting wide mouthed alongside his duffel bag. The clock! Of course! "Quickly!" urged Stube. Everitt pushed the cigars back into his own bag and dropped the little clock, now wrapped in paper, into the yawning jaws of Stube's music case. It only took a second and the swift exchange was masked by the table and by Stube's body, blocking the mouth of the booth.

Stube turned to go. "Good luck" said Everitt in German.

Stube stopped and looked at him, nodding slowly.

"Many thanks," said Stube. He shook Everitt's limp and damp hand, and returned to the bar. Everitt heard the words "*Nederlandse Zigarren*" and the group looked at him in his booth for a moment before returning to their conversation.

Everitt felt drained. He'd done it! It was all over. He stared down at the Jenever, then gulped it back. The warm glow reflected his mood as he looked across at the party at the bar. Someone was telling a joke, and a roar of laughter rocked the puddle of light around the group.

Everitt noticed that his fingers were trembling. No need; not now. It was all over. How long could he stay here, safe in Rotterdam? he thought idly. At least another couple of days, for sure. Then a nice safe neutral Dutch packet boat from The Hook to Harwich. Yes, he'd spin it out until the weekend.

Anyway, he deserved a holiday. Hadn't "C" himself said so? He smiled to himself and drank his beer.

On the far side of the room, he noticed Stube staring at him.

The British Secret Service's most secret agent, A34, didn't look happy.

CHAPTER 24

BEF GHQ MONTREUIL

THE CHIEF OF STAFF'S OFFICE

Thursday 14th March 1918

"Well, it looks like Fifth Army. And soon. I don't think that there's any doubt about that now?"

Brigadier General Edgar Cox nodded. General Sir Herbert Lawrence, Chief of Staff to the BEF, stirred one of the aerial photographs on his desk. "Amazing. How d'you get these, Mackenzie?" he demanded.

"Twenty-five Squadron, Sir. Yesterday afternoon. Special mission. We'd got a tip from the *Dame Blanche* network that Bruchmüller's train was booked through to the Peronne. So I got them to get us the German rail staff timetable and talked to Twenty-five Squadron direct. Told them it was a special GHQ mission. There wasn't much time. They flew to Wattignies and caught them in the station on the second day."

"Good job the train was on time. Eventually," observed Cox.

Lawrence smiled and nodded in his turn. "Trust the Hun to be punctual eh? Good work. Well done." A thought struck him. "It's definitely him? We're sure it's his train all right?"

"Oh yes, General. *Dame Blanche* were adamant. And it tallies with Bruchmüller's other sightings, too. Lieutenant Powell here has been keeping an eye on Bruchmüller for months." He jerked his chin at the fourth occupant of the room. "He knows more about the Hun push than most of the Huns, I'll wager. As you may recall from last week, sir." He added tactfully.

Lawrence grunted. He remembered the last intelligence briefing and Gough's pigheadedness only too well.

Cox went on, "Where those two carriages go, Bruchmüller goes."

Powell nodded and interrupted them, pushing a magnifying glass to the Chief of Staff. "If you use this sir, you can even read the numbers on the carriages."

Lawrence nodded slowly. "Good work by *Dame Blanche*." He had stood in as temporary Head of BEF Intelligence after Charteris' sudden dismissal four months before, so knew all about the secret underground spy network in occupied Belgium. The *Dame Blanche* train-spotting network was a pearl among the BEF's intelligence sources.

"Well, it all fits." Lawrence scrubbed at his face. His next problem was to warn Haig and Gough, Fifth Army's commander. He was quite looking forward to that. He smiled grimly to himself. "Any further news about timings? Dates?"

Cox and Mackenzie looked at each other. "Well, Powell here thinks he's got the answer, general. As you know he's been watching this whole subject for the last three months and there's no-one who knows more about it."

Cox gestured to his junior intelligence officer.

Powell cleared his throat. "Yes, Sir, We've been looking at it very closely. I''ve been monitoring all the transcripts of the German intercepts for over two months and checking them against all the other things we know. There are two whole armies, that's well over twenty divisions, probably more, over 300,000 men, stacked up opposite Fifth Army." He realised that he was nervous and gabbling.

He calmed down. Lawrence – old Lorenzo – was on his side, he remembered. He went on more slowly.

"All the photo-reconnaissance confirms hundreds of new ammo dumps and artillery sites, some of them well forward. There are underground stollen – that's forward bunkers – everywhere, Sir, and all leave has been stopped. In addition, I've got a report from London – not confirmed – that all the Huns' Army Training schools behind the lines are to cease operations and close down on 20th March, except for the one in Army Group Flanders, in the North." He took a deep breath. "Bruchmüller and his artillery train are really the final pieces of the jigsaw. So our money's on 20th to 25th March for the date of the German attack on General Gough's army." He stopped, slightly breathless and looked at Cox, who nodded encouragingly. "Sir."

"Next week, eh?" Lawrence looked keenly at Powell then examined the photographs of the Bruchmüller HQ train through the large magnifying glass.

His brain was absorbing the implications of all that the young ex-don had said. He liked Powell, and hadn't enjoyed watching a member of his staff, however junior, being sneered at and chewed up by Gough five days ago. Unlike the arrogant commander of Fifth Army, Lawrence had a healthy respect for the young intelligence officer and his expertise on the Germans.

He noticed a tiny group of German officers frozen on the platform by the camera. It looked as if they were smoking. In another picture, one of them was pointing at the aeroplanes. He picked up a magnifying glass and looked more closely. He wondered which one of the grainy blurred figures was Bruchmüller, the great artillery expert. "I'll bet it's you," he thought, looking closer at the pointing shape. Impossible to see any rank, of course, at that distance. "Humph! Pity they didn't bomb the train. Might have got the bugger."

Powell looked surprised. "Sir?"

"Brookmiller, or whatever his name is. Pity we didn't kill him instead of just taking his picture. Might have forced a bit of delay; change of plans, that kind of thing." A thought struck him. "By the way Mackenzie, whatever happened about your idea? The one the Chief wrote to London about? Having a go at their High Command? Trying to kill Hindenburg and Ludendorff? All we got was a vague reply, signed by the DMO, saying that London would investigate and do its best or somesuch nonsense."

My idea? thought Mackenzie wryly. He shook his head. "I've heard nothing. Nothing at all. As far as I know, general." He looked enquiringly at Cox, who nodded agreement.

"Nothing, General. Not even Drake's people ever have heard a word back about it."

"Oh, well," said Lawrence. He scratched his face. "It was worth a try, I suppose. Probably just as well. Don't think Sir Douglas really approved of trying to kill Commanders in Chief", he added, in a rare flash of humour. "Well, it's down to us now. Or rather Gough and his chaps. They're in the firing line. Have we warned them? And Third Army, too?" Byng's Third Army was the BEF formation to the north of Fifth Army.

"Yes, Sir," said Cox grimly. "Many times."

Lawrence nodded and scooped up the pictures. "I'll hang on to these for the moment. The C-in-C's due back in a couple of days." If he gets back, he thought. He wouldn't be surprised if Lloyd George didn't try and sack the BEF's C-in-C. London was seething with politicial intrigue these days. Pity you can't sack a few politicians.

"I'll brief him myself." He looked kindly at Powell. "And well done, Powell. Well done. Good work. I'll see that the Commander in Chief knows about your contribution. Well done, my boy."

Powell glowed. After his mauling by 5th Army's braying commander last week he had begun to lose confidence in both his abilities and his place in the HQ. For him the Army had always been a strange world, full of arrogant, snobbish senior officers and even stranger rules and pointless inconveniences. Gough's sneering dismissal of his careful work had convinced him that most of them were boneheadedly stupid as well. Only the absorbing puzzle of the German Army and the German offensive had really kept him going over the past few days. He liked Mackenzie and enjoyed the work of the intelligence branch. Praise now from General Lawrence, Haig's Chief of Staff, was praise indeed. He blushed like a girl, muttering, "Thank you very much sir…"

The Int men left the office, leaving the BEF's Chief of the General Staff alone with his thoughts. He strolled to the window and looked down at the courtyard. The bustle of a busy headquarters was all around.

Two soldiers carrying rations for the kitchen round the back of the chateau; a driver washing a car from a bucket and whistling cheerfully; a fussy quartermaster reading from a list to a puzzled looking senior NCO; a farrier serjeant, braces hanging down, leading a glossy back charger round to the stables.

Lawrence watched the soldiers blankly. "Who posted you here?" he thought. "How did you all get such cushy billets?"

The Chief of Staff shook off his thoughts and drew hard on his cigarette. It was fate, the luck of the draw that decided where a man soldiered. He knew that. No point in brooding about it. It was chance; pure luck. He'd soldiered in India and South Africa. He knew that the Goddess of Chance determined what happened to soldiers, from the most humble to the most exalted. Sometimes good chaps just got in the way of what was just damned bad luck. It was all chance.

His mind rolled on. Take young Powell there, down in Int; thoroughly good chap. Pure chance he worked for the BEF HQ. Clever; not quite a gentleman, but damned good at his job. You could always turn a good chap into a decent officer if you took the time and trouble, he mused. The fact was that Powell may be one of the self-styled "irregulars" but he was a jewel, whatever that bloody fool Gough thought. In fact, thought General Sir Herbert Lawrence, they were damned lucky to have clever young men like that in the headquarters…

He sighed and looked down at the photographs and map left on his desk. Like iron filings round a magnet, black German divisions clustered opposite Fifth Army in the south. It looked like Gough's men would soon need a little luck, too, he reflected.

He wondered how Haig would react to the news when he got back. Assuming that Haig did come back. Lawrence wouldn"t have been surprised if Lloyd George decided to sack him. Untrustworthy little Welsh shit. Bloody politicians. Well, if he had sacked Haig then they'd all expect Henry Wilson as C-in-C. Another shit. He'd sort Gough out though, that's for sure. He hoped it was Haig: at least you where you stood with Dougie. He ground out his cigarette viciously in the overloaded ashtray. He completely agreed with young Powell: whatever happened, the Germans were coming. That was for sure…

"Talk your way out of this one, Goughie," he thought with a sudden stab of malice for Fifth Army's arrogant leader.

"Your boys are for the high jump now."

CHAPTER 25

The Man who Knew too Much
ROTTERDAM

Thursday 14th March

Stube gently guided Van der Horst to a corner seat, waving aside a jovial offer of another beer from the cheerful press pack thronging the bar.

The Dutchman eyed him carefully. As Stube's secret link with London, Holland's Reuters correspondent was playing with fire, meeting him in public and they both knew it. Equally, both knew that Stube would not have dared risking a face to face with his Dutch courier without some very pressing and urgent reason. The fact that he had stayed on an extra day in Holland would need explaining when he got back to OHL, too. He'd cabled earlier to say he was delayed, hinting at preparing a big story for the international press.

"Get your notebook out," said Stube loudly, as they settled in the booth. "Look busy. I've got a big story for you."

Van der Horst pulled out his journalist's pad. He and Stube were keenly aware of the curious glances from the other correspondents at the bar. The two men made an odd couple: the cadaverous Stube, tall, angular, black as an undertaker; and the plump, pink-faced Dutchman, a latter day Pickwick. He licked a pencil and smoothed a page.

"Well?" They spoke in German.

"I've got a really good story for you. About this *KaiserSchlacht*. This is a very good story, for Reuters only at this stage." Van der Horst looked at the press man. They both knew they were being watched. He started to write. The Dutchman already knew the official German line on the impending KaiserSchlacht – the whole press pack knew.

"So what is so special about this story, *Herr* Stube?"

"This story is exclusive." Stube dropped his voice. "Exclusive for my old friends. Especially C."

Van der Horst looked up sharply.

"Start writing," hissed Stube. "Make it look good, for God's sake. We've got a little problem. There's trouble. That man that I met yesterday evening, the one I spoke to about the cigars."

"Oh, the one in the booth over there? The sailor? With the ginger beard? I remember…" interrupted van der Horst, without looking up.

"Yes." Stube was impatient, short. "Well, he's recognised me; he knows my name. He knows who I am and he knows my name."

The Dutchman stared over his spectacles at the pale-faced German. Comprehension slowly dawned in his eyes. "He knows your *name*?"

"Exactly." Stube glared at him. "Exactly – he knows what I look like, he knows where I work and and he knows my name."

"Shit." the Dutchman looked at the bar crowd. "Shit," he repeated with sudden vehemence.

"*Ja*. I couldn't have put it better. Shit. We are in the shit. Or, to be more precise, *Mijnheer* van der Horst, *I* am in the shit."

Van der Horst shook his head. This was a disaster. Stube was the British Secret Service's greatest secret. He knew that. "But how…" he began.

Stube cut him off "Apparently some customs man pointed me out to him at the border. Or so he says," he added savagely.

"Do you believe him?"

"It's possible. I've been coming across for nearly a year now and they know I've got a Kaiser Headquarters pass, signed by Ludendorff himself. No, the border people know me…"

"So how does this stranger know your name?"

Stube pulled a face and lowered his voice. "Because one of the border guards told him, and because he's not a stranger, my dear friend, he's one of *you* supposed to be meeting me on business. He's a *friend*." He emphasised the "*friend*".

The Dutchman nodded slowly. The "friends" was slang for Britain's Secret Service. "What's the connection? Can he be trusted?"

Stube shook his head violently. "No, no-one can be trusted. You are the only other man who knows me. Even C's courier. That's what he was; it was supposed to be a blind meeting." He shrugged. "That's what he was. A courier from London. And now he knows exactly who I am. And where I work. And you can wager your father's farm that he has worked out what I do."

"Shit," intoned the Dutchman. There was a long pause. The babble of voices from the bar seemed suddenly louder. "You call this a *little* problem? I call it a damned big one. What the hell do we do now?"

Stube frowned. "Well, the first thing is to get a message back to London and let them know: fast. Second, we must find our friend and make sure he knows how important it is to keep his mouth shut." They both looked up as a cheerful German voice broke in. Standing over them was Kominsky, Nord Deustche Shipping's Rotterdam agent, beer-pot in hand, looking impatient.

"Come on you two. We've got another round in back at the bar. Haven't you fellows done enough scribbling for one day, eh?"

Van der Horst shut his notebook. "*Ja*, Kominsky, you are right. Enough scribbling. Time for action." He stood up. "Leave it with me, *Herr* Stube. I will deal with your little problem. You can be sure I will handle this matter with the utmost discretion."

"And expedition," added Stube.

Van der Horst bowed. "And expedition, too…"

"Dear Christ," said Kominsky. "Discretion? Expedition?" He shook his head in disgust. "You two sound like a pair of pox doctor's clerks. Or God-damned lawyers. Come and have a drink…" and he ambled back to the bar.

"Warn C – *tonight*," hissed Stube and returned to the press group. A foaming lager was thrust into his hand as a worried van der Horst slipped out into the night.

If anyone knew that Britain's secret service had a high-level agent planted in Germany's General Headquarters there could be bad trouble; and if anyone knew just who it was – well, thought van der Horst, that really could spell disaster.

Stube's great secret had been compromised.

CHAPTER 26

C's LITTLE PROBLEM

LONDON

Saturday 16th March

"This is bad news, Freddie; thoroughly bad news."

C smoothed van der Horst's "MOST IMMEDIATE" telegram on his desk and read it for the tenth time. It spelled nothing but bad news. He shook his head. "How the hell did this happen?"

Freddie Browning eyed his boss carefully. He hadn't worked with Cumming long enough to gauge his temper, or his moods. But this looked bad. Well, it wasn't his fault.

"Well, C, from what we can make out from van der Horst, A34 was recognised by Everitt as he passed over the timer…"

C banged his fist on the table. "But how the blue bloody hell did he find out that A34 was *Stube* – eh?"

Browning rushed to mollify him. "It looks like an accident, C. It seems that Everitt and Stube were on the same train at the border checkpoint and according to him, a customs man told him his name…"

"But how? Why, blast it?"

Browning shrugged.

Enraged, C went on. "Don't stand there bloody shrugging, Browning. This is a disaster! We've spent years getting Stube into that place – years! He's one of our best men. And now someone tells one of our chaps his name…"

"… And Everitt meets him, puts two and two together," added Browning, "So he knows who it is."

"Exactly. Exactly. It's a damned disgrace. All that careful work, and now this." C subsided grumbling, looking round for a paper knife to plunge into his cork leg. He couldn't see one. "Bugger!"

Browning tried to calm him down. "I didn't see the whole A34 file, C. I mean, when we picked him for this Duo job. Is he that important? Has he been on the books long?"

"Oh, yes." Cumming was calmer now. "Henderson spotted Stube in South Africa back in '03 and tipped off the old Secret Service Bureau. Long before my time. We've been grooming him one way or another ever since. Never thought he'd end up in their High Command headquarters, though; that was a stroke of luck. But, by God, we were pleased when he did. What a stroke!" He smoothed the telegram again. "And now this!" A sudden thought struck him. "Could the decoding chappies have got it wrong?"

"No, C. I checked it myself. Van der Horst's message is quite clear. He used our commercial telegram code. Asks you to 'take all necessary action'"

"Hmm." C looked at the signal again, willing its text to change.

"Do you want to take any action?" enquired Browning. "Pull A34 out somehow?"

"Good God man, no! Absolutely not. No, he's far too valuable where he is in OHL. Think about it. Our man in the heart of their headquarters. At a time like this?"

"But surely his position is at risk as long as Everitt knows about him? What if he's caught? What if he blabs?" Browning stared at C. "What if the Huns get their hands on Everitt? You saw the feller, C. Thought he was a nervous wreck, m'self. On the edge and so forth."

Cumming nodded. A sudden thought struck him. "Where's 'Jim' – Everitt – now?"

"Still in Rotterdam. Due back on the Dutch packet in a couple of days" time. Do you want his arrangements changed? Get him out sooner? You were going to send him on leave, if you remember."

"No." Cumming shook his head. He stood up and looked out of the window at the Thames.

Browning waited.

"No. No. There's another way of dealing with this, Freddie." He nodded, came to a decision. "Oh, yes, I know how to deal with Stube's problem.

Everitt needs bringing back, though. Soon as possible. No doubt about that." Cumming went back to staring out of the window. Christ, this wasn't easy, he thought. "Ask Mrs Anderson to get me Major Rice, will you?"

"Rice?" enquired Browning. He'd never heard of him.

"Yes,"said C, swinging round. "He's a sort of bodyguard. Does special jobs for me sometimes. She'll know who I mean. Tell her I've got another job for him. Escort, sort of. I know what to do about A34." He nodded. "Sooner we get Everitt safely out the better all round. It would be a disaster if Stube's identity leaked out. An absolute disaster."

*   *   *

A feeling of imminent disaster swept over Roberts as he tried to guide his DH4 towards the boundary hedge.

The propeller windmilled idly in front of its dead engine. Like most RFC pilots, Roberts had been in an air crash before. The unreliable engines of the day virtually guaranteed a crash landing at some point, in a service that killed 20% of its trainee pilots. What was making him gulp was the knowledge that he had misjudged his glide approach and undershot badly. The silent engine and Timmy's nervous queries from the back seat didn"t help. He tried juggling the fuel mixture lever to restart the engine, but to no avail. Dead as a dodo. The airfield began to grow larger, but they were too low. The DH4 could glide; but without power they couldn't climb. What had started as a normal bombing operation had gone badly wrong from the start and now looked like coming to a disastrous conclusion.

"Well," he bellowed over his shoulder, "at least we got rid of our bombs."

"Wonderful, Skipper," came the voice from behind. "I think we've made a balls up of this one; bit of a washout…"

Desperately trying to hold the nose level while still maintaining airspeed, Roberts had to agree. Despite Major Duffus' remonstrations about the low cloud and driving rain, Wing had ordered them to bomb a railway yard south of Lille and the three available DH4s of A Flight had endured an uncomfortable half-hour in the rain. Attempts to get above the cloud had proved fruitless and dangerous. In an age without proper instruments, flying in cloud could be suicidal. Three minutes in a cloud and you could be upside down and not know it.

They had slid across the front line half hidden below the cloud ceiling to be met by a furious barrage of "archy", German anti-aircraft fire. The only way to locate the rail yard in the murk had been by peering over the side through the driving rain to follow the railway lines. Their bombs had rained down to little effect and the return flight, against a strong headwind had taken them twice the time it had taken going out. To add insult to injury, the returning DH4s had been greeted by another deadly barrage of pom-poms, archie and even machine-gun fire as they struggled back to the British line at less than a thousand feet. Twisting and turning to confuse the German gunners, they had got split up in the gloom. Then the borrowed DH4's engine had suddenly cut out and now Roberts and his observer were trying to land a strange, heavy, rain-soaked aircraft, without power and unable to climb, a good half mile short of the airfield.

"I think we're going to have to risk it," shouted Roberts. He was freezing cold, soaked to the skin, and the driving rain blurred his goggles. "I daren't turn and that wood'll smash us up." The trees beneath looked alarmingly close and the airfield still far off. A strong gust of wind tipped a wing and he used it to grab some precious height. An idea came to him. "Hang on, Timmy!" and he pushed the stick forward. The DH4 nosed down sharply, heading for the forest and gathering speed.

Ignoring the yelp of alarm from the back seat, Roberts plunged the aircraft earthwards, gathering speed until at the last minute he hauled back hard on the stick and the DH4 soared up, trading speed for height for a few vital seconds. The useless propeller windmilled in front. The plane slowed, staggered and, just on the edge of a hammerhead stall, Roberts nosed her over to line up on the field ahead, now much closer. They might still just do it.

"Think we'll make it?" floated from the back seat.

"Might do, just…" Roberts was concentrating on holding the soggy airframe on the edge of a stall as they sank towards the green field ahead. Thank God the DH 4 had a flat glide angle. That's what comes of being given other chaps' kites, he thought. Old 164 was a rubbish kite. Always had been. That was why it was the squadron spare… The trees below whipped by faster and faster, rising to meet them until they became a blur. They were still too low. They weren't going to make it. The trees rose up to brush the undercarriage. At the last second Roberts hauled back on the stick and the wallowing DH4 rose one last time to clear the forest before dropping flat to meet the ground at the edge of the airfield.

They nearly made it. With a shattering crash that punched their spines and jarred their teeth, the aeroplane's tail hit the boundary hedge and collapsed on the ground, speared by the thick hedge. The undercarriage buckled under the near-vertical final descent, and Roberts saw stars as the DH4 crunched down, impaled on the hedge and stopped dead. The silence that followed seemed to Roberts the quietest thing he had ever heard in his life and seemed to last forever.

He shook his head to clear it. The stars faded and he could hear Timmy. The petrol was switched off, and apart from a ripped and missing tail-plane, the aircraft seemed surprisingly intact. The bottom wing lay flat along the ground, which seemed unnaturally close.

"You all right, Timmy?" he said, checking around. A distant lorry was driving through the rain towards them, he noticed, tiny figures holding on to the sides. "You all right?"

"Oh, absolutely," came the voice from the back. "Apart from having my spine pushed through the top of my head. D'you call that a landing! Bloody pilots …"

Roberts smiled. Timmy's voice betrayed his relief. Undoing the straps, they clambered out to survey the stricken aeroplane as a Crossley tender splashed to a stop beside them. Sjt Doughty squelched across the grass, his eyes taking in the wreck.

"You"ve done it this time, Sir. This 'un will not fly again, that's for sure." Looking at the airframe, Roberts had to agree. Flat on its belly, 164 would never fly again, borrowed or not. He noticed a gaping hole in the side of the nose by the engine. They'd been hit by archie. He looked into the engine space. A large piece of the engine block had been blown off. Half the engine seemed to be missing. So that was why it had stopped. Suddenly, he felt cold and very tired. The lowering clouds and gathering gloom added to his misery. He rubbed his head where he had banged it against the front of the cockpit and discovered to his astonishment a lump the size of a pigeon's egg on his forehead. It was very tender, and he winced.

"Better let me have a look at you, Robbie." Doc Moon emerged from the group around the stricken DH4. "You've taken a crack on the head."

"Good thing," said Timmy, clambering into the back of the Crossley. "Might knock some sense into him." He reached down a hand to help his pilot up. "Actually it was a damned good effort, Robby. I didn't think we were going to make it."

Contemplating his throbbing head, Roberts had to admit to himself that he had had his doubts, too. "Nor did I; damn lucky, we were." It never occurred to him that he had displayed consummate skill in nursing the crippled aircraft back to the aerodrome, or in squeezing the last 100 yards out of the ailing airframe to miss the trees. His thoughts were interrupted by the doctor.

"Well, no flyin' for your for a coupla days, boy. How're you feelin'?" Doc Moon probed his head as the Crossley lurched to a stop outside the squadron hut. "Headache? Blurred vision? Double vision? Feeling sick?"

"Just a headache, Doc. A bit sick. Dizzy."

"Hmm. Ah'm gonna take you off flyin' for a day or so, Robbie. See how that head of yours sets. We don' want you flyin' with concussion, now do we?"

"No, we damn well don't," said Timmy with feeling, as they got down into the gathering dusk. "I'm not sure I could go through that again. Tell you what, Robbie, you go and get your head down, and I'll do the flight report for the CO."

"My sentiments exactly, gen'lmen," said Doc Moon. "Ah'll give you some aspirin and then git to your cot, Robbie. There's no flyin' for you tomorrow. Take y'self a nice quiet day, now. Doctor's orders. And that was some flyin' by the way; we were all rightly impressed."

Despite his pounding head, Robbie smiled. Maybe this way he would get to see Françine again down at the café. That was good news.

For at least 24 hours, he had no problems.

*   *   *

Two hundred miles away in London, Manfield Cumming was dealing with Stube's "little problem". London knew exactly what to do with

244

problems like this; or at least Manfield Cumming knew. He had decided the previous morning what he had to do. The man who could look after Everitt sat across from him, smoking a cigarette and listening intently.

Cumming looked over his man carefully.

The officer the world knew as Major Angus Rice of the 60th Rifles was as good a man as you'd find for a job like this, he thought. Officially a member of the War Office's "Military Operations 2" branch, Rice's credentials for Special Operations were impeccable. He had volunteered from university in 1914 and gone over the top at Loos in 1915. Two days later, the lean dark subaltern was commanding the few shocked survivors of his company, and by the end of that year was leading his own Greenjacket company as an acting Captain. He had gone into the hell of the Somme in 1916, taking over as a battalion commander after all his senior officers had been killed or wounded, and won one of the new-fangled Military Crosses in the process. By the time he was wounded at Vimy in spring 1917, the skinny intense ex-university student had filled out and matured into a hard and rather grim-faced young man, with an air of taciturn maturity that belied his years.

Now, as a 25-year-old acting major in Meinerzhagen's Special Duties Section, he was tipped to become the first head of the joint "Special Operations Officers" organisation that C was trying to set up with the War Office. Dark, quiet and with a brooding air of menace, Rice didn't look like the sort of man you would like to cross, thought Cumming.

Rice stared back at the Head of the Secret Service. He'd done a couple of what he called nurse-maiding jobs for C before. Nothing too difficult. In fact, he wondered why the Navy made such a fuss about these things. Didn't they realise that there was a war on? He became aware the Cumming was speaking.

"So, d'ye think that you can do this, Rice? I can't really order you. Neutral territory and so forth. But it's definitely your territory; Dutch mother and you've got the language."

Rice examined his cigarette. When he spoke, his voice was very low and very quiet. "I don't see any problem at all, Sir." He pulled at the cigarette and looked at Cumming. "When would you like me to talk to Everitt?"

C was slightly taken aback by the younger man's calm and self-assurance.

"Well, as soon as possible, Rice. As soon as possible."

"Will you telegraph him to let him know I'm coming?"

"Of course. He'll probably be grateful for an escort. He was quite jumpy, you know – before he left."

Rice nodded. "Well, he'll be pleased to see me then?"

"Absolutely."

"Just like the last chap?"

Cumming nodded. "Just like the last one." He looked hard at the young major. "You know what to do."

Rice nodded, stood up and smoothed his uniform. By 1918 uniform was the best camouflage for the more secret denizens of Whitehall. "I'll be on my way then, Sir. Can you let him know that I'll meet him at the docks tomorrow? I haven't much time. I'll get the night packet boat to the Hook"

"Of course," Cumming responded mechanically as the lean figure adjusted his cap, saluted and let himself out.

"Goodbye," Cumming said to his empty office.

That young man rather scared him, truth to tell.

CHAPTER 27

Stube's Unusual Cheese

OHL FORWARD HEADQUARTERS

Saturday 16th March

At OHL, Stube was a little scared.

If Wendel – or anyone else for that matter - comes in now, he thought, I'm finished. For the umpteenth time he checked the door of his hotel room to reassure himself that it was locked ,and that the chair he had wedged under the door handle was still in place.

The OHL Security Officer would have been astonished if he had been able to see into the Press Chief's room. On a blanket across the bed lay four small sticks of dynamite, the length of a man's finger. Stube himself was busy scooping out a hole in a large flat yellow Gouda cheese. The label and a circular plug of cheese lay to one side and he was using a spoon to delicately carve out an exact space for his bomb inside the cheese. A pile of discarded strong smelling *oude Gouda* lay on a cloth. Satisfied with his efforts, he tried inserting the explosive tubes once more into the cheese. He still couldn't fit all four in. Grunting, he returned to his strange task.

Stube had originally planned to plant his bomb on 20th of March - just five days away – for maximum effect. Hindenburg and Ludendorff had called a final *KaiserSchlacht* staff conference for noon on that date. Stube had originally planned for the bomb to primed and waiting in the staff meeting too. He himself was not invited. However, since Everitt had recognised him, he felt the need to hurry and bring things forward. You never knew. The big Dutch cheese had given him another idea.

He wasn't too worried. He felt he could talk his way out of any allegations coming from a half-drunk English spy, desperate to save his own skin, should the need ever arise. But he just didn't want to take unnecessary risks. So the sooner he did what he had to do, the better. He went on hollowing out a space in the cheese. Occasionally he picked up a piece and nibbled it. It was excellent cheese and went well with the glass of *oude Jenever* liqueur gin on his bedside table. He tried fitting the tiny clock timer inside the yellow wheel and smiled. At least his job gave him access to the better things of life, like good liquor and good cheese, even in the middle of the biggest war the world had ever known.

As he fitted the dynamite sticks into their hollows he smiled again. Major Wendel had been almost speechless the day before when Stube had presented him with a Dutch *Maasdam* cheese of the highest quality, a kilo of real coffee and half a dozen bottles of cognac. Wendel had insisted on paying for the brandy, so in order to allay suspicion he had accepted the Security Major's money. He suspected the Bavarian aristocrat could well afford it, although his Jewish orderly had grumbled when he had been given Wendel's newly acquired booty to lock away. Now, *there* was a sharp one, thought Stube. Weissmüller might only be a Corporal, but he was no fool. One to watch, and close to Wendel, too, Stube thought; he might be able to use Weissmüller one day.

With a grunt of satisfaction, he slotted the timer into its place. Now it all fitted tightly. There. Apart from the detonator, the cheese bomb was complete. Stube smiled. He liked the idea of a bomb made of cheese. It appealed to his sense of humour. Now all he had to do was smuggle it onto the Command train tomorrow and get it into Ludendorff's dining car. The First Quartermaster general and Hindenburg were planning a final inspection at Rupprecht's Army Group HQ, going from Avesnes north to Mons by train. That was a perfect chance of getting access to the Duo.

Stube eased the detonator in and made sure the bomb was safe. Getting his hands on four half-sized sticks of military dynamite had been easy enough, even for him, and detonators were two a penny in wartime, but the timing clock was the vital piece. He lacked the skill to rig an alarm clock. However, the purpose built mechanical timer inside the Gouda cheese would do the job perfectly. As he checked and set it carefully, he marvelled again at the carriage clock's tiny golden precision. It was a beautiful piece of workmanship. A shame it had to be destroyed. He looked down at it for one last time and pressed the label in to cover his excavations.

The dynamite had begun to sweat, and the marzipan stink of it on his hands made his head ache. Still, a shame the little gold clock had to go. It really was beautiful. And he was going to destroy it. It was like burning a painting. But that, thought Stube grimly, was the madness of war. At least, after too many years, he could now do more than just spy and report on the idiots who had caused this madness.

He let his memory roam back to that dreadful hot evening in Berlin in 1914. He had been horrified. Ambassador Wallenstein, normally the gentlest of men, had been pink with excitement, shouting, "War at last! *Der Tag*! Now the day of reckoning has come! Victory!" Bloody fool. How could getting mired in a war with the rest of Europe be a *victory*? Idiots. He rocked back on his heels and let the tide of memory flood over him.

That supposedly secret Conclave in Potsdam on the 5th of July 1914. According to an excited Wallenstein, proud to boast of his presence in the inner councils of the Reich, that militaristic idiot Warlord of a Kaiser had gone round the room, asking all the senior generals and financiers if they were ready for war. Stube had met a General Staff officer later at the War Ministry and asked him if it was true that there had been a *KaiserKonferenz* the day before. With true Prussian hauteur the Colonel had refused to answer, apart from saying that Prussia – *Prussia* mind you! – and the Army was always ready for war, and that journalists who dared to ask impertinent questions of the Great General Staff were mere scum who deserved a good thrashing.

A good thrashing! Stube felt himself grow hot with the memory. He remembered his father, angry and red-faced, always shouting; his father waving his belt, about to thrash him for some trivial childish misdeed; his mother, scared and afraid. Always afraid. Oh yes, he remembered the old tyrant. Stube remembered the long diatribes about the glories of Germany and the Greater German Reich. He remembered his father extolling the virtues of the Kaiser and Germany's destiny. "*Prussia, whose stern people alone knew how to lead Germany to her golden place in the sun: and you, my son, must learn the harsh discipline of a good German*". The memory of a hundred petty brutalities from his childhood flooded into his mind.

Stube had been amazed at the English when he had first met them in South Africa. They were completely unlike anything he had seen. At first he had despised them. They were everything the Germans derided and the Americans were not. The English were casual, lazy, relaxed and clever. They didn't try too hard and even laughed at their own stupidities. Even the harsh realities of Imperial expansion had been almost apologetic. After a while he had found himself liking the English, even the snooty Milords of the cavalry, who had welcomed him into their tents on the Veldt and laughed at the battles they had to fight. These were no arrogant conquerors, but rather diffident bringers of law.

If one single thing had made him realise where he wanted his loyalties to really be, it was on the night of the peace in South Africa. The British had treated the vanquished Boers with incredible leniency. All the international war correspondents were agreed on that. The British had behaved very decently towards their foes. When that night at the end of the war, Colonel Henderson had raised his glass to the Boers and proclaimed a toast to, "*a truly gallant foe*" and all the English – and the Scottish officers – had raised their glasses, Stube knew. That hot night at Pretoria, Stube had looked around and suddenly realised that here were truly the men of the new century; decent, brave, magnanimous and genuine *gentlemen*. The English had meant it, too. Unlike the Kaiser's *Reich*, these were good people.

But later, Brinkmann the *Frankfurter Allgemeine* man, had been scathing. "Weak!" he had boomed in the hotel bar, his red beefy face flushed by drink and sun. "Weak. Weak! *Weak!* The English are weak and decadent and soft. That is why Germany will one day crush this ridiculous empire of theirs." He banged his fist on the table, reminding Stube of his father all those years ago, as Brinkmann glared round at his three German press colleagues. "I drink to the Greater *Reich*! A real Empire of hard men and iron rule. And to The Day! To Germany!" and they had all risen and cheered.

Suddenly the rebellious soul of the little German boy of so long ago had seen something truly better than the harsh brutalities of *Preussens Gloria*, "Prussia all Glorious!" For Stube, loud-mouthed pigs like Brinkmann, Prussian militarism and its entire works had to be opposed and stopped, just like his father's petty brutalities and household tyrannies. Now he saw, at last, his chance to really make a difference. Prussia was a bully, as his father had been. Brinkmann was a prime example. Germany was in thrall to a militaristic bunch of Prussian madmen.

Stube had realised that his loyalty was to something better than the bullying bombast of Prussia and the Army. A "real empire"? Well that meant British decency, with justice and fair play. Now that was something. They had even treated the natives like human beings most of the time, which was more than the Boers ever did. He smiled. The British were even relaxed about their timings, he thought as he set the little golden clock for 13.00 – one o'clock – precisely. Hindenburg might be a little erratic; but everyone knew that Ludendorff ruled his life, his staff and his family, by the clock. Very Prussian. Just like father, he thought with a grimace.

He held his breath and pressed the timer. It clicked softly into place. Done.

There – it was done. The cheese bomb would go off at one o'clock precisely the following day, on Ludendorff's staff train. That would show them. A final thought obtruded into his mind: Really, he should try and keep Wendel out of the danger area. The Bavarian major was a decent chap and deserved better; but as for Ludendorff, von Zelle and the rest of that stiff-necked bunch… He finished the Jenever and began to tidy up. What to do with the pile of cheese scrapings? He couldn't eat it all. He'd have to throw it out. Pity.

Suddenly, like a toothache, the memory of that *verdammte* courier with the ginger beard in Rotterdam came to mind. Bloody man, sitting there gawping up at him like a fool. He could ruin everything. Well, he'd warned London.

As he put the prepared cheese with its sealed plug and label back in place under the bed, he could only hope that London knew how to deal with it. He'd got his own problems to deal with now. And sleeping above a primed time bomb seemed about the most dangerous.

*   *   *

Next morning, Stube ambled across the tracks to the waiting OHL command train. Further down, all was bustle and activity as staff clerks and officers prepared for departure.

It was a grey morning with fog drifting in patches. He could see baskets of files and documents being passed up into the *StabsHauptQuartier* officers' carriage, with its half windows and closed off sides. It looked like a buffet car, he thought wryly. Stube's personal target really was the buffet car, or to be more accurate, the kitchen car in the middle of the train. Before that all was headquarters staff and senior officer territory; in the middle was the second kitchen car for the junior ranks, and their quarters in the last six carriages. Someone had put a set of steps alongside the open central door of the senior officers' kitchen car. Climbing up, he met a white-coated chef, a wicked looking meat cleaver in his hand.

Stube knew him. It was Senior Cook Serjeant Redl, who had worked before the war in the Adler Hotel in Berlin and was now head chef in the Officers' Mess at OHL.

"*Herr* Redl. Good to see you."

"*Herr* Stube, likewise." The chef beamed and gestured at the large canvas bag Stube was carrying. "What have you got there? We don't often see you in the kitchens." He liked Stube.

"Ah. Well, it's a surprise, Redl." Stube swung the bag onto a serving trolley and reached inside. Further down the kitchen car, a couple of junior cooks looked up curiously then went back to their work. Stube took out the big yellow-grey *Oude Gouda* cheese and laid it on the table. It was well over a foot across and four inches thick. The bright yellow label in the centre concealed his excavations to hide the dynamite.

"Now that's what I call a cheese." Redl stroked it admiringly. He cocked his head. "*Oude Gouda*. You don't often see that nowadays. What a cheese, *Herr* Stube!"

"Only from Holland, Redl." Stube's manner was easy, relaxed. "I promised it as a surprise to the generals' table from my last trip." He reached inside the canvas bag again and took out another couple of packets. "And something extra for you, I think. One, that's two kilos of real coffee. Two, there's some real gerookt haring – that's not for the *prominenten*, you understand, that's for you and the cooks." Redl muttered a "thank you" as he took the Dutch smoked herring but Stube continued, "and three, here's a bottle of Scotch whisky and a packet of real Earl Grey tea for *you*, Herr Redl."

Redl beamed, his large moustache moving sideways as his teeth gleamed. "Earl Grey? Wonderful. Outstanding! *Vielen Dank, Herr* Stube!" He stroked the pile of groceries on the table. "Ah, what it is to see real stuff again. What with the rationing it is all rubbish nowadays. Even for the High Command. And Earl Grey?"

"That, Herr Redl, is for you, not for the officers, you understand. I know how much you enjoy your tea." This was greeted by a scornful, "Ha!" from one of the junior chefs down the kitchen car. Redl's weakness for Earl Grey tea was a running joke between the two men. When Redl had wished he could see real Scotch whisky and real English tea once again, Stube had jokingly asked the chef which he would prefer, to which Redl had replied, "The tea, naturally," to much laughter.

"Now," said Stube, "to business." He patted the cheese. "What time do you serve lunch?"

"Twelve thirty. *Herr* Ludendorff is very exact about these things - most exact."

Stube knew that. Most of the headquarters knew Ludendorff's clockwork-like routine by heart. "Well, I want you to take the cheese in at the end of lunch. It's a surprise. What time will that be?"

Redl knew exactly. "The coffee must be served at one o'clock precisely, *Herr* Stube. Then the General eats a little cheese, perhaps some fruit with his coffee. Lunch ends at one fifteen exactly. You can set your watch by the general."

"Excellent! Well, Redl, take the cheese in with the coffee and place it on the table. I want it to be surprise. Herr Ludendorff likes his cheese, I know."

Redl nodded and reached for a knife.

"No, no!" exclaimed Stube. "Don't cut it! Let them have a sight of it whole. They can cut it at the table. Tell them it's a very special cheese and I promised to bring a whole cheese. Show it to them."

Redl shrugged. "As you wish. I expect that they will be grateful. Do I tell Altmann it came from you?" Altmann was the generals' butler.

"No need. Just tell him not to cut the cheese before he takes it in. You understand?"

Redl shrugged. "As you wish."

Stube turned to go down the steps onto the railway siding. It was a misty morning and the watery outline of the OHL *Château* loomed ghostly through the fog.

"Aren't you coming?" asked the cook.

"Oh yes," said Stube. "But my place is in the first car, with the staff officers, not back here with your smart set, *Herr* Redl." Redl grinned and tossed the tea in the air to catch it. "Earl Grey, eh? Many thanks, *Herr* Stube."

"Nothing to thank me for, Redl, my friend. See you at Mons." With a wave, Stube and his now-empty canvas bag went into the mist to get his overnight bag, just in case. Experience at OHL had taught him that it was always best to be prepared. In war, anything could happen. Even the First Quartermaster General's OHL Command train didn't always run on time.

Now that, thought Stube, would really piss old Ludendorff off.

CHAPTER 28

The Bomb

OHL COMMAND TRAIN,
THE FRENCH BELGIAN BORDER

Sunday 17th March 1918

By 11.00, exactly on time, the Command train was chugging slowly north heading for Mons.

Hindenburg had come on board at the last minute, his ponderous progress marked by a small platoon of aides and anxious staff officers. The *FeldMarschall*'s mere presence had a way of making his immediate staff nervous. Not as much as Ludendorff though, thought Stube. The First Quartermaster General was already on board, fussing over the agenda for his meeting with Rupprecht at Mons.

Stube was in the second carriage back, with the middle ranking staff officers. The carriage had been opened up into a single large room and equipped as a travelling office. Stube had nothing to do and lounged in a wicker chair in the corner, idly flicking the pages of an old French magazine and watching the bustle of the staff. Clerks came and went carrying papers.

"Ah, paper," thought Stube, "Where would we be without it? How could the war be fought without paper?" He chuckled at the thought.

"A humorous magazine, *Herr* Stube?"

Stube looked up to see the short, immaculate figure of Major Wendel standing over him. "Ah, *Herr* Major. Nothing so good, sadly. What brings you forward to this travelling post office?"

Wendel smiled. Stube's description of the General Staff office car was apt. "A small announcement." He clapped his single hand on the carriage side for silence. The chatter stilled. The slow clack of the train's wheels could be clearly heard as it swayed over some points.

"Pay attention!" he called. "We've just heard that the Tommies are bombing the railways up ahead, so we may be delayed."

"Bombing? In this fog, *Herr* Major?" said a voice.

"*Ja*. In this fog. Maybe it's not so foggy up there. The airmen tell me that the sky is a big place. Anyway, we may be delayed." Wendel looked at the clock on the wall. It read 12.15. "I came back to tell you that *Oberst* von Zelle says that we will now plan to be at Mons for about 13.35. So get your lunch meal on the train. And if we stop it's because of the English bombers. All understood?"

A hubbub of nods and chatter greeted his announcement. Wendel turned back to Stube. "Will you lunch?"

Stube shook his head. "No, I think I'll give lunch a miss today. I'll just wait until Ludendorff and Rupprecht have sorted themselves out and I've something to say about *der Tag*."

Wendel smiled at the press man. "Not long now, Stube. Not long. And this mist will help us on the day, if it stays." He turned to go. "Now I must get my meal. Some of us have to eat, you know."

A sudden stab of alarm hit Stube. "Not with the Generals?"

Wendel guffawed. "*Nein, nein*, Herr Stube! The likes of mere staff majors don't get invited to the senior officers' mess. No, I will eat with the general staff in the staff dining car. You sure you won't join me?"

Stube shook his head. The clock read 12.20.

*   *   *

At exactly 12.30, the door of the senior officers' dining car swung open and Hindenburg and Ludendorff walked in. Four places were set at the polished mahogany table in the middle of the half-carriages reserved for the senior officers' mess. Silver and glasses gleamed and white napkins were neatly folded. Altmann, the Mess Serjeant, stood rigidly to attention at the entrance to the kitchen car. Ludendorff grunted his approval.

"Just us?" rumbled Hindenburg.

"*Ja, Herr Feldmarschall*," Altmann nodded obsequiously. "General Bruchmüller went on ahead."

Ludendorff grunted and sat down heavily, studying the handwritten menu: goulasch, noodles, salad. A glass of Rhine wine. cheese, fruit and coffee. He nodded his approval. A simple meal was all that was required of soldiers. With men fighting and dying, the High Command and General Staff should set an example of frugality.

He nodded to Altmann to start serving and addressed Hindenburg, still officially his superior. "Is Rupprecht still complaining about lack of stores?" he began.

Altmann started to pour the wine. The clock said 12.32 exactly.

*　　　　*　　　　*

The squeal of brakes and the blowing off of steam surprised the whole train. After the first lurch, it glided gently to a stop. Signal stops were not unusual in wartime, but after about 5 minutes, curious faces began to stare out of open carriage windows. The engine had stopped alongside a signal box and eventually the officer of the day came back towards the train commander. Von Zelle was annoyed. He knew that delay would infuriate the Duo, particularly Ludendorff. The Staff Colonel leant out of the door window, scowling at the hapless Captain standing to attention down on the track.

"Well?" snapped von Zelle.

"English bombing, *Herr Oberst.* The Tommies have bombed the rail yard up ahead near Valenciennes."

"Where are we now?"

"The signal box is Artres Sud, *Herr Oberst.*"

Von Zelle compressed lips with irritation. "How long a delay, *Kapitän?*"

The duty officer looked blank. "They said they didn't know, *Herr Oberst.* Not long, though. We have the highest priority on the line." He looked up. Somewhere above them in the fog they heard the drone of aero engines, gradually fading. "That's probably them now, *Herr Oberst,*" he added.

"*Lieber Gott!*" von Zelle cursed. "I'd better inform the *Feld Marschall.* We're going to be late." He pulled out his pocket watch. It read 12.49.

*　　　　*　　　　*

Stube was watching out of the train window at the discussion on the trackside and saw the orderly officer trudge back towards the panting engine and the signalbox at the front of the train. He looked at his watch. Not long now. His mouth was suddenly dry. What if the cheese was discovered? What if it didn't work or didn't go off? He shrugged the thoughts aside. The train panted and waited. It was 12.51.

*   *   *

Von der Zelle's assessment that Ludendorff would be angry at the delay was entirely accurate. Ludendorff turned pink with rage. "But we'll be late for *Prinz* Rupprecht!"

Hindenburg looked at his companion mildly. "My dear Ludendorf, not everything can be controlled in war," he said, swilling his Rhine wine and gesturing to Altmann. "Remember your Clausewitz, neh? *"The friction of war"*." Ludendorff glared at him. In his view, Paul von Hindenburg was too damned easygoing, too… He spluttered at the thought – too Austrian sometimes.

Altmann cleared away, studiously ignoring the tension in the air. Cheese, gentlemen?" he enquired.

"Ja, ja," Ludendorff said absently. He pulled out his watch. 12.55. They were going to be late. And all because of a bunch of damned English flyers! This was intolerable. He snapped at Altmann, "Get me General Marcks, or his Air Service representative. Now!

"Immediately, *Herr* General," Altmann opened the door to the rest of the train and spoke in a low tone to Ludendorff's personal staff officer, who pulled a face and disappeared down the train. Altmann went back to his silent generals. The atmosphere was poisonous. The butler looked at the small wooden clock on the sideboard. 12.56 – time for cheese and coffee. He went through the carriage door into the kitchen car and re-appeared a minute later wheeling the trolley with Stube's yellow cheese and the fruit decorating it.

Ludendorff looked up, his face choleric. "No, no," he snapped. "No cheese today; just get us coffee."

Hindenburg looked as if he might remonstrate with his subordinate and colleague, but decided against it. When Ludendorff was like this it was better to humour him. He nodded to Altmann, who wheeled the cheese trolley out of the mess carriage towards the kitchen. Overhead, above the fog, an aeroplane droned on its mission.

"And cut the cheese, Altmann," shouted Ludendorff after the butler. "Don't serve it in great chunks like that again. This is a gentlemen's mess, not a grocery store!"

Altmann muttered under his breath and pushed the trolley into the steamy kitchen car. Redl, the chef, looked up.

"No cheese today?"

"Baby's in a bad mood, Redl. No cheese today and it's to be cut in future."

The Cook Serjeant grunted. "Not again. Oh well." A sudden thought struck him. "*Herr* Stube will be disappointed." In the next carriage the Westminster chimes of the clock on the mess sideboard struck one. Ludendorff pulled out his watch and frowned at it.

Further down the train, Stube casually took out his watch, braced himself for the explosion and tried to compose his features. One o'clock precisely. His heart thumped under his ribs.

Nothing happened.

*   *   *

Ludendorff was working himself into a rage. They had now been stuck at the signals for over 20 minutes. They were definitely going to be late. Worse still, the coffee was filthy muck. "Altmann !" he bellowed.

The general Officers' butler was at that precise moment next door in the kitchen car pushing a large, shiny kitchen knife into the Oude Gouda cheese. If the *Feld-Marschall* wanted cheese cut, thought Altmann, then he would get it cut. But, butler's privilege, he got to taste the cheese first. He sliced a small thin V -haped segment for himself and bit into it, handing the kitchen knife to the head chef. It really was excellent cheese. Altmann nodded to Redl, who plunged the knife deep into the heart of the cheese.

Whether the timer clock was running late or broken we will never know. Whether Redl disturbed the detonator or cut the trip switch will always remain a mystery.

With a blinding flash and a roar, two pounds of military-strength dynamite exploded in a confined space.

The strong steel underframe of the carriage directed most of the blast upwards. Altmann and Redl died instantly, blown to obscene lumps of unrecognisable bloody flesh. The wooden roof and sides of the kitchen car were blown upwards and outwards. The two assistant cooks in the kitchen car were hurled against the back wall, maimed, deafened and burned. In the next carriage, Hindenburg and Ludendorff were almost thrown from their chairs by the blast. The connecting doors between the carriages swung open, blowing in a billow of reeking smoke into the generals' mess room.

The explosion played strange tricks.

Colonel Von Zelle, standing by the signal box up ahead and remonstrating up at an imbecile of a Belgian signalman, heard it as a dull boom, followed by a mushroom of greasy grey-black smoke blowing away on the breeze. He stood open-mouthed, irresolute, as fragments of wood and wreckage pattered down. Falling glass tinkled all about him. As if in slow motion a wicked looking spike of broken glass suddenly embedded itself in his forearm, sticking up like a dagger. Von Zelle looked down with astonishment at the pink film of blood slowly soaking through his grey uniform sleeve.

Wendel, inside the train, two carriages up, heard it as a thud that made the carriage shake, and jumped out to run back towards the commanders' carriage.

Further up the train, Stube had put his watch away, wondering what had gone wrong; he heard the explosion as a kind of "crack".

What everyone could hear in the silence that followed was the receding drone of an aeroplane engine far overhead. Then everything was chaos and shouting.

Thank God, thought Stube. I've done it. Now the war really will be ended. We've got rid of Hindenburg and Ludendorff.

The war was over.

*   *   *

Wendel sprinted back to the stricken carriage.

He had jumped down onto the track to make better progress and it was hard to run well on the crunchy ballast. His single arm made running feel unbalanced. A group of shocked onlookers was already scrambling around the wreck, officers and soldiers mixed together.

The front half of the wooden kitchen coach had been blown away, exposing the built in stoves and kitchen units to the sky. The underframe seemed intact on its wheels, but splintered bits of wood stuck up and half the carriage roof was gone. Glass crackled underfoot. Hindenburg and Ludendorff were standing on the track by their coach, looking back. As he skidded to a halt, Wendel heard Ludendorff say, "… the hand of Providence is upon us. Truly this is God's miracle." He gestured to the sky where a faint drone could still be heard above the clearing mist. "Another ten metres and we too might have been victims, too, *Herr Feld Marschall*."

Paul von Hindenburg was saying nothing, his chin low on his collar, his bull neck wrinkled. He was watching the train guard platoon passing down the two wounded under-chefs and laying them on the trackside. One of them was whimpering with pain and fright. A medical orderly was bending over them.

Stube walked back.

By the time he got to the scene, he realised he had failed.

With a sense of shock, he saw it was his two intended victims deep in conversation by the train. The kitchen car stood ragged, smoking, one end blown open to the sky, a crowd of soldiers staring and talking. A Signal Corps NCO was already up a telegraph pole, clipping telephone cable to the wires. He heard crackling glass beneath his shoes and stopped. The debris of the explosion was scattered all around the wrecked car. With a feeling of disgust, he noticed a bloodied eyeball lying on the trackside and ominous red lumps of what looked like raw meat lying around. What on earth had gone wrong?

He walked forward, just in time to hear Ludendorff speaking to *Major* von Körtge, the train commander standing to attention in front of the little knot of senior officers. "… leave you here to sort this mess out. We'll uncouple the back carriages and proceed to Mons. Any questions?"

Von Körtge clicked his heels. "*Jawohl, Herr Feld Marschall.*" He saluted and spun on his heels, snapping orders and pointing. Körtge was from the 4th Prussian Guards Regiment, a no-nonsense, common sense young man. If anyone could sort the mess out, he could.

Ludendorff saw Stube standing by and beckoned him over. "Not a word of this must come out, Stube. You understand? The papers must not get to hear of this."

Stube nodded. He was still in shock. What the hell had happened?

Ludendorff was still speaking. "…if the Tommies get the slightest hint that they only missed us by a split second, they will try again; depend on it. How they found us in this fog is a mystery. None of this must appear in the press, Stube. You understand?"

Stube nodded again.

Ludendorff turned to Wendel. "And you, Wendel, find out who knew our route. The English airmen must have known we were coming. The train, the time, everything."

Stube couldn't believe his ears.

My God, he thought, he doesn't realise. He thinks it was an aeroplane bomb! A wave of relief washed over him.

"And you, Wendel."

The Security Major stood to attention as Ludendorff addressed him directly. "You find that spy, and quick. He must be something to do with the railway people. These wretched Belgians and French hate our guts. The swine would betray their grandmothers to the English. Let us hope that he hasn't given away the *Kaiserschlacht* attack date as well, for all our sakes. Now let us proceed to Mons. We are already behind schedule. And not a word!"

He looked back at the scene of organised bustle. A shocked von Zelle was having his arm bandaged by an orderly and complaining about the damage to his uniform. Another colonel with a double Iron Cross was telling him that it was an honourable wound, and he'd probably get a medal for it. A grim-faced Hindenburg was starting to climb back up to the general officers' carriage. Two soldiers were uncoupling the wrecked kitchen car. Ludendorff was nodding with satisfaction. Amazing! Thought Stube. He hasn't even asked about the dead, let alone the wounded. How very Prussian. He caught Wendel's eye and they returned to the front carriage. Wendel crunched along the ballast beside the press man.

"So, Herr Wendel, we have a railway spy?"

Wendel shrugged. "These damned railwaymen report everything they see, Stube. You know that. Spies, pigeons… And then again, with a plane bomb it could have been pure chance."

Stube agreed. Anything to put Wendel off the scent. "Yes, I heard the plane distinctly…"

Wendel stopped at the carriage steps. "One thing bothers me, though…"

Stube looked down at Wendel as he clambered up to the door.

Wendel shook his head. "*Ja*. It was a very small explosion for an aircraft bomb."

Stube reached down to take Wendel's good arm and help him up the steps. "Maybe it was one of their little ones."

The security major dusted his jacket down. "Maybe. It's odd, though." He glanced up at his orderly. "Ah, Weissmüller, just the man. Get me all the details of the OHL train orders, please. We must find out who knew about this journey. And when."

"Apart from the people on the train, *Herr* Major?"

"Of course." Wendel paused. "For the moment, anyway."

Weissmüller started to go, then stopped. "By the way, Herr Major, who was hurt?"

"Oh, didn't you hear, Weissmüller? I thought you staff clerks knew everything first. It was old Altmann, the butler. And that nice cook Serjeant – what was his name? Ah yes – Redl, that was his name. Poor devils. Blown to bits." He shook his head. "Ah well, at least it was quick."

Stube suddenly felt slightly sick. He'd liked Redl. He was a good man. Inconsequentially he wondered what had happened to the chef's Earl Grey tea he'd passed on. Bloody Ludendorff.

The great bomb plot had failed. What the hell had gone wrong?

CHAPTER 29

Everitt's Homecoming
THE HOOK OF HOLLAND

Sunday 17ᵗʰ March 1918

"I was beginning to wonder if something had gone wrong. The overnight boat isn't usually late," Everitt addressed his guest.

Major Rice was a big man. Unsmiling he looked the ginger-bearded sailor up and down as they shook hands. "No, just a bit of delay off the harbour, old man. We had to dock in daylight, apparently."

Everitt smiled. "Submarines. They're always worried about them. Well, now you're here. Am I pleased to see you, old man." He lifted Rice's valise grip and walked towards the terminal. The wind off the North Sea was cold and a shrieking pack of seagulls pecked and worried at something on the dockside. The black hull of the Holland line ferry, "*De Jong*", loomed over them, a huge Dutch flag painted on the side.

They tramped across the quay. "What time are we due out?"

"We sail back at eight o'clock tonight." Rice looked at his watch. "That's twelve hours to kill."

Everitt was excited, pleased at the company. "Come on, old man. I'll show you Rotterdam. It's only 10 miles down the line, and a damn sight better than the Hook for killing time, I can tell you. We've plenty of time." Everitt dropped his voice. "By the way, what's your cover? Just in case I have to introduce you."

Rice grunted. "Dutch. *Mynheer* Meiner Reisz. I'm in beef. South America. But don't you worry, I've got all the right papers. Speak the language."

"Good man. We don't want you getting interned as an undercover combatant by the Dutchies, now do we?" Rice lapsed into silence as Everitt chattered on.

The truth was that he found his unexpected visitor's manner a little off-putting. He'd been delighted – no, he thought, relieved – when C had sent the telegram saying he was sending someone to act as a bodyguard. Even in neutral Holland, he still felt at risk. The Germans could still kidnap him, spirit him over the border, and then what? He shivered. And he had been looking forward to the companionship of a fellow officer. Truth was, it was a lonely life as a spy.

But this new bodyguard from London wasn't at all what he had expected. Not only was he a large man who somehow exuded an air of menace, but his brooding, dark presence made Everitt feel distinctly uncomfortable. Even on such a short acquaintance it was clear that Major Rice was a singularly unapproachable companion. They shared a pot of coffee in silence in the buffet as they waited for the tram to Rotterdam.

Everitt contemplated the steamed-up windows and desperately tried to think of something to say. "So, what were your orders?" he began. "C didn't say much."

Rice stared at him. "What did his telegram say?"

Everitt blinked. "That he was sending someone out to keep an eye on me, and help me home. In veiled speech, of course. Commercial code."

Rice nodded slowly. "Well, if that's what he said, that's exactly what I'm here to do, Everitt."

There was another long pause. Everitt broke in, "What do we do if there's any trouble?"

Rice smiled, if a mirthless sideways pull of his mouth was indeed a smile, and opened his coat. A pistol nestled in a holster on his waist-band. "We're prepared. But there won't be any trouble." He let the coat flap back and patted the gun, staring at his companion.

Everitt found himself gabbling, even more nervous. The grim Major Rice was a disconcerting colleague, let alone a guest for a run ashore in Rotterdam. "What sort of gun is it?"

Again, that eternity and the searching stare before Rice replied. "It's a point three-two Colt hammerless automatic pistol, model 1905, if that means anything to you." The enigmatic Major Rice patted his waistband again. "American. But I don't think we'll be needing it, do you?"

Everitt shook his head. Rice and his gun made him nervous.

The visitor sat back, his eyes flicking round the near-empty buffet. The seconds stretched to minutes. Everitt's sense of bafflement and unease increased. "Look," he said, "I think we should forget going into Rotterdam. What say you that we wait here until we can board? They'll let us up the gangplank at noon, and then we can rest in our cabin."

"Now that's a good idea." Rice looked Everitt up and down. "Better not to take any unnecessary risks, old chap. After all, we've got to get you back safe and sound, haven't we?"

Everitt nodded fervently. "I'll get us some more coffee."

Major Rice's unfathomable eyes watched him go up to the counter. The bodyguard's permanent watchfulness made Everitt distinctly uncomfortable, but he supposed that that was what these people did. He seemed a pretty tough customer, that was for sure. Perhaps C knew more about the risks than he was letting on? Everitt began to worry about just how safe he really was. Rice's presence brought his fears of a last minute German snatch to the surface again.

He chewed at a bitten fingernail as he waited for the coffee, aware of Major Rice's unblinking stare on him.

*   *   *

Everitt needn't have worried.

At just after noon, "Nils Pedersen", Norwegian ship's officer and Mynheer Meiner Reisz, "Uruguayan Beef Factor" of Fray Bentos, were allowed on board the Holland Line ferry, and spent the afternoon lounging in their cabin. Everitt offered Rice a glass of his schnapps, but the bodyguard refused and watched in silence as Everitt gulped it down in one. When at two o'clock, Everitt said "How about a spot of lunch?", Rice declined, and when the sailor went to the cabin door added, "Better stay in the cabin, old man, what? We don't want to take any unnecessary risks in harbour, do we?"

So Everitt lay on his bunk all afternoon, listening to his stomach rumbling, drinking schnapps and dozing. Rice sat in the corner, idly flicking the pages of a magazine and saying nothing. He ignored Everitt's feeble attempts at conversation and they both lapsed into silence. As a travelling companion, thought Everitt, Major Rice left much to be desired. That was the Army for you. But at least he felt safe with such a grim guardian.

At eight in the evening, their ferry sailed.

*　　　　*　　　　*

The morning's stiff breeze had abated, and the huge arc lights illuminating the Dutch flag painted on the ship's sides were reflected in the darkness of the sea as the SS *de Jong* set out on its illuminated overnight run from the Hook of Holland to Harwich. Neutral, Holland may have been, but the ship's careful owners were taking no chances of any unfortunate mis-identification by a prowling German U boat. The SS *de Jong* was positively ablaze with lights.

On board, all was light and noise. The mainly international passenger list thronged to the restaurant. The sea was calm, the food was good. Led by a hungry Everitt, Major Rice carefully locked the cabin door and followed. At their table for two, Everitt ordered gin, and worked his way through the menu, helped by a bottle of red wine. A careful observer would have noticed that Rice drank little, sipping a weak whisky and water, which he managed to make last the whole meal. All the time his eyes watched Everitt and their fellow passengers.

Everitt began to relax. With a bodyguard like Rice, and on a neutral ship in international waters, at last he felt safe. Pouring the last of the wine, he decided that Rice wasn't such a bad chap after all. A bit serious perhaps, but, he thought in his semi-drunken state, as good a fellow as you'd get, considering the job he had to do. A fellow would need to be pretty watchful if he was a bodyguard.

"You're sholly good bodyguard, y'know, Rice," he slurred. "Why don' we finish the evening off with a glass in the saloon?"

Somewhat to Everitt's surprise, Rice agreed. "Why not?" he eyed Everitt closedly. "You look as if you deserve a decent drink after all you've been through; and we're safe enough now. Follow me."

Everitt was even more surprised when Rice plonked a bottle of whisky and two glasses on the saloon table. "Fancy a cigar, old man? A real Havana, not those Dutch things." He handed Everitt a cigar, and splashed whisky into the glasses. As they lit up, Rice proposed a toast. "To England."

Everitt was astonished. Rice was actually smiling. "To England," he repeated mechanically and drained his glass.

Rice refilled it. "Must have been a hell of a time for you, old man, over there. I mean, what with the strain…"

Everitt waved his second glass before drinking heavily. "You're damn right. I don't think I've ever been so glad to see anyone as you this morning."

"Glad to hear it, old chap." He sipped his whisky and blew cigar smoke in the air. "By the by, d'you have your papers on you?"

"Courshe," slurred Everitt, patting his pocket. "Papers. Courshe."

"Can I see them? I've orders to give you a new set. Can I see them?"

"Courshe you can ol' man…" Everitt handed over his papers and temporary passport. Rice looked at them briefly and put them in his inside pocket. Everitt stared bleary eyed. "New papers?"

"In the cabin, old man; I'll give you the new set there." Rice raised his glass. "Well, here's to England, home and beauty. Drink up." They drank.

*   *   *

By one o'clock, Everitt was very drunk. The saloon was empty now and the sea getting up. The steward polishing glasses behind the bar bade his last two customers goodnight as Rice helped Everitt stagger out on to the deserted deck, rolling gently as the *de Jong* ploughed through the waves.

"Where'sh cabin?" he enquired.

A cold moon glinted high above. The freshening breeze had put a slight chop on the sea and the dazzlingly lit *de Jong* ploughed a white wake dead astern. The decks were deep in shadow as the lights reflected in the sea on either side, lighting up the huge painted Dutch flag. The chonk-chonk of the reciprocating engines and the surge of the sea were a steady noise, drowning out all other sounds.

Somewhat to Rice's surprise a solitary seagull was perched on the railings of the deck above them, one sleepy eye watching the two men below.

"Whatta moon," slurred Everitt. "I like the moon. Lovely moon. Beautiful."

"Are you all right, old man?" enquired Rice.

"Yesh, yesh. Jusht want to see moon. Nice moon. Beautiful moon, love the moon…"

"Here, let me help you," said Rice, as Everitt staggered to the side and looked up at the sky.

The stars were very bright, occasionally misted by high scudding cloud. The nearly full moon sailed between them. Everitt leaned on the rail and stared out to sea. He sighed deeply, taking in the blackness of the water, the splash of the waves below and the steady beat of the engines. He was happy. It was all over at last. Even in the shadow of the lifeboats, Rice could see the agent's eyes glittering with tears. They were alone on the deck.

Everitt sighed. "I'm drunk." He looked up at the sky again.

"You certainly are", said Rice. That made Everitt laugh.

"Anyway, it's all over now," he said.

"It certainly is," said Rice.

With one flowing movement he bent down, lifted Everitt's hips and slid him head first over the rail.

Everitt was too surprised and too drunk to resist or even to call out. He hit the water with a barely audible splash and went under as smoothly as a diver.

"It certainly is," Rice repeated to the empty deck, straightening his jacket. He looked around. No-one. He walked away.

Above his head, a solitary witness to the murder blinked in astonishment.

Then the seagull went back to sleep.

*   *   *

Everitt was too drunk to realise at first what had happened. To his dying moment he never realised that Rice had pitched him over the side.

Falling through the air for a second he thought he was flying. He had just started to react but the shock of hitting the icy water drove him under, gasping and spluttering for air. By the time his waterlogged clothes allowed him to wallow gasping to the surface, the *de Jong* was already a hundred yards away and receding fast in a blaze of lights. The freezing water drove the air from his lungs as he tried to shout when a wave splashed into his mouth and he choked. The cold bit into his bones as the lights of the ship went further and further away. Everitt splashed and futilely called for help for a minute or so.

The North Sea in March is an unforgiving place.

Gradually he felt the cold beginning to fade as he got used to it. Whether it was the drink or the sea, he suddenly realised he was very tired. He didn't care. Someone would be along to rescue him. Rice must have known he was in the water. He'd be up on the bridge in a flash, telling the Dutchie captain to turn the ship round and get help. Good chap, Rice. A bit grim, mind, but first-rate chap... Just had to stay afloat. His legs felt numb. He was tired and sleepy and floating. He relaxed and allowed sleep to carry him off, where he couldn't feel the cold. The lights of the ship went wavy. There! It was turning round.

His last sight was of the SS *de Jong*'s lights far off in the distance. The ship was still heading firmly on course for Harwich. But Everitt couldn't see that. A wave splashed in his face. It didn't feel cold at all...

Then Nicholas Everitt closed his eyes and quietly went to sleep.

*   *   *

Next morning, Freddie Browning came into C's office, his knock unanswered. He found Cumming at his desk, head down in his hands.

"You all right, C?" he enquired, anxiously. Cumming looked up. Browning thought he looked older and more tired than usual. The man was working too hard.

"Yes," He drew a deep breath. "Yes, I'm all right, Freddie." He sat up. "What can I do for you?"

"I just came in to see if that chap, Everitt, was back."

A flicker of something Browning didn't recognise flashed across C's face. Fright? Surprise?

"Oh yes, he's back all right. Rice telephoned me from Harwich earlier." He shuffled some papers on his desk, looking down. "Yes, it's all fixed."

"Rice?"

"Yes." Again Browning thought that a shadow passed across Cumming's face." He was the – er – bodyguard I sent out. All sorted now."

"Will he be coming here for a debrief?"

Cumming shook his head. "No, no. No need for that."

"What about Everitt? When's he coming in?"

Cumming shook his head. "He's not. Feller's gone on long leave. Needed it. No; we've put him out to grass at last."

Browning was astounded. "What, no debrief of an agent just returned from the field?" His voice trailed off. "Security?"

"Something like that."

Browning considered. "Last mission? Well, that's what you promised, C. That's what you promised, after all."

Cumming brightened. "Yes, I did, didn't I?"

"What about Major Rice? Will he be coming in – to report?"

Cumming's face darkened.

"No. No need. The job's done. It's all done and dusted. Don't need to see Rice; and young Everitt won't be working for us any more. Out to pasture for good this time. Earned a rest. Feller did his bit."

He dropped a pile of papers into the out-tray. "Now look, Freddie, be a good chap and go down to the message room for me, will you? Dame Blanche have apparently sent a pigeon saying that the Air Service bombed Ludendorff's OHL train. Go and see if it's true for me, eh?"

Baffled – for he had been expecting a debrief on such an important mission as Everitt's – Freddie Browning went off on his errand. He wondered what that civil servant chappie… *Neville*, that was his name – would make of it all.

*   *   *

A couple of days later, purely by chance, Browning was taking a file back to the Registry. On an impulse he asked Margaret Coombs, the severe head-matron type who ran the Registry Room if he could see Everitt's file.

"Certainly, sir. It's right here." She reached down behind her desk. Puzzled, he looked at her. "It's just come back from C's office," she explained. "It's going to be closed."

He raised his eyebrows, took the blue folder and glanced inside. A photograph of a younger, unbearded Nicky Everitt stared dispassionately up at him. He flipped back to front through a mass of papers. Some were press cuttings, some were in incomprehensible Scandinavian languages. There was a hastily printed German handbill in heavy black type. "Quite a career," he thought. He flipped to the final entry on the front of the thick bundle of foolscap.

It was a freshly typed discharge certificate. His eyes flicked down to the signature, a hastily scrawled green ink "C", then wandered back up the page. He stopped at a line marked,

"Reason for Discharge: DD."

"What's DD?" he asked.

"Oh that," said Margaret. "It's rather sad, really. C likes to use naval terms. Well, you'd expect that from a sailor, wouldn't you? It means "Discharged, Dead". She glanced at Browning's shocked face. "Why, sir, did you know him?"

"Not really," muttered Browning. A thought struck him. "When did he die?"

"Don't know." Margaret shook her head. "It's only just come back from C's office. Mind you," she added, dropping her voice, conspiratorially. "DD usually doesn't mean that, does it?"

"Doesn't it?"

"Lord, no. Sometimes it's just his clever way of closing an agent's file. That way, no-one ever knows where they've gone, do they?" Margaret took back Everitt's file and selected a rubber stamp from a carousel on her desk. She breathed on it, and stamped CLOSED FILE in red firmly across the cover, underneath the handwritten "Everitt, Nicolas James".

She beamed up at him. "No, Mr Everitt could be anywhere now. The rumour is C's sent him to Canada… or Scotland."

On a sudden thought, Browning asked, "Do you have Major Rice's file?"

Margaret frowned. "Major Rice... Major Rice…" Tongue between her lips, she rifled impatiently through a box of filing cards. Puzzled, she took another box out of a locked drawer and checked it carefully, shaking her head. "I don't think we have Major Rice on the books, Sir. Not as an officer of this service, anyway. Hang on a moment, though".

She called across to a younger woman standing at the back of the Registry Room over a table packed with long trays of cards. "Miss Belfield, do we have a Major Rice, R-I-C-E?"

The young woman flicked through a box of cards at the back, near the window. Shaking her head. "No, Mrs Coombs. The only Rice we have on the files is a lady. Lives in New York, married to Mr Aloysius Rice, a banker."

Margaret turned to Browning. "Sorry, Sir, no Major Rice."

"Wait a sec, though, Mrs Coombs," called the younger woman. "What about Captain Reisz? R-E-I-S-Z. He could be a major now. Might that be the gentleman?" She looked at Browning then back to the Head of Registry. "It's a red file," she added.

Margaret's face cleared. "Ah, Captain Reisz." She nodded. "Yes, that could be the gentleman, Colonel."

"Have you got his file?"

The Registrar shook her head. "Oh now, Colonel. We don't handle Red files, dear me, no." She smiled at him. "No, the Red files are highly confidential. They get special handling. We don't hold them down here."

"Well, who does?" began Browning, impatiently.

Margaret laughed. "Well, C of course, Colonel Browning."

She put the "Closed File" rubber stamp carefully back onto the carousel with its fellow stamps. She looked up at him.

"They're all in the Chief's private safe. C holds the Special Operations officers' files personally. I think they do all his special jobs for him."

She smiled. "Fancy you not knowing that, Sir."

CHAPTER 30

Problems

OHL HEADQUARTERS

Monday 18th March

Wendel rubbed his missing eye socket.

"Well, I can't make head nor tail of it, Weissmüller."

Unshaven and with his uniform jacket unbuttoned he looked like a man who had been up all night – which he had. Around the OHL security major and his clerk, a litter of files and half-empty bottle of brandy gave silent testimony to a long night.

It was a blessing that von Zelle was away at the Field Hospital. Freed from the staff Colonel's nagging interference, Wendel and Weissmüller has been able to check the personal files of every member of the HQ staff undisturbed to see if they could identify the source of any leak. They had interviewed each member of the Transport Branch and questioned the Railway (Movements) clerks in great detail, Wendel asking the questions and his orderly writing the answers down. Now, nearly 24 hours on, they were little wiser and much tireder.

It had been Weissmüller who had noticed the key detail.

The Command train had originally been scheduled to depart for Mons at 1030 on the Sunday morning. But Hindenburg or Ludendorff had changed its departure time for 1100 – thirty minutes later – only the previous evening. Weissmuller had looked up from a sheaf of nearly 20 transportation orders and realised that the change had been ordered late on the Saturday night; barely 12 hours before the train had left Avesnes siding, heading for Mons.

"*Herr Major?*" At six o'clock in the morning, Wendel was blurred and tired. At first he hadn't grasped the significance of his orderly's discovery. When it dawned on him, he woke up sharply.

"*Jesu, Maria und Josef!* he swore. That's means the Tommy fliers must have been well prepared; outstandingly well prepared. That's too quick. How could they have got the message? Wireless?" Weissmüller shook his head.

"So it's either a traitor on the railway with a pigeon…"

"Too slow, Major" broke in Weissmuller, shaking his head. "In the dark, and then getting the message down to the fliers on the other side? No." He thought. "Or someone with a wireless?"

Wendel pulled a face. "That rules out the railway staff. They don't have wirelesses. Only we have those. And there's no telegraph lines across the front lines. So, how the devil could the Tommies have been in the right place at the right time? We were a long way back from the Front. It doesn't make sense…"

Weissmüller dragged a file off the floor and re-read a page. He pulled a face. "And, *Herr Major*, the official re-scheduling is only finally signed off at one o'clock in the morning – look."

"Who knew, then?" enquired Wendel sharply. "Who signed it, the final authorisation?"

A grin spread over Weissmüller's face. "You'll never believe it, *Herr Major*." He pushed the file across to his boss. Wendel frowned, then looked up in astonishment. "*von Zelle?*"

"Ja. He was Staff Duty Officer that night. They had to wake him up to get a signature. I remember that *StabsFeldwebel* Sulzback told me that old Zelle chewed him out for waking him up in the middle of the night. Do you think that *Oberst* von Zelle is our secret OHL traitor, *Herr Major?*" he added michievously.

Wendel treated his clerk to a look of withering contempt. "Stop," he said. "Of course not. Let's just go through the timings. The Chief changes the train time just before midnight on Saturday night, right?" Weissmüller nodded, checking the file. "The duty clerk in Transport types up new orders?" Wendel was making a list. "The orders get taken to von Zelle at one o'clock for signing…"

"And are released from the headquarters at about two," added Weissmüller.

"And it's all done on a secure telephone line," Wendel finished.

The two men looked at each other, baffled.

"It just doesn't make sense," Wendel muttered. "No headquarters could react that fast and plan a bombing raid against a moving train. We certainly couldn't."

They stared at each other. Weissmüller shrugged. "You're right, Herr Major. It would be quite some trick to get the Tommies" Air Service informed and at the right place in that time…"

"Unless," Wendel mused, "unless it really was an accident."

"Accident?"

"Yes. Why not? What if it was just a coincidence? Say the Tommies are off on a bombing mission anyway? They're bombing railway lines, we know that, right? And they see a train below. So they bomb it. That makes sense."

Weissmüller nodded. "*Ja.* Just a coincidence. Bad luck." He pulled a face and shrugged. "Do you think so, *Herr Major?*"

Wendel muttered, "*Ja,* it fits. But…" He hesitated.

He was tired and puzzled. His stump was throbbing and his good eye felt as if it was full of sand. He tried to think clearly. Could it really have been bad luck, pure chance? Weissmüller was right. It did all fit. The British Flying Corps had been active buzzing about that morning, so it could easily have been bad luck. And yet, and yet…

Major Wendel tried to imagine the Chief of Staff's reaction when he told him that his investigation had officially concluded that the bomb had all been pure chance, bad luck. He pulled a face.

Ludendorff wouldn't wear that for a second, he was sure. They'd all heard him raving on at the trackside about the hand of God and Divine Providence. He wasn't going to buy "mere chance" under any circumstances. *Christ!* he thought, as a stray idea flashed across his mind. What if Ludendorff's suddenly got religion? Wendel had seen stranger things happen in the war. The man was already a hot-tempered fanatic, convinced that he alone was right and effectively the co-ruler of Germany. A religious maniac in charge of the country, convinced as a lawyer that he's always right…

That's all we need, he concluded grimly. But if Ludendorff *really* believed that it was the hand of God that had saved him, then he must equally believe that it was *enemy* action that was against him. And for that he would certainly want a big investigation, whatever the real truth. Mere coincidence would seem feeble explanation to his puritanical Prussian soul.

No, Wendel decided with a sigh, he daren't leave his investigation just like that. As Security Officer, he'd have to pretend that he was still working on all possible avenues, like a good General Staff Officer should.

Major Wendel was not an introspective man.

The harsh disciplines of the Imperial General Staff discouraged unnecessary self-indulgence and idle thinking among its carefully selected officers. However, he was no fool when it came to his brother officers, especially the Prussians. Hard work was seen as the path to virtue; or, Wendel thought cynically, the *appearance* of hard work. Very Prussian. He realised that his reputation depended on being seen to be taking vigorous action, as much as on any successful outcome. This, he decided, was a case where the appearance of diligence, lots of activity and the illusion of forceful action were the only military methods that the Prussians could really understand. The last thing Ludendorff and his colleagues wanted to be told was that the bombing was just pure chance; bad luck. Good Prussian generals didn't believe in bad luck – they just believed in bad planning and bad staff work.

Well, he reasoned, if it's *action* to keep Ludendorff happy, action is what I'll give them. If being a good German staff officer meant pointless work for the sake of work, then that's what they would get. It wouldn't be the first time. He came to a decision.

"Right, Weissmüller. Get me an interim – interim, mind – report typed up for the eleven o'clock staff meeting."

He got up and began to pace the office.

"Say that – ah – preliminary indications appear to point to an unfortunate coincidence in that the British bombers were active in the area at the time the HQ train was passing through. However, these initial conclusions cannot be accepted until all other avenues have been explored and discounted. No – make that *thoroughly* explored. Questioning the French railwaymen, examination of fragments of the bomb casing, statements, etc., will establish whether the train was merely a target of opportunity or something more sinister… Further investigations and in depth interviews continue by the HQ Security Staff, blah, blah." He waved his good arm. "You know the kind of stuff."

Weissmüller grinned. "*Jawohl, Herr Major.* I know exactly what you mean. I'll have it ready for your signature. Do you want to order any further action? For the recommendations."

Wendel paused, then rattled off a list; "*Ja.* We better had, to make it look good. Say I need to see the Military Police *Kommandant.* Get him to talk to all the local town mayors along the line. Say I want the Ammunition Officer's report on the carriage, bomb fragments, that sort of thing; all the statements from the arrested French railwaymen; any sudden absentees from the civilian work force; the Air Service's log of British air activity for Sunday morning; access list – everything! I'm sure you know."

Weissmüller smiled slyly. "My, we are being a busy security office, *Herr Major*, aren't we? Are we trying to tell someone something, by any chance?"

Wendel looked his orderly up and down. "Certainly not, Weissmüller. What an extraordinary idea."

Weissmüller returned Wendel's haughty stare. "Well, *Herr Major*, if you're going to the staff meeting in two hours' time you'll want to wash and shave. And a clean uniform?"

Wendel smiled slightly at his orderly, and began to button his jacket with his good arm. "No, Weissmuller, I think I will attend the 11 o'clock staff meeting just as I am."

"But *Herr Major*," protested Weissmüller, "You look as if you've been up all night!"

Wendel's face cracked. "Precisely, my dear Weissmüller, precisely. Working hard, as a good General Staff officer should."

CHAPTER 31

WHITEHALL

17th March 1918

Wendel wasn't the only individual whose workload had been dramatically increased by Stube's unsuccessful attempt to splatter Hindenburg and Ludendorff across the French countryside.

In London that morning C's sense of depression over his "solution to the Everitt problem" had been further deepened by the realisation that the bomb plot against the German high command had failed. He was also uneasily aware that Major Reisz had now "disposed" of two of his agents on his personal orders, and Cumming was worried that his tame assassin now knew far too much. Was "disposing" of his agents even legal? He gnawed at a fingernail. To make matters worse, a flurry of urgent requests for information from the BEF and the War Office about the impending German attack had virtually swamped the Secret Intelligence Service. Thus it was with something approaching desperation that C looked at the neatly hand-written note from Neville, asking for a *"brief meeting to discuss the situation"* as a matter of *"no little urgency."*

What Cumming did not know was that Neville himself was under pressure.

As the civil servant had so accurately predicted the previous week, he had now been given a task directly from the PM; or at least, initialled by him. To Neville, that innocuous little memorandum had, in his mind at least, got Hankey's empire-building fingerprints all over it. He read it again carefully, as a student might read an exam question:

> *"Be so good as to provide a short intelligence briefing for the War Cabinet at 2 p.m. on Wednesday 20th March to outline any information we have on any impending German assault on the British Expeditionary Force in France and Flanders; what action we have taken so far and make such recommendations as you think fit."*

Yes, thought Neville, the little confidential sheet of No. 10 Downing Street notepaper had Hankey's grubby fingerprints all over it; no doubt about that. Someone had put Lloyd George up to this. He suspected that someone had been tipped off about the failure of the bomb plot and was going to use it as a chance to drag intelligence and its failures into the very public gaze of the politicians – and that could only benefit Hankey, he thought. The next full Cabinet met at 11 o'clock on Thursday morning – the very day that the German attack was now expected, if all Neville's sources were to be believed.

Neville thought hard about the implications. If a shocked Cabinet met on Thursday morning to discover the news that the German barbarians were unexpectedly at the gates, heads would have to roll. Unlike Gough, Neville had a strong suspicion that the weakened BEF would bend, if not break, under the onslaught of half a million well-trained German assault troops hurled against its weakest army. Thursday could well be a day of decidely unpleasant news. A panicky Cabinet would undoubtedly be looking for scapegoats.

It was, he realised, the moment to use the impending German storm to his own advantage to ensure that he was not made the sacrificial victim of any political game of pass the parcel. His urgent note to Cumming for a meeting to discuss the failed attack on the Duo reflected a desire to protect himself against just such a possibility.

However Hankey's – or the *Prime Minister*'s – note, he thought wryly, raised the stakes. So, like the cautious man he was, Hubert Neville decided that a few bureaucratic counter-measures of his own would not come amiss. He sat down and penned a careful reply back to No. 10 in his neat donnish hand:

> *"Thank you for your note of the 17th March. I can confirm that we will be ready to brief the War Cabinet at 2pm on 20th on the matter you raise. Please be aware of two points:*
>
> *1. I share your obvious sense of urgency and can confirm that this is a subject we have been following with close attention for the past three months. I therefore welcome this opportunity to bring you and the War Cabinet up to date.*
>
> *2. Please be aware that on your behalf, and at the request of the Commander of the BEF, the responsible officers have already set certain contingencies in motion to ameliorate, if not disrupt, any planned German assault."*

There, he thought, blotting the note, that little bureaucratic masterpiece should give Hankey, and anyone else coming after Hubert Neville's scalp, pause for thought.

He sealed the envelope himself with red wax and carefully addressed it to "*The Prime Minister*" adding, "*Most Secret*" as an afterthought. He banged the little brass bell on his desk and instructed the grave young man who acted as his private secretary to deliver the note.

Afterwards he sat, chin on hand, staring at out of the window for the best part of two minutes. An observer might have observed dryly that they could almost hear the ex-Don's mind whirring as his brain clicked over. However, there were no observers present to witness Neville's slight smile as he eventually took up his pen to draft another short note, this time to Hankey personally.

Ju-jitsu, he thought; Ju–Jitsu. That was the secret; to turn an opponent's strength into his weaknesses. If Hankey was going to make a play to bring intelligence under his control he'd better think again. Neville's smile deepened as he penned the letter:

"*My dear Hankey,*

Just to confirm that I have, as requested personally by the PM, put the necessary steps in motion to brief the War Cabinet on the grave threat the BEF will undoubtedly face in the very near future. As you are aware, I have been warning of the seriousness of this matter for some little time and I am delighted that you have finally succeeded in bringing it to the War Cabinet's attention.

This subject does, however, bring the importance of the overall coordination of our various intelligence services to the fore once again. Events clearly demonstrate the growing importance of coordinating <u>all</u> confidential information in order to bring it to policy-makers' attention in good time."

Neville's smile broadened, as he added the final paragraph:

"*Clearly such a full-time task cannot be carried out from No. 10, being both time-consuming and requiring an extensive range of daily contacts both in Whitehall and certain other places. In the circumstances, I would be grateful if you would ask the PM if I might have half an hour of his time as soon as possible, to outline some proposals we have been considering on his behalf for the more efficient coordination of intelligence matters.*"

That, he thought, is a Whitehall masterpiece.

Again he dinged the little brass bell, and his secretary, a good-looking young man, came in. Hubert Neville rather enjoyed the company of intelligent, well-bred, good-looking young men.

"Ah, Asprey," said Neville, peering over his glasses. "I want you send this letter to the Secretary to the War Cabinet's office."

Asprey took the proffered sheet of paper. "Urgently, sir?"

"No, no. Not at all. No need for unnecessary haste, my boy. Completely routine. This one through the normal channels, I think."

"Very well, sir."

Charles Asprey turned to go. He glanced at the text and realised immediately that as a result of this slower delivery Hankey was unlikely to see the note before the War Cabinet's briefing in two day's time. During that briefing Neville would undoubtedly ask for a personal meeting with the PM on intelligence matters and refer to the note. Lloyd George was hardly likely to turn down such an offer. But Hankey wouldn"t receive the request until it was too late to block it in advance. So Neville would get his one on one access to Lloyd George. And probably without Hankey being present, if Neville pleaded that universal catch all, "security". It would completely wrong foot the ambitious Hankey. Clever.

He looked round; Neville was speaking. "…Oh, and one other thing, Asprey. I would be grateful if you would make three copies, personally. One for our files – for the records in case the letter gets mislaid. These things do have such a habit of disappearing in No. 10, don't they?"

Asprey nodded. "And the others, sir?"

"Yes," mused Neville, sitting back in his chair and seeking inspiration from the ceiling, "the others. See that one goes to Manfield-Cumming over at the Secret Service, and send the other to Mr Winston Churchill. Mark them both 'Personal'. Oh, and I'll initial all the copies, by the way." He beamed at his aide. He had chosen his allies well for the coming fight.

Asprey nodded slowly and went out. There was no doubt about it - what they said in the Whitehall mess was absolutely true: old Doc Neville was a wily old bird, and no mistake. Charles Asprey reckoned that he had just witnessed the first shots fired in a battle over one of the most fought over pieces of territory in Western Europe: Whitehall and control of British intelligence.

He'd back Neville to win.

CHAPTER 32

THE WAR OFFICE

WHEN THINGS GO WRONG

19 March 1918

It was, therefore, with the invigorating prospect of imminent action that Neville stepped across Whitehall the following morning.

The coming battle may have been merely a bureaucratic one but it did not diminish for one second his relish for the coming combat. A thoughtful man, who speculated endlessly on his own and other's motives, Neville was genuinely surprised by his own pleasurable anticipation of confrontation at last. It put a spring in his step as he bade a jaunty welcome to the War Office porter who greeted him and the over-enthusiastic Boy Scout who guided him to the office of the Director of Military Operations.

It was a gloomy group he found sat around the DMO's desk.

They welcomed him as philosophically as men could when they report the disastrous failure of some long-cherished cherished project. To their – and it should be said, his own – astonishment, Neville was surprisingly cheerful. He actually smiled and nodded when Browning and Cockerill told him of Stube's coded despatch sent by God alone knows what secret method. Cumming's Secret Service might use their most cherished agent to further Whitehall's Macchiavellian schemes, but they were most certainly not going to risk his neck, or their priceless agent's usefulness, by revealing the inner secrets of their devious trade. So Neville and the DMO had to be content with listening to Browning reading out a short text outlining Stube's version of Sunday's events at the German OHL command train and his failure to assassinate the German war-lords.

When he had finished this bald narrative, Neville chuckled. "Well, well, gentlemen. It looks as if we've given the Duo quite a shock, what? Ludendorff especially. '*Divine providence*' indeed!" He shook his head and turned to the fifth occupant of the room, a young captain from the Royal Flying Corps Headquarters, the wings on his breast proclaiming his trade and the two medal ribbons his professional qualifications.

"So, Captain Scott, what has Air Operations got to add to this extraordinary saga?" Neville had the air of a tutor waiting to hear a student's essay, as he sat back, eyes closed, his fingers steepled together.

Scott was baffled. He had been dragged into this very senior meeting at short notice, sworn to secrecy and hadn't understood half of what he had just heard. He thought that the Flying Corps was being blamed for something. Despite his junior rank, he launched into a spirited defence of his Service.

Somewhat startled by the vehemence of the young man's eloquence, Neville, who had taken on the unofficial mantle of chairmanship of the group, stopped him mid-sentence with a raised hand. "Captain Scott, no-one is blaming the Flying Corps for attacking the OHL train."

Scott, deflated, looked around. "Oh, but I thought…"

"No, no," said Neville. "On the contrary, we merely need to ascertain precisely," he emphasised the word, "which operations the Flying Corps was doing in France last Sunday morning. In particular, at one o'clock on that afternoon."

Scott opened the file in front of him, revealing a thick stack of flimsy messages sent in answer to his unusual query of the previous day.

"Well, Sir, there's the dawn patrols. You know, scouts all along the Front…"

Again Neville stopped him. "Just the bombers, Captain Scott. And at one p.m. if you please."

Scott riffled through his signals. "Well, there's the Royal Naval Air Service in the north. They had a go at noon against Oostcamp and Ostend…"

With a slight air of exasperation, Neville again halted the RFC Captain's voluble flow. Cockerill and Browning exchanged amused glances. General Maurice leaned forward and intervened. "I think what Mr Neville's really asking, Scott, is, were there any RFC bombers active around the Valenciennes area at lunchtime on Sunday?"

The DMO went on, "Just a simple, straightforward answer to a straight-forward question." He looked at Neville, who inclined his head gratefully.

"Ah," said Scott, thoughtfully. "That should be easier." There was a long pause while he shuffled through his file. Finally, triumphantly, he produced a flimsy. "Yes, here we are, sir. Nine Squadron, DH4s, six of them; ground fog; but took off at 11.20 ack emma; attacked and bombed the Valenciennes rail yards; 15,000 feet; clear visibility over the target; all bombs released over target; all aircraft returned safely; no EA encounters."

"EA?" said Neville.

"Enemy Aircraft, sir," said Scott, looking up.

"And that's all?" said Neville. "You're sure?"

Scott looked at his papers again, then nodded. "That's the only activity all day in the Valenciennes area, Sir. As far as we know."

Neville resumed the contemplation of his inner eyelids. Suddenly his snapped eyes open. "The timing's wrong, surely. They, this 9 Squadron, couldn't have been flying over the OHL train at one o'clock. It's far too late..."

"Actually, it isn't, Sir," said Scott. "The Huns are at least an hour ahead. Berlin time."

Neville breathed a sigh of quiet satisfaction. "So it does fit. The RFC could have done it."

"No, sir," said Scott doggedly. "The DH4s unloaded all their bombs over the railway yards. No-one bombed the train down there at _" he looked at a folded map in his file, "at Artres." He stumbled over the name. "They were coming back empty – no bombs."

"But could they have bombed the OHL train? Theoretically?"

Scott looked around somewhat desperately at the senior officers for support. "No, sir. They couldn't have bombed that train. They had already dropped all their bombs, you see."

"What exactly are ye'drivin' at Neville?" said the DMO.

Neville assumed a beatific smile. "Nothing. But are we not fortunate therefore that although the Flying Corps clearly did not bomb the train in question – having already unloaded all their bombs, as Captain Scott has so eloquently pointed out - the OHL gang believe that they did?"

Browning got the point immediately. "I'll say! They think we did it! And long may they believe it, too!"

A baffled Scott was dismissed, with old world courtesy, by Neville.

When he had gone the civil servant addressed the group.

"This may not be such a – ah - *setback* as at first we may have thought, gentlemen. There are two extremely valuable outcomes from even this abortive enterprise." He noticed the puzzlement of his audience.

"First," he leaned forward on his stick, "we can look the C-in-C of the BEF in the eye and say they have done our best. Browning's service - with your invaluable War Office support, Cockerill - has clearly done its damndest to do precisely what General Haig asked us to do. Am I correct?"

The others nodded dumbly. And the Cabinet would appreciate that point, too, should anyone ask, thought Neville.

"Second, we now know that the OHL and its command train is a very tempting target for air attack in the future. Do you agree?"

The others agreed Neville's logic. "So what are we saying?" enquired Cockerill. "Leave it to the Flying Corps?"

"No, my dear Cockerill, most certainly not. But what this little escapade has proved beyond all doubt is that, if at some future time we get good intelligence and a suitable target, then airmen can be trusted to go after such a high value target. And far more speedily than any mere secret agent, as I'd sure you would agree. They have the ability to react quickly if tasked."

The others looked at each other, acknowledging the truth of Neville's argument.

"Good point Neville," said the DMO. "But how will we know in future when we've got a chance if a suitable target comes up?

Neville stood up to go. "Clearly, we have to pool our information. I suggest that we have no choice but to continue to work together, gentlemen. We will need good intelligence, obviously." He favoured them with a slight smile. "Might I suggest that the best way of accomplishing that is to keep this little group together? It has certainly proved most useful, I think we all agree?"

They nodded. "We could even dignify it with a suitable title, for we're certainly something more than an *ad hoc* group now. Perhaps something like the 'Senior Targets Intelligence Committee'?"

"Bit obvious for secret work," said Walter Kirke from his corner, without looking up. "How about 'The Intelligence Planning Committee'?"

"Excellent!" said Neville. "Capital! What a good title. Just the right note, and with all the key Whitehall offices represented. Perfect! We should be able to co-ordinate our various intelligence affairs far better."

"With proper minutes?" asked Kirke.

"But of course," replied Neville now only to well aware of the civil servant mentality – "provided General Macdonogh can spare you occasionally from your work for military intelligence?"

Kirke nodded.

"Good scheme," muttered Browning. He could see immediately that any committee could lobby for SIS's money and influence across Whitehall and share out the blame when things went wrong. "C will like that. I agree. And we'll need a chap from the Admiralty, of course... But it's just what we've needed for months: years. Work together. Good idea, Neville."

"So," said Neville sweeping round the room. Are we all agreed?"

They were.

And with a cheerful smile, Hubert Neville departed and stepped out briskly across Whitehall. Now he'd have something really solid to brief the War Cabinet on Wednesday. Not just the coming storm of the KaiserSchlacht, either. That was certain to happen and equally certain to bring bad news, followed by gloom all round. They'd be looking for a saviour. But now he alone could offer a solution to all the government's intelligence woes. He was now Chairman - by acclamation - of Whitehall's new, "*Intelligence Planning Committee*".

Let Maurice Hankey try to get his hands on that – if he dare.

CHAPTER 33

The *KaiserSchlacht*

THE WESTERN FRONT

21ˢᵗ March 1918

The final decision to launch the *Kaiserschlacht* was officially taken by Field Marshal Paul von Hindenburg of the Imperial German General Staff at the daily staff meeting at his headquarters on the 18ᵗʰ of March.

In fact, the real decision was taken by his co-commander, Erich von Ludendorff, but only the Commander in Chief von Hindenburg could endorse it. It was a momentous decision. Not just because by the time the great German 1918 spring offensive petered out in mid-summer, it would have condemned 800,000 Germans to death or mutilation, but also because of its timing. Germany's great spring offensive was a day late.

For, despite the best efforts of the German railway staff and their over-worked engineers, plus the surly efforts of hastily impressed un-cooperative French and Belgian railway workers, the vital supply trains on which the attack depended were delayed. Armstrong and 25 Squadron's dive-bombing raid had bought a vital 24 hours. It was therefore with a sense of irritation that Ludendorff jabbed at the map and ordered Operation Michael to begin at 4.40 am on 21ˢᵗ March. He surveyed the expectant faces of the key staff officers and the imperturbable fierceness of Hindenburg, his titular master, and stabbed his hand down a second time.

"One day's delay will not worry us, gentlemen. It gives us extra time to stockpile the stores we will need." He glanced at his team. A little convincing is needed, he thought.

"Our aim is to split the British from French armies once and for all. We will attack up both sides of the Somme river and split them like an axe splits a log! And once Operation Michael has got the British on the run, we will push them and push them, until we drive them back to the sea. England, France's right arm, will be knocked out of the war. Whenever they stop, we attack elsewhere. It will be a series of hammer blows the like of which this war – any war – has ever seen." He crashed his fist on the map. "1918 will go down in history as the year in which victory is ours!"

A growl of approval greeted this little speech. Ludendorff noticed Wendel at the back of the map room. "Ah, Wendel, what progress on the bombing of my train?"

My train? thought Wendel. He risked a quick glance at von Hindenburg. But that Olympian visage remained impassive. Wendel clicked his heels. "Preliminary indications confirm that it was an English air raid, *Herr Feld Marschall*."

Ludendorff nodded impatiently. "We know that."

"With respect, sir, as security officer it is my duty to explore all possibilities. There are a number of puzzling features about this air attack that are still under investigation. For example, how did the Tommies coordinate such a precise attack in the time between you ordering the departure time and the bombing?"

"*Ja* – that is a surely a puzzle, Wendel."

"That raises the thought that it might have been merely an opportunistic attack."

Ludendorff's eyebrows knitted. "You mean that it *wasn't* intended for the OHL command train?"

"The Tommy fliers seem to be attacking every train these days, Herr Feld Marschall. It could have been," he swallowed hard, "just bad luck."

Ludendorff's heavy jowls became mottled and red. "Are you suggesting this attempt on the lives of the High Commanders was a just a chance attack, Wendel? Pure chance? Do you really suggest that?"

Hindenburg's great granite head came up as he stared at Ludendorff.

"No, sir," Wendel went on, "I am merely suggesting that we in the Headquarters security office are examining every possibility. As a professional General Staff officer I keep an open mind in these investigations until I am sure of all known facts, sir."

Hindenburg's gaze swivelled towards Wendel. He nodded slowly and spoke. "Quite correct. Continue your investigations, Major Wendel. I am sure you will identify the real cause in due course." Hindenburg's manner was judicial, the voice a deep rumble. "We have every confidence in your security measures."

"Thank you, *Herr Feld Marschall!*"

For a second, Wendel thought that Ludendorff would speak again. Then the junior member of the Duo grunted and turned back to the map. He leaned both hands on the table, and addressed the staff.

"So, back to the business in hand. Everything is now ready, gentlemen. The fate of the German Empire rests on the bayonets of our soldiers. Prussia and her King will not permit the German people to even contemplate failure, despite the socialists, trade unionists and Red defeatists in Berlin. It is we now who must be strong for Germany! God is with us! Let this attack begin, with the Lord's blessing on us all!"

Christ Almighty, thought Wendel. Prussia? The Lord's blessing? The bloody man thinks he's on some divine cause. He thinks he's Frederick the Great – another mad bastard.

He personally thought that Ludendorff was now an over-strung, over-worked neurotic, liable to a nervous collapse if pushed too far. However, it didn't pay to question, let alone antagonise, such a dangerous despot, especially if he had religion too. He eyed his master closely. This mad Prussian really thinks he knows best for all Germany, thought Wendel – with 'the Lord of Hosts' help", of course. He suddenly remembered who Ludendorff reminded him of. Not Frederick the Great.

The bloody man thinks he's Oliver Cromwell.

*   *   *

Just before dawn on Thursday 21st March 1918, Operation Michael burst like a thunderbolt on General Sir Hubert Gough's 5th Army.

On a forty-mile front Ludendorff's storm troops assaulted along an axis from St Quentin towards Montidier, 40 miles away on the River Somme. Seven thousand guns unleashed the greatest single concentration of shells the world had ever seen. For over four hours Bruchmüller's carefully orchestrated hurricane bombardment fell like a torrential rainstorm of high explosive on the hapless British positions. Men, horses, dugouts and buildings were blown to bits and hurled into the air.

A keen observer would have spotted several unusual features, however. Much of the bombardment fell well behind the British lines as the German gunners searched out headquarters, artillery lines and even ammunition dumps in the rear. Amidst this storm of high explosive and steel was also mixed the deadly whisper of gas shells as key crossroads and routes forward were drenched with poison gas. At 9.30 the bombardment switched to the forward British trenches and ripped away the barbed wire before moving like an iron flail back across the shell-shattered trenches to surprise those unwise souls in the rear areas who had foolishly chanced emerging from cover.

And, behind this remorseless barrage, despite Sir Hubert Gough's prediction of a long barrage, the first specially trained elite units of German storm troopers began to flit forward through the fog to begin their creeping advance.

*　　　　*　　　　*

Serjeant Len Arkwright and his half platoon of Lancashire Fusiliers peered apprehensively into the drifting mist.

The twenty-odd men had been stood to since before dawn and listened to the barrage roaring over their heads and crashing into the fog and darkness. Puzzlingly, it was falling miles behind their positions in the front line battle zone. Apart from one brief interval when they had been pelted by huge trench mortars for about ten minutes, the Fusiliers' trenches had been remained remarkably unscathed. Only one of the fat black aerial torpedoes had done any serious damage, dropping smack into one of the platoon's forward trenches a hundred yards to their front. A white-faced Second Lieutenant Hitchcock had scrambled back down the wrecked communication trench about ten minutes later, hands red with blood, to tell his platoon Serjeant that four men had been killed outright. Young Mr. Hitchcock had been near to tears, reflected Arkwright as he sipped his mug of scalding hot tea. He himself knew only too well what the bodies of men who have been blown apart by high explosive looked like. Poor little sod. First week in the battalion and now this. He was nothing but a lad, really. Not like the regular officers back in 1915; now all gone. Arkright wondered what would happen next.

"'Ere, Thompson, where's that bloody rum?"

"We've not 'ad permission to issue it, Serjeant."

"Sod that. Give every man a tot in his tea and then carry the jar forward to Mr Hitchcock. Lively now!"

"Right-oh, Sarge," and with that, a grinning Private Thompson from Oldham had splashed a generous portion of thick dark service rum into the grateful mugs of his mates and disappeared forward carrying his stone jar of rum, marked "S.R.D.", standing for "Service Rum Diluted". The soldiers said it really stood for "Seldom Really Distributed" or "Soon Runs Dry". Arkwright smiled and pulled on his pipe, staring out into the shifting mist.

The truth was that the platoon serjeant was baffled by the German barrage. He had been out since December 1915 and had seen many bombardments, but nothing quite like this one. Through the mist, the explosions far to their rear blended into one continuous roar and occasionally a brief red glow flared through the gloom as some massive explosion lit up the grey dawn. Arkwright was only too pleased that, as he put it so succinctly to Fusilier Thompson, "*Soom oother bastard was coppin' it,*" but his professional soul was genuinely puzzled by the fact that he and his men were not. There was definitely something wrong.

The arrival of Captain Cook, the Company Commander, merely added to his bafflement. "Cookie" and he went back a long time; to the Somme at the end of 1916 and through the Salient and Ypres the previous year. They were nearly the last survivors of the old C Company. Now as they peered into the grey shifting mist, they were both bemused and a little worried. Where were the Germans? Far off they could hear the rattle of machine guns and occasionally the whispering *crack, crack, crack* of bullets overhead. But these were merely spents and overs from someone else's battle. Whatever else was happening, no-one was attacking the Lancashire Fusiliers, and after an anxious hour, Captain Cook took himself off down the trench to the neighbouring platoon of his company; but not before confiding in Serjeant Arkwright that there was "*something bloody odd going on*".

Arkwright silently agreed with his company commander and resumed his vigil. Like the good senior NCO he was, he ordered his men to get some food and sleep while only sentries manned the trench. He himself stayed on the parapet smoking his pipe and scanning the drifting mist, but to no avail. Once, as the fog cleared for a few seconds off to his right, he thought he saw distant dark shapes flitting through the watery clouds but then the mist thickened and he could see no more.

By noon, it was clear that something really was badly wrong. A runner from Company HQ said that the Battalion had lost all contact with Brigade and runners going back to find out what was happening had all mysteriously disappeared. The rattle of machine gun fire was all around them; most of it distant in the fog, some of it startlingly close. To Arkwright's experienced ear, the rattle of German machine guns and explosions to his rear was deeply troubling.

By two o'clock, his patience was exhausted. Padding forward down the communication trench he found a worried Mr Hitchcock standing on the parapet staring blankly into the drifting fog towards the barbed wire and the German lines.

"What's going on, S'arnt Arkwright?" were his platoon commander's first words, to which even Len Arkwright had to confess complete bafflement. They held a hurried conference in the trench and agreed to send out patrols to front and flank to see what was happening. A flight of stray bullets whispered through the grass in no-man's land and a stray shell droned overhead on its way to some luckless target far to their rear.

"I'll lead one," said Hitchcock, anxious to prove himself to his new platoon.

"I'd not do that if I were thee, Sir," Arkwright advised. "Your place is 'ere, wi' the lads. Let corporals do it."

So three of the platoon's corporals led four-man groups into the fog; one to left and one to the right, while a third advanced forwards into the grey blanket that shrouded no-man's land. Arkwright and his officer strained their eyes into the blankness. Suddenly, the crump of grenades and bursts of automatic fire rang out from their front. The firing continued until a lone figure sprinted out of the mist, running hard for the trench.

"Don't shoot!" bellowed Arkwright as the helmetless figure of Private Smethurst slid over the lip of the trench and crashed to the bottom, panting and shaking.

"What happened?"

"Huns, Sarge. Fookin' 'undreds! Just lying there, by the wire. Wire's blown to fookin' boogery. 'Undreds of the fookers."

"Cpl. Mulholland?"

"Dunno, Sarge. They were chuckin' grenades and firin'. Fookin' 'undreds." Smethurst controlled his breathing. He was white-faced and shaking. The firing to their front died away.

"Where's your rifle, Smethurst?" demanded the Platoon Commander. He remembered that casting away one's arms was a court martial offence.

"Fookin' search me, sir," said Smethurst, closing his eyes and leaning back against the trench. "I didn't stop to look." His legs were trembling. He sat down on the floor. "Fookin' 'ell!"

Arkwright suppressed a smile. "Don't worry, sir. There's plenty of bucksee rifles. Best give the lad a couple of minutes to get 'is breath. 'E needs it."

Hitchcock looked shocked. "But shouldn't we…? I mean… Running away? Deserting post? Losing his rifle?"

Arkwright reassured him. "Don't thee fret about it, Sir. At least Smethurst reported back. As for the others? We"ll need all the lads soon, I'm thinking." He peered over the parapet and swore quietly at the murky gloom. A crackle of rifle fire close to the right made him duck down. He rubbed his chin. "I don't like it, sir, and that's the truth. There's summat bloody queer goin' on, and I don't know what."

They peered forward into the fog. The ominous crackle of small arms fire now rattled in the distance from every direction. He could swear he could see figures in the fog off to the flank.

"I wish I knew what was going on," began Second Lieutenant Hitchcock.

"Perhaps I can enlighten you," said a harsh voice from behind.

The twenty odd men lining the trench turned round to see a slim, steel-helmeted German officer standing above them, pistol in hand. Even as they turned, a line of German assault troops emerged from the mist to tower over them from the rear, machine guns and rifles pointed down into the trench and with potato masher grenades poised, ready to throw. The surprise was complete.

Charlie Smethurst, a man of few words, summed it up best of all: "Fookin' 'ell!"

"Put down your arms and move away," said the German. His English was hardly accented at all, Arkwright noted.

Young Lieutenenant Hitchcock stared up belligerently at the German looming menacingly above. He clawed at his pistol holster. "I'll be damned if I will!"

"No, Sir, no!" screamed Arkwright, but it was too late. The German fired. Two rapid shots. A professional double tap, thought Arkwright. At that range the German could hardly miss. The bullets hit the young officer smack in the middle of the chest. Hitchcock staggered back and looked down with horror at the holes in the front of his new uniform. Bright red arterial blood spurted out for a second then pumped out in steady jets.

"No! No!" the young man tore helplessly at his tunic buttons as he sank to his knees. The front of the tunic was already black with blood. Then he held up his crimson hands before his face in disbelief, choked, "Oh God!" and crashed forward onto his face. His legs struggled and wriggle-kicked for a couple of seconds, like those of a trapped rabbit, then he was still.

The German officer looked up and down the trench. "Any more heroes?" he enquired. He raised his pistol theatrically and fired again, arm outstretched, this time deliberately smacking the bullet into the trench wall between Arkwright and Smethurst. The bang of the pistol sounded flat and loud in the fog. "Well?" Paralysed, the platoon looked at their leader.

Arkwright was frozen. He couldn't save his men and they had nowhere to run. He raised his hands. Smethurst copied him slowly raising his hands. All down the trench, the platoon followed suit.

"Very wise," said the German officer sardonically. "You're all prisoners. Now get out of the trench. Come on, Tommy, *los, los.*" The platoon scrambled up onto the top, hands held high. The bucket-helmeted Germans searched them none too gently, taking everything they could. Arkwright noticed with surprise that first field dressings and every tin of British rations disappeared swiftly into the Germans' packs. A row broke out down the line and a brawny German belted one of the Fusiliers with his rifle butt. The man collapsed to the ground and the German kicked him hard before wrenching a bottle of whisky from the soldier's pack. Another German held up a tin of cigarettes in triumph.

Very odd, thought Arkwright. What was so attractive about tins of bloody bully beef and a few fags? And why were they stealing the lads' first field dressings? Were the Germans so short of rations?

The officer came up to him. "Are you in charge?" He waved at his Serjeant's stripes and new medal ribbon.

"Yes," said Arkwright. The German was thin-faced, pockmarked, with mean lips. "Sir," he added, noticing the Iron Cross. He gestured back towards the rear. "What happened to…?" He was going to say "Company HQ," but thought better of it.

The officer smiled and followed his glance towards the British support line. "All prisoners; you are the last."

"All?" said Arkwright, startled. "All? But how?" He wondered how the German officer could speak such good English.

The German's smile broadened. "*Ja*, all. In their beds and their holes. Even your Colonel. Better to attack from behind, I think." He holstered his pistol.

"Now you, Serjeant. You are now our prisoners. Take your men and go. Join the rest. That way." He pointed through the fog towards the German front line. There was a crash from the trench below. A German had thrown all the platoons' rifles into a dug-out then flung a grenade down after them. Grey smoke billowed from the entrance. Mr Hitchcock's body lay sprawled face down on the trench floor, a widening pool of blood framing the torso.

"I'd best write to his family," said Arkwright.

The German followed his gaze down. "*Ja*. Fortunes of war. He was stupid."

Arkwright nodded. "Yes, he was. Poor little bastard. He wor only a lad." He met the German's eyes.

The officer shrugged. "He was a fool. You had more sense, I think?" Serjeant Arkwright nodded dumbly. He realised that the sight of young Hitchcock's stupid and unnecessary death would haunt him all his days. And now he and the lads were prisoners. Alive, but dead inside. What a way to end his war.

The German officer waved his pistol. "Now, take your men and go. Müller!" he yelled at a bucket-helmeted giant, festooned with potato-masher grenades and holding a new black machine pistol. A burst of incomprehensible German followed and the giant laughed, pushing Arkwright towards the German lines. "*Marsch! Los – marsch!*" He fired a machine gun burst at their feet, and the platoon, hands held high, shuffled blankly back into the the the fog of no-man's land and captivity.

In the trench behind them a German was carefully putting all Lt. Hitchcock's belongings into a sandbag. He held up the wristwatch with a query, but the officer curtly ordered him to put it into the bag. The soldier shrugged and did as he was bid. However, when he held up a bundle of letters, wet with fresh red blood, the officer shook his head. The soldier threw them away. The thin blue female handwriting slowly began to dissolve in the puddles on the trench floor.

Then the soldier laid the sandbag reverently alongside the body and pinned Hitchcock's identity discs to it. Someone stuck a discarded British rifle, bayonet down, on the lip of the trench to mark the boy's body.

Then the German storm troops, led by their thin-faced officer with the Iron Cross, marched away to victory, heading back west, towards the now distant sounds of battle on the horizon. The *Kaiserschlacht* was proceeding to plan.

The British were beaten.

CHAPTER 34

Armstrong Moves On
25 SQUADRON

Late March 1918

The great German Offensive impacted on more than the British front lines. Even the Royal Flying Corps were aware that something unprecedented was happening.

Far back at St Omer, the German attack dragged fliers from their beds that morning. As Roberts and his sleeping comrades tried to forget their fears and the war, a distant eruption of noise dragged them to the surface of their dream-charged sleep. Roberts had been in his cubicle, wrapped in a warm fantasy involving a pink and naked barmaid, when he became aware of low voices and a rumbling noise like thunder.

Throwing on a greatcoat and wellington boots, he stumbled out of the hut to find his fellow airmen standing outside looking south-east in the pre-dawn blackness. Still bleary from sleep, he asked the nearest shadowy figure, "Where's the storm?" to which Archie Watts, looking pale, had pointed to the horizon to the south, which was awash with a flickering red glow and a continuous low rumble.

"There's your storm, Robbie."

Roberts took in the sight and became aware, as his eyes adjusted to the dark, that all over the airfield black shadowy figures were looking at the skyline, talking in low, hushed tones.

"Well," said an unseen voice, "it's started."

Someone yawned and clattered back up the wooden steps to the hut, "I don't know about you fellows, but I'm going back to my pit. If they keep this up for a week, then we'll be needed – bet your life on it."

*   *   *

But the Germans didn't keep it up for a week. For the whole of the 21st artillery rumbled to the east, but nothing happened. No-one in 25 Squadron knew anything as the 22nd dawned, and the aircrew waited for orders.

By mid-morning rumours began to circulate that something very odd was going on, of unusual breakdowns in telephones, and of panicky staff officers at HQ. Robbie's request for a pass into the town was curtly turned down by a harrassed Peter Coachman, back at St Omer for a couple of days, with the warning that all leave passes were cancelled and the whole squadron was on permanent standby.

As the day wore on, fantastic reports began to circulate. A muddy despatch rider on a motorcycle brought a package from Wing for the Adjutant. While waiting for Cauchemar's reply, he regaled the orderly room clerks with horror stories of a German breakthrough on the Somme, lost units and whole forward brigades out of contact. Clutching a steaming mug of tea, he relayed his news, with all the gloomy relish of his breed, to a growing audience – until Jack Armstrong told him to "chuck it".

"Don't talk rot, Corporal. Of course the Hun hasn't broken through. So they've pulled a fast one and started early; but it'll take days before anyone starts retreating, even if they have got into some of the frontline trenches. And even if they have, we'll jolly soon kick 'em out and back to where they came from."

He looked round for support. "So stop talking piffle, spreading alarm and scare stories. The Hun'll be a week before he can start any real attack."

A low rumble of agreement greeted his words.

The despatch rider opened his mouth to say something but the door of the Squadron Commander's office opened and Peter Coachman limped in, envelope in hand. He looked startled at the crowd. "What's all this? Here." He thrust the envelope at the despatch rider. "Get this to Wing as quick as you can. Right," he said, eyeing the throng crowding the orderly room. "As you're mostly here, saves me a job. You're all on standby with immediate effect." A groan went up. "Never mind that. No-one's to leave the airfield. We're doubling the guard and you're all to be ready to fly out at one hour's notice." He noted the shocked expression on the faces.

"What about me?" asked Robbie from the back.

"You, too, Roberts. Bang on the head or not, you fly. Everyone flies. It's all hands to the pump, gentlemen." He took in the startled faces of his audience and mellowed his tone. "This is serious, chaps; it looks as if the

Hun's broken through down south."

By the next morning, it was clear to the whole squadron that the Adjutant was right; something serious was happening. The appearance of a reserve squadron of Camels, who flew in for lunch and then, tight lipped, departed for the south, added to the air of unease. Apparently they had been sent to the Rouen depot the day before to have bomb racks fitted.

The news that Camel fighting scouts were being turned into ground attack bombers at short notice added to the general air of bewilderment and apprehension. Rumours abounded, but no facts and few orders, most of those contradictory and overtaken by others. By the time Coachman had sorted the muddle out, the anxious 25 Squadron aircrew were going to bed and with a warning to prepare for a dawn bombing raid on the morrow.

*   *   *

At daybreak on the 24th, the rump of the squadron flew out, headed for Doullens, via a raid on the railway yards at Cambrai. Only the three Special Duties crews were left in St Omer, kicking their heels and starved of news. Peter Coachman stayed behind as well, to supervise the day-to-day administration at St Omer, and to field the questions of a steady stream of RFC squadrons passing through on their way to the battle.

At one point, even a flight of Royal Naval Air Service DH4s from Conderkerke on the Belgian coast flew in and departed, almost as soon as they had arrived, to add their weight to the fighting in the south. One of the pilots told Robbie that their intended target was the canal bridges near Cambrai, and that all four squadrons of 22nd Wing had been hastily redeployed to Champien aerodrome down on the Somme. As the SD aircrew went to bed that night, they learned that they were to be packed and ready to fly to Bertangles near Amiens next day.

By dawn on the 25th, everything had changed yet again. Robbie, Armstrong and Archie Watts were ordered to take off and bomb the bridges over the Somme as soon as possible.

"What about our kits, Coachie?" asked Armstrong.

"Leave them behind."

"So, we're coming back here, then?"

"For the moment." Peter Coachman stared at Armstrong, noting the large plaster on his forehead covering the slash cut he had received in his crash the week before. "And no stupid heroics, Armstrong, you understand?" He looked at the three officers. "We need every manjack who can fly – and the planes too. No-one knows what's going on. The Huns are through Fifth Army and heading for Amiens, by all accounts."

"*Amiens?*" interrupted Watts, a dark-haired, laconic senior observer. "Christ! That's nearly halfway to the coast!"

"Well, he isn't there yet, according to Wing, and we're going to see he can't move forward. So it's the bridge across the Somme at" – he looked at his orders – "at Peronne. And the 15,000 foot height restriction is lifted. Wattie; you're the senior. You're in charge. But no stupid heroics," he repeated, pointing at Armstrong, "you understand. Just be careful."

Armstrong coloured and nodded.

"Good." Coachman stared at them. "One other thing. Wing has told us that Richtofen's crowd have been called in to cover the Somme. So be careful. Good luck. I'll see you when you get back."

The aircrew assembled at Armstrong's DH4. Watts spread a map on the wing. "It's about half an hour's flying," he began, "That's if we go straight. But I'll wager that the Huns will be thick as fleas on a dog over those bridges. Stands to reason. And they'll have packed the area round the bridges with all the archie they can get." He looked at the other five airmen. "So, it ain't going to be easy."

The others nodded soberly.

"But there's another way of doing this stunt." He drew a gloved hand over the map tracing a line due east. "If we cross to our east, here," he indicated the front line at Armentières, "Then turn *south* well behind the Hun lines, we can come in from the rear. It's longer flying, I know, but the Huns won't be expecting an attack from the east, from behind them. With any luck, all their archie will be facing west, towards our lines. We should take 'em by surprise. What d'you think?"

Robbie nodded slowly. "How high do we bomb?"

"As low as we dare. Come downhill nice and steady, straight onto the bridges and away. Line astern, and fast. With luck no one can catch us."

Armstrong grinned. "Just like last time, eh?" He rubbed his hands.

Robbie stared at him. "You go as fast as you like, Jack, but I'm going to take it steady. And we' ll not follow you too close and get blown up again, that's for sure. I think we've had enough of your fathead stunts."

Armstrong's jaw dropped in surprise. "Fathead?" He exploded. "How dare you bloody call me a fathead, you young tick. I'm your flight commander and I've been out here a damned sight longer than you, let me tell you. Fathead? I'll give you bloody fathead…"

The frustrations of the Lesquins sortie boiled over. Robbie lost his temper. "Yes. A fathead! And a stupid, dangerous one too. You nearly killed Charlie Barton the other day. Stunting your kite. Showing off. Everyone thinks so. Don't we chaps?" The others looked away, embarrassed. "And we won"t forget that stupid stunt you pulled, two weeks ago, dive-bombing the railway-yards. Nearly ripped all our wings off let alone nearly blowing our bloody tail off too. Everyone knows you're a dangerous bloody maniac."

Armstrong stepped forward, threateningly.

Archie Watts broke in, putting his arm up between the two men. "That's enough! We've got the bloody Huns to fight, without squabbling among each other. Sort it all out when we get back." He stared at Armstrong, red with anger and glaring at Robbie. "Anyways, Jack, you've only got yourself to blame. All the fellows know that."

Armstrong frowned at the rebuke. He jabbed a threatening finger at Robbie. "I'll sort you out when we get back, young Roberts."

Timmy tried to change the subject. "How long are we over Hunland, Wattie?"

"I estimate about 50 minutes." The others looked up, startled. "But we've got two advantages," Watts went on. "One, we'll tuck ourselves just below the clouds, so no-one can surprise us out of the sun. Two, we'll be flying on the wrong course and in the wrong area for RFC kites. With any luck, the Huns won't be looking for us, and if they do see us, chances are they'll think we're Hun two-seaters. They'll be concentrating over the Somme, not fifty miles to the north, you can bet on it." He looked round at the other five men, sensing the tension in the air. "Now let's forget about this nonsense and get going. We've a real war to fight."

Armstrong glared and jabbed his finger at Robbie. "You've not heard the last of this, Roberts. You mark my words." He spun on his heel and they walked to their planes.

*   *   *

The take-off, with a 112lb bomb on the centre line, plus four 25lb Cooper bombs under the wings, was sluggish. Robbie held the labouring DH4 down as long as possible before lifting heavily over the boundary hedge and beginning a gentle bank to the left to head east. Far below, hands on hips and looking up at the DH4s, was the unmistakable figure of Peter Coachman. Ten minutes steady climbing brought them just under the cloud layer at 10,000 feet and to the accompaniment of a desultory salvo of black archie bursts the three DH4s flew east deep into German-occupied France.

Another ten minutes of scudding just below the cloud banks brought them north of Lille. Robbie saw Watts stand up in the rear cockpit of the lead DH4 and gesture to the right. The formation slowly banked to head due south. They were now thirty miles behind the German lines and over half an hour from the bridges. Robbie and Timmy scanned the sky below to see if there was any sign of German aircraft. Except for a cluster of glinting wings sliding west and far below as they crossed over Lille, nothing was seen.

The next twenty minutes was spent in anxious silence as the little formation droned on, occasionally flitting though wisps of cloud hanging lower than the rest. Once a fighter appeared far behind and followed them for a full five minutes before eventually turning west and dropping down out of sight.

They relaxed. Robbie looked around for the others. They had become spread out. Above and ahead was Wattie's kite. He looked back. Armstrong was quite a long way back. Although he never relaxed his constant vigilance of the sky, Robbie allowed his mind to drift over the subject of Jack Armstrong and his threat to "sort him out" when they got back. A cold anger came over him. There would be a row when they landed, that was for sure. After all, the cocky little bugger had nearly killed Charlie Barton with his stupid stunts. Robbie gritted his teeth, remembering Barton's seared face, like burnt meat, and the stink of burnt hair. Well, it was about time that someone sorted bloody Armstrong out, once and for all. He shook his head and tried to concentrate on the business in hand.

Cambrai slipped below the left wing and the DH4s angled slowly to their right. Not long now. Far ahead, Robbie could see a cluster of minute specks in the sky swirling like darting midges. As the minutes slid by they resolved into a tumbling, whirling aerial battle as distant planes jockeyed for position. Instinctively, the three DH4s drifted upwards to hug the protection of the cloud ceiling.

As he tore through the broken wisps of fog, Robbie occasionally lost sight of Watts' aeroplane. On emerging from a particularly blank ten seconds of grey nothingness, the leading DH4 was nowhere to be seen. Startled, he looked around. To his relief, a thousand feet below a DH4 was heading down to the right. It was Wattie. He banked his plane to follow.

As he did, a two seater RE8 suddenly hurtled vertically out of the clouds barely yards away, followed a split second later by a brightly-coloured German Albatross fighter streaking in hot pursuit of the British observation plane. The two aircraft plummeted down to disappear far below. Seconds later, Timmy's voice echoed in his ear. "Crashed. Poor blighter. Just went straight in."

Robbie nodded grimly and held his height. He intended to keep as close underneath the cloud base for as long as possible. Growing ever closer to Peronne, he could see the dancing specks of aeroplanes and the black clusters of Archie bursts dead ahead. He headed straight for them, knowing that the bridges must be below. Sure enough, he suddenly saw the glint of the river and the distinctive towers of Peronne's medieval castle. He pushed the nose down. "Right, Timmy! Here we go!"

The DH4 dived and picked up speed.

Ahead there was a melée of aeroplanes which slipped smoothly past as Robbie's aircraft dived through them. A couple of black-crossed fighters skidded away and tried to turn and follow them only to fall rapidly behind the speeding bomber. A trio of brightly painted Fokker triplanes burst apart like a covey of surprised pigeons as the racing DH4 hurtled straight through them down towards the bridge, now clear and dead ahead. It was packed by a black snake of men, horses and vehicles stretching for miles on either side. Mercifully there was no archie coming their way, although far ahead a positive barrage of grey and black puffs marked someone's passage. A sparkle of lights and smoke puffs on and around the bridge. Someone's bombs. Burst of tracer floating by. Another, faster.

Robbie lined his plane up, angling straight down the road for the bridge growing rapidly bigger, dead ahead. At less than 100 feet and well over 150 mph, the DH4 swept over its target and soared as the bombs dropped away. Robbie shoved the stick hard forward to keep the aircraft's nose down as they roared along the column of grey men, horses and guns, streaking by below, diving for the ditch, some shooting. Very fast. A blur of faces and men. Behind him, Robbie heard Timmy's twin Lewis guns hammering away. One hundred and fifty mph. Still very fast. Robbie's mouth was dry. He swallowed hard and pulled up a little.

Then they were banking hard to the right and swerving as a pair of black-crossed fighters hurtled in from their right, golden tracer spraying everywhere. A flash of bright red and green wings and they were through, heading for the British lines. Timmy's guns blasted away again. Robbie risked a glanced behind.

For a second, his heart stood still. Behind the racing DH4 was a swirling cluster of multi-coloured German aircraft desperately trying to catch up with the sprinting DH4. But even as he watched, Robbie realised that they were turning back one by one to blend with the blossoming puffs of pursuing archie over the bridge they were protecting. Further back still, a huge pall of black smoke billowed up over Peronne from a hellish red fire. Ahead, the Somme twisted and glinted to the west and safety in the watery sunlight. In the distance the front lines were growing closer. They were through. Safe. His heart was hammering. He let out a gust of pent up breath and throttled back. All clear. Automatically he swept the sky ahead.

There, to his astonishment, about a mile ahead and slightly above, he spotted a lone German Aviatik cruising on its artillery-spotting mission, drifting gently from his left to right, looking away towards the distant front lines. They hadn't seen the lone British aircraft, far below to the East, behind them.

Almost without thinking, Robbie nosed down and swung right to position himself below and to the rear of the two seater, throttling back to drift slowly upwards into the Aviatik's blind spot. He looked around. No German fighters. Any escort would be far above, watching out to ambush British scouts coming in from the West. The last thing they would be expecting was a British plane sneaking in low from the German lines.

The DH4 crept closer as they slid up from below the German's tail, growing larger by the second and hanging above their heads. It was like some deadly game of grandmother's footsteps, Robbie thought. He was surprised to discover that he was holding his breath. He cocked the single forward firing Vickers carefully and lined up the nose for his shot. The Germans had still not spotted them. He had the Hun plane cold. Nearly there. Now!

Suddenly, without warning, a DH4 roared in diagonally in from their left.

It was Jack Armstrong. His Flight Commander swept in front, blocking his shot. Robbie frantically pushed his aeroplane's nose hard down to avoid a collision. Armstrong's hand waved derisively. For a second Robbie could swear that he could see the flash of Armstrong's teeth as he cut in, boring in close to steal Robbie's kill.

At the last minute, the Aviatik noticed them. Whether it was Jack Armstrong's or Robbie's aeroplane, they never knew. Robbie suspected it was his, because the black-crossed two-seater suddenly reared to its right like a panicking horse, standing on its wing to escape, a crucifix in the sky. A horrified Robbie shrieked "*No!*"

Armstrong's DH4 smashed smack into the middle of the fleeing German.

The two aircraft froze, merged into one single wreck of wood and canvas and spars to hang still in the air for a split second like a broken kite. Robbie saw a goggled face slowly turning round to stare at them. Then the strange tangle dropped vertically like a stone.

"Oh my God", came Timmy's voice from behind. "What the hell…?"

Robbie continued his turn. Far below, the doomed wreckage plummeted earthwards, shedding broken fragments of fabric and wood to flutter in the air like blowing rubbish. The DH4 nosed down to follow the strange shape of the two locked-together airframes. After what seemed an eternity they thumped into the ground, scattering wreckage bouncing everywhere for a second before flashing into flame and sending an oily column of black smoke skywards. Robbie circled the funeral pyre. There were no survivors.

"Christ!" said Timmy from the back seat. A stunned Robbie checked the sky and automatically set course for home.

With a sense of shock he realised that he would never have his row with Jack Armstrong now. Jack Armstrong was dead. Gone forever, along with David Blair, his ever-loyal observer. Armstrong had killed them both. He would never speak to his flight commander again. He wondered what Peter Coachman would say. Jack Armstrong was *dead*.

Ludendorff's great offensive had just claimed four more casualties.

CHAPTER 35

Kaiserschlacht – Progress?

26ᵗʰ March 1918

"Casualties? I'll say there are bloody casualties…"

General Sir Hubert Gough frowned in irritation and held the telephone away from his ear, pulling a face at his Chief of Staff standing at his side.

"Now look here," he said in his slightly high-pitched drawl. "I'm sure you're exaggerating, Mountford. I can't believe that you've really lost so many guns. It's impossible; quite impossible. Probably what's happened is that you've just lost contact with your fellows as they pulled back. What?"

His senior gunner was panicking, he thought. It was bad enough the Huns breaking in without getting into a muck sweat about a few batteries out of touch. Damn' feller'd lost his nerve. Have to go. Whole bloody army was in trouble. What was the matter with them all?

"Now look here, Mountford…" he began.

"No, general, you look here," said the angry voice on the 'phone. "You've not the faintest idea what's going on. There are Huns everywhere. I've seen 'em. They're pouring through. I've bin from Bapaume to God knows where over the past week. The front's as good as busted all along the line. We've lost over 400 guns and Christ knows what's happened to the infantry…"

"Pull yourself together, Mountford," said Gough crisply. Damned man really would have to go, he decided. Obviously lost his nerve. "Of course we haven't lost 400 guns. Don't be ridiculous." He came to a decision. Time for some firm leadership. "You're relieved. Relieved. Hand over to your Chief of Staff immediately and report to me here. Immediately – d'you hear?"

The voice on the line laughed shrilly. "Report to *you*? How? I'm surrounded by Huns, you damned idiot. Don't your realise, Gough, that we're cut off?"

"Cut off?" Gough was startled beyond his gunner's insubordination.

"Yes, *General*," blazed the tinny voice, its rage audible even over the handset. "Germans. All over the bloody gun-lines. We're firing over open sights direct onto Hun guns at 400 yards in some places. Can't you understand that?"

"Impossible," muttered Gough. "You're with 18 Corps…" He glanced at the map on the wall. "You're back with 39 Division's gun line."

"Impossible?" shouted the irate voice. "Impossible? By God! Listen, you idiot, if I stuck the telephone outside you'd hear 39 Div's bloody 60 pounders firing over open sights at the Huns' artillery! What's the matter with you, for God's sake? The Hun is through on the Somme. They're all round us. There is no Eighteen Corps, man. We're fighting for our lives. We've got infantry running away up here."

"Impossible," muttered Gough weakly. "Not my soldiers… not Fifth Army…"

The voice at the other end recovered its composure. "Impossible is it? Well, you'd best come up the line and see for yourself, General, before you meet some of your soldiers coming back to see you, I think. The infantry's running back. Running. Whole brigades have gone. And if my headquarters wasn't surrounded by bloody Germans – I'd join them and give you a piece of my…" The phone cut off abruptly. Two pink spots glowed in Gough's cheeks.

"More trouble, General?" enquired his Chief of Staff.

"Yes. Mountford. Damned feller's lost his nerve." He pushed himself petulantly away from his desk. "Says the infantry's running away. Damned fool." He stood up and rounded on his ever-patient BGGS. "You get on to the Gunners at 39 Division and get Mountford back here. Tell him from me he's relieved of command. Now!"

But, despite the best efforts of both his staff and HQ's harassed Signals Section, General Sir Hubert Gough, KCB, KCVO, Commander Fifth Army, was unable to make contact with the cut off gun lines of 18 Corps. The Chief of Artillery was already a German prisoner.

Two days later, to his own surprise, it was "Goughie", the "darling of the cavalry" who was summarily relieved of what was left of his wrecked and ruined command.

*   *   *   *   *   *   *

It took the German Army just one week to rip the British and the French armies apart. Despite heroic efforts by both British and French reinforcements flung in on either flank of the breakthrough, the Germans flooded up the valley of the Somme, pushing hard for Amiens and the Channel coast. Only exhaustion and a marked tendency to loot the well-stocked captured British depots slowed the German advance until finally it sputtered out at Villers-Bretonneux, at the very eastern gates of Amiens itself. By that point the *FeldPolizei* was reporting that half the surviving storm troopers were incapably drunk on looted whisky and service rum. It appeared that no one had anticipated the disintegrating effect of victory - even upon well-disciplined forces.

No sooner had the hard-pressed Allies restored some semblance of order than Ludendorff struck again, this time in the north, against Ypres. A Portuguese division collapsed and "Daddy" Plumer's 2nd Army infantry barely managed to stem the stormtroopers from seizing the Ypres Salient itself. Even as Haig shored up this disaster, another befell him. Armentières was evacuated, as everywhere the British pulled back. For the British Expeditionary force, April 1918 was a time of defeat and trial.

The newly formed Royal Air Force was no exception. The rebadging from Royal Flying Corps to become the new Royal Air Force on the First of April went virtually unnoticed by the fighting squadrons, as day after day they were launched to try and halt the advancing Germans. Robbie's log-book recorded a brief note on 1 April 1918 commemorating his new allegiance, before submerging itself into a long list of operational entries and records of bombing raids.

Surprisingly after the shock of Jack Armstrong's death, 25 Squadron suffered no more casualties. There were several reasons for this, despite the constant rate of flying. On one no-flying day towards the end of April, Robbie totalled up that he had done no fewer than 37 sorties since 25th March. Yet no-one had been lost. GHQ's stern admonition to maintain the 15,000-foot bombing height for DH4s played its part, as did the growing experience of the crews, and Major Duffus's careful leadership. 25 Squadron was tired but efficient. On one occasion, three DH4s from St Omer on an unescorted bombing run towards Courtrai had seen off nearly ten assorted German fighters, without loss to themselves. After two of the attacking Germans had been downed on their first pass the others hung back, occasionally darting in to be driven back by the concentrated fire of twelve well-directed Lewis guns. Eventually one too-daring German was hit and exploded earthwards, twisting and turning in a stream of burning petrol.

The sight of their comrade flaring earthwards like a thrown down match was too much for the remaining attackers. They banked and flew off. That night, Twenty-five Squadron's crews got very drunk. But nothing could mask the overall feeling that the German steamroller was winning, as April turned to May.

The merest glance at the map of German gains proved that.

*   *   *

At OHL, Major Wendel, like all the German HQ staff, was buoyed up by the prevailing mood of victory. However, while it was clear that the British were in deep trouble, there was an undercurrent below the surface that worried him. Behind the boastful reports of success at every daily staff conference – only that morning, "Operations" had reported that of the 59 identified British divisions, 53 had been engaged, of which 15 had been destroyed – Wendel sensed an unease in the High Command.

Even Ludendorff's habitual optimism seemed muted. The triumphant announcement by Intelligence that they had calculated that the British had lost a quarter of a million men, 10,000 officers and over a thousand guns since the *Kaiserschlacht* had begun hardly seemed to dent Ludenforff's air of self-absorption. The First Quartermaster General seemed more concerned with his own army's defects than its victories. While it was undeniable that there were too many reports of indiscipline, and units seemed to be disappearing as fast as they were committed, the fact is, thought Wendel, we're winning! But somehow, he thought, something's wrong.

He raised the subject with his orderly as they pored over a pile of reports one evening.

Weissmüller's reply surprised him. "Of course there's a mood of pessimism, *Herr Major*. Everyone knows that we've lost the war."

To say that Wendel was scandalised was an understatement. "Weissmüller! Lost the war? How *dare* you? How can you say that? We're winning. The greatest victory in the Fatherland's history, and you sit there and calmly tell me we've lost the war? My God, what kind of defeatist talk is that? Are you mad?"

The Rhinelander rubbed his face and laid down his pen. "Forgive me, *Herr Major*. Please don't think I don't want Germany to win this *verdammte* war. Of course I do; it's just that we can't. Not now."

"Weissmüller, how can you say that? First, it's treacherous talk, and second, you're wrong. For Christ's sake! We're winning, man."

Weissmuller looked at his boss sadly. He liked Wendel and felt as close as any Jewish trainee schoolmaster from the Rhineland could towards a Bavarian aristocrat and a pre-war professional soldier at that. In a way he loved Wendel. He liked the cavalry officer's decency, his sense of duty and honour, his wry sense of humour and the way he turned a blind eye to his orderly's all-too-frequent utterings of disrespect for things military and contempt for Prussian bullshit. Above all, Weissmüller respected Wendel for his ability to tolerate the pain of his wounds without complaint. "Oh, *Herr Major…*" he began.

There was a knock at the office door. The long dark figure of Stube, the press man, opened it. "May I come in?"

"Of course," muttered Wendel, mechanically.

Stube stopped, sensing the atmosphere. "Is something wrong?"

"Ja, you could say that, Stube. My orderly has just told me he thinks that we're going to lose the war." Wendel waved his arm at a chair. "After I've just recommended him for promotion, too."

Weissmüller looked up, surprised.

"You'd better enlighten him before he's shot as a traitor once old von Zelle gets back from convalescent leave."

The word "traitor" made Stube's stomach tighten. "May I sit down?"

"Of course. Have a drink." Wendel indicated a tray in the corner with a bottle and glasses.

"The good news is that old von Zelle won't be coming back." Stube looked up to catch the glances of Wendel and Weissmüller. He poured himself a generous brandy and one for Wendel, too. "The gossip is, he's to stay on in Potsdam at the War Ministry and oversee prisoner-of-war administration."

Weissmüller snorted with laughter and even Wendel smiled.

"There's more," went on Stube. "Apparently he's now giving heroic interviews about life at the Front. 'Our gallant soldiers…'; that kind of stuff." He smiled and swilled his brandy. "That's how I found out. Clearing an article for the *Allgemeine*… And he's been awarded a medal." Wendel and Weissmuller looked at each other, then burst out laughing. Stube joined in.

"Weissmüller," said Wendel, wiping his eye. "Pour yourself a drink, you idiot. Even an insubordinate traitor like you should join your officers in our loyal toast." He raised his glass. "To *Oberst* von Zelle, heroic soldier of the Reich: and to Germany's ultimate victory!"

They drank.

"Now," said Stube, when the hilarity had subsided. "What's all this about you being a traitor, eh, Weissmüller? You don't seem the type to me."

"Oh, I'm not a traitor, *Herr* Stube. It's just that I don't believe we can win the war now."

Stube looked at Wendel, who raised his eyebrows and poured more brandy into all three glasses.

The lanky journalist pulled a face. "Have you decided who you want to represent you at your court martial, Weissmuller?" he added sarcastically. "Because if anybody else hears you talking like that around here, I believe that the good major here will soon be looking to find another orderly. Never mind. I'll tell your mother that you were a good soldier when they come to shoot you. I think you'd better explain yourself, Weissmüller. Explain."

Weissmüller looked down at his glass, then stared at the two staff offers. "I am just a corporal…" he began.

"Stop," said Wendel. "Stop now. If *Herr* Stube and I order you to explain your views then it is your duty to do so. You are not "just a corporal". You are an intelligent German non-commissioned officer who has been wounded in the service of the Reich. You have the Verdun clasp. God knows there are few enough front line soldiers around here. So say your piece, corporal. Without fear or favour. That's an order, by the way. An *order."*

"Very well, *Herr* Major." Weissmüller's manner was formal, thoughtful. He cleared his throat.

"It seems to me that if we really were winning, then we should have done more by now, much more. *General* von Ludendorff said we'd split the British and French; we haven't. He said we'd defeat them before the Amis arrived; we haven't. Even the HQ daily orders sheet admits that the Americans are fighting in the battle line down south now. And we have taken a lot of casualties. A *lot*," he emphasised. "*Feldwebel* Stozback in Personnel tells me that his branch has recorded 300,000 casualties so far. 300,000!" he repeated. Wendel and Stube looked at each other, shocked.

Weissmüller took a sip of his brandy and continued. "Even I can see that we can't go on. And have you seen the battle replacements coming up from the depots? They're rubbish. You should see them. Old men, kids, socialists preaching defeatism, mummy's boys who can't wait to desert. Oh, you should hear them talking in the soldiers' lines. I had to threaten one the other night; an ex-navy apprentice from Kiel – full of it, he was: the Red Flag, soldiers' councils, end the war, overthrow the Kaiser, set up a socialist government. All that sort of rubbish. I tell you…"

He swilled his glass and drank deeply. "And then there's the stuff from home. Strikes, shortages, unrest, workers jailed, rationing. My mother tells me that they're putting sawdust in the bread now. The only thing not in short supply is turnips, from what she says. Turnips!" He spat out disgustedly, then looked at Stube. "You're our pressman, Sir. It's true, isn't it? You should know. It's true – back in the *Heimat*?"

Stube nodded.

Weissmüller shook his head. "There you are, then. And the Tommies live like lords. Never mind that rubbish about our heroic U-boats having brought them to their knees." He reached down for a haversack in the corner. "This is what Herling, the *StabsFeldwebel* in the QM's branch, brought back last night from his inspection of the British dumps we've captured. Finished, are they?" He emptied the pack carefully. Wendel's eyes widened as chocolate, tea, whisky and tins of ham spilled onto the desk. "I don't think so. And that's just my share. Oh," and he reached into a side pocket. "And here's a couple of the Tommies' First Field dressings. Cotton wool and real bandages. No crêpe-paper wound dressings for the

English, even the common soldier."

He looked up. "That's why I think we can't win now, short of a miracle. We're losing the *materialschlacht*, the supplies war. The Tommies have more of everything we're running out of and it's getting worse every day. Even when they're supposed to be beaten…"

He put his glass down on the desk with exaggerated care. "You asked me what I think *Herr* Major. Well, that's what I think. I think our real situation is much worse than we are pretending, victories or no victories. And once the *Amis* join in, we're sunk."

Wendel was speechless. He looked at Stube.

The journalist's mind raced. He sensed a big advantage in the conversation. "Well, Weissmüller, that's not defeatist talk. It's just… Well, dangerous stuff to say in public. The truth often is." He glanced sideways at Wendel. "Of course we have problems at home, serious problems. No one could deny that. But we are a long way short of defeat, surely? Don't you think that the Reich can still get an honourable peace?"

Wendel was about to say something but Weissmüller cut in.

"I don't honestly think we have time, *Herr* Stube. We should have won this war by Christmas 1914. A fast knock-out blow to France, like 1870. Then turn on the Russkis and it'll all be over. Remember? That's what old von Schlieffen always wanted. That's what the Kaiser said. Everybody remembers that. But once we came back from the Marne in 1914, we'd failed. Even a trainee schoolmaster from the Rheinland called up as a reservist grenadier can see that…" He leant back, eyes closed. "The rest, *lieber Herren*… I'm sorry." He opened his eyes and drank deeply of his brandy.

He stood up to go. "The rest is merely the truth, *Herr Major*. You ordered me to say my piece. I'm sorry if I spoke too freely. I've said too much, but I'm only an NCO. I've been out here since 1915 and I'm worried about my family back home. I hope you understand. I pray to God that Germany can still win, I really do."

"Sit down, Weissmüller." Wendel's voice was surprisingly gentle. "Sit down," he commanded. Glancing at Stube, he said "You should know, *Herr* Stube. Is Weissmüller a traitor to say these things? Or is he right?"

Stube sensed his moment. He knew full well that the Bavarian major was no Prussian stooge. His mind raced. Had he found a genuine waverer on the Command Staff of OHL? Now, that would be an incredible ally to recruit; but how? He measured his words with care. "In the first place, do not apologise, Weissmüller. Sadly, you are only saying what is true. *Herr* Wendel is the headquarters Security Officer. His job is to keep the lid on this particular cookpot. But my job is to report what is going on, and nowadays even that is difficult; sometimes impossible." He looked down at his hands.

"The truth is, we do have problems, bad ones. Back home, Germany is not the place we left to come to this war. The *Reichstag* is up in arms about the power of our commanders here. The Parliamentary Deputies are calling for peace, quite openly. And they're screaming for the end of what they say is a military dictatorship. The army and police are rounding up deserters and agitators in thousands and packing them off to forced labour battalions. That's not going down well, I can tell you. There's a lot of anti-army stuff going on back home. The public just laugh at the official army *communiqués* now. Quite openly. Sometimes they rip the posters down. I tell you, the gap between soldier and civilian back home has never been greater, or more bitter, I must say. I know these things, as a professional journalist should. But I would never print them for fear of damaging national morale."

He looked at Wendel, straight in the eye. "I know my duty as a good German as well as any officer of the General Staff. But I also know the truth. The real truth." He leaned back, transferring his gaze to Weissmüller. "That is why I don't think you're a traitor, Weissmüller, merely a clever NCO who's a bit too observant and far too open-mouthed."

Wendel was silent for a long second. "*Lieber Gott!* Is it really as bad as that? Back home?"

"Oh, yes." Stube nodded emphatically. "Worse, in fact. Did you know that Hindenburg has threatened to execute black marketeers, deserters and strikers, shoot them out of hand, imprison their families? Civilians, to be tried by court martial. There's uproar back home."

Wendel fiddled with his pens. "You should see the Censorship reports I see, Stube. They're terrible. The soldiers moan, they complain they've lost confidence in the High Command, their officers. I spend half my day fending off calls to court martial the moaners. You wouldn't believe it."

The group fell silent.

Stube sensed his chance and risked it, as delicately as a fisherman dropping a fly on a trout stream. "You know, if what you say is true, then I think that we should work together. For the good of the Headquarters. Compare reports; that kind of thing. I see all the stuff from back home and from the international press. You see all the security reports and the internal stuff, Wendel. And Weissmuller has the run of the soldiers' lines. You hear all the gossip. No-one is better placed to keep their finger on the pulse, the real truth, than we three here. Am I right?"

He held his breath. Wendel scratched his stump moodily, and gestured to Weissmüller for more brandy. "To what purpose, Stube? What's the point? We can't put it right."

"True, *Herr* Wendel. But we can report honestly on the real state of affairs to the Chief…"

"Háh! Much good that'll do," burst out Wendel. "The last thing Ludendorff wants to hear is the truth. All he's interested in is victory, victory. Never mind the real state of affairs, Stube. Even that bomb on the train…"

Stube's stomach tightened again at the mention of his unsuccessful attempt to murder the Duo. "What about it?"

"Oh, Ludendorff's always asking for an update on how well my investigation is going. Traitors, spies, even Reds and Bolsheviks. You name it, Ludendorff's convinced he knows best, whatever the truth about that bomb."

"Which is?"

"Bad luck. Sheer chance. Tommy aircraft bomb. But old Ludendorff won't have it." He banged the pile of files on his desk. "It's a plot. So poor old Weissmüller and I have to spend hours going through endless reports pretending to look for the real truth and some non-existent spy. Something that'll satisfy Ludendorff."

Stube relaxed. "Any luck?"

"Nah," scoffed Wendel. He looked at his clerk, quiet in the corner. "Weissmüller and I have flogged through hundreds of things. But there's nothing, there's never was any phantom spy, and we're still at it. Waste of time."

Stube pulled a sympathetic face. "Sorry I can't help," he began untruthfully. He returned to the matter in hand. "So do you think we should work together in future? Pool our information?"

Wendel shrugged. "Can't do any harm." He looked at Weissmüller. "What do you think?" Weissmuller had recovered some of his composure. "Me, *Herr* Major? I am just a humble staff corporal ..." he began.

"Shut up, Weissmüller," said Wendel. "I'm asking you if you think it will help. Don't give me that 'I'm just an NCO' stuff. The NCOs round here know a damn sight more than most of the staff officers about what's going on."

"In that case, yes, *Herr* Major. If Herr Stube can tell us what's really going on outside the HQ, then we can judge better what the real state is among the soldiers. It'll show us if those security and morale reports, the bad ones, are really justified. I think it's a good idea."

"And I benefit," cut in Stube quickly, "because I can put all my reports about unrest back home against the context of what's really going on on the battlefield, without having to rely on all that optimistic pap that Operations Branch and Ludendorff keep feeding me for the official *communiqué*."

"Seems sound enough to me," said Wendel.

"Good." Stube stood up. "Thanks for the brandy." He slapped Wendel's orderly gently on the shoulder. "I wouldn't worry too much about being accused of being a defeatist, Weissmüller. It's just that round here the truth could be dangerous. Guard that tongue of yours, eh?" He nodded to Wendel. "I'll pop by tomorrow and let you know what the Tommies and the French press are saying." He thought for second. "And the Swiss reports." He shook his head. "Now they're really depressing."

"Good," said Wendel. "And Weissmüller here will let you see the full operational and security reports. See if they match, eh?"

Stube closed the door and stood outside smiling as he shrugged on his coat. Non-existent spy? Well, the "non-existent spy" had just recruited a spy ring inside OHL, the German GHQ for the Western Front.

That should please London.

CHAPTER 36

A Second Chance?
LONDON

May 1918

London, as Stube had forecast, was indeed impressed.

So much so that Cumming felt that the need to tell Hubert Neville – in strict confidence, of course – of his Service's success, as they walked across Whitehall to the meeting of the Intelligence Planning Committee.

"By the way, Neville before we go into the meeting, you ought to know, A34's become active again."

"Oh?"

"Yes. Bit of a coup, really. Just between you and me, he's recruited the Huns' security officer at Ludendorff's HQ. Good, eh?"

Neville was astounded. "The OHL Security Officer? Good God, why?"

"Why, as in why recruit him? Or why, as in why the Security Officer?"

"Yes," said Neville. "Both." A thought struck him. "Won't it put your A34 in danger? Compromise him?"

"Well, as far as we can make out, the chap doesn't realise he's been recruited. Doesn't realise what A34's up to. Just thinks he's helping the cause. You know, better Germany, concerned citizen, that kind of stuff."

Neville raised his eyebrows. "He sounds a remarkably stupid man."

Cumming shook his head. "A34 doesn't think so. He rates him very highly as a source. Good chap. Bavarian; regular officer - General Staff, badly wounded in East Africa with Lettow-Vorbeck's lot. Likes him. He says the man's just worried about the future. And his Serjeant clerk, too. Ex-school teacher; Rhinelander; Jew. Clever feller, according to A34."

He stared down at Neville.

"No, A34's done us proud here. Says it gives him lots of access to their High Command documents. Mainly morale, unrest among the staff – that kind of stuff. Damned useful to your people, I'd say."

Neville considered this as they strolled up Whitehall. "Does anyone else know?"

"Not likely! I'd rather cut my own throat. Only you. No, I just wondered if it's worth raising in the meeting. That's why I ran it by you first."

Neville was silent for a few paces, a look of concentration on his face. Eventually he spoke. "No, I don't think you should, Cumming. With Maurice gone, better the Committee doesn't know. Certainly not at this stage."

This would be the third meeting of the Intelligence Planning Committee. General Maurice, the late Director of Military Operations would not be attending. His patience had snapped. He had written to the newspapers to tell them that Lloyd George had lied to Parliament back in February about the explosive subject of shortages of Army manpower. The fact was that the Prime Minister really was starving the BEF by secretly holding one hundred thousand soldiers back in Britain to keep them away from what he saw as Haig's bloody clutches. However, Maurice had made the mistake of telling the world the truth; the PM was lying.

The PM's revenge had been swift and savage. General Maurice, a senior serving soldier, had been peremptorily dismissed on the orders of a vengeful PM. The Army Board pensioned him off overnight on Lloyd George's express orders. As a result, relations between soldiers and politicians were on a knife-edge of mutual detestation. The Whitehall atmosphere was even more explosive than usual. In dark corners generals and politicians were even muttering "*Who's running this war?*"

In such a poisonous atmosphere, as Neville had suspected, Lloyd George had been only too grateful to accept a personal, private briefing on secret intelligence matters when Hubert Neville had raised the subject at the end of his deliberately pessimistic briefing to the War Cabinet. They had been shocked at his gloomy prognostications of German intentions and had been only too ready to clutch at straws when Neville had offered the PM some solutions in private, "as I set out in my memorandum, PM…"

Neville had been even more delighted at the sight of a puzzled Hankey flipping through his briefing file, obviously searching for some unseen memo. Out of the corner of his eye – for he was naturally giving Lloyd George his whole sympathetic attention – Neville saw Hankey's head slowly come up to stare at him. The War Cabinet Secretary, as Hubert

Neville had so acutely calculated, had obviously just found the missing memo – too late.

Hankey's offer to "take the minutes at the meeting, PM" had been courteously declined by Hubert Neville on the grounds that "these are matters strictly for your ears only, Prime Minister". Lloyd George had readily agreed, as Neville knew he would – the old goat would do anything for a whiff of secrets and intrigue – and Hankey had been left in the dark, just as Neville had planned.

But, as he later pointed out to young Asprey, over a congenial glass of dry sherry in his office, "You know Asprey, Hankey's the sort of man who'll write a book to try and make money when the war's over. You mark my words. And I am very much afraid that he will somehow contrive to write something that elevates the role of Maurice Hankey and just what an important part he has played in this war. It will be all about "power" if I'm any judge and probably not a word about "intelligence". The fellow just doesn't understand the subject, I'm afraid."

Asprey had smiled and remarked dryly, "You mean that Colonel Hankey lacks intelligence, Dr Neville? In which sense?" Hubert Neville had thought that was rather witty.

Cumming and Neville turned into Whitehall Place.

"So, what's top of the agenda today, Neville?" boomed Cumming. "Still trying to get the Admiralty on board?"

"Oh yes," said Neville. "But their Lordships will come on board, as you put it, sooner or later, especially when they realise that Haig's asked the BEF to be represented in future. They think we're important enough to send a Colonel Mackenzie across from G Intelligence in Montreuil to join our little committee. Observer status, of course."

"I didn't know that, Neville."

"Oh? Didn't I tell you?" replied Neville, vaguely, waving his stick at the doorman. "Didn't think it was that important."

But Mackenzie's presence at the meeting was important, and was to change the course of history. For, after the customary exchange of views and wrangle over who should write to Admiral Blinker Hall, the Royal Navy's irascible Chief Intelligence Officer, to encourage him to join the

Committee, the members of the IPC turned their minds, in the manner of all committees, to thinking about what to do next and prolong the Committee's existence. Inevitably it was Neville who lit the fuse on a chain of events that would eventually have far-reaching consequences. This time, however – unusually for an agile mind – it was by accident, not design.

As the meeting drew to its close he asked Mackenzie, more out of courtesy than anything else, if there were any particular subjects on which they could assist the BEF, now reeling under the double hammer blows of Ludendorff's great offensive. Mackenzie equally casually asked what – if anything – had really come out of Haig's vaguely phrased request for assistance against "strategic targets" earlier in the year. The last he had seen was a vague reply from the Maurice, the now sacked DMO.

The committee looked uneasy. It was Cumming of SIS who broke the silence. It was, he reasoned, his business, and his alone. After all, A34 was his man and the memory of Everitt's sudden demise still kept him awake at night.

"Well, I don"t know if Freddie Browning has explained…" he looked at his deputy, who shook his head. "Fact is, we *did* have a crack at the Duo. Very secret. Unfortunately it didn't work. Good scheme and nearly came off, but failed by a whisker. Shook 'em up, though." The others nodded. Mackenzie sat transfixed. Not a whisper of this had got back to the BEF.

Cumming went on. "I've not told General Cox, or even Drake, nor anyone else over in France for that matter, MacKenzie. Seemed safer, really. Kept it here in London. But that's what happened. We really did have a bash as requested by you chaps in the BEF. Didn't work. Sorry."

Mackenzie interrupted, "What did you do exactly?"

C harrumphed and looked at Neville. The civil servant interposed smoothly, "We decided to plant a bomb. Unfortunately it was moved at the last minute and exploded next door. A 'near miss' might be the appropriate sporting analogy, I believe."

"Did they know?" spluttered Mackenzie. "The Duo, I mean?"

"Oh, yes," said Neville. "In the circumstances of the explosion, and its – ah – proximity, I understand that they could hardly miss it," he added and was rewarded by a chuckle around the table.

"Good God," said Mackenzie. "Shall I brief the Chief, when I get back?"

Neville looked round the faces. "I don't see why not," he began, gauging the mood. "I think anything that reassures Haig that we are doing our best on his behalf can only be of help in these difficult times, don't you agree? But nothing on paper, please and no detail. But you can tell your C-in-C that we tried."

"But this is tremendous news, Mr Neville," Mackenzie said. "Absolutely terrific. When are we going to have another crack at them? Or…" he broke off, looking round the table.

They all stared back at him open-mouthed.

Because the truth was that all the conspirators had regarded their attack on the Duo as a one-off event. Once it had failed they had individually and collectively assumed that there could be no further attempt. But the minute the BEF's intelligence man had spoken, they realised – as if curtains had suddenly parted – that they had all missed the obvious. For they knew, as Mackenzie did not, that the German High Command believed the bombing of the OHL train was a chance attack from the air.

As busy men with departments, pressures and daily responsibilies to fill their minds, the possibility of planning a second attempt on the Duo had simply not occurred to the members of the Intelligence Planning Committee. Suddenly they had seen the tantalising prospect of another chance of success. Instinctively they looked to Neville for guidance.

The fact was that Neville himself had missed the obvious as well. The failure of Stube's "cheese bomb" had, to his mind at least, made all future attempts impossible. His mind had been so cluttered by Hankey and the PM and the doings of Whitehall that he had overlooked the fact that there was still another chance at attacking their unsuspecting targets. While he had been mulling over bombing headquarters and trains, the Duo's continuing vulnerablity had completely passed him by. It drew a rare oath from his lips.

"I'll be damned, Mackenzie, you're absolutely correct! Of course we could have another shot at them. They still don't suspect a thing." He slapped his hand gently on the table. "How could we have been so blind? What do you say?" he enquired of his fellow committee members.

Unsurprisingly, the group was all for a fresh attempt on the Duo. The gloomy news from the front made it more imperative than ever to put a spoke in the *Kaiserschlacht*'s ever-rolling wheel and Mackenzie from the BEF was, inevitably, a more than willing ally. As the discussion roved around the table however it became obvious to them all that something more was required, however. Someone was going to have to devote himself exclusively to such a sensitive subject.

Neville put his finger on it. "I believe that this is now too important to be left to fortune, gentlemen. We're going to need someone to deal with this full time, I believe. What do you think?" They looked at each other, torn (like all ambitious men) between the desire to grab whatever glory might be going and the equally strong desire to avoid the blame if it all went horribly wrong.

Mackenzie who, representing the BEF, had no stake in either, spoke up first, "Why don't I give you one of my fellows full-time, to help out? He's just the man for the job." He looked around. "Bright young man. Doctorate at Cambridge - German studies or something. Speaks German like a native; understands them. My best order of battle analyst. Damn' good. Predicted the big attack to the hour. Just the chap to keep an eye on the Hun…"

Thus it was agreed that Lieutenant (temporary Captain) Dr Charles Powell, late of the University of Birmingham and General Staff (Intelligence) BEF, would become secretary of the Intelligence Planning Committee Study Group on "Targets of Value". He would work directly for Dr Hubert Neville.

It was a decision that would have far-reaching consequences and change many lives.

*   *   *

Charles Powell's call to report immediately to Brigadier General Cox's office both astonished and delighted the young intelligence officer. The news that he was to be taken off all other duties in GHQ and work directly on secret service work for London came as a genuine shock. He liked working in Mackenzie's Intelligence Branch, and Drake's secret service work behind the green baize door had long been a source of speculation among the junior intelligence officers. So it was with something approaching genuine relish that he approached his new secret task.

Even that came as a surprise. He had expected that his order of battle work would be his prime role. But both Cox and Mackenzie had made it plain that something new was expected.

"You see, Powell," Cox had said, "we can't give you clear orders, because we don't know what you'll find. He smiled at Mackenzie. "All we can tell you is what we want you to look for."

Mazkenzie took up the briefing. "Don't look so puzzled, Powell. Intelligent chap like you. Do you remember that conference in the Blue Mirror Room back in January? The one where Marshall-Cornwall and Bobbie Purfitt suggested having a pop at the German High Command?"

"Very well, Sir."

"Well, we followed it up, or rather the Chief did, with London." He paused and looked for guidance at Cox.

Powell broke in. "Good Lord. I never realised. We did? That's ripping! What did London say, Sir?" MacKenzie looked at Cox who nodded fractionally.

Mackenzie continued. "They said to go ahead, but they, London, took over the running of the – ah - the operation. Pretty secret stuff, y'see."

"And what happened, Sir?" Powell was breathless with excitement.

"Well, it didn't go according to plan, I'm afraid. Worked all right, but missed the target, if you see what I mean."

Powell didn't, entirely, but had the good sense to keep his mouth shut while the Colonel looked at his own boss for help.

"Truth is, Powell, you don't need to know all the details, but basically London organised a crack at the Duo ..."

"Hindenburg and Ludendorff?" asked Powell, incredulously. "Golly!"

Cox smiled at his youthful enthusiasm. "…and it misfired," he went on.

"Gosh," Powell repeated. "I mean, good Lord. What went wrong? How did they…" A hundred questions tumbled into his brain.

Cox held up a pacifying hand. "Doesn't matter. You don't need to know, any more than we do. What does matter, however, is that we're still free to have another go."

"And that's where you come in, Powell," said Mackenzie. "No-one knows the detail of the Huns' order of battle, and how they work, better than you do. You're to act as the I.O. responsible for seeing if we really can have another crack at them. Dedicated, full time. Track their high command's movement plans, see where they're going, find a weakness; that sort of thing."

"Target them, Sir? The Duo?"

"Exactly – target them."

"But who will do the attack?"

"Don't you worry about that, Powell. Not our concern. Your job is just to look out for any chance we might have of having a go at them and let us know."

"Good heavens," said a stunned Powell. "Who do I report to? Where will I work?"

Mackenzie looked at Cox. The BEF's intelligence chief picked up his ruler and spoke to it rather than to Powell.

"You'll work direct to Colonel MacKenzie of G Int. Personally. He's your boss. In strict confidence, mind. As for *where* you'll work…" He looked at MacKenzie, who took up the dialogue.

"You'll work out of an office in Colonel Drake's section in Int 1B. You're to run it on your own, without a clerk, and without any unnecessary paperwork. All files – everything, mind – is to be kept under strict lock and key; absolute security. You're free to ask to see any papers you like on OHL and their High Command out of any BEF Intelligence office. You're looking for anything that gives us an opening, some kind of chance to mount a direct attack on the Huns' headquarters and their top generals…"

"Ideally with as much notice as possible, obviously," broke in Cox.

"But anything with a 24 hour lead time is acceptable," added Mackenzie. He looked at Cox, who nodded and pointed the black ruler at Powell. "Twenty-four hours' notice, that's all we need; but more if possible, naturally."

Powell was absorbing the practicalities of his new task. "Who do I report to, Sir?"

"Me," said Cox and Mackenzie, simultaneously, and then both laughed. The Brigadier General put the black ruler down carefully.

"Actually you'll report mainly to a chap in London. Mr Neville - Hubert Neville. Professor Neville, really. Works directly for the War Cabinet and Number 10."

Powell's eyebrows shot up.

"Yes," said Cox grimly. "So you'd better be careful, young man. And keep your mouth shut in the Mess, too. No-one's to know about this, except us."

"And Colonel Drake. He knows; the outline anyway," added Mackenzie. "He'll help you all he can with his Intelligence 1(B) team. He's got access to all the secret service networks behind the Hun lines, and his chaps even work with the French intelligence people. They don't know what you're up to, and they don't need to either. They've been told you're doing a special research project on the Huns for Sir Douglas Haig himself, so they shouldn't ask too many questions."

"Any bother," said Cox grimly, "and you see me. Understand?"

"Yes, sir!"

And so, with a distinct thrill of excitement and a willingness to work every hour God sent, Charles Powell threw himself into the work of tracking the movements of the German High Command. Brigadier General Cox's last words, "and get yourself a special GHQ movement pass, so that you can travel to and from London as often as you need to," was a welcome endorsement of the importance of his new role.

His first visit to Whitehall reinforced this view. Hubert Neville swiftly warmed to this clever young man, as he warmed to all clever young men, and they spent a genial half hour discussing Schiller and Goethe over a glass of sherry before the conversation turned to Nietzsche. Coming from an older generation, Neville was prepared to accept the German philosopher's dark view of the world. Powell was more critical of the sage of Basel. Hubert Neville eyed his new young assistant with interest. "I didn't know that you were interested in moral philosophy, Powell?"

"Not with Nietzsche, Doctor Neville. I'm afraid I think Nietzsche's philosophy rather immoral."

Impressed with this *bon mot*, Neville chuckled and walked his protégé over to the War Office to meet the other members of the Intelligence Planning Committee. They too were suitably impressed with their new young recruit and Powell left for France with the final words of the Head of the Secret Service himself, no less, ringing is his ears: "You just find us a good target that'll knock the Huns out of the war, Powell, and we'll do the rest. Give 'em the shock of their lives, young man."

Charles Powell went away, determined to do just that.

CHAPTER 37

Nasty Shocks

OHL

Mid May 1918

The second week of May, however, brought a nasty shock for Major Wendel. The OHL Security officer had relaxed his investigation into the "train attack", as the German Headquarters called it, and had kept any queries from Ludendorff at bay by insisting that he was still investigating the matter. Ludendorff had merely grunted and turned away to examine the doings of "Operations" and its harrassed chief, von Wetzell.

However, Weissmüller's breathless warning of a rumour that "old von Zelle" was due back sent a ripple of panic through the more indolent corners of OHL. Old files were dusted off, offices tidied and uniforms spruced up. Even Weissmüller, newly promoted to *Feldwebel* or Serjeant (Staff Assistant) made an effort to make himself presentable for the return of such a stern disciplinarian as Oberst von Zelle, sporting his new Iron Cross.

The arrival of the HQ Colonel (Staff Co-ordination) came, therefore, as a surprise. For it was not the redoubtable von Zelle who stepped up the steps of the OHL headquarters but the small square figure, in a fashionably pale uniform, of *Oberst* Kullmann, General Staff and *Pour le Mérite*, lately commander of two whole regiments in the east and recognised throughout the army as a "soldier's soldier". Moreover, Kullmann was a native of Hesse, not Prussia, and his style was crisp, no-nonsense and highly efficient. On being told that a serjeant major, newly returned from a gruelling liaison tour around the attacking armies, had lamentably long hair, he replied – in a sentence that would be quoted many times as proof of the new colonel's common sense and military wisdom – that "H*auptfeldwebel* Drewienkiewicz could get his hair cut after he had reported. Until then, the high command was more concerned with what was inside, rather than outside, the heads of senior *HauptFeldwebels.*"

Such military sagacity in an operational military headquarters was rewarded with a collective sigh of relief by OHL.

It was with genuine pleasure, therefore, that Major Wendel and Serjeant

Weissmüller greeted his arrival in the OHL Security Office. After the formalities he sat down, insisted Weissmuller stay in the room, and accepted a small glass of cognac. "Now then, Wendel, how's that arm of yours?"

Taken aback, Wendel stuttered. "Good, *Herr Oberst*. I am fine."

"No, you're not. The Head of Medical Services tells me you are in constant pain and refuse morphine. He says that's why you drink brandy in the office instead. To dull the pain. True?"

Wendel nodded.

Kullman sipped his cognac and looked slantwise at Weissemüller. "Well? Is it?"

Weissemüller looked alarmed and wheezed. "The *Herr Major* does his duty *Herr Oberst*. He does not get drunk. I see him suffer. I help him. In the office and out. We may be wounded but we know our duty."

"I know. No-one questions your dedication or your work. Both of you. On the contrary." Kullman smiled and turned back to Wendel. "So, what's your office up to?"

Wendel, who was now well aware of the new Colonel Staff Coordination's methods through the bush telegraph of the General Staff, pushed a neatly typed report across the desk. "It's all in here, *Herr Oberst*."

"*Ja*, I'm sure it is. I read very well. My teachers in kindergarten were very proud of my reading ability. But I want to hear it from you. That's why I am here and not reading reports in my office. Speak"

Wendel took a deep breath. He had been warned of this, too. "We have three major preoccupations in the HQ Security office, *Herr Oberst*…" he began.

"And the first of those is doubtless your need for extra staff, *nicht wahr*?"

Wendel was taken aback. "*Jawohl, Herr Oberst*. I am desperately short of…"

"Forget it," cut in Kullmann, crisply. "It isn't going to happen. No extra staff, *Herr Major*. I know that you are the smallest branch in this HQ, and that's how you'll stay. At the Front they need an extra half-million fighting men, so *General* Ludendorff and *OberstLeutnant* Wetzell in Ops tell me. If you want extra staff, Major Wendel, I suggest you ask the Americans. They seem to have brought unlimited manpower, according to the Intelligence Staff's briefing." He smiled at Wendel. "Now, how can I really help you?"

Amused, Wendel couldn't help grinning. "How did you know I was going to ask for extra staff, *Herr Oberst*?"

"Because every other staff branch has already done so, Herr Major." Kullmann smiled back. "So why don't we stop pissing about and you can tell me what your real problems are? Maybe those I can solve for you. So far as a mere O*berst-in-GeneralStaß* can?"

Wendel told him. Mindful of Stube's warnings of the international press, he emphasised operational security for the great attacks and then the sloppy handling of secret documents inside the headquarters. Kullmann took notes in a black pocketbook. When he had finished, he tucked his small silver pencil away in a breast pocket and picked up Wendel's report. "So that's it?"

"*Jawohl, Herr Oberst.*"

"Hmmm." Kullmann buttoned his pocket. "And how goes the great investigation? *'Quid sub terra est'*, eh?"

Wendel was thrown. "What?"

"'That which the earth conceals...' Among other things I taught classics before this war dragged me back into uniform once more, Wendel. The rest of the quotation reads, *'In apricum proferet aetus'*, if I remember rightly 'Aright' is better. 'That which time reveals'. So how goes your security investigation into the 'Great OHL Train Bombing', eh? What has time revealed to us? Or more particularly, to you?"

Wendel was thrown. He considered bluffing. Somehow, he thought, a man like Colonel Kullmann would see through a lie in a heartbeat. He came clean. "To tell you the truth, *Herr Oberst*, it hasn't been my top priority. Investigations are continuing."

Kullmann raised a sardonic eyebrow. "Really, *Major* Wendel, you surprise me. *General* Ludendorff's number one security concern, and you tell me it isn't your top priority? I'm surprised at you, Wendel."

Wendel's jaw sagged. "His number one security concern?"

"*Ja.* Hadn't you realised? The Chief particularly enquired how is the OHL Security Office's most important investigation was proceeding?" Kullmann's mouth crinkled, as he tried vainly to suppress a smile. Wendel looked shocked. "I think I had better tell him that you are giving it urgent attention, *Ja?* Why don't I inform him that you are giving it you are giving it your fullest attention, that your investigations are proceeding well and that you will render a full report for – ah, let us say – the 31st of May. Yes?"

Wendel clutched at this lifeline. "*Ja,* naturally, *Herr Oberst.* The 31st of May; a full report. Thank you. Yes, of course."

"Then, good!" Kullmann rose. For the first time he turned to Weissmüller. "So. They tell me that you are a free thinker, Serjeant Weissmüller. Is this true?"

"*Jawohl, Herr Oberst!*" Weissmüller stood to attention.

"Good, good," said Kullmann. A ghost of a smile flickered across his face. "I like good men who can think for themselves. Particularly men who really know what soldiering is all about because they have seen the reality. How is your chest?"

Weissmüller stumbled out an astonished, "Good, *Herr Oberst.*"

"Good," said Kullmann. "Glad to hear it. Verdun gas leaves scars inside, they tell me." He fixed Weissmüller with a sharp eye. "But just remember that it's clear thinking, not just free thinking, that counts in the end, if Germany is to win this war, Serjeant. Thank you, *lieber Herren,*" he said, putting his hand on the door. Wendel and Weissmüller crashed to parade attention. "I have every confidence in this office. It may be the smallest branch in the headquarters, but it is by no means the least significant." He turned to go. "Just let me see the draft of your report on the train bombing on the 27th. Then I can see if it reassures *General* Ludendorff that we are taking the train bombing seriously. Reassure me; we are taking the train bombing seriously, aren't we, *Herr* Wendel?"

"*Jawohl, Herr Oberst.*"

"Good, good." Kullmann nodded cheerfully. "I knew I could rely on you." He swept out, leaving Wendel and Weissmüller eyeing each other.

"Some Colonel," began Weissmuller. "I think I'd better dust off that train bombing report, hadn't I, Herr Major?" And for once he really meant it.

Wendel sighed and poured two more brandies. "*Herr* Weissmüller, I think you better had. We'd better given them a proper answer. We have much to do. I see some late nights ahead."

CHAPTER 38

GRAND QUARTIER GÉNÈRALE

FRENCH ARMY HQ

21ˢᵗ May 1918

"I'm afraid that I don't speak much English." The speaker was a tall, lean French cavalry officer with dark hair, who was rising from a very cluttered desk. "*J'espère que vous parlez Francais?* I hope you speak French."

Charles Powell shook his head. His French was of the wine-ordering variety. "*Malheureusement, non.*" he began. "*Je suis,*" he sought for the word, "*professeur d'Allemand.*"

"*Allemand?*" The French officer smiled broadly and lapsed into fluent German, to Powell's amusement and relief. *Capitaine* Jean-Noël de Romcourt was the intelligence officer responsible for tracking the Germans' order of battle at *Grand Quartier Génèrale*, the French version of GHQ. With his ancestral home in Alsace on France's eastern border, he spoke German like a native. The irony of a British and French officer conducting their business in the language of their common enemy was not lost on either. Heads turned at neighbouring desks on hearing the guttural tones of the hated Boche in France's most secret room.

Powell looked around.

The Intelligence Branch of the French HQ at Chantilly reminded him of a large schoolroom. One of the grand salons of the *Château* had been converted into lines of desks. Rows of horizon bleu-uniformed officers scribbled away, looking for all the world like schoolboys taking exams. Only the maps on the wall and a group of officers standing debating some point over their coffee cups in a corner broke the illusion. One or two looked in his direction, curious at his strange uniform. He felt uncomfortable, as if he were intruding in some strange monastic order.

"So," began Jean-Noël. "We are to work together to help your great project. Remind me; what exactly do you need? May I call you Charles?"

"Of course."

"Me, I am Jean-Noël." He waved Powell to a seat at his desk. "What can

I do to assist you?"

"It's their HQs. German Higher HQs. Above corps; armies, even OHL itself. Especially OHL."

De Romcourt raised his eyebrows. "Just the HQs?" He looked shrewdly at the British officer. "You don't want to see our latest update on their divisional order of battle?"

"No. Just HQs. We've got a good handle on their orbats. Thanks to the train watchers."

"Indeed. The train watchers are a pearl for us all. Outstanding. Your *Dame Blanche* material is highly regarded. But just the headquarters? That's unusual, I think. He cocked his head on one side. "May I enquire why British Intelligence is suddenly taking such an interest in the *Boches'* higher headquarters? Purely as a matter of record, you understand." he added dryly.

Powell was torn. He instinctively liked de Romcourt, and felt that the French captain to be a man who would help, not merely regard his work as just as another wearisome staff task. But secrecy made him cautious.

"We think that we can work out their intentions from the movements of their HQs," he lied.

De Romcourt's eyebrows shot up. "Yes. That would theoretically be possible." He stared Powell straight in the eye. "If they ever moved their higher HQs, that is. But they hardly ever do, as I am sure you know, Captain, as I am sure you know." He picked at a blue file. "For example, Rupprecht's Army Group HQ has moved about once per year - if that. And your BEF is as aware of that as we are, I think. So?"

Powell said nothing. The Frenchman leaned back in his chair, his mobile face impassive. His fingers drummed on the desk. Their silence hung heavy in the air, and Powell was suddenly aware of the chatter of the busy room and the strong smell of French tobacco.

"Captain Powell. What exactly would you like to know? That is, that you don't know already?"

Powell had the grace to feel uncomfortable. He had been warned not to tell the French anything, but this was clearly going to be impossible. Sensing his discomfort, the Frenchman let his chair fall forward with a bang and reached for his pale blue *kepi*. "Come. Let us got to the officers' club and discuss this over an early lunch. Does that sound a good idea?"

Powell agreed with relief. As the two strolled in the spring sunlight across the Château's park, de Romcourt talked of the progress of the German offensive and of his next posting, to take up a post in Foch's headquarters.

"Good for my career, they say. But not perhaps as interesting as the service of intelligence, I think?"

Powell agreed.

"So perhaps you could enlighten me, Captain Powell. I have been ordered to assist you. I will follow my orders. But, I repeat, what exactly do you want from us? The *Boche* headquarters? *Pas de problème*. But - more importantly – why? Tell me what you really need and I can help you. But if it's just common liaison..." He shrugged. It was a very Gallic shrug. It conveyed resignation, hopelessness and the whole futility of man's existence. It made Powell feel inadequate, clumsy and not very co-operative; which was precisely what de Romcourt meant it to do.

"So," the Frenchman returned to the question. "What is it that you really want? And why?" He grinned. "After all, we are allies, yes?"

Powell was nonplussed. His mind raced desperately as he tried to work out what he could say and, more importantly, what he could *not* say.

"We think we could hit the Germans hard, disrupt this offensive of theirs, if we could, well, find and neutralize some of their HQs..."

"Find them? The BEF doesn't know where the enemy headquarters are? Really? You surprise me. Now, 'neutralise', eh? That's an interesting word. 'To make impartial? Colourless? To render permanently inoperative.'" The German synonyms rolled off the Alsatian's tongue. "Which of them is the most accurate do you think, *Monsieur* Charles?"

Powell was embarassed. "I think 'render permanently inoperative' is our aim."

"Ah." The Frenchman's eyebrows went up and he nodded. They walked in silence. "Tell me," he enquired. "Would it help us if we were to - ah – destroy these German headquarters? For that is theoretically possible. That might 'render them inoperative'?"

"Of course."

"Hmm." They were at the steps of the officers' club. The Frenchman stopped and turned to Powell. "So... we could shell them. Or bomb them. But a big HQ is like a church, or a cathedral. It's not the building itself that counts, my friend, but those who worship inside, *ja*? So if we were to render the occupants of German HQs 'permanently inoperative' – I think you said? – then that would be a ideal course to follow. I'm sure you agree?"

Powell agreed.

De Romcourt ploughed on, his logic remorseless as one of the French army's new Renault tanks.

"And the best way of rendering the inhabitants - the senior ones, the ones who count - of a big HQ inoperative would be to attack them, not the clerks and telephone operators, or the building." He paused. "But not just any HQ. There are lots of German HQs. For such a concept to make sense it would be best to go for the controlling brain, the highest HQ of all..." He snapped his fingers in triumph. "Of course! OHL. You really want to know about OHL and their higher headquarters staff. Yes?"

Powell saw little point in denying it. He nodded.

"You are thinking of doing something about Hindenburg and Ludendorff. Or their command staff."

It was a statement. It was Powell's turn to shrug. Delighted at his own cleverness, the Frenchman's mobile face lit up with excitement.

"But what a wonderful idea. Of course we must help you. How will you attack such a target?"

Powell shrugged again. "I don't know," he replied truthfully. De Romcourt stared at him appraisingly. He came to a decision then slapped the Briton on the back.

"Come. After lunch, I will show everything we have. But first, my friend, *à table*."

*　　　*　　　*

After an excellent lunch, de Romcourt led Powell back to his desk. The

French officer declined a cigarette, explaining that since Verdun he had stopped smoking. "A bullet through the lung at *Morte Homme* does not assist these matters," had been his only amplification. Powell glanced at the Frenchman's medal ribbons and asked no more.

True to his word de Romcourt produced a series of fat files from his desk drawer and dispatched a cheerful but scruffy staff clerk to bring more. For Powell it was a treasure trove. The French had up-to-date aerial photographs of every German headquarters on their sector of the western front and spare copies for him.

"Jean-Noël; these are amazing. How did you get them?"

"It's not a problem, Charles. Every month we have a regular photographic reconnaissance flight to check on every HQ, from division to OHL. It's just a routine intelligence task for *l'Armée de l'Aire.*"

Powell picked up a stack of photographs of OHL's headquarters at Avesnes. "What about the trains? Railway lines? Railway movements?"

"We spot them, too. When we can. Sometimes their HQ train comes in to a special siding. Here," de Romcourt picked out one photograph. "Look, here. Here's where they were building a special railway spur from the main line to a *château*. They sometimes do that."

Powell pored over the photograph through a magnifying glass. "What's this?"

The Frenchman turned it over and read the back. "OHL. That's the railway spur they built in the first week of March. Nothing special. It turned out to be the connection for their new forward HQ at Avesnes." He pulled a file out and flicked through a pile of pictures. "Now, here's another one. Being built last week. Something strange, though. This is Trélon, near Hirson. You see," he indicated a spot. "… and here, the Boches" construction workers are building another of their railway spurs. Here."

"What's so special about Trélon? Is there an HQ there?"

"Non. Not at all. It's a mystery. There's no HQ, nothing. Just a château. A nice one too, *Château* Trélon. *Tres chic.*"

Powell looked up, mystified. "Maybe they're going to move an HQ there. To Trélon?"

De Romcourt shrugged. "It's possible. But it's not a good spot. Too far south for OHL: much too far back for an Army HQ. Wrong place, Trélon. No; it's just a mystery." He stared down at the photograph. "To be honest, I don't know why they are wasting their time. All I know is that the *Château* Trélon is supposed to be one of the smartest country houses in the area. Here, have a look." He handed Powell a pre-war picture postcard from the file.

Powell glanced at it without much interest. A typical sepia tourist postcard; taken in winter, judging from the bare trees. The *château* didn't look anything special, but it certainly looked imposing. He looked at the date: 1911.

"Nice place. Bit small for a major headquarters."

De Romcourt put the photographs back in the folder. "I agree. It's a mystery. If I didn't know the Germans are anything but stupid, I'd say they were wasting their time. But the Germans rarely waste their time on anything. But what it is," he shrugged. "It's a puzzle. We'll keep an eye on it though. Now here," and he pulled out a fat file clearly marked "OHL", "here's what you're really looking for: OHL's new set up at Avesnes. Where do you start?"

*   *   *

By the time Powell got back to GHQ at Montreuil next day, he had formed three clear conclusions; he liked Jean-Noël and could trust him; secondly, the French had a terrific intelligence set-up; and lastly they would help him. He reported as much to Mackenzie.

"But no intelligence on train movement plans?"

"Not that I saw, Sir."

"Or internal HQ staffs, officers, movements?"

"They didn't show me that, Sir. But they must have some material, I would have thought. Maybe next time."

"Hmm." Mackenzie stared out of the window. "Probably highly secret. Agents' stuff: spies in the HQ, secret service, that kind of thing. Probably want to keep stuff like that to themselves: close hold. Can't say I blame 'em." He folded his arms. "We would." He came to a decision.

"Right then, young Powell. Best be off with you. See what that Neville fellow's got up his sleeve in London, and let him know what you've found out."

CHAPTER 39

Converging Destinies?

Late May 1918

While Powell travelled north via the ferry and train to Whitehall, the missing piece of his intelligence jigsaw was, unbeknownst to him, being placed on the table. Ironically, Germany's greatest secret was being leaked by none other than Oberst Kullman of the German General Staff. With an even greater irony, he was being driven by that highest of motives, the need for national security.

Major Wendel sat in a wicker chair in Col. Kullman's office, wondering just why he had been sent for. The Staff Colonel came straight to the point.

"*Herr* Wendel, we have a problem. A security problem. And that means, as the HQ Security officer, it's *your* problem, yes?"

Wendel nodded and guiltily ran through all the unreported security breaches he was aware of. Kullman was talking.

"...security of the highest order. We cannot afford for anything to go wrong. Do you agree?"

"*Jawohl, Herr Oberst.*"

"Good. Then when I tell you that the visitor is the Kaiser himself, then you'll understand my concern..."

"The Kaiser?! Visiting? Here?" Wendel couldn't suppress his astonishment.

"Not here, Wendel. Haven't you been listening?" said Kullman irritably. "To a place well forward. Where he can visit the troops, present medals. That kind of thing."

The implications of Kullman's words began to sink into Wendel's thoughts. "How long is the All Highest staying?"

"I don't know. Not at this stage."

"But he'll be coming on his train, *Herr Oberst?*"

"Of course."

"Good. So he'll be staying on the Royal train?"

"No, Wendel. That's my point. He won't be staying on the Royal train. He's stopping off for two nights at –" *Oberst* Kullman fumbled for a telegram flimsy on his desk. He picked it up. Wendel could clearly see 'Streng Geheim' - Top Secret – stamped across it in red.

"Ah, here we are. *Château* Trélon; near Hirson. That's where he'll be."

"The dates, *Herr Oberst?*"

"Next month. Arrive on the first of June, depart on the second, perhaps the third. So you've got about a week to organise the security for the visit. Anything you need. Full guard battalion – there'll probably be a ceremonial guard from 18th Army anyway; air squadron nearby on standby; anti-aircraft guns. Talk to the *FeldPolizei*. Tell them to give you whatever you need. Just go and check the place over and make sure that the All Highest is well guarded while he's in the Army's care. Report back to me and we'll both go and brief Ludendorff himself. Any questions?"

Wendel shook his head. "Not at this stage, *Herr Oberst.*" He stood up to go.

"Oh, Wendel. One other thing. How's that investigation of yours into the train bombing coming along?"

"Fine, *Herr Oberst.* Nothing to report. We've been very thorough. Truly. Over 200 statements and reports, with more to come. It all seems to point to the Tommies' air force." He paused. "One odd thing, though. They couldn't find any of the bomb fragments. You'd expect to find some evidence of an air-bomb casing, wouldn't you?" He shook his head. "Not a scrap. The Ammunition Technical Officer couldn't find one piece of it."

Kullman looked puzzled. "Maybe it was all blown to tiny chunks? Isn't that a possibility?"

"Oh, yes," Wendel agreed. "But you'd still expect to find something. It's a bit odd. I'll have another look at it before I present my final report, Herr Oberst."

"Good. By the 27th to me, please. But the Kaiser Visit is now your number one priority, Wendel. The Kaiser comes first."

*   *   *

"Always let the lady come first."

As he trudged across the dew soaked grass towards his aeroplane Robbie was thinking about women and sex. Since he had first taken the bad news of Charlie Barton to Françine at the Arche du Soleil, he found he could think of little else but the sweet-smelling young woman who had sobbed her heart out and left his tunic damp with tears. "Please come and see me again," she had begged. But how could he? After Charlie? He knew little of women; but it made him think. And the attraction was strong, no doubt about it. He shook his head as he recalled the conversation in the mess hut the previous evening. Two of the older pilots had been reminiscing about their last leave in Paris and, unusually, the conversation had turned dirty. Peter Coachman had eventually stopped it by the simple expedient of lowering his three-day-old copy of The Times, glowering at the two and saying "I don't hold with that kind of mucky talk in my mess, you two. You're supposed to be gentlemen. Now cut it out!"

Lester and Jones had slunk out looking slightly embarrassed, but had left Robbie to absorb their overheard pearls of masculine wisdom. Having listened to the explicit tales of his colleagues, he clearly had much to learn. But surely, sex was just like any other physical activity, after all. Tenderness, was that it? Tenderness and lust. Was that love? He could hardly ask Lester and Jones. All they were interested in, if last night's conversation was anything to go by, was "getting their end away". Pair of oafs, particularly Hugh Lester. Awful man…

"A penny for your thoughts, Robbie?"

Robbie looked up, startled. Timmy was trudging across the turf with him, a bulky flight bag in his hand.

"I said, a penny for your thoughts. You looked as if the op was worrying you."

Robbie blushed and returned Sjt. Doughty's salute as they reached their DH4. "No. I was just thinking." He swiftly changed the subject. "How is she, Sarn't Doughty?"

"She'll do, sir. Wi' Cooper away wi' his burns, I've got young Henries from Sarn't Mac's ground crew to check engine out. He says it's hundred percent. Goin' nicely."

Robbie nodded.

"How is Corporal Cooper by the way?" asked Timmy.

Doughty smiled. "He's all right, sir. Back at the base at Rouen, accordin' to t'lads. Just burned 'ands. We'll have him back soon enough, never fear."

"Changed your opinion then, Sarn't Doughty?"

"I 'ave that, sir. He may be a miserable, cocky little booger, but he's got balls, I'll say that. And he's good wi' engines. We'll be glad to see him back, won't we lads?" The rest of Robbie's ground crew chorused their agreement.

"And the CO's put him up for a medal, I hear," said Timmy, clambering into the rear cockpit.

"Bloody deserves it, too," said Doughty. "Aye, aye." He looked across at the next DH4 in line and coughed politely. Lindley, the pilot, was being sick on the grass. Robbie walked across.

"I say, are you all right, old man?"

Lindley nodded his head as he wiped his mouth.

"I'm all right, Robbie. Truly."

"Something you ate?"

"No. Just…" Lindley stood close to Robbie and dropped his voice. Robbie could smell the vomit on his breath. "It's just… Well… You know. Before… I sometimes get a bit… Well, you know." He waved his arm helplessly at his DH4, where Watts his observer was studiously checking the twin Lewis guns in the rear cockpit.

"Ah." Robbie understood. Lindley's aeroplane had been shot up in his last op and they had barely made it back. He tried to encourage his fellow pilot. "Don't worry, old man. We all get a bit jumpy sometimes. Coachie says that anyone who doesn't get a bit of the wind-up before an operational flight is a damned fool. Get a bit, well, tensed up myself, to be honest. Don't worry." He slapped Lindley reassuringly on the back. "You'll be all right old chum, once we're up there. You'll see."

"Thanks, Robbie." Lindley clambered up into the cockpit.

"You all right, sir?" enquired his ground crew Serjeant.

"Yes, yes, Sarn't Smith. Just something I ate. I'll be fine. Contact!"

Back at his own DH4, Robbie met Timmy's eye. "Linners alright, Robbie?"

"Yes. He'll be fine. And he's got Wattie with him. He'll be all right."

Timmy grunted. "Just the wind up, I suppose. I get nightmares sometimes. What about you?"

Robbie considered. He was scared sometimes, it was true. But he didn't want to admit it. The nightmares remark worried him. He himself had been having some terrible dreams lately. Burning and golden fire. Must be the Charlie Barton crash, he thought.

But, barring accidents, he felt he was capable of facing anything he met in the air. Except archie, perhaps. He'd seen an escorting SE5 just explode in the air only two weeks before, victim of a direct hit by a German anti-aircraft shell. It had literally burst apart, fragments blown like leaves. He remembered the leather-suited body of the pilot falling straight down like a stone, arms and legs slowly waving as the body turned over on its last flight... into eternity. He shuddered, remembering how he had hoped that the unfortunate airman was dead or at least unconscious from the blast of the shell. Recalling those slowly waving arms, however, he doubted it. What a dreadful way to go. His mouth was suddenly dry and his legs felt weak. He realised Timmy that was staring at him.

"Yes, I get the wind up too, Timmy. Sometimes. Best not to think of it, eh?

As the DH4 lumbered across the airfield turf to line up for take-off, Robbie suddenly bellowed a snatch of song into the wind, a grin across his face.

"Good God," said Timmy's voice from the backseat. "You're in a damned good mood this morning, Robbie. Anyone would think you were in love."

347

No, thought Robbie, as he gunned the throttle, but I had a very sexy dream last night. The memory of the girl in the café was strong. What was her name? Françine. Yes, Françine. And with CB gone…

I need to find a girl to love.

CHAPTER 40

A DATE WITH FATE

22ⁿᵈ May 1918

"Selfless love, the highest of all the emotions. *'Agape'*, as the Greeks called it."

Hubert Neville sipped his rather fine Manzanilla and eyed Charles Powell closely. Despite his short dark hair and that rather unfortunate accent, Powell was an attractive young man, he decided. Quite bright, too. For a Cambridge man.

The BEF intelligence officer was swirling his own sherry and trying to shake off the feeling that Neville was subjecting him to some kind of impromptu *viva voce* examination. He tried to drag his thoughts back to Neville's suggestion that national characteristics and ideas are most clearly identified by linguistic differences. "I think I agree with you, Dr. Neville. I do believe that there is a higher concept of love than mere affection, procreation: call it what you will. I suppose that you could argue that Christ himself was the greatest exponent of selfless love, self-sacrifice… *'Agape'*, to use your Greek word." He watched the sherry swirling round his glass. "Did you know that there's no single word in German for such a concept? Interesting isn't it?"

"Yes, it is rather." Hubert Neville was enjoying the conversation, He, like Powell, was not convinced that all things German were intrinsically evil, or at least had magically become so in August 1914. Christchurch High Table still served some decent hock. But it really was a pleasure to have a civilized conversation with a fellow academic once in a while on an abstract topic – if indeed it was really abstract….

"However," he said, dragging himself back to the matter in hand, "we really must address ourselves to your – our – little problem before all else. You say that the French are being cooperative?"

"Yes, sir. Their desk officer could not have been more helpful." Knowing the French, Hubert Neville doubted that, but let it pass without comment. "Chap by the name of Jean-Noël de Romcourt. Cavalry captain. Pretty bright. They"ve got aerial photographs of every German HQ plus all the unusual activity in the area. See…" he opened his briefcase and pulled out a handful of photographs. "… If you look here you can see everything."

"And OHL?"

"Yes, OHL as well, sir. Here's their latest location… Avesnes."

Neville studied the photographs and picked one up. "What's this one?"

"Ah, that one's a bit of a mystery, according to the Frenchies. Apparently the Huns are building a railway spur out to some *château* or other out in the wilds." He consulted his notes. "Trélon: that's it. The *château* at Trélon. No one knows why. It's miles back, behind St. Quentin." ˙

Neville studied the image and laid it aside, picking up another. "Well, I don't suppose we'll ever know. Now what's this one?

*   *   *

But Hubert Neville was wrong, for at that precise moment, Major Wendel of the German Security Staff was unwittingly informing a British Secret Service agent exactly what the mysterious railway spur would be used for.

"The *Kaiser*?!" Stube was speechless.

"*Ja*, I know. The man's a damned nuisance. He's coming by train to visit the Front on the first of June and they are building a special railway line to get him to some château. It's down near the border at Hirson. Haven't you been told about it? I expect you will soon enough. There'll probably be lots of press stories once he's arrived. Presenting medals, parades, bands, that sort of thing."

Stube's mind was racing. "Maybe he'll be giving *Oberst* von Zelle his Iron Cross," said Weissemüller from the corner, where he was busy listing everyone's movements on the 15th and 16th of March.

"Shut up, Weissemüller," said Wendel absently. The NCO grinned and went back to his task.

"Well," said Stube. "I certainly will need to know about any visit from the All Highest." And not just for press *communiqués*, he thought grimly. London would give their right arm to have this particular piece of information.

The unofficial collaboration between the Press Office and "Security" had worked well. Every day Stube deliberately brought armfuls of the worst stories he could find about disasters on the Home Front. While the censors back home ensured that the papers themselves carried little of value, the underground radical and the neutral newspapers were full of woeful stories outlining the German citizens' growing plight, some of them in harrowing detail. The Swiss and Swedish papers in particular were full of doom and gloom.

Wendel had been shocked, a cynical Weissemüller less so. "Told you so," he responded to his major, thrusting one particularly graphic account of a Potsdam war-widow being sent to jail by a military courtmartial for stealing coal dropped by a passing railway train. "Told you so," he'd added triumphantly.

"*Mein Gott*, I didn't realize it was as bad as this." Wendel looked helpless and wiped his hand over his face.

"I'm afraid it gets worse, *Herr Major*." Stube selected a piece from a Swiss German language newspaper. He plonked the *Züricher Zeitung* on Wendel's desk.

"Deserters Flee the Reich," read the Gothic headline. Wendel read on. "Twenty thousand deserters… German military authorities demanding immediate repatriation… Military dictatorship… Starvation in the northern cities…." He looked up. "*Lieber Gott*, is it truly as bad as this?"

Stube had been calm. "It gets worse. You should see the Scandinavian papers. Especially the Danish ones. Oh, it's this bad all right."

Wendel shook his head and reached for a file.

"Here. You'd better read this, then. God help us if the papers ever get their hands on that."

Stube opened the buff "G1" Branch file. His eyes widened. Paydirt. He was looking at a German Army Top Secret report on "*Morale and Growing Disaffection in the Ranks*". He glanced at the distribution and his eyes widened even further. Four copies only: Lüdendorff, The War Ministry in Berlin, OHL HQ Security and a file copy for the Personnel Branch. "Even the Kaiser hasn't seen this," Wendel added. "It's dynamite."

Skimming the contents, Stube had seen why. The report had chapters on casualties, morale, discipline, court martial statistics, subversion by the Bolshevik-Socialists, pacifism in the ranks. There were graphs, statistics, conclusions, and recommendations. Stube had to agree. Wendel was right; it was explosive. The dry official tones of the General Staff report in his hands recorded a litany of disaster. He read it through then handed it back with the dry observation that "things could only get better". This had drawn a sardonic sniff from *StabsFeldwebel* Weissemüller. Immediately afterwards, in the privacy of the lavatory, Stube had scribbled down everything he could remember from the report. London would be pleased with that, he thought.

But now, he mused, a secret Kaiser visit to tell them about as well. He was positively spoiling the unknown denizens of Whitehall. He grinned as a thought struck him - maybe he should ask for a pay rise...

*   *   *

Cumming blinked. He read the de-coded flimsy carefully. "The Kaiser," he muttered. The significance of the information he held in his hand hit home. "Good God" he said out loud, standing up and pacing the office. He looked at the trees and the Thames far below and read Stube's brief report again:

```
Secret.  Flash.  Urgent.  Personal  for  C.
Security  Office  OHL  informed  that  Kaiser,
repeat  Kaiser,  due  official  visit  Chateau
Trelon Hirson 1 to ?3 June. Confirmed 100%.
A34.  Secret."
```

He came to a decision and thrust the flimsy telegram into his pocket. "Mrs Anderson! Get Dr. Neville on the telephone!" he shouted to his secretary. "Tell him I need to talk to him right away. Now! At my Club." And with that, the Head of the British Secret Service grabbed his walking stick and limped out to meet the Chairman of Britain's Secret Intelligence Committee.

He had had an idea: one that could change the course of history, although he didn't know that. But he hoped that Neville would be impressed.

*   *   *   *   *   *   *

Hubert Neville was impressed, if somewhat irritated. Neville distrusted hastily convened meetings and, much worse, the hasty decisions which so often flowed from them. But when Cumming had – rather breathlessly, Neville thought – explained the urgency and had shown him the message, Neville was converted.

He held the flimsy carefully, and re-read it. "The Kaiser, indeed?" He looked cautiously around the RAC library. At this time of the morning they were the only occupants. He waved the slip of paper.

"How reliable is this information?"

"A34's never been wrong. A hundred percent, so far. I'd say that it's as reliable as we're ever going to see."

Neville nodded. "Who else knows?"

"No-one. 'cept the code chappie who decoded it, and you can trust him."

Neville pondered and look at the date. "That gives us just over a week."

"Plenty of time."

A long silence reigned. Neville's eyes were fixed on the piece of paper. Eventually it was Cumming who broke the spell.

"Are you thinking what I'm thinking, Neville?"

Neville looked up and their eyes met. "Yes," he said slowly. "I do believe I am. Strategic targets?"

Cumming nodded. "They don't get more strategic than this, Neville."

The little civil servant stared up at the ceiling. "Tell me. Could your man, this A34, could he…?"

Cumming stopped him, a warning hand in the air. "No. Absolutely not. He's my best man and he's where he can do the most good. In his case, that's smack in the middle of their HQ…" He broke off as a white-jacketed club servant entered the library. "Coffee, Jackson." said Cumming. "Morning coffee for two, please." The servant left.

"No." Cumming returned to his point. "It's taken us years to get him where he is and I'm not going to risk my best asset. Can't afford to lose him. Sorry." He was emphatic. "He's had one go and it didn't work. I'm not going to tempt fate after the last time. No, we must find some other way."

"A pity. However, I do understand and I fully trust your judgment, Cumming." Neville smiled beatifically. "And I believe I may know that 'other way'. You remember young Powell?"

"BEF chappie? Of course. Nice young feller; pretty bright."

"Yes. But what do you suppose he just brought back from his visit to the French?"

C looked blank.

"An aerial photograph," went on Neville. "That's what. Taken recently of *Château* Trélon, amongst others, that's what he showed me." Neville slapped his knee as realisation dawned. "Of course. It all fits. That's what the mysterious construction is, in that photograph. The railway siding that nobody could fathom... It'll be for the royal train." He slapped his knee again. "Of course. We've got him. The Kaiser. The Kaiser! Well I never…"

Cumming looked uneasy. "Steady on now, Neville. I know what you're thinking and I must say I agree – in principle. But popping off at the Kaiser…" He broke off as Jackson entered the library with their morning coffee. When he had gone, Cumming returned to his theme.

"What I'm trying to say, Neville, is that it's a jolly good idea and the chance of a lifetime and all that, but we can't set up a stunt like this off our own bat. There'd be a deuce of a row if this ever got out. I mean, the Kaiser? You know there would."

Neville nodded slowly.

"I understand your concerns. You're quite right. There would indeed be a deuce of a row. However, if you could get official authorization to 'pop off at the Kaiser' as you so elegantly put it, would you still countenance such an operation?"

"Well of course. I should say so! It's not every day you get a chance like this. Why, it could end the war. But, let's be realistic. Face facts, Neville; no-one round here's going to put their name to a stunt like this. And we certainly couldn't order it."

"Could we not?"

"Well, think about it, old chap. Assassinating the Kaiser? We can't just go doing something like that off our own bat, now can we? Come on, now! Consider the repercussions. Something like this would have to be cleared by..." He paused, as the enormity of the proposed project washed over him. "My God, you'll have to clear this with the King, the War Cabinet, the PM, Heaven knows who. I'm right, aren't I?"

"Perhaps. On the other hand, perhaps they might prefer not to know."

"*Not* know? What d'ye mean?"

Neville tasted his coffee then put the cup down with an expression of alarm. "What I mean is that sometimes in life it may be better *not* to know about some matter whose outcome we fervently desire. We *will* the end result, but not the means, if you take my point. We are, to put it crudely, often prepared to let others do our dirty work for us without enquiring too closely how that which we want has been achieved."

Cumming was genuinely puzzled. "So how would that affect this operation? *Potential* operation?" he added, lamely.

Neville suppressed a sigh. For a man with "one of the sharpest brains in Britain" – to quote one of his friends – it was tiresome to have to spell out a concept whose totality he had grasped in an instant, particularly to a respected colleague. "Let me give you an example. Have you ever thought about what happens to those lamb chops you so enjoy?"

Cumming, mystified, looked blank. "Lamb chops? What on earth has that got to do with…?"

"I mean, have you ever heard the lamb screaming as it goes to the slaughterhouse and its fate on the block? The knife; the blood?

Cumming's eyebrows knitted. "Well of course not!"

"Exactly. And you, forgive me, go to the lavatory daily. Do you ever enquire into what happens in the sewers?"

"For God's sake, Neville. That's disgusting!"

"I rest my case, my dear Cumming. You'd much rather *not* know about such things. Quite rightly so. You need the events to occur, but you prefer to close your mind to the rather unpleasant reality which lies behind them. We all do. Which, I suspect, is the case in this extraordinary chance with which we have been so felicitously presented. Everyone wishes it. For us a dead Kaiser is a good Kaiser. But I strongly suspect that no-one is willing to lend his authority to such…" he paused and thought carefully. "Such a dramatic act, with such far-reaching consequences." Hubert Neville smiled and leaned back. "So I suggest that *we* order the deed in the interests of other people. In the interests of political expediency. What do you say?"

Cumming was speechless. "Good God!" he finally spluttered.

Nevile looked at his companion's astonishment. "After all, you and I do have that power."

Cumming was mystified. "Do we?"

"Oh, yes." Neville sat back in his club chair and took another experimental mouthful of coffee. He pulled a face and pushed the cup away with an air of finality.

"I know: dreadful stuff," muttered Cumming. "Sorry."

"You see, when I saw the P.M. last month, I told him about our little committee and how we may be able to help him. He seemed very taken with it, I must say. Showed quite an interest. For a politician."

"What are ye drivin' at, Neville?"

"Ah, well. You see the PM effectively gave our little committee the power to order special operations. 'Special operations designed to bring the enemy to its knees', I think was the exact phrase. I have it in writing somewhere," he waved a vague hand. "And if an operation such as this fails to bring the enemy to its knees, I fear nothing will. Don't you agree?"

"Yes, but dash it all, Neville. This is different. Ordering a shot at the Duo off our own bat's one thing. But the *Kaiser*? There'd be hell to pay. HM would never agree to such a thing.   And who'd approve it even if we did order it?"

"I would." Neville replied matter-of-factly.

Cumming rubbed the back of his neck. "What? …You?"

"I will sign the order," Neville went on "on behalf of the committee, using the powers delegated to me by the PM. No-one else need to know. Indeed, I suspect most of them would prefer it that way. So there you are, Cumming. It's perfectly straightforward. I'll take full responsibility. May

I take it that that is an agreeable course of action?"

Cumming shook his head in disbelief. "Are you serious?"

"Perfectly serious."

"Heavens above, man. Are you sure? If it were to go wrong and it all came out, you'd be for the high jump, surely? Finished. It's the devil of a risk. I mean the King, the newspapers… Well, everything!"

"I appreciate all that. But it's a risk that I'm perfectly prepared to take. If you'll back me, I promise that you, and your service, will take no blame should it fail or become public knowledge. The total responsibility would be mine, and mine alone." He cocked his head on one side like a sparrow. "Well?"

Cumming looked at Neville.

Funny, he thought. You could work with a chap for a long time and still not really know him. Quiet little civilian, professor or something, Oxford. Wouldn't say boo to a goose; but clever, mind. Damned clever. And here he was, calmly sitting here in my own club talking about giving the order to murder the German Kaiser off his own bat and to hell with the consequences. Well, well… Extraordinary.

He shook his head ruefully, in genuine admiration. "Neville, you're quite some feller!"

He came to his decision.

"Aye, I'm with you. Let me shake you by the hand."

*   *   *

Hubert Neville walked back across Horse Guards Parade towards Downing Street considering his actions with a sense of mild astonishment.

He had been, for the first time in years, impulsive. He had surprised himself at his own resolution, his own ruthlessness. But then again it was obvious to him what had to be done. Nonetheless, he had just agreed to order a murder. And not just any old murder, either. The killing of the German King, their Emperor. An assassination of a head of state. What at was it the Cumming had said? "There'll be a deuce of a row?" True. But only if it got out, he thought grimly. Only if it ever got out.

He walked on, considering the problem and turned towards the Park, deep in thought, hardly noticing the curses of the frightened taxicab driver who nearly ran him down. Then he'd better make sure, win or lose, that any order to kill the Kaiser never did get out, decided Hubert Neville.

And he knew just the man to help him: Maurice Hankey.

CHAPTER 41

SECURING THE KAISER

25ᵗʰ May 1918

It is one thing to have an idea or to give an order. It is quite another to see that it is carried out and ensure that things happen. That, thought Major Wendel, was always the problem.

He looked over the dozen or so reluctant security staff standing in the slight drizzle on the steps of *Château* Trélon with a feeling approaching that of exasperation.

However, as several of the individuals in question were senior to him, he would have to be tactful. And, to add to his troubles, his missing arm was aching like blazes. How the hell could anyone still feel their fingers when they were buried in some Godforsaken jungle 5,000 kilometres away? A powerful glass of cognac seemed a wonderful idea.

He cleared his throat.

"So, gentlemen, everything appears to be *almost* in order." He raised the stakes, "There are, however, certain points on which *FeldMarschal* Ludendorff has asked for particular assurances"

His audience shifted uneasily at the mention of Ludendorff's name. Risking the wrath of a Field Marshal was quite a different a different proposition from that of a one-armed security major from headquarters. Even one with a *Pour le Mérite*. They glanced at each other as men will do when they are gauging their chances of being found wanting in public. Wendel smiled grimly. That was the beauty of the *GeneralStaß* he thought; he might be a mere major – but he could wield the power of a field marshal if and when the need arose.

"So, *liebe Herren*. *StabsFeldwebel* Weissmüller here has the security checklist. Let us go over it, so that everybody knows everyone else's duties, and exact..." he let the word hang in the air for a split second before continuing, "...responsibilities."

"Weissmüller." He invited his assistant forward. As he did so he noticed a large and very blond Serjeant from the Guard battalion sneer and whisper something into his company lieutenant's ear. The officer nodded and sneered back, jerking his chin towards Weissmüller. Odd; thought Wendel. What the hell was that all about? He listened as Weissmüller ran down his checklist, revealing a sorry tale of duties left undone. When he had finished, he turned to Wendel and snapped to attention.

"*Herr Major*! One company will be missing from the guard battalion. The air fighter squadron will not arrive until the day of the Kaiser's visit itself… The first, and not before. And the *Feldpolizei* can only provide thirty military policemen. Sir!"

Wendel sniffed and took the list. He caught the eye of the *Oberstleutnant* from the Air Service and raised his eyebrows.

"All we can spare, Major," said the airman. "These are all we can spare and even they will have to be double-tasked in order to do this." His manner was defensive and surly. "The Air Service is too stretched with the front fighting to allow for a whole squadron to be detached for, well… *Ceremonial duties*. So we will double-task the St. Quentin *Staffel* to guard the Kaiser's country house. It's just re-equipping with the new Fokkers. The D–7s. That's the best we can do."

Wendel said nothing and turned to the Captain commanding the *FeldPolizei*. The MP officer looked Wendel brazenly in the eye.

"This is the total men I can provide, *Herr Major*. I have lost over twenty NCOs in the last month. Most of them blown to pieces by the Tommy artillery at some Godforsaken crossroads whilst directing traffic towards the fighting front." "So, although of course it is an honour to guard the All Highest, this is all I have left of my Military Police company. To tell you the truth, we are looking forward to this mission. It's not everyday my men are given the opportunity to get away from the line and share the pleasures of the rear areas and the staff."

Wendel sense of unease increased. This barely-veiled criticism of the Higher Command was unprecedented, especially coming from the Military Police, the most disciplined and well-regulated of any part of the army. He noticed suppressed grins from some of the group. In desperation, he turned to *Oberst* Paulus, Commanding Officer of 63 Infantry Regiment, who had been selected to provide the guard unit for the Kaiser visit. "And your second battalion, *Herr Oberst*?"

Von Paulus grunted. "They're good enough, Wendel. But at most, only 400 strong. This bloody Spanish influenza is going through the Regiment like a dose of salts. That's why Major Jagow can't be here today. And most of the reliefs coming out are just kids. *Leutnant* Stresser here, will be the HQ Company Guard Commander." He pointed at the Lieutenant who had sneered at Weissmüller. "A year ago he was doing his Abitur in High School. Now he's guarding the All Highest with about 50 men and pretending to be an infantry company. Times are hard."

Wendel looked puzzled. "Pretending, *Herr Oberst*?"

Paulus looked at Wendel almost with pity. "Look, Wendel," he began. "You're a decent man and you've got a job to do. We understand that. And you've obviously soldiered," he said pointing to Wendel's *Pour Le Mérite* medal. "We all know that those things are not given away for sitting on your fat arse in a *château* somewhere, doing nothing. But things have changed now. We're down to our last gasp up at the front. My whole Regiment's only got about 1,100 men. Oh yes!" he went on, noting Wendel's shocked expression. "That's *three* battalions. And that's on a *good* day. Christ, man, I know of whole divisions that only have about 3,000 men. *Divisions!* But on the ops staff wall maps at HQ they're still marked with a full divisional pin. Correct?"

Wendel nodded dumbly.

"So it's hard to provide a full battalion, even for a Kaiser Guard. Oh, we're glad of the rest and the break, but I tell you, I can't raise any more men. They just don't exist." He pointed to the lieutenant and the NCO. "Look at Hartmann there. Two months ago he was a line trooper. So he shot an enemy spy and got the Iron Cross. He's a good, loyal soldier. But now he's gone from *Gefreiter* to Staff Serjeant in just two months. All the other senior NCOs in his company are dead, wounded or promoted. So suddenly after just eight months at the front he's the acting Company Serjeant Major, the *Spiess*, first spear of the Company. And a *verdammt* good one, at that. But he's only been here for eight months and he's a veteran. You see what I mean? Eight months!" Hartmann grinned at the discomfited security officer. He wondered how the one-armed major had won that blue enamelled PLM. He'd like a PLM, too if he could get one. Now that would be something. It would go well with his Iron Cross.

Wendel looked at the little group.

"I understand. Thank you, *Herr Oberst*." He took a deep breath. "It's a long time since I was in the field." He wagged his throbbing stump. "But I too have made my contribution. I understand how you must be feeling. However, I have to reassure *General* Ludendorff that we are mounting a proper guard on our Kaiser. You know the security of the All Highest is paramount. I will report back to OHL that you are all doing your best – but with the restricted resources available…" Looking directly at the others, he said "And you will all give your utmost support to the *Kommandant*." He pointed at *Oberst* Paulus. "The ultimate responsibility is his, not mine."

Paulus nodded. "Ja. Fair enough, Wendel. We'll do our best. Tell the *FeldMarschall* that." He looked around the group. "He smiled at Wendel. "But I can't see any trouble. Can anyone here?" They all chorussed in agreement. He looked back at Wendel, who stood to attention. Paulus set his jaw. "Thank you, Major. Dismissed!" The group saluted and broke up.

Weissemüller walked across to the big blond Serjeant major. He was puzzled about the earlier exchange. "What's your problem?" he began. Hartmann cut him short.

"Piss off, kyke!" Weissmüller reacted as if stung. Hartmann went on, "We don't like your sort, so push off." Weissmüller was speechless. When this is all over, we're going to see that you and all the rest of you fucking Yids are sorted out once and for all." He jabbed a finger at the shocked Rhinelander. "It's your lot who started this fucking war – everyone knows that. So now you've got yourself a cushy staff job away from the fighting and you're feathering your nest along with all your rich fat Yiddish friends. I don't like Jews, I don't like you and when we're through, Germany will send you back where you belong."

Weissmüller began to protest, but Hartmann once again cut him off.

"Piss off, you greasy Jew. You're not a real German at all and when the war's over we'll deal with you lot for good!" He clenched a surprisingly large fist and waved it menacingly at Weissmüller. "Now fuck off back to your cosy headquarters and leave the real soldiering to real Germans." He turned on his heel and walked away. The Lieutenant sneered at Weissmüller and hissed, "You heard the *Spiess* – Jew!" and sauntered off. He said something to Hartmann who nodded and guffawed.

Weissmüller stood open-mouthed.

As a Jew, he had of course encountered prejudice before. Every Jew had. But in the past it had always been based on ignorance, stupidity or sometimes even simple, misplaced curiosity. He had never before been subjected to such blatant malice and hatred from his fellow countrymen. He was a German just like them, surely? He'd been badly gassed at *Côte* 304. He'd even got an Army Commander's commendation for Verdun. His mouth was dry and his legs felt weak from the shock. He shook his head in disbelief at the retreating infantryman.

Wendel was talking to the Military Police captain. Out of the corner of his eye he had noticed the exchange.

"What was all that about, Weissmüller? What's going on?"

But Weissmüller turned away, tears of anger and humiliation pricking his eyes. "Nothing. Excuse me, *Herr Major.*" Weissmüller walked away, fists clenched.

"Now what was all that?" thought Wendel. "What on earth?"

CHAPTER 42

THE BEGINNING OF THE END

26ᵗʰ May 1918

Powell's second and last visit to *Grande Quartier Générale* was briefer than the first. A hasty telephone call from de Romcourt brought him speeding southwards to the French headquarters. He arrived to find it a scene of bustle only just short of confusion.

"Today has been some day", was de Romcourt's enigmatic greeting in German to his visitor on the steps.

Once inside, he explained why. Foch and Petain had been holding an urgent Commanders' in Chief conference. Pershing, the new American C-in-C., was rumoured to be on the way and even the Premier, Clemenceau, the Tiger of France himself. The reason for all the bustle quickly became apparent. The Germans had broken through in the south on the *Chemin des Dames*. The new, now familiar, formula of a hurricane bombardment, drenching the rear areas with gas, followed by storm troopers infiltrating deep behind the front lines had once again proved unstoppable. Everywhere on the Aisne the French, for the second time in the war, were falling back towards the Marne, outposts over-run, field guns abandoned.

"It's a disaster," said de Romcourt. "That stubborn old fool, Duchêne at 6ᵗʰ Army wouldn't listen to Pétain. Idiot. But we shall hold them." He pulled out a graph. On it was charted the record of German losses. The line was curving up, ever more steeply. "Look." He pointed to the figures. "Over four hundred thousand casualties already. And it's getting worse. France will bleed; but they will fail. It's unsustainable." He sat back. "Ludendorff is finished. Happily for us, the Boches' capabilities don't match his ambitions. I think we have won the war, my friend."

Powell noticed that the big intelligence room was as busy as an anthill and that de Romcourt's eyes were dark rimmed and his cheeks unshaven. He came straight to the point. "You have your own duties, I expect, Jean-Noël. You must be busy. What was it you had for me?"

De Romcourt grunted. "Ah yes, the package." He pulled a fat unsealed envelope out of the clutter of files colonising his desk top. You will find this interesting, I believe. It's for you. Look."

Powell pulled open the flap and slid out the papers. It was an absolute treasure trove of intelligence on OHL. He flicked through the contents, eyes widening.

The Frenchman yawned. "It's mainly the Kaiser's visit. He's coming to present medals. The first of June. It's all there. Maps, photographs of the *Château* Trélon, his itinerary, timings – which could change, I understand." De Romcourt flapped a languid hand. "It's all in there. The plan of the *château* is very good. A real coup."

"How on earth did you get all this?" asked Powell.

De Romcourt shrugged. "We have a man in their HQ; OHL," he stated matter-of-factly. He's very reliable. Forget I told you that", he added tiredly. "Pretend we don't have a man in there. I didn't say that."

Powell looked down at his hoard. The Frenchman rubbed his face and yawned again. A French major walked over to them, clipboard in hand. He stood by the desk looking impatient. Powell stood up, politeness struggling with his excitement over the chance to examine the priceless intelligence.

"I must go."

"Good," said de Romcourt simply. "And I must check the latest reports for the five o'clock briefing. So we must say goodbye, *Capitaine* Charles. I hope that it helps you."

He stood up and gestured towards the envelope. "Use it wisely, mon ami. It's all there. But don't lose it! Good luck. Until next time" He shook hands then sat down heavily, opening a file bulging with telegrams and messages. The impatient looking major began to say something incomprehensible.

Powell found his own way out.

*　　　　　*　　　　　*

Wendel's arrival back at Avesnes from *Château* Trélon was not a success. *Oberst* Kullmann was unimpressed by the Security Officer's report on the security arrangements for Hirson. Eventually, in some exasperation, Wendell suggested tartly that if the Colonel was dissatisfied with his security arrangements, perhaps the best course might be to speak directly to *Colonel* Paulus, the responsible officer? After all, he was the *Kommandant*, not Wendel. Kullmann looked at him for what seemed an age, then nodded. "You are quite right, Wendel. You have done your duty." He picked up a pink security office folder marked "*VERTRAULICH*" – Confidential.

"Now, about your draft report on the attack on the OHL train; there are some things I don't quite understand." And the two men had turned to the strange tale of the train bombing.

The original source of Kullmann's puzzlement was the report of the Ammunition Technical Officer. Harried by Wendel for a report five weeks earlier the ATO had actually called on the security officer to check if his perfunctory offerings were satisfactory. "If it's thorough enough," had been Wendel's enigmatic reply. He then explained that the final report was to go to Ludendorff himself, no less. At this revelation, Captain Schulz of Ordnance Services had looked thoughtful and offered to have another look at his original one-page scribble.

"I thought you might," smiled Wendel, and thought little more about it.

When Schulz came back a week later with twenty pages of dense typescript, including annexes and a graph, Wendel had smiled still more broadly, thanked Schulz – who had gone from OHL mopping his brow and cursing all HQ staff officers for wasting everyone's precious time – and promptly passed the report to Weissmüller.

It was his NCO who actually read Schulz's literary masterpiece and drew Wendel's attention to the mystery of the missing bomb casing.

> One of the peculiarities of this incident is the complete lack of evidence of any fragments of the original bomb case

This had been the ATO's finding.

Wendel, ever thorough in his desire to fend off Ludendorff, had then – unusually – ordered the Medical Service to provide an autopsy report.

"But we know what killed them, Wendel," wailed a harassed *Oberst* of the Medical Corps, and grumbled. "They were blown to bits, for God's sake! What more evidence do you need?"

But Wendel had been insistent, blaming Ludendorf, and a hard-pressed junior doctor was forced to spend a hot afternoon probing in the disinterred fragments that were the stinking mortal remains of the general officers' chef and butler. His terse report was even more puzzling. Apart from an ugly chunk of kitchen worksurface embedded in the mangled leg of Redl, the chef, there were no pieces of bomb in either of the two dead men's bodies. Only "the remains of what appears to be a small gold clock", blown into the reeking lower bowel remnants of one of the victims.

Baffled, Wendel had passed the problem to the Special Investigations section of OHL's Military Police. By sheer chance, they had a *Leutnant* Müller on their staff. Müller had been, before the war, a crime scenes detective-lawyer for the Frankfurt Police. Ex-*KriminalRath* Müller had welcomed the chance to practise his old forensic skills and had done a thoroughly professional report on the wreck of the bombed-out coach, now rusting in some God-forsaken siding far behind the lines. Müller's report had found no evidence of British Flying Corps activity and deepened the mystery still further. It was the main course of the final conclusion in Wendel's comprehensive report.

> In the absence of any hard evidence of enemy action from the air or the ground, it is concluded that the bombing of the OHL train at Artes remains an open case.

Colonel Kullmann re-read the paragraph out and looked across the desk at his Security Officer. "An open case? You mean you're saying you still don't know?" he said in disbelief.

The Bavarian met his gaze with equanimity. "That's exactly what were saying, *Herr Oberst*."

Kullmann waved the thick report. "After all this, you're telling me that you still haven't been able to discover what happened?"

"Exactly, *Herr Oberst*; it's a mystery. No-one can explain it. There are no fragments of an air bomb, and if it wasn't an air bomb…" He stopped and looked at the OHL Coordination Colonel. Suddenly, an awful possibility began to occur to him. *Lieber Gott!* How could he have missed the obvious? His stomach knotted. How could he have been so slow?

"So it might be something else?" went on Kullman.

Wendel swallowed, and adjusted his eye-patch. "Exactly, *Herr Oberst*."

His mind was racing.

Kullman smoothed the report's pages and stared down at it in bafflement. "Like what? If it wasn't a Tommy aeroplane, then what else could it have been – the gas?"

Wendel shook his head. "No, all the three gas bottles in the kitchen carriage were undamaged. They were in the middle. One was blown onto the other track, but it was intact. It wasn't a gas explosion. I'm sure."

"Then what?" Kullmann stared at Wendel. "I've got to tell Ludendorff something. If after six weeks and all this effort…" he lifted the heavy report then let it drop. "Well…" He left the sentence unfinished. The two men stared at each other. "Is there no indication?" began Kullman.

"Well," said an increasingly uneasy Wendel. "There's one odd thing; if you look at the Medics' report – that's Annex C, *Herr Oberst* – they say that they found a clock in one of the bodies."

"A clock?"

"Yes, a small gold clock. Badly damaged, but still recognisable."

"You mean a watch – a pocket watch?"

Wendel shook his head. "No, it looks like the remains of one of those little carriage clocks, according to the doctor." He leaned forward over the desk and flicked through the pages. "Here, even the maker's name on the brass frame: l'Epée, Paris. And bits of gold clock casing; too big and square for a watch. Almost a cube it says – ah, here. Four centimetres by two point five, by …"

"By five," completed Kullman reading the report, "That's a damned big watch, Wendel."

"Exactly, *Herr Oberst*."

"Could have been on the table?" mused Kullman.

Wendel swallowed again. The awful possibility was growing stronger by the minute. "An expensive clock for the kitchen, I think." He took the bull by the horns and began to outline the dreadful thought that was going through his mind. How could he have been so blind? "Unless…"

"Unless?"

"Unless it wasn't just an ordinary clock, Herr *Oberst*. What if it had been some sort of timer for a bomb?"

Kullmann looked up, blinking in astonishment. "A little clock? A time bomb? Are you serious, Wendel?"

Wendel nodded. Now that he had recognised the possibility, all the facts fell into place with a sickening clarity. "Oh yes, Oberst, think about it. It's the only other possibility. If it wasn't gas, or a Tommy aircraft bomb …"

"Sabotage?" exclaimed Kullmann. "Bloody sabotage? Are you serious?"

Wendel nodded. The two men stared at each other across the dusk, comprehension dawning on both.

"*Ja*, sabotage, *Herr Oberst*. It's the only other explanation."

"But that means…"

"Those bloody Belgians!" cursed Kullmann, banging the desk with his fist. "Fucking sabotage! Again! Bissing will hang the bastards." *General* Freiherr von Bissing was the Governer General of the Occupied Territories, and a savage dispenser of justice when required. His ruthless treatment of Belgian saboteurs and terrorists was legendary.

Wendel stood up. "Well, at least we know what to do now, *Herr Oberst*." Both Kullmann and Wendel were professional soldiers. They were the type of men to whom decision and action comes naturally. Once having admitted the possibility of sabotage they would both instinctively direct action to root it out without the need for any further discussion.

"Right!" Kullmann began. "I'll hold onto this draft. You find out everyone – everyone, mind – who had access to that damned kitchen car once the order to go to Mons was issued. It has to be one of them."

Wendel was already heading for the door "*Jawohl, Herr Oberst*." Weissmüller's already got the complete list of everyone's movement on the day. In there; Annex H, I think."

"Excellent, Wendel, excellent! I knew I could rely on you." Kullmann's enthusiasm was infectious. OHL's security officer went out with a grim smile on his face. He had been made to look a fool. Woe betide the guilty man when *Herr Major* Wendel laid his single hand on him.

CHAPTER 43

SETTING THE TRAP

27ᵗʰ May 1918

Mackenzie's telegram, telling Neville that the BEF intelligence officer was on his way to London by the first available means, arrived on the same day that Neville's own hasty telegram calling for an urgent meeting reached Mackenzie's empty desk in France.

By five o'clock, Mackenzie, Powell and Cumming were closeted in Neville's elegantly furnished little office in Whitehall. The atmosphere was tense with barely suppressed excitement. Even Neville was aware of the electricity in the air. To his surprise he found that he was rather enjoying the novelty.

An onlooker might have observed that the group had the air of conspirators, for that is precisely what they were. Like all would-be assassins, they were only addressing two fundamental questions: could they do the deed; and secondly, could they get away with it?

In the nature of all secret conspiracies, some of the plotters knew more than others. Mackenzie and Powell genuinely believed that the deed to which Neville was suggesting, and to which they gave their support, had been sanctioned at the highest levels, and were concerned only with getting a clear order to strike. On the other hand, Neville and Cumming were more concerned with finding unwitting tools to execute the deed. All four men, however, realised that they were involved in a dangerous game, and of the need for absolute secrecy.

Mackenzie and Powell had assumed that, having brought good intelligence to what they thought of as "the committee", their role was finished. It was with a degree of surprise, therefore, that they found themselves caught up in the details of the operation itself.

"You say that the French have a man in OHL?" Neville enquired.

"That's what de Romcourt said," replied Powell.

Neville glanced at C who, who shook his head infinitesimally.

"And he didn't say who it was?"

"No, Sir."

"Hardly surprising," grunted Cumming, adding, "I damn well wouldn't say who it was, if we had an agent in the German Kaiser HQ either."

Neville ignored Whitehall's Secret Service chief and turned to the BEF's Mackenzie. "How best do you think we should mount such an attack?"

"Well, that's really for Special Ops or Drake's people to say. Best thing would be a chap on the inside, a shooting, or a bomb."

Well, let's assume we don;t have a man on the inside," broke in Cumming, earning a sharp glance from Neville.

"Well then, that leaves us with either sabotage – a servant, a locally employed civilian, something like that – or a direct attack."

"We haven't got time to recruit someone on the inside. The Kaiser's visit is only four days away." Cumming was adamant.

Mackenzie shrugged. "Then it's an air bombing. Mind, you'd need a lot to be sure. A whole squadron, at least."

"How many aeroplanes is that?" asked Neville.

"Twelve." Christ, thought Mackenzie, these damn' civilians really don't know anything. "That's twelve 112 pound bombs – possibly a bit more," he added.

"Would that be enough?"

Mackenzie pulled a face. "Should be. If they all find the target. Let's face it, Neville, it'll be an operation of war. There are no guarantees."

Neville nodded slowly. "But it should be enough?"

"Yes," said Mackenzie. "But it would still be better to have it done by someone on the inside – if we can."

Neville studiously ignored Cumming's eye. "I think bombing is the only course then. If we have to order an aerial attack, how do you suggest we do that? Quickly I mean."

"Oh, that's straightforward enough. Just get Salmond to issue an order. He's head of the RFC in the BEF, sorry, Royal Air Force, so that'll be no problem."

"You couldn't order it yourself?"

Mackenzie was puzzled. "Why would I? I mean, it's just a G (Ops) matter for GHQ."

"Ah." Neville paused. "But if we wanted to keep those who know to a bare minimum?"

"Then if you'll take my advice don't go anywhere near HQ RFC – or RAF, I should say now – or GHQ at Montreuil," said Mackenzie, earning a chuckle from Powell. "Every staff officer in France will know within a week. Why not just go straight to the squadron?"

"Could we do that?"

"Oh yes. Just get 9 Wing to order a special op order on behalf of the Director of Military Operations back here in London. No problem if DMO's involved."

"Nine Wing?"

"Special Operations", grunted MacKenzie.

"And we can do that?" probed Neville.

"No problem whatsoever. After all, isn't DMO represented on your committee? The Director of Military Operations can authorise what he damn well likes; virtually order anything."

"So he is," said Neville, exchanging glances with Cumming. "So he is." He sat back. "So if we ask DMO to order your 9 Wing to do a special task over the heads of the BEF they just get on with it; is that it?"

"Absolutely. The War Office, DMO's word, is law. They'll just tell 25 Squadron to do a special job, no questions asked."

"25 Squadron?"

"The GHQ Special Duties outfit. DH4s, I think. Probably hot stuff. Secret missions, night flying, dropping agents, that kind of op. Good people." He remembered his visit to St. Omer with young Craig. Whatever had happened to him? he wondered. Never heard from him again, according to Drake. "Yes, it's a good outfit. Run by a Canadian; Duffus, I think. Good man."

Neville persisted with his point. "So, to be clear; if the DMO at the War

Office here in London issues a secret order to your – 25 Squadron? – they will execute it? No questions?"

Mackenzie looked blank. "Of course. Provided 9 Wing, their bosses, know. And they don't need to know the details." He looked at Powell, who nodded.

Neville sat back, impassive, and risked a glance at Cumming. The Secret Service chief writhed in his chair. "You're sure about this?" he demanded.

"Of course," shrugged Mackenzie.

Cumming and Neville's eyes met. "Thank you." Neville addressed Mackenzie with great courtesy. "Thank you. A most valuable contribution from the BEF. I am most grateful." He began to collect his papers. "I wonder if I could trouble you to come back tomorrow at – shall we say eleven o'clock? In the meantime I will see if I can ask the committee to issue the appropriate orders as you suggest."

As I suggest? thought Mackenzie. Me? Hardly. Odd. Deuced odd. He wondered if he should tell Haig. Perhaps not. That was his boss's job. Rather Cox than me, he thought. Haig was damn keen on protocol, that sort of thing. Wife was Lady-in-Waiting to the Queen, or somesuch. Haig might not approve of any bombing attack on generals in principle, but he'd certainly close his eyes to any attempt to pop off the Duo. Yes, that made perfect sense…

*   *   *

The hastily convened meeting of the Intelligence Planning Committee next morning in the DMO's room in the War Office (a venue deliberately selected on Cumming's advice) was a brief affair. Neville explained that Hindenburg and Ludendorff were to visit *Château* Trélon at Hirson on the second of June – which was perfectly true, for it was inconceivable that the Duo would completely ignore their Kaiser when he visited the Front – and would his colleagues agree to another attack, this time by RAF bombers? Cumming, secretive as ever, amplified the point by explaining that he dare not risk his agents being compromised by ordering any Secret Service operation against OHL – and anyway, there wasn't time. All of which was perfectly true.

Believing that they were going for Hindenburg and Ludendorff once again, the small committee agreed without hesitation. Two high-ranking generals? It was a perfectly legitimate target. Was this not precisely the sort of task for which they had agreed to come together? And had they not already ordered a previous attempt? The only awkward moment came when Walter Kirke asked why couldn't they just ask HQ BEF to get on with it? The new DMO, unskilled in the ways of Whitehall, had nodded in agreement.

"Secrecy," explained Neville, tapping his nose. "Security. The fewer people who know about this the better. Probably best not to mention this in any minutes, either," he added to Kirke who was taking notes.

"Absolutely. Don't want to put the birds up, eh?" Cumming had added, nodding. "Absolute secrecy."

The Committee looked at each other and collectively shrugged and nodded. It seemed a lot of fuss for what appeared a very routine affair.

"Good," purred Neville. "I'm so glad we agree." He produced a letter from a folder and handed it to the DMO. "I took the liberty of asking your Serjeant Briggs to get this typed up for us earlier - to save time, you understand. Colonel Mackenzie has to hurry back to France today."

The DMO glanced down at the piece of paper. It was a brief letter on his own headed writing paper, headed "Secret" and ordering 9 Wing to mount a special operation on behalf of DMO and DMI (Special Operations). He read the second brief paragraph aloud,

```
Detailed target briefings will be provided
directly by the Intelligence officers of
Int 1(A) HQ BEF directly to the Commanding
Officer and aircrews of the nominated
Special Duties squadron.

Due to the highly secret nature of this
operation, the need to know principle must
be rigorously enforced.
```

Cumming was particularly proud of this last sentence, for the idea had been his. "Need to know". That sounded good. Nice phrase. He might use that again.

The DMO read out the final sentence again and looked up.

"Seems pretty straightforward to me. Any problems?" The other members of the committee shook their heads. "Good!" He signed with a flourish, delighted to be able to demonstrate his new-found authority publicly.

"There you are, Neville. Give that to Mackenzie. And good luck to – er – 25 Squadron, eh?"

Neville took it. A close observer might have seen him release a tiny breath, as if relaxing after a moment of acute tension. But there were no acute observers present in DMO's office – only men relieved to have finally set in motion an enterprise of which they had high hopes and in haste to get about their other duties.

After the Committee had dispersed, Serjeant Briggs asked his new general if he had a carbon copy of the letter to 9 Wing, RAF.

The DMO shook his head. "No, I'm afraid I haven't, S'arnt Briggs. I thought Dr Neville had a copy."

But Dr Neville had gone.

*   *   *

Neville, Mackenzie and Powell were not the only men with the Kaiser's journey to Hirson at the forefront of their minds.

With *Oberst* Kullmann's final injunction to "make sure that everything is in order for the Kaiser Visit," ringing in his ears, Major Wendel and his chief clerk made their way to *Château* Trélon. The importance of their duty was emphasised by the use of an OHL Mercedes running on captured British petrol. Wendel had extended his good fortune to Stube and an MP Captain who had been ordered to reinforce Hauptmann Koenig's depleted band of military police at Hirson. The large open car swept along the sun dappled tree-lined roads of northern France in all their summer glory. Stube voiced their collective thoughts when he said that it was hard to believe there was a war on.

Evidence of that war came brutally to their attention just outside a small village near La Capelle. A wrecked artillery wagon lay half in the ditch, half in the road and two dead horses were sprawled in the dust, their terrible wounds already black with crawling flies. A pale gunner, with no tunic and a bandaged shoulder, came to attention on seeing the car.

Wendel stopped and asked him what had happened.

"Tommy flyers, *Herr Major*. About an hour ago. One of their *scheisse* aeroplanes just flew down the road, dropped a bomb and flew on. There was nothing we could do." He waved helplessly at the ditches on either side. The battery's gone on to Cambrai."

"Casualties?"

"Two dead and two wounded. And me. This was just a chunk of metal. The medics took it out but the Battery Commander ordered me to stay with the wagon until the salvage party arrives."

Wendel took in the stink, the flies and the dark stains in the dust.

"Here," he said to the driver. Give this man your water bottle."

The driver opened his mouth to argue, then saw Wendel's face. He glanced at Weissmüller by his side in the front and reached sullenly for the spare water bottle on the seat beside him.

"*Vielen dank, Herr Major.*" The soldier drank thirstily, stopped, sniffed the bottle, then drank again, more deeply.

"Keep it," said Wendel. "I have been wounded myself". Stube nodded agreement. The driver compressed his lips.

"Be careful," the gunner said. "They're all over the place now. Tommy *terrorflieger*. Where are you headed?" He looked tired and drained.

"Hirson. *Château* Trélon."

"That's not far. But keep an eye out. They come from anywhere, those sodding planes; even back here."

Stube looked back as they drove off. The wounded gunner was drinking deeply from the upturned water bottle.

The driver's secret mixture of stolen English rum and water tasted like nectar.

*   *   *

Stube's main concern on reaching *Château* Trélon was to find his room and check the message he had received from London. His leather music case had the vital copy of yesterday's Dutch newspaper – *de Telegraaf* – with its innocuous advertisement alerting him to the Reuter's report, waiting to be decoded. Fortunately, what with the bustle of guards, the noisy band parading outside, and the servants and orderlies preparing the country house for its eminent visitor, no one paid much attention to the semi-civilian Press Officer. He found his way to a small room at the back of the house, which had a desk, chair, camp bed and a hastily-written "Presse" chalked on the door.

Locking himself in, he began to unbutton his orders from "C", the only distraction coming in the form of a sharp bang on the locked door and a Sachsen voice shouting "HQ Coordination conference at 1700 hours, in the Grand Salon! All officers!" Its owner then went away, leaving Stube listening to the sound of his heart hammering in his chest. The message from London, cunningly concealed in a report about Romania's role in the war was frighteningly clear. He looked down at the newspaper and his decoded scribble:

> "FLASH. ALERT. AIR ATTACK ON TRELON PLANNED DAWN 2 JUNE COINCIDE WITH KAISER VISIT. BE CAREFUL. IF RAID FAILS TRY DISCREETLY FINISH JOB YOURSELF. C. END"

Stube checked the pricked out letters one last time to ensure that he hadn't made a mistake. Then he burned the scrap of paper in the ashtray. *"de Telegraaf"* was consigned to the pile of foreign newspapers on the floor. It, and van der Horst, his contact in Rotterdam, had done their job. He wondered how the hell he was expected to do his. Discreet? Careful? The Kaiser? He'd be careful all right…

*   *   *

"You see, it's all about being careful."

Hubert Neville dusted a chair and sat down, stick between his knees. From the other side of the desk, Maurice Hankey raised his eyebrows.

"How do you mean, Neville? What's to be careful about?

"May I put to you a hypothetical question, Hankey? Concerning the Prime Minister?"

Hankey disliked hypothetical questions, especially coming from a slippery eel like Neville. Bloody man should have been left at Oxford where he belonged… Too damned clever by half and always up to something. Hankey couldn't stand the fellow. He gave him his friendliest smile, "Of course, Neville. Delighted. How can *we* help?"

Neville noted the plural pronoun. "It's your advice I'm really after, you see. Concerning the Prime Minister. You are, after all, the one most close to him."

"What about the PM?" Hankey asked warily.

"It's a matter of considerable delicacy: hence my need for caution. The point is, well… I need to check details of a highly confidential matter, but I'm not sure that the PM should be made aware. It may embarrass him."

"Never a good idea to embarrass LG, Neville. Don't forget what happened to Maurice when he wrote that silly letter to the Times. Ruthless."

"Quite. However, I do feel I need to alert No. 10, but I don't quite know whom to tell," Neville said blandly.

"Why not let me be the judge?"

"Would you? That's most kind. You see, it really is of the utmost secrecy…"

Hankey's appetite for secrets was well and truly aroused, just as Neville had intended. In Hankey's world, secret knowledge was the golden commodity, which if carefully hoarded, usually paid rich dividends in the future. "Well?"

"Permit me to ask you this question, Hankey. If LG were aware of something going on that could possibly blow up in his face, would he prefer not to have known?"

"There are always things the PM must not be seen to know or have known – officially, anyway. What's the big secret?"

"It's something he himself ordered."

"Even worse, Neville. By far better that he is not made aware in advance, especially if you think that it could go wrong…"

"So that he could truthfully deny all knowledge?"

"Absolutely."

"So who should I inform? In his stead, I mean. I can't just do things because he's told me to without informing him, can I?"

Hankey was exasperated. "Well, of course you can. You tell me. Let me be the judge. After all, that is what I'm here for." He was becoming impatient. "Is it that Duo stunt of yours?"

So Hankey *did* know about that, thought Neville. He affected surprise. "Why, yes. I didn't know you knew about that, Hankey."

"Oh yes," said Hankey airily, "there's not much I don't know about these days, Neville. The PM tells me everything."

Liar, thought Neville. He continued, "Then you will know that the Cumming operation against the Duo – because it was his idea, not mine – failed last time. But we wish to remount it, as sanctioned by the PM. In great secrecy of course. Do you believe that I should let the PM know that we are ready to proceed?"

"Certainly not." Hankey was most emphatic. "No. That is something he must never know – officially. If things don't work out he must be able to look the House of Commons in the eye and say he didn't know. Absolutely."

"Not even if he agreed it – in fact, told us to mount special operations to support Haig and the BEF?"

"Even more so. Best to leave it there. Take my advice. Just get on with it. What the PM doesn't know officially, he can honestly deny."

Neville nodded thoughtfully. "But should I send a note to let *someone* at Number Ten know. Officially? For the record?"

"No, no. No need. Best not commit these things to paper, eh?" No, you've told me. That's good enough, given the circumstances. That way the PM's protected."

"I see!" Neville paused. "But you'll make a note of it? You see, I've got to report to someone, haven't I? I mean PM's orders and all that…"

"Well, you've reported to me, old chap." Hankey was expansive, relaxed. At last. He'd got Neville under control. Reporting to him. About time too, from the sound of it. Going behind his back to Lloyd George indeed.

Neville looked doubtful. "Well, Hankey, if you're sure…"

"Absolutely."

"And it will remain confidential? I can proceed? The PM's special operation?"

"Absolutely. Trust me. The less LG's told the better. You can leave it with me."

Neville stood to leave. "Well, thank you very much for your time, Hankey. Most helpful. I can see that the PM is well served. Thank you. I really am most grateful."

"Not at all my dear chap, not at all. Delighted to be of assistance."

Hankey accompanied Neville to the office door and saw him out. When it was closed he leaned against the woodwork and looked heavenwards. At last! He'd got Neville reporting to him. He smiled grimly. So the PM's ordering special operations now is he? Well, well, well. So that's what this little secret committee of Neville's was all about…

On the far side of the door, Hubert Neville stopped, leaned on his stick and looked back at Hankey's office for a moment.

A faint smile spread across his face.

CHAPTER 44

THE LONGEST NIGHT ?

The Eve of Battle - 1ˢᵗ June 1918

Charles Powell stood on the veranda of the wooden squadron hut and watched the sun set off to the west. He felt drained, elated and apprehensive all at the same time. It had, he reflected, been a hell of a week. Paris, London, back to France, and now on a front-line aerodrome. And to make things worse, he was still reeling from what Neville had explained to him. Trying to kill the Kaiser!

The faint thudding of the guns, like far-off thunder, marked the distant front line away to the east. The door behind him opened, lamplight streaming from within as MacKenzie waved to him.

"You're on now, young Powell. Time to earn your pay."

He entered the briefing room to meet the curious stares of the two dozen seated airmen. Major Duffus and Dr. Neville stood at the far end in front of two blackboards and a large map. MacKenzie addressed the group.

"Right, gentlemen. Here's Captain Powell, our expert on the Germans' HQs and everything to do with the Hun. He'll brief you on your target. Listen carefully, because what we've laid on for tomorrow is the chance of a lifetime. What you'll be doing is nothing less than having a crack at *the* top German HQ on the Western front. And, with any luck, we'll catch a couple of their top people. If that doesn't help to win this war, gentlemen, nothing will. Captain Powell…"

As Powell stepped forward, a murmur went round the room. Raising his voice he pulled back a blanket which was covering a large photograph on one of the blackboards.

"Here's the target, gentlemen: *Château* Trélon, near Hirson." A buzz of voices arose. "And here is a map of the target itself." He ran through all the intelligence details of the target while the assembled aircrew scribbled vigorously. He concluded by handing out a bundle of photographs of the map provided by de Romcourt. It showed Trélon in great detail, including the *château* and the spur with *"train impérial"* clearly marked. The observers and pilots looked at them closely.

"What's our exact aiming point?" called a voice.

"The train and the *château*."

The aircrew buzzed. Duffus stepped forward. "Which is the more important? According to this, they're nearly a thousand yards apart."

MacKenzie intervened. "Go for the *château* first. Then, if you can, go by the train. Can you do that?"

"Sure," said Duffus. "What's this Imperial train doing there anyway?"

"It's just parked there, we think." Neville looked up at MacKenzie, who continued, "It'll probably be empty. But if you can brass it up as well, then so well and good."

Duffus stared up at the staff colonel. "The Imperial train, huh? At this château?" A light slowly dawned in his eyes. He opened his mouth to speak, but Neville suddenly stood up and raised a hand. The room fell silent.

"Gentlemen, what you are being asked to do on behalf of London is totally, absolutely secret. Do I make myself clear? There must be no discussion of this raid whatsoever. Ever. I cannot emphasise this enough. No-one is allowed off the aerodrome – no one – until this mission is over. And when it is over the subject is to be forgotten."

The buzz arose again and Neville held up his hand for quiet again.

"You know the target. You have an excellent detailed plan. We can do no more. From here it is up to you. I will now hand you back to Major Duffus." He sat down.

Duffus stood, hands on hips and surveyed his men. "Right. I will be leading this raid." This announcement was met with incredulity – RAF squadron Commanding Officers were forbidden to fly on ops over the lines. "Quiet!" he shouted. His Newfoundland accent was strong. "You heard Mr. Neville: it's too important to be left to anyone else. Anyway boys, I need the flying practice," he grinned. He turned to the map and pulled a coloured thread across to show the planned route and pinned it firmly to the target.

"And here's how we're gonna do it." Observers and pilots alike began to make notes.

"Take off at 04.30. Load, one 112-pounder and two Cooper bombs each."

A groan went up. "I know: it's heavy. But we're only going to need half tanks of fuel. It's not far." He jabbed at the map. "We fly south-east, 115° for Arras, Cambrai and Le Cateau." He banged the map at each point. "That's about 70 miles."

"At Le Cateau we carry straight on, still on 115° for another 35 miles. That takes us just over the Belgian border to…here!" He indicated a spot well to the east of Hirson.

"But that's way past the target, skipper", a voice interrupted him.

"Sure it is," grinned Duffus. "We're gonna come in on the bastards from behind. Where they'll be least expecting it. And we'll be coming out of the morning sun too, going downhill and out of it before they know what's hit 'em…"

A buzz of voices arose. He banged the map again with the pointer. "So it's left wheel, north-east: follow the road to Chimay. About 45°." *Bang!* The emphatic pointer came down again.

"Then it's hard left, 270° - due west. That's your attack heading. Hell, even I can remember a compass bearing of due west. And that's your way home, too. Straight, fast and low." He looked at Peter Coachman standing at the back with Smith, the squadron's intelligence officer. "What's the forecast?"

"Warm, no rain. Light winds, little cloud." called Smith.

"So that's about 100 miles in, 20 for the raid and 80 miles back. No head winds. Let's say two hours flying. Two-and-a-half at most?" A couple of observers nodded.

Archie Watts raised a hand. "What about recovery, Skipper?

"Good point, Archie. Once you're across our lines coming back, take a dog-leg north. You'll be crossing between Bapaume and Albert, so keep your wits about you. One final point…" he looked around the room. "This is a low-level attack. We'll cross in the dark at approximately 800 feet. Stay low all the way, and only climb as we take the dog-leg northeast for Chimay. We'll probably have about 10,000 feet by then. After that it's downhill all the way, gentlemen, maximum speed out of the rising sun and get the hell out. It's a Jack Armstrong job, this one. Just follow me. I'll be in front."

"Opposition?" called a voice. Duffus looked at the BEF Intelligence Officers.

"There's a squadron of the new Fokker D-7s fitting out at Cambrai and some other scout outfit re-fitting at St Quentin," replied Powell. "At least they were up to two days ago. But they'll still be on the ground when you go in and only just climbing up for their routine dawn patrols when you're coming back. From what we know of their patrol patterns they'll be up very high, maybe well above 15,000 feet… And the new D-7s even higher still. So they may not even see you."

"That's the whole point of this raid, boys," said Duffus. "We go in low in the dark, we're a long way behind their lines as dawn breaks and we come in fast from the east, with the sun in their eyes *and we keep going*! They'll be expecting any trouble from the west, not the east. We'll take them by surprise, from behind and run out fast and low before anyone can react."

He turned to the three Intelligence Officers at the front. "Anything else?"

MacKenzie shook his head. "No, I think you've had it all, Duffus. Powell?"

"No, sir. We've covered the target, the photographs; every observer has a copy of the French plan of the *château*. No, if the Major is happy, I think we are."

They all looked at Neville. He slowly got to his feet and walked forward to the aircrew. They fell silent.

"Look," he began, leaning on his silver-topped cane. "I'm not one for big speeches. I just want you to know that what you're being asked to do is vital. It might even help to end the war. I know you'll do your best. I think I can honestly say this is the most important thing we have ever have asked anyone to do, and I suspect it will be the same for most of you. I just want to end by saying thank you, and good luck." He turned to Duffus. "Thank you. Come, gentlemen." He led Powell and MacKenzie outside, bowing slightly as Sjt. Pickthall held the door open for him. "Thank you."

Once the intelligence trio had departed, a hush fell over the room. Duffus looked at his men.

"Well, boys, there it is. Looks like we've got ourselves a party. Take off at 04.30 ack emma. Just follow me and you'll be all right. I suggest that we all get some sleep. And remember, this is secret. No blabbing about it to anyone, not even to the ground crew!"

"One question, Skipper," called Robbie. "If it's so secret, what do we mark in our log books?"

"Good point, Robbie," said Archie Watts.

Peter Coachman spoke from the back. "Just put it down as a 'special mission'. No more. That should do. I'll sign it off for you. Now you heard the CO. Get to bed as soon as you're ready, get some shut-eye. And remember – no loose talk! Get some sleep; four o'clock comes early."

CHAPTER 45

A NIGHT TO REMEMBER
1ˢᵗ- 2ⁿᵈ June 1918

"You should really get some sleep, *Herr Major.*" Wendel and his aide were seated in a stuffy back room at the *Château* Trélon.

"Weissmüller, you are absolutely right. It's just this damned OHL Train Bomb file… *Es steht mich etwas deutlich vor den Augen* - there's something here staring me in the face." Wendel shook his head and scratched the stubble on his cheeks. "What's the time?"

"Gone midnight."

"Go to bed. No. Wait… Pass me that list; the one with all the people who had access to the generals' restaurant car."

Weissmüller handed over a thin folder.

"Can't it wait 'till morning, *Herr Major?*"

"Probably, but by morning we'll all be fussing about the All Highest and his programme." Wendel yawned. "No, I'll do it while it's still fresh in my mind. The Kaiser's safely in his bed, so I've got some time to think."

"Strange place for the Kaiser to sleep: I mean having his bedroom in that drawing room on the ground floor."

"Well, it's not really a bedroom, Weissmüller. It's just that Oberst von Paulus thought it would be easier to guard, not to mention better access control than all that fuss upstairs. Anyway, go and get your head down, there's a good fellow… I'll take another look at this."

"Goodnight, *Herr Major.*"

"Goodnight, Weissmüller."

But Weissmüller didn't go to bed. He unbuttoned his tunic and dozed off in an armchair in the room next door, just in case his one-armed major needed a hand in the night. He usually did.

While the HQ slept, Wendel ran through the well-thumbed train bomb file. First he listed all those who had visited – or had had access to – the restaurant car. He struck from the list *Hauptmann* von Körge

– the Prussian Guards Commander; the Military Police captain; then Hindenburg and Ludendorff. The latter two he ruled through with a wry smile. He eliminated the two dead men as well as the two wounded sous-chefs. Suicide, he decided, was an unlikely option. He totalled up the remainder: storemen and guards: 14. Railway workers: 2. These were the German train guard, checking that all was ready to move, and a Belgian railwayman, responsible for testing the gas bottles – one hour before. Both however had been closely supervised by a German military policeman.

He rubbed his face. Who else? Wendel's eye ran down the list – Stube. He re-read the press officer's brief statement. "...*handed over a packet of tea... to my old friend cook-Serjeant Redl...*" Something niggled him. He reached for the statements of the two wounded sous-chefs. There. Both confirmed Stube's visit. He read on, "*....laughing with cook-Serjeant Redl... Handing over his gifts of Dutch goodies...*" He read the other and found that both accounts tallied, "*...laughing and joking... A really big Dutch cheese... Earl Grey Tea... Whisky...*"

Wendel froze and with a growing sense of disbelief reached for Stube's statement again. He read again the inventory of items the journalist claimed to have passed to Redl. "*Coffee, smoked herrings, whisky, Earl Grey tea...*" He picked up the second chef's statement, given from his hospital bed: and there it was, staring him in the face. "*Herr Stube had a canvas bag and gave cook-Serjeant Redl some gifts from Holland. Tea, coffee, a big yellow cheese – a big one, shaped like a wheel – and whisky...*"

Why hadn't Stube mentioned the big yellow cheese? Odd.

Cheese! *Wendel put his hand to his forehead. Stube had brought a cheese* back for him, too. *Lieber Gott!* Stube had even told him that he had given a cheese to the HQ Mess. He remembered the press man saying, "*...and a damned big one, too.*" Wendel suddenly realised how a bomb could have been smuggled on to the train; in that big yellow cheese. How else? He clutched at the statements. Hindenburg and Ludendorff were far too grand to "make statements" but the MPs' report recorded what the Duo remembered of the incident.

Yes, there it was...

> Ludendorff: ...the FirstQuarterMaster General
> had just sent the cheese back after lunch when

the British aircraft struck...

Hindenburg: ...the Chief of the General Staff observed that if Herr Altmann had not been sent out to cut the cheese, he might have survived the blast...

It was the cheese. The bomb must have been in Stube's *verdammte holländische käse!* He sat back in bewilderment. How the hell could Stube have failed to mention the cheese? Unless... He shook his head, disbelieving.

In all fairness, Wendel did not at first suspect Stube.

His first instinct was that the Press Officer had been used as an unwitting instrument for someone else's plan, or had simply forgotten. Someone must have planted the cheese on Stube, surely? There was no "Eureka!" moment. Then the realisation that Stube must have deliberately omitted the cheese from his statement only dawned on him slowly as he stared down again at the paper. After all, he reasoned, there was no other reason for it *not* to be mentioned. You could hardly miss a cheese like that. He'd mentioned everything else. Even a miserable little packet of tea. So why had he not mentioned a half metre wide cheese, the size of a small wheel? He must have omitted it deliberately. Why wasn't Stube telling everything?

That was the point at which Wendel realised that Stube must be the man with some questions to answer.

Once he had absorbed the idea, the enormity of its implications hit home. He suddenly remembered the report he had shown Stube only days before... "*STRENG GEHEIM – TOP SECRET.*" What else had Stube seen? What else had he and Weissmüller shown the press man? Christ! Not Stube? He began to feel sick. Clumsily, because of his missing arm, he buckled up his pistol belt with the wooden handled Mauser and went looking for Stube. *Herr* Stube had some big explaining to do...

*   *   *

Neville and Powell stood in the pre-dawn blackness, staring out at a line of improvised flares, nothing more than tins of sand soaked in petrol. The roar of aircraft engines hammered off the unseen buildings.

Occasionally a black shape would blot out a flare or two, then soar into the indigo sky and fade off to the east.

Unlike MacKenzie, seasoned campaigner that he was, Neville couldn't sleep: not on a night like this. When the last DH4 had disappeared into the darkness, he turned to Powell.

"Well, I wish them luck," said Neville. "I had no idea it would feel like this – they are very brave young men."

Powell said nothing. He was still grappling with the fact that the Kaiser was the real target.

"When are they due back?"

"Anytime after half past six, Doctor Neville."

The last faint engine noise faded into silence. Even the far-off guns went unheard or were quiet for once. A chill breeze ruffled the canvas hangars.

"Have you ever flown?"

Powell shook his head in the darkness. "No, never."

"Neither have I." Neville stared pensively east at a dark horizon. "I pray that they all make it back."

"It's in the lap of the Gods now, Sir."

Neville laughed quietly; "…or the Germans."

Powell looked at Neville's face, anxious in the gloom. "If they pull it off - I mean actually do kill the Kaiser, what do you really think the effect will be?"

Neville considered his response. "It is hard to tell. Germany is already facing red ruin. This war has wrecked her economy and her political system. The common people are already up in arms in a dozen cities already. The loss of the Kaiser will undoubtedly add to her turmoil. I have no doubt about that…"

"Could it really end the war, do you think?"

"Possibly. They have lost anyway, now. Prussian militarism started this madness. Or, to be precise was instrumental in creating the conditions that led to it. So, let us hope that striking at the very fountainhead of

German militarism will help to end it as quickly as possible. The Duo may try and fight on but the German people will not support a military *Junta*, I suspect. Not with the way things are developing."

"Or we wait for the Americans?"

"Ah yes, the Americans… The answer to all our problems, according to my newspapers. I'm afraid that I do not share your enthusiasm for our American allies, Powell. I distrust their motives. Watch them, my friend. Remember, they're not in this war through their choice. They are reluctant allies, and in it for their own reasons."

Despite the darkness, Powell swung his head to try and see Neville's face more clearly. "But, I thought they joined…"

"No, we tricked them into joining in. Or, to be more precise, Admiral Hall and his clever codebreaking people did, with that foolish telegram from Zimmermann, which they managed to intercept. No, President Wilson and his new American Army are in this war for one reason and one reason only."

"His fourteen points? Putting down militarism? Democracy?"

Neville snorted with mild derision. "*Democracy*? Certainly not. How can you be so naïve, my boy? The Americans are not fighting to make the world safe for the sake of *democracy*, Powell. That is tendentious hypocrisy. Americans are rather good at that, and Wilson's better than most. Mere propaganda to appease the masses." He waved a dismissive hand. "No, the American people believe in their heart of hearts that they are fighting to ensure the best interests of America. And American big business is only too delighted with it all. Bankers, big money men, manufacturers of goods. They have invested heavily in Britain and France. They dare not let us lose. They will ensure that America and its money men do very nicely out of this war, believe me."

"How?"

"Look at the gold transfers. Do you know how much this war has cost us?"

Powell shrugged. "Millions, I suppose."

"Forgetting the human cost, financially it has cost us five million pounds a day. *Five million!* If my arithmetic is correct, Powell, that's about 13,000 million pounds that the British Empire alone has poured out. And a very great deal of that money has been transferred from London in *gold* across the Atlantic. When this is all over, I think you will find that America and her bankers have made a very tidy profit from their little European adventure. Whoever prevails, and I do believe we shall, American will be the only real victor from… All this." He waved a hand into the darkness to the East and sighed.

"This European war has been a disaster for us all. A complete madness. Nothing can ever be the same again: not Europe, not the Empire, *especially* not Russia, after the Bolsheviks have seized power… Nothing. This idiocy will be the ruination of everything that we went to war to preserve. Only the Americans, revolutionaries and bankers are benefitting. It has been a calamity. A European disaster. Mark my words."

Powell was silent.

The first streaks of light appeared on the Eastern horizon. "Anyway," said Neville, stabbing his cane on the ground. "Enough of this. Let us go in. Perhaps we can find someone who can get us a cup of coffee. Dawn will soon be here."

CHAPTER 46

THE KAISER'S DAWN

2ⁿᵈ June 1918

Once over Le Cateau, Duffus began to climb very gradually. As they climbed, the rising sun suddenly illuminated the dark shapes of the other DH4s. He checked his watch – just 0500. At nearly two miles per minute... He spun the calculation in his head. Two miles per minute... Just under 50 miles to go... Say 20 minutes, give or take. He squinted into the red furnace door that was the sun exploding over the eastern horizon, dead ahead. The earth below was still dark in shadow. Twenty minutes. Perfect timing. He waggled his DH 4's wings and kept on climbing.

*　　　　*　　　　*

Stube couldn't sleep.

The hot, airless little pantry that served as the Press Office was dark and oppressive. He pulled on his boots and walked outside to catch a breath of cool air. The dew was heavy on the grass and the first fingers of dawn were visible in the east. He stood in the shadow of the building.

The Duo were coming to visit the Kaiser this afternoon. The place would be as busy as hell. He might have to make his move today. But how? He stood calm, supremely confident watching the sentries and wondering just what the day held in store...

*　　*　　*　　*　　*　　*　　*

Wendel decided that he had better get some help. The Military Police detachment room was empty, so he went looking for someone to help arrest Stube. The more he thought about the press man's behaviour, the surer he became of his guilt. Why the hell hadn't he listed that cheese? He certainly did have some questions to answer. He toyed with the idea of waking *Oberst* Kullmann, but what was the point? Later. He had to be sure. And bloody Ludendorff and Hindenburg were due at 16.00

At the corner of the building a couple of the sentries were silhouetted against the sky. His boots crunched on the gravel.

"Excuse me," he began.

"Password!" snapped a voice.

Wendel was embarrassed. "I've no idea. It's *Major* Wendel." He recognised one of the sentries as being the big blonde Serjeant major from the 2/63 Infantry Regiment, the one with the Iron Cross who had upset Weissmüller. He must be on early duty, checking the guards at stand-to. His embarrassment increased. "It's me, *HauptFeldwebel. Major* Wendel. The Security Officer."

Hartmann smiled, his teeth white against the darkness: then he snapped to attention. "*Herr* Major!" He saluted. 'Reiniger here could have shot you! Better to know the password, I suggest. As OHL Security Officer. On a day like today, *Herr major*? Is everything in order?"

Momentarily thankful for the semi-darkness, Wendel flushed. "I need an armed guard to come with me. I think we may have a spy in the house. We may also need to make an arrest. All the MPs are out," he added lamely.

Hartmann almost laughed out loud. Officers! Spies! Whatever next? He decided to humour the Bavarian Major. "A spy, *Herr Major*? *Ja*, That is serious. Then I must accompany you myself." He ostentatiously cocked his rifle and put the safety catch on. He winked at Reiniger, his face now more visible as the sun began to light up the front of the château. "I am ready," Hartmann announced. "Now where is this spy, Herr Major?" He winked again at Reiniger behind the major's back. Officers!

*   *   *

Half-blinded by the dazzle of the rising sun, Major Duffus banked to the left and began to swing due west. About ten miles ahead, *Château* Trélon suddenly stood out in the increasing sunlight. He checked his height: 11,000 feet. Looking behind against the blinding brilliance of the rising sun, he could see the other eleven DH4s tightly holding their position in staggered line astern. He sliced a white-gloved hand vertically over his head, pointing forwards.

"Right, Billy," he shouted to his observer, "Here we go! He pushed the stick forward and the DH4's engine note rose. Duffus looked at the big fob watch he kept clipped to the dashboard. It read 5.23 exactly.

*   *   *

Wendel rounded the corner of the *château*, with an amused Serjeant Major Hartmann trailing behind. The Security Officer had decided to go round behind the building and enter via the rear entrance rather than try and explain his way past a series of guards in the hall and kitchens. Stube and the Press Office were quartered in the back. Ahead was a steel-helmeted sentry in full battle order, rifle at the high port, guarding the glass French doors of the Kaiser's ground-floor suite.

"Halt!" called the sentry, then slammed to attention on seeing the unmistakable form of the one-armed Security Officer and his own Serjeant Major.

Wendel suddenly became aware of a noise. He stopped and looked round. The buzzing grew louder. Shielding his eyes, he peered up at the rising sun, Hartmann and the sentry doing likewise. There were specks, high up in the sky.

"What's up?" said a voice.

Wendel turned to see Stube, braces dangling and collarless, coming round the other side of the building, rubbing his unshaven face. For a second, he paused and their eyes met. In that glance, Wendel knew. From the look on Stube's face, and he realised that Stube knew too. Wendel clawed for his wooden-handled Mauser.

'Stube!" he shouted. "*Halte!*" The press man fled round the corner.

Wendel's bellow was drowned out by the roar of an aircraft engine.

A dark shape swept overhead, followed by a massive explosion. As if in slow motion, the *château* windows blew in as a bomb ripped through the courtyard, blowing Wendel to the ground, along with Hartmann and the sentry.

Stube ducked behind the corner as another blast blew apart two of the parked staff cars. An apparently constant stream of aircraft thundered low overhead, bombs and bullets crashing everywhere. A sentry fired up at a retreating aircraft, its RAF roundels clearly visible, and was cut down by a chattering burst of fire from the air.

Flames and debris erupted around the *château*, interspersed only by the barrage of explosions and the thunder of aero engines as a procession of DH4s roared in to burst through the rising pillar of smoke. Somewhere a man was screaming. A riderless horse suddenly bolted through the gates, disappearing into the park. Stube pressed himself to the ground behind the wall and cursed as bullets smacked against the *château* walls above him. Bits of stone showered down.

A bomb burst on the gravel drive outside the entrance and a hail of machine-gun fire ripped across the façade of the building as another DH4 roared over, lower than the rest, its machine guns chattering. In the park, a platoon of infantrymen were standing on the lawns, firing up at the receding bombers. A retaliatory blast of machine-gun fire chewed across the grass, spinning two men over.

There was a final blast of firing from the direction of the Imperial Train. The planes vanished, their noise fading into the distance.

Then silence.

Stube looked round the corner; Wendel and the two infantrymen lay sprawled and lifeless on the ground. Shattered glass glittered everywhere. Nothing moved.

A thick curtain of smoke rolled slowly over the courtyard. There was no-one else in sight. It was now or never. Stube sprinted across the grass, stumbling over the body of the blond Serjeant major. Hartmann lay face up, still breathing, his rifle by his side. Stube scooped it up. A few feet beyond him lay *Major* Wendel, face down, half the back of his head blown away, brains oozing out like porridge. The other sentry lay silent in a widening lake of blood. Somewhere far off an invisible man was moaning.

Stube checked the Serjeant major's rifle and crouching, ran to the Kaiser's rooms. Bursting through the wrecked French doors, broken glass crunching underfoot, he barely avoided tripping over the body of a young Guards officer, face ripped and tunic bloodied beyond recognition by the flying glass. Of course! There would have been an officer guard inside the locked Kaiser Suite.

Sitting up in bed straight ahead was Kaiser Wilhelm, the Second Emperor of the German Reich, very much alive, and ridiculous in a nightshirt and nightcap.

Even more ridiculous, his moustache was held in a kind of hairnet, secured with strings behind his ears. Germany's All Highest and Supreme

Warlord was whimpering with fright. Stube stood in the shattered doorway and became aware of a thunderous knocking at the bedroom door. It was now or never. He raised the Mannlicher 7.92 to his shoulder, and aimed directly at the Kaiser's chest.

"*Nein*," screamed Wilhelm. "*Nein! Bitte! Gott sei mir gnädig!*" (No! Please! God have mercy on me!")

Stube took the trigger pressure. "Now, you son of a bitch!"

There was a single gunshot. The Kaiser screamed.

Stube snapped his head up and lowered the rifle. A look of total surprise crossed his face. He stared at the Kaiser and opened his mouth to speak. As he did so, two more shots rang out. Stube jerked forward like a puppet.

He wanted to say something but he couldn"t. He wanted to say something to the Kaiser, staring terrified up at him. But he couldn"t speak because of the salt in his mouth and those gunshots had made his ears sing. His chest felt very full, very tight. Hard to breathe. He felt weak. To his surprise, very slowly, Stube found himself slumping to his knees, the heavy weight of the rifle dropping away with a clatter from nerveless fingers. His startled eyes looked up at the Kaiser, and his mouth was working – but all the Kaiser heard was a gurgle. Then Stube fell forward, to finally crash face down and silent.

The Kaiser squeaked in fright.

Another grim figure loomed out of the smoke and stood framed in the shattered French windows, Wendel's wooden-handled Mauser pistol in hand, pointing directly at him.

The thunderous knocking on the door redoubled and became a crashing noise. The Kaiser backed up the bedhead, desperately trying to pull away. "*Nein. Bitte.* Please…."

Weissmüller looked down at Stube, sprawled out and silent at the end of the big bed. The three bullet holes were clearly visible on the back of his blue-striped shirt. At that range, the press man had been impossible to miss – even with an officer's toy pistol.

He took in the bloody remnants of the officer guard at his feet. Then, slowly, Weissmüller transferred his gaze to his Kaiser, backing up the bed head to escape. From the spreading dark stains on his nightshirt, the

Kaiser, of all the Germans, had obviously just wet himself with fear. Poor Major Wendel's pistol was still in the NCO's hand, trained straight at the Kaiser's head. Weissmüller's mind seemed to be working in slow motion. He would never see Major Wendel again, he thought. A pity. A great officer. There was a lot of noise outside. And there was the Kaiser. My God, he thought, one bullet now and it could all be over. All this madness and killing could be stopped. No-one would ever know… They'd assume it was Stube who'd done it. He could be a hero… The man who tried to save the Kaiser and managed to shoot his killer instead. He'd be a hero. The war would be ended… He became conscious of the terrified whimperings of his monarch and the battering at the door.

Weissmüller recognised his duty as a good German. He instinctively did what a real German soldier should do.

He snapped to full parade attention at the foot of the bed.

"*Eure Majestät! StabsFeldwebel* Weissmüller, OHL Security Staff! At your orders, Your Majesty!"

The door burst open. A flight of German fighter planes roared uselessly overhead.

*   *   *

Twenty miles away, Twenty Five Squadron's DH4s were racing for safety and closing in on the front lines.

With the exception of one "B" flight aircraft, which had gone down to make a forced landing near Cambrai, they were all heading for home, urgent as pigeons heading for the loft. High overhead they could see the flash of the early morning sunlight on the wings of patrolling German fighters. But nothing could catch the DH4s now, almost on the deck, sprinting for home at full throttle. Robbie's aircraft was lagging behind a little, but it was still in sight of the rest of the formation. The front lines slid below the aircraft, marked only by a single lazy burst of golden tracer that curved up and then fell slowly, miles behind.

"Well, that's one for the books, Robbie!" shouted Timmy from the back. "What a stunt! I must have fired four whole magazines."

Robbie didn"t answer. He was concentrating on holding the DH4 steady. The plane seemed sluggish. Now that the mission was over, he realised how deathly tired he was. And it was cold up here, very cold. He shivered and yawned. The bellow of the big Rolls Royce seemed so far away. God, he was tired. It was still dark flying towards the west. The aircraft yawed.

'Steady on, old man!" shouted Timmy. "No time to fool around now." Robbie didn't reply and the plane's nose started to drop. That was better. He yawned again and shivered. He felt cold, tired and he ached all over. It shouldn"t be this cold surely? It was hard to hold her on course.

"I say, Robbie. Are you all right?" Timmy noticed a couple of bullet holes in the wing. "Looks like something hit us, old man. Nothing serious, though."

Robbie didn't reply and now the aircraft began to climb. Timmy noticed oil seeping back along the cockpit floor from the front. The oil tank must have been hit. That could be tricky. Never mind; they were the right side of the lines at least. He glanced down again at the dark liquid oozing along the floor and froze. That wasn't oil... It was too red. It was blood. Blood? A long trickle ran underneath his seat, dark against the pale canvas. Christ! Suddenly there was gallons of the stuff, pouring back now as the plane climbed.

"Robbie! Robbie! Are you all right? Robbie!"

But Robbie couldn"t reply. He was staring straight ahead into the fading light, which seemed to be growing dimmer by the moment. Funny... He checked his compass - 270°- due west, that was good... Should be getting lighter now though, surely?

Far off, he heard Timmy shouting to him, like the distant piping of a child. He tried to concentrate on holding the kite straight and level. She was very sluggish. Difficult. Perhaps controls damaged. They must have been hit. He remembered a bang as they'd flown over the *château*.

Then suddenly, he saw it.

The spot of light, straight ahead. Growing bigger. The most glorious, radiant light he had ever seen in his young life. Like the sun. He thought of Françine the barmaid, back at St. Omer. And Charlie Barton. Wonderful! The blinding glow was growing stronger, opening up before him, golden white and dazzling... Growing ever bigger and brighter, enfolding him in its welcoming softness. The DH4 roared on towards the light.

Robbie's dull eyes tried to focus on the unseen compass. Funny, he thought, something's wrong... Course 270 degrees, skipper had said... Must fly straight. Couldn"t fight it. Cold, so tired... But that light... Beautiful. Fly into the golden light...

Robbie's final dawn would rise for eternity in the West.